Selected Works
of
Sacheverell Sitwell

Sacheverell Sitwell

Selected Works of

Sacheverell Sitwell

THE BOBBS-MERRILL COMPANY, INC.

Publishers

Indianapolis   New York

ACKNOWLEDGMENTS

The author, as a matter of courtesy, would like to express his thanks to the following publishers for the extracts quoted from the books below:

"Dumb Tones, and Shuddering Semitones of Death," from *Dance of the Quick and the Dead,* Faber and Faber Ltd.

"Ames Damnées," from *Splendours and Miseries,* Faber and Faber Ltd.

"Djemaa El Fna," from *Mauretania,* Duckworth and Co.

"Nuns of the Fondouk," from *Sacred and Profane Love,* Faber and Faber Ltd.

"The Golden Reign of Saturn," from *Splendours and Miseries,* Faber and Faber Ltd.

"Fugue," from *Splendours and Miseries,* Faber and Faber Ltd.

"Hurdygurdy," from *Splendours and Miseries,* Faber and Faber Ltd.

"A Picture of Bucharest," from *Roumanian Journey,* Batsford Ltd.

"The Areöis," from *Primitive Scenes and Festivals,* Faber and Faber Ltd.

"Mexico," from *Southern Baroque Art,* Duckworth and Co.

"Festival at Nola," from *Primitive Scenes and Festivals,* Faber and Faber Ltd.

"Battle in the Steppe," from *Splendours and Miseries,* Faber and Faber Ltd.

"Finale in Form of a Bacchanale," from *Sacred and Profane Love,* Faber and Faber Ltd.

Thanks are due to Messrs. Batsford, of London, for their kind permission to quote "Feria at Seville," from *Spain.*

CONTENTS

INTRODUCTION

This book has been planned for the American public exactly as though it is an exhibition of selected paintings. Designed, that is to say, so as to show the writer in differing moods and phases. There is a lot of material to choose among, and it has not been easy to make the selection, or, in the sense of arranging it in some sort of order, to hang the exhibition. Certain pieces, from a similarity in treatment or in subject, to some degree flow into one another and must be placed together, while others stand by themselves and are seen better in isolation. There are portraits, landscapes, still lives of fruits and flowers, and even, where images and metaphors are concerned, flights of fancy which might be termed abstractions. Even so, the collection is not complete since from reasons of space it omits the writer's architectural and theatrical pieces. And, of course, being an exhibition of prose, no poetry is included.

In the collection taken as a whole, there are certain things with which we in England are familiar and that need no footnote, but which require some preface for the public in America. This Introduction is written, therefore, by way of commentary, to be regarded as though printed in the catalogue in the form of program notes. But at least it is in the words of the writer, who must be aware of his own intentions. It carries, therefore, the seal of authenticity.

The book opens with a pair of episodes of macabre nature. Every Englishman of my generation was brought up in childhood to look upon the Pre-Raphaelites as the most recent school of English painting. Rossetti, Burne-Jones, William Morris were familiar names, and remained so until the first Post-Impressionist exhibition at the Grafton Galleries in London in 1911, of which I can remember at thirteen years old the early repercussions, and being told by my brother and sister who are older than I of how Gauguin, then their favorite, threw up his employment in a bank

9

and went out to paint the South Sea Islands. Shortly after, Russian music and the Russian ballet altered the whole focus. But we must forget all that and remember that for many years Rossetti, Swinburne and their circle of friends were famous names—to those at least who, like ourselves, loved poetry and hoped even at that early age to be writers and poets and leave a name behind us.

I do not think that the first episode of this book requires further explanation. There can be no doubt that Miss Siddal in her pathetic way inspired Rossetti. And how English is her phantom! How much, even, a part of London: the specter of Kensington, Hampstead, Chelsea, wherever there are artists! We seem to behold, in her, Keats's *"La Belle Dame sans Merci."* If brotherly affection has prompted me in this episode to attempt a portrait of a yet more remarkable and wonderful woman, one of the greatest of our poets, the reader must forgive me and forbear with what I prophesied of her future more than eighteen years ago.

"Ames Damnées" is another and murkier chapter than that concerning Rossetti and Miss Siddal, but it too is Pre-Raphaelite in treatment. The case of Madeleine Smith is the most romantic of our English murder stories. She can become somewhat of an obsession with those who think of her. But for all my inquiries, I have been unable to discover the color of her hair. She should have had for the story's sake bright auburn hair. But persons whose parents remembered her at the balls in Edinburgh, or at her trial, described it, carelessly, as red or black. I am bound to admit, too, that the daguerreotype portrait of her is far from beautiful. But beautiful she was by all accounts. Of her guilt I have no doubt at all. I only hope I have made her history as romantic and curious as it seems to me to be.

"London Charivari" is a study of the streets of London in the time of Cruikshank. It was begun, as I mention in a footnote, on the day the Germans entered Paris, when London, it could be said, seemed "next upon the list." The first pages are in description of a drawing by Cruikshank, one of his "Fashionable Monstrosities" which it has not been possible to reproduce; but hoping my words will be description enough, I have left it as it stands. This leads on to a note on Lord Petersham, one of the bucks of the Regency and a very odd character indeed, and to what I would term the geography of snuff. We then proceed "window-shopping" down the Strand, on a day in the 1820s or 1830s. I describe the cats'-meat shop which was in existence behind Oxford Street until a few years ago; and the piece ends with the etchings of Jacques Callot, superimposed, as it were, on George Cruikshank. The subject is, in fact, that sacred area of the theater round Drury Lane and Covent Garden, still haunted by the ghosts of Peg Woffington and Edmund Kean.

The next three episodes run together and form almost a separate book of their own. There can be no public spectacle in the world today to equal the Feria of Seville. This formed the first chapter of my book on Spain, and was written, I could say, with the music of Albeniz, Bizet, Chabrier sounding in my ears, together with the crackling of ten thousand pairs of castanets, a noise of intoxication, played by the women and children of Seville as they walk in the evening to the fairground. I try to describe, too, the midday parade of cavaliers and amazons, all in Andalusian costume, in the blazing heat. I have written of the Gitanas and their flower-decked eating places, and of how they push forward into the crowd to try to drag you in. But the Feria of Seville is at its best in the early hours when you can see and hear hundreds of *seguidillas, sevillanas, siguiriyas,* in every direction in the scented night.

The Spanish scene is intended to alter, without interruption of more than an interval for refreshment, into the Djemaa El Fna, the market place of Marrakesh, in Morocco. Seville, let us remember, was the summer capital of the Sultans, who moved their court to Marrakesh to spend the winter. The Giralda of Seville and the Koutoubia of Marrakesh were minarets, built by the same architect, Jebîr the Moor. The Djemaa El Fna is the Times Square, the Piccadilly Circus of Africa, but as Oriental as can ever have been the market places of Bagdad or Isfahan. These two episodes, then, are crowd scenes, and I have tried to make them exciting and full of color for the reader.

There follows "Nuns of the Fondouk," an interior study of the "reserved quarter" of an African and Oriental town, written in the pastel colors of the dresses and turbans worn.

"The Golden Reign of Saturn" is a fantasy built round the frescoes of Benozzo Gozzoli. This Florentine master of the *quattrocento* is well known to all Americans who have been to Florence from his paintings in the Cappella Medici. But my study is based more particularly upon his frescoes at Pisa, much damaged in the last war, which had for subject Noah's Vintage. Those were among the most beautiful early paintings of the Italian Renaissance, lovely in their rendering of the cypresses and stone pines of Tuscany, with vineyards and little far towns gleaming on the rounded hills—indeed, a kind of fairyland, for it has few but fair-haired angels and children for inhabitants. In the frescoes at Pisa, Benozzo's models are young men and women (*contadini*), and beautiful play is made of them ascending and descending ladders or treading in the wine press. I only wish there had been space to put in, as pendant, an account in *The Gothick North* of Signorelli's frescoes at the monastery of Monte Oliveto Maggiore, outside Siena, where his young warriors wear the black and white magpie dresses of the Palio. However, the scene changes and Benozzo's cypressed hills give place to a landscape in the manner of Francesco di Giorgio, a painter who, like Leonardo, was military engineer as well, and his brand-new fortifications appear with men in armor standing in the doorways. This, in turn, changes to the frescoes in the Spanish chapel of Santa Maria Novella at Florence; and I end with "The Triumph of Death," that marvelous fresco of the Middle Ages, which was one of the worst of all the war losses at Pisa. It is interesting to remember that the "Triumph of Death" was Liszt's inspiration for his "Todentanz," too seldom performed but tremendous in its fanfares and noises as of rattling bones.

There follow two pieces which I call, collectively, "Orpheus and his Lyre." They are studies of music, and are the best things which my only amateur interest in music has achieved to date. The first is an essay on Bach's organ music, which I have tried to describe visually, yet, were it possible, in the formal language of the fugue. Above all I tried to apprehend the "meaning" of the music. I hope and believe that my analysis of the Fantasia and Fugue, the tremendous and awe-inspiring Prelude and Fugue in C major, the Passacaglia and Fugue, and the terrific— there can be no other word for it—Prelude and Fugue in E minor, a work of art equivalent to a "one-man" Chartres Cathedral, may be not wholly inadequate to their subject. A pity that there is no room, as well, for a study of Bach's Goldberg Variations, published elsewhere. I think that being a practiced writer upon architecture helped me to describe Bach's organ music.

In the pendant piece called "Hurdygurdy" my ambition was to take the opposite pole of music. For a long time I played with the idea of making either of the Hungarian Gypsy musicians, Czermak or Bihary, the hero of it. Any reader who remembers "The Visit of the Gypsies," or "The Wandering Sinte," different episodes I have written, will know of my interest in the Gypsies and their music. This goes hand in hand with a love of virtuosity for the sake, it could be said, of the virtuoso, as proved by a book on Liszt and a chapter therein on Paganini. Musical dictionaries, the perusal of which was a pastime while waiting for other books to arrive in the Reading Room of the British Museum, at length gave me what I wanted in the person of Gusikov, an impromptu player of Russian-Jewish origin, now forgotten entirely —indeed, no one has heard of him—but he would seem from contemporary accounts to have been the greatest of all musicians of his kind.

Part of the fascination of this particular subject is its Russian or, rather, Ukrainian background. In order to achieve it I had to steep myself in accounts of childhood in the country, out of Russian memoirs. I can see the traces in it, too, of my reading of "Pan Tadeusz," the Polish epic of Miczkiewicz, which has beautiful and poetical accounts of the rye fields, and of picking mushrooms in the forest. Also, of the ceremonial dancing of the mazurka in the evenings, with the Polish nobles hand in hand with their ladies, and with their other hand twirling the long ends of their moustachios, as they processed to music down the long halls of the castle. The town of Mohilev, where our Russian-

Jewish musician passed his childhood, I described from personal
knowledge of near-by Hotin, a town with a Jewish population on
the Dniester, formerly Roumanian and now in Russia. I tried to get
into the soul of the Russian folk music, carrying its sophistication
a little further than it can ever have got in the time of Gusikov,
by following the strains of Gypsy orchestras into the Novo-
Troitski Traktir, and the Moskovski Traktir, Moscow restaurants
famed for their Gypsy bands and Gypsy singers. Tunes were
played there such as the famed "Zigeunerweisen" of Sarasate,
heard by the Spanish violinist in Moscow and written down by
him. Similar tunes, one or two of them by bandmasters, but in
the Hungarian idiom, were used by Brahms for his Hungarian
Dances. The peculiar nature of the special instrument played
by Gusikov, and the wonderful effects drawn by him out of its
slender structure, made me think, inevitably, of that magical
clavichord player Mrs. Gordon Woodhouse, whom I had known
from childhood, and my account of him ends with what is, in
fact, her playing of Mendelssohn's "A Midsummer Night's
Dream," a musical experience of immortal and breath-taking
loveliness, only the more immortal because it perished so completely at her lamented death. In this episode, as in several
others, the reader will notice undercurrents of the war and of
the dread and apprehension of those six years of isolation.

The haunting strains of Slav music give place to "A Picture of
Roumania," where the survival into modern times of the equivalent of an outlying province of the Byzantine Empire is the topic.
Bucharest and its polyglot population, its bastard churches, its
Gypsies and Sephardim Jews are described; and there is a study
of the weird Russian sect of the Skoptzi who were droshky drivers
of the Roumanian capital. All this reads, now, as if it were re-
moter even than the pantomime splendors of the Turkish Sultans; it seems, indeed, as though it were a study of life under
the Comnenus, or the Palaeologus; yet it was written in 1937!

"The Areöi Society," which may strike the reader as a curious
name, is perhaps a prime instance of nostalgic writing. It was
written during one of the worst and longest stretches of those
interminable war years, when it was a memorable treat to get as

far away as the next village. A rare visit to London was as audacious as a journey across Siberia. The full forces of that long imprisonment, and the absolute cessation of most of those things that made life worth living, must have pressed hard on and spurred the imagination. In the effect, "The Areöis," a piece of unashamedly "escapist" writing, pleases me more than anything else printed in these pages. Written in the manner of Gauguin's paintings, it is a fantasy on the South Sea Islands. I took immense trouble with the fruits and flowers, and with trying to get the colors of the landscape. In one detail there is an inaccuracy, for it appears that the narwhal is an inhabitant of the Northern Arctic Seas. Shortly after writing it, a friend told me of his experience during the First World War when he met a man—I think a Scot—who made his livelihood by going every year, as his father and grandfather had done before him, to buy narwhal tusks—"sea ivory" as it was called—from the Eskimos in Baffin Bay and Greenland. This must have been the most unlikely and picturesque of businesses to remain in private hands. When the Royal Academy held their exhibition of a hundred years of painting, a year or two ago in London, pictures were on view by William Hodges, who accompanied Captain Cook on his second voyage. "On his return," according to the *Dictionary of Painters,* "Hodges painted for the Admiralty some views in Otaheite (Tahiti) and the other islands in the Pacific Ocean." His pictures of the huge war canoes of the Oceanians, full of tattooed warriors, with the high hills of the islands rising at the back tufted with strange palms, could have been another source of inspiration, but at that date I had not seen them. In *Dance of the Quick and the Dead* (1936) I had written descriptions of the Maori warriors in their rustling war cloaks, formed of feathers, always of red, black or yellow, never green nor blue, with their jade scepters in their hands, based on Angas' *New Zealanders Illustrated,* a book of colored lithographs of rare excellence by one of the first Englishmen to reach New Zealand. In the section called "The Armada, or the Shoal of Maidens," I wrote of the Maori maidens swimming out to the schooner and climbing on board crowned with flowers. But this was another civilization from that of the Areöis and required a different treatment. To the many Americans who have had the opportunity of going to Honolulu and appreciating its paradisal flowers and climate, I hope my Oceanian chapter will not come amiss.

"Mexico," which formed the concluding portion of my first prose book, *Southern Baroque Art,* published in 1924, was written many years before I ever went there. This is, I trust, no argument against it. I followed the same practice sometime later in writing *"Valse des Fleurs,"* a description of a ball in the Winter Palace of St. Petersburg during the reign of the Czar Alexander II, and found ignorance of the locality no impediment. To deny a writer authority to do this would be to say that no author must describe a scene or persons living before his own era. My ambition to go to Mexico was only gratified thirty years after writing of it, in December 1952, when I was there for five days only, but that was long enough to have my hopes fulfilled. It is, of purpose, the only specimen included here of my writings on Baroque art. Having been labeled as "Futurist" in early days, I find that a ticket with "Baroque" inscribed on it seems ever since to hang around by neck. But, in fact, I addressed myself to the subject only because I was looking for material to sharpen my pen on, and at this time of day little fame is to be had by writing on Botticelli or Fra Angelico. But "Mexico" is as much a description of the landscape as of the buildings.

After this lapse of so many years, some discrepancies are evident. Much more is known, now, of the Churriguera family of Spanish architects whose name was seized on in order to discredit a whole movement. Salamanca, their main center of activity, is a townful—that is the only word for it—of magnificent late Gothic and Renaissance architecture in golden stone. Their works, which complete the building cycle, certainly reflect little ignominy on their name. This extreme "Southern" style—for it is an exuberant expression of the South, however perfected in Salamanca—is, if anything, wrongly labeled with their name. The most splendid specimen of Churrigueresque is the glorious western front of the cathedral at Santiago de Compostela, high, golden towers, rich as the pagodas of a Hindu temple, nodding with flowering weeds and snapdragons, above terraced landings and ceremonial flights of stairs. This is by a local architect, and typically enough, Santiago, far from being in the South, is in Galicia, the northwest corner of Spain, above Portugal. Nevertheless, it *is* a Southern style, to be appreciated at Murcia and along the sunlit Levante with its blue ocean and its orange groves; in little towns like Lorca, or like Elche in its forest or oasis of date palms. And from Spain it passed to Mexico, and *is* the style of Mexico. I was lucky enough, while I was there, to see perhaps the three most splendid examples: the church at Tepozotlán, the Santuario de Ocotlán on a hill outside Tlaxcala, and the church at Taxco. These are, certainly, as magnificent and romantic as I could ever have imagined them in youthful enthusiasm when I was little more than twenty years old. And in those few December days they could not but be enhanced by the ten-foot scarlet poinsettias that grew against their walls. I find, however, that I never even mentioned the extraordinary glittering white façade of the Santuario de Ocotlán, between its towers, which have bases of scarlet lozenge-shaped bricks, set in white mortar, giving an effect as of scarlet shagreen.

Taxco, as old residents in Mexico remember, was then three days' ride by muleback over the mountains of Guerrero. It is now some two hours' drive along a motor speed road through an earthly paradise of flowers and flowering trees. I wrote of Yucatán and the ruined Mayan cities, but seemed to have attached no particular importance to Chichen-Itza or Uxmal. But this was many years before American enterprise and public spirit had restored the ruins. My source of information was that centenarian authority, Stephen's *Yucatán*, familiar to me since childhood, for we have a copy with my great-grandfather's name in it. I may add that the bullfight with which this chapter ends, forming the finale of *Southern Baroque Art*, was modeled on Stephen's account of a bullfight in Mérida. The further extension of the subject down to South America, and particularly Brazil, was written in ignorance of the eighteenth-century rococo towns and churches at Ouro Preto, and elsewhere in the province of Minas Geraes, and no one at that date seemed to have heard of the sculptor El Aleijadinho, who is now the rage. To this extent can aspects of a subject alter in the space of half a lifetime. How sad that it should be half over! There is some mention of the Jesuit settlements, the Misiones, in Paraguay and Argentina, a subtopic of extreme picturesqueness, but how interested I would have been had I but known more! It is, for instance, only within the last year or two that it has been discovered that Domenico Zipoli, most talented of Italian composers for the harpsichord after Domenico Scarlatti, resigned his post as organist to the mother church in Rome, joined an expedition to Rio de la Plata as missionary, and became the organist of the principal church at Córdoba, in Argentina. (This is the town where Manuel de Falla died in 1946.) And Zipoli, with little of his music published, died at Córdoba in 1726. He had lived in Argentina for nine years. So many Americans now go to Mexico that I hope this description of it by an Englishman who had been there of instinct only may be interesting. After many years I found my essay on this unseen subject, made real by enthusiasm, rings true.

"Festival at Nola" is written in Neapolitan style, inspired, that is to say, by the climate, the architecture and the music of Naples, the one town in Italy which has come down to us with a large population from classical times and conveying, therefore, in its vociferous hurly-burly something of the ancient world of Greeks and Romans. Rome itself is forever, now, the ecclesiastical city; and it could even be true that at certain periods its population was outnumbered by its statues. The scene of the festival is not Naples itself, but the near-by town of Nola, in the Campania, where what is nothing more or less than the Festival of Adonis is still celebrated, doubtless with ever-diminishing resemblance to its original, but still an extraordinary living relic of the ancient world. This is a crowd piece, as are those at the beginning of this book describing the market place of Marrakesh and the Feria of Seville. I spent several winters at Amalfi, near Naples, as an appreciative onlooker of the Southern scene, and used to know well the country round Naples, towns like Torre del Greco, Torre Annunziata, Nocera de' Pagani, Sorrento and all those places, actually or in spirit on the slopes of Vesuvius, and warmed by volcanic as well as solar fires. This was an occasion, then, to give free rein to fancy in a description of a *fiesta* in a Southern Italian town.

The penultimate episode in this collection, "Battle in the Steppe," was inspired by a photograph, taken by a German soldier, that appeared in one of our illustrated papers at some date in 1943 or 1944. I suppose it had been found on his dead body. How or why it was released for publication I do not know. It was the forcing of a river (Dnieper, Don or Volga?) under a heavy smoke barrage by the German army invading Russia. My old classical dictionary, with a preface by Dr. Lemprière (dated Pembroke College, Oxford, November 1788, at a good period in the writing of English), under the heading Tartarus, puts: "One of the regions of Hell, where according to the Ancients, the most impious and guilty among mankind were punished. Its entrance was continually hidden from the sight by a cloud of darkness, which is represented three times more gloomy than the obscurest night. According to Hesiod, it was a separate prison, at a greater distance from the earth than the earth is from the heavens. Virgil . . . says that it was surrounded by the impetuous and burning streams of the river Phlegethon." And under Phlegethon, Dr. Lemprière speaks of "a river of Hell, whose waters were burning." This photograph of a Battle in the Steppe could be interpreted in no other words than these. It even seemed incredible that anything so ephemeral as a photograph could have survived this epical and Stygian struggle. When I further consult the dictionary, under the heading Styx it tells me: "A river whose waters were so cold and venomous that they proved fatal to such as drank them. A river of Hell . . . whose waters even consumed iron, and broke all vessels." This seems to be a complete and entire interpretation of that battle scene, in all the heat *and* cold of Hell.

In its conception there is some influence from Brueghel's paintings; and where the harvesters are described eating their midday meal among the stooks of corn there is an obvious reminiscence of Brueghel's picture in the Metropolitan Museum.

But it was my own invention to have the battle going on at the same time in the distance, and to put the workers from the collective farms into dancers' practice dress. Miss Dorothy Sayers, now engaged on translating Dante, wrote to me that one of my images of dying persons in the cornfield was exactly paralleled in *The Inferno.* I tried to add the horrors of air battle in terms of the aerial monsters to be described in Hieronymus Bosch's paintings. And the flame throwers, in the end, advancing slowly through the ruins while they spray their liquid fire, are certainly an afterthought of which the medieval masters of *diableries* would have availed themselves had they but been able. I think that a detailed and close copy of Brueghel's "Triumph of Death," in the Prado at Madrid, which forms an episode in my *Dance of the Quick and the Dead,* may have been of help to me in this "Battle in the Steppe." There are accurate studies in it of the sounds of distant bombing, and of the hurtling of "dead" airplanes to the earth, "with screaming engine, as though the metal cried in pain and fear." But the supreme invention of all was still to come. For in 1943 we had not the atom bomb.

"Finale in Form of a Bacchanale," which is the ending of *Sacred and Profane Love,* is not difficult to deduce from the last movement of Beethoven's Seventh Symphony. That apart, it is of interest that Beethoven, in a memorandum which he wrote in 1818 about two symphonies he thought of writing, says, "the orchestral violins, etc. to be increased tenfold in the last movement—in the allegro a Bacchus festival." On another occasion Beethoven said, of himself, "I am Bacchus." In spite of this, the last movement of the Seventh Symphony, which is unquestionably a bacchanale, is said by some authorities to be based upon a Cossack tune. Bacchus, or Dionysus, it will be recalled, invaded India and taught the inhabitants "the use of the vine, the cultivation of the earth, and the manner of making honey." This is exactly the sense in which I interpreted the bacchanale; and it is used here after that Tartarean battle for a happy ending.

The first thoughts of any conscientious author must be of his own shortcomings. These are hideously and woefully apparent when he reads his proofs. Nothing, ever, is the equal of his own expectations. Proofreading can take on the aspect of an eternal and perpetual wet day with no sun and, as day fails, but a weak globe in the electric light. Nevertheless, I have tried hard for warmth and clarity. I have mentioned that "The Areöi Society" is my own favorite among these pieces, precisely, I think, because of its warmth and clearness. But there are so many other passages with which I would wish to tempt the reader. I would have liked to include the total of what I have written on Venice, which is the most beautiful city in the world, even in its poverty and decay. I wrote of the Festival of the Bucintoro and of an August thunderstorm in Venice with the different sorts of thunder booming, all night long, from all over the town; and have written many passages on Carpaccio and on the Bellinis. I believe that my most sustained flight of imagination is "The Shoal of Pearls," part of *Sacred and Profane Love,* inspired by a most glorious old book on shells from the East Indian Seas.

Among other things, not presented here, I would mention "La Vie Parisienne," a fantasy built round the first night of the operetta of that name by Offenbach, on a certain summer evening during the Second Empire. Then, if the component parts of books are in question, and not their total, I would name the episode "Chrysorrhoas" in *The Hunters and the Hunted,* an evocation of the palace of the Byzantine Emperors, probably the most splendid of all buildings there has ever been with its golden mosaics of lion hunts and towers of porphyry built in the form of pyramids; and from the same book the fantasy on the castles of "Les Trés Riches Heures," loveliest of all French medieval manuscripts. That is a calendar of the twelve months with as many paintings of the old Louvre, the Château de Lusignan, and others of the Royal castles. A companion piece to this would be the chapter on the Crusaders' Castles in Lebanon and Palestine from *The Gothick North:* Mirabel, Blanchgarde, Nigraguarda, Toron and Scandalion. From *The Hunters and the Hunted,* again, I would mention the "Chasse Royale de Louis XV," based on that set of tapestries. For I have written much on tapestries, as in my book on Spain where the tapestries of Zaragoza are described, as also the Wars of Troy at Zamora and the "black" Burgundian tapestry to be seen there, which is one of the minor wonders of the world.

Not to weary the reader with things which are not within his hands, I would like in a final paragraph to recall "The Oracle of Dodona," in *Primitive Scenes and Festivals;* "Red Indian Warrior Customs," a chapter built up in that same book from George Catlin's paintings of Red Indians; studies there also of the Mayas and the Maize Goddess; and would in the last resort recall what I have written on flowers and birds, on dancing, on architecture and on music. I would have included a study of the night quarter of Barcelona, the Paralelo, which seems haunted still by figures from the "blue period" of Picasso. This comes in *The Hunters and the Hunted,* while, from *Primitive Scenes and Festivals,* I would have liked to reprint "à la Polikare," which is a study of Albanian warriors and shepherds in their white fleece coats. Many books are not quoted here at all. Yet there is enough, one hopes, to satisfy most tastes.

The pieces here included read, of course, disjointedly, for there is no string of narrative attaching more than two or three of them together. It is an exhibition with, perhaps, no more cohesion than a one-man show of paintings, or a concert of one composer's works. The task has been to render it as little repetitive as possible, and to throw wide the net so as to draw in material from far and near. Some accumulation of knowledge and experience, however little compared to what could be, has accrued to me up to the time I write this. It is my belief that I have informed myself of nearly all works of art in the known world. I cannot think that anything considerable is missing. Where I have not been in person, I have read and studied. I have heard most of the music of the world, and seen nearly all the paintings. But, in order to create, it is necessary to remember it all with one part of the mind and forget it with the other. The sensation of being born anew every morning is a necessity. One must be alone and by oneself, the first human being in the wilderness. That is, perhaps, how to look at the wonder and beauty of the world. I believe that poetry, and as much of poetry as enters into all the other arts at their highest level of imagination, should be an aim in itself over and above all other considerations whatever, a religion of its own with its own rewards and punishments, and conveying no other threats or blandishments than the sum of its own achievement. It is the beauty or the poetry in the creations of the human spirit that is more important than the faith, however strongly and to whatever degree that was the motive. Their greatness as works of art is judged by that. The reward of the art is enough in itself, and all other motives are in decline from that. Those works of art are greatest which can be admired "absolutely," as an end in themselves. This law is universal, applying to all faiths and creeds: the devils of Notre Dame look down over the city, leaning their elbows on the stone parapet at the angles of the towers, inspired by the same spirit that dragged the stone figures of oxen into the belfries of Laon; that by extension of faith, coursing along other channels, raised the minarets of Grand Cairo and Istanbul, dressed the domes of Isfahan and Meshed in glittering tiles; or built Tibetan lamaseries among the rhododendrons and the snows.

The spirit animating these writings is, perhaps, that of the whole world civilized and accessible, and poverty and war abolished. Those were my ideals when young, and I think they are still the aim of most Englishmen and Americans. Without two wars, what could the world have been? What might it be, even now, if all the wounds were healing! One lives but once, and I have tried during this one life to celebrate its splendors and its miseries. It is a pity, in my opinion, that I have not been to India and to Persia, for it would be particularly good for me to see the Persian buildings. But there exists, unfortunately, no organization to dispatch persons where they ought to go. In default of that, which is too far for my own resources, I have watched and studied all I can. Now comes the moment, with a career half over, when the truth is borne in upon me of Pope's remark that "the proper study of mankind is man," and I know that I should now address myself more to persons than to things. In view of which I close this book of my old writings, take up my pen, and begin anew.

Sacheverell Sitwell

DUMB TONES, AND SHUDDERING SEMITONES
OF DEATH *

At about six o'clock of a February evening a man and woman enter the Sablonnière restaurant, in Cranbourn Alley off Leicester Square, London. It is the night of 10 February, 1862. The four-wheeler can be heard driving away, and they come across the floor to a little table out of the gaslight. Now that he has hung up his hat and coat, his red or auburn-red hair falls nearly to his sloping shoulders; for he is very small and had a peculiar walk, just now, and the most extraordinary shoulders. They slope straight down into his body as though their construction was for some particular physical purpose, in order to play some instrument, perhaps, and as if to justify this guess he is forever fluttering his hands. They are never still for a moment, and he has a voice that is alternately shrill and sonorous. So extraordinary is his whole appearance that the clothes he is wearing are of little moment; and in any case they are conventional clothes of the day. There is no difference in them: all the difference is in himself. In fact, he is the most peculiar being ever seen, and calculated, what with one thing and another, with his clothes, his voice, his hair, his hands, to be stared at wherever he goes, and not least of all in this restaurant. He is talking in elaborate French to the waiter, and in the end a lot of wine is ordered, and not much food.

They neither of them eat when it comes. She plays with a knife and fork and pushes the plate away, and to keep him company with his wine pulls it back again in front of her. But they talk without ceasing, even if at times it is his monologue and she only sighs or nods her head in agreement, or as if listening to a verse of poetry that he is reciting. Her spells of silence draw attention to the pallor of her face. She is older than he, or it is

* From *Dance of the Quick and the Dead*, 1936.

25

that she is ill. She might be nearly thirty, and he must be twenty-five.

Her appearance is no less different, no less estranged from the ordinary. Her character is in her beautiful neck, long and delicate, in the heavy lidding of her eyes, and in the long folds of her dress. She has full lips, but they are pale and bloodless, and so are her cheeks, which with a little color would disclose her youth and freshness. But everything about her is blanched, artificially blanched with illness—pale, it might be said, like celery that has been hidden from the light to make it tender. And then in a moment she will flush red. The beauty comes back into her lips and cheeks, but it is only momentary and in the excitement of something said. Even so, this happens often enough to be a perpetual reminder of her youth, to anyone who watches her. We have said that the character comes also from the long folds of her dress. The lines of this are altogether outside contemporary time, however much they may since have become a part of it whenever we think of her. It is of some striped material with long sleeves, long waist, and everything done to it that could revoke the age they hated and give to it the semblance of belonging to another time. This was the aim in mind, but its end is only typical of herself, and makes her as noticeable and peculiar as her companion. Also, there can be little doubt that the dress was made by her own hands, and it shows the shortcomings of this, and the faults of a slender purse. Perhaps, as well, she may be too ill to bother much. Even so, it does not need the peculiar lines of her dress to make her remarkable. This she would be anywhere and in any company. Perhaps there is a consecration, a sacrament in all her actions, something in her which is as if she is already dead and is only lingering until she can see the end of something she has loved. But in spite of her air of sadness, there is nothing cadaverous or disembodied about her; and this is because she is young, and looks a little older than her age, through illness, and is naturally simple and unaffected. It is noticeable that while the poet never ceases from agitating his hands, her hands are generally folded as if she is patient and used to waiting. Also, at times and for a long while together, she will close her eyes. When she speaks, her voice is soft and low so that it hardly carries as far as the next table in the restaurant. And this is in marked contrast to her companion, who talks as if to be overheard and has, indeed, something flaunting about his whole manner and appearance. Yet, for all the physical difference in them, they are alike and the one is counterpart of the other. Their relationship is that of brother and sister more than that of lovers. But, even so, the vital difference of birth divides them. He could be nothing but aristocratic in his origin, while she has the humility of something that has been hidden for a long time, obscured by poverty and darkened rooms. She has been brought out into the light, and this it is that is killing her.

It is to be seen by anyone who watches them that there is some close bond between them. They are not lovers, they are not brother and sister. It is clearly enough one of those situations in which their affinity is complicated by difficulties that bring them together only to separate them again. Or it is one of those cases in which persons who are in constant contact together meet in their souls but never in their bodies. If she is unhappy because of him they would not be talking together quite in that way. When she shuts her eyes it is obvious that the cause of her misery, on which she is now thinking, is outside this present relationship. It is, in fact, her husband. A moment later she has opened her eyes again and listens more attentively because her companion is reciting poetry to her. This love of poetry is one of the links of their friendship. At the same time something in her air of sacrifice and consecration tells that her husband, on account of whom she is suffering, and who is, therefore, her lover still, must be someone possessed of the same qualities that she admires in this friend with whom she is dining. He must be a poet or an artist, and probably he is older than her companion. This is all surmise from their behavior and appearance. And, indeed, this young man and woman in all their actions and in everything that they say or do are invested with an air that makes them different from the figures in everyday life. Not only their personalities but even this particular occasion make an extraordinary event and attract the attention of everyone who witnesses it. But before we pursue our inquiries any further into their history, let us remember the time and place. In that day there were nothing but family hotels in London and the only restaurants were two or three of this character, in the foreign or cosmopolitan part of the town. It is chiefly foreigners who frequent them, and a young man who brings a lady here for dinner is prepared for something of an adventure or is, at least, asserting his knowledge of Paris, where restaurants are already the rule. No other man of his acquaintance would be here unless he was either trying to escape being seen or was dining with someone whom he could not take elsewhere. This much must be said in order to establish that they are no part of the ordinary clientele of the house. But, in truth, both of them are so outside life that in any and every environment they would be exceptional.

Now she closes her eyes for so long a time together, while he goes on talking and appears not to notice it, that one wonders what is passing through her mind and what agony of thought can be afflicting her. It is, however, a thing that she has power to put away from her, for a moment or two later she is talking earnestly to him, and even smiling. Also, she has flushed red again and looks young once more. The quick recovery of her spirit is a sign of her nervous condition. This is, also, the secret of her beauty, though, as soon, she relapses again and sighs deeply, as if too sad to weep. But this is the moment to disclose her identity. It is Miss Siddal, the wife of Rossetti, dining with Swinburne. He had called that evening to fetch her, as he often did, at the house in Chatham Place; and now that we know they are among the most remarkable men and women of our race who have lived, we are better prepared to look at them and never to forget the picture of them on this tragic evening. We may well watch them carefully, for an entire phase of poetry depends on their persons. The creation of this must be the physical purpose behind their strange appearance. And this must sound as if we are about to say that they are lovers, but of that there has never been even the suspicion. Yet no woman ever loved Swinburne except Miss Siddal; and it is clear that he loved no one, not Miss

Siddal, not Adah Menken, not any woman whom he ever met or saw. His life of love was in his own mind, twisted, it may be, into peculiar and unprofitable directions into which it is no part of another writer's business to probe. The center of his own tragedy lay in himself, out of which, or whom, he was never able to emerge and extricate his emotions, and this is all that need be said about the secret of this greatest poet of that century—always excepting Keats, from whose early grave the flower of this fresh apparition has appeared. No less is this true of Miss Siddal, who is the physical incarnation of the poetry of Keats, of its maladive loveliness and doomed youth. The poetry of Keats, who had been dead for forty years, had just become the intoxication of Swinburne. This is to be found, transmuted by his own genius, in such poems as "August," "In the Orchard," "Anactoria," the flower of that year or two during which he was one of the greatest poets there has ever been. It is just at this time that we see him; and it may have been under the influence of his friendship with Miss Siddal that he wrote these poems. They are, therefore, in some sense the products of her personality, or ghost, working through him, and this thought gives an additional poignancy to our sight of them both.

To her this dinner in Cranbourn Alley off Leicester Square is less of an adventure than it would be to most other women, for the reason that she had worked in a milliner's shop near by in Cranbourn Alley. It was there that the painter Deverell saw her through the window, and coming back announced his discovery to Rossetti, who was quick to profit by the information. She was so much the incarnation of his ideals that she became the obsession of that lively mind to the exclusion of everyone else. Soon they were engaged to be married, but already she was ill with consumption and the wedding was put off from year to year while it was supposed that she was gaining strength and would soon recover. Thus it came about that though they were incessantly in each other's company, the marriage became, as it were, indefinitely postponed. All this time she was agitating, more perhaps than he realized, for it to take place; and when at last they were married, it was to a dying woman that he was tied. This was little more than eighteen months before the evening on which we see her; and she had first met Rossetti nearly ten years before. She had left her home to become a shopgirl only a year before Deverell saw her in the shop window. This had been when she was nineteen years old, so that for all her adult life she had known this quarter of London in which they were dining. She was used to its ways; and the peculiar reserve of her nature made it easy for her to protect herself against its dangers, which were more real then than they may seem now. This same trait of character in her made it essential that Rossetti should marry her and insisted on the delay of this until it was, in effect, too late to be anything but fatal to her health. This was the tragedy of Miss Siddal, and the implications that grew out of it make her the figure of romance that she must always be and, as certainly, brought her to her death.

On this night she is, indeed, very near to it. The immediacy of it depends only upon herself; and of that we cannot be quite certain whether she has decided or not. It is when she closes her eyes that she is practicing, as it were, for eternal sleep, and then she will as suddenly open them and talk and laugh as if to let anyone say that it was, in half, a happy evening that they spent and that they talked and laughed together without concern. Once or twice she bites her lips, and she has a handkerchief screwed tightly into the ball of her hand, but these are signs that pass without notice from the unworldly being who talks to her, and pours out more wine, and talks again. The air of tragedy deepens because of this monologue into which, from time to time, she interposes a few words or opens her eyes and listens to poetry. It is evident from this that she will do nothing to disturb him or break his mood. He calls for more wine, and puts the bottle in front of him, and calls for brandy. So far as he is concerned there are no other diners in the room; and if there were they must listen to him, for he grows more and more excited and querulous and his voice ranges from basso to falsetto, up and down the scale, as he speaks. Also, his hands are incessant in their fluttering and now even his shoulders move spasmodically. All of his body is on the quiver and vibrating, so that he is like someone in a religious ecstasy who is about to give prophecy and become the mouthpiece of the god. The double intoxication of wine and poetry shakes and seizes him. It is like watching someone in a fit. The only outlet of this force is in talking, and after a while the spate of it ceases, leaving him exhausted and wanting still more brandy. It is very seldom that she has interrupted this monologue, and the quietness of her few remarks shows the authority that she has over him and is the proof of how often they must have talked together. Therefore it seems, in a sense, as if she has come to this restaurant against her own inclination. She has eaten little or nothing; and, as she is so unhappy, there could be no other reason for coming out to dinner —since this was no clandestine meeting between them—than simply the desire on her part to please him. Also, it draws her far enough outside her own orbit to let her think over her life. And if we knew the truth of that, we should realize at this late date in her life how seldom she comes out at all.

It was just ten years ago that she had started work in the shop. And then one day that young man looked through the window and came in to see her and brought his friends. That was the end of one life and the beginning of another. This was her rebirth, or at least it was her entry into the life predestined for her. Of this she had never a doubt. Neither could anyone else who knew her deny that the very mold into which she had been cast made her separate from the rest of mankind. Her destiny was to be brought out into the light and to die of it.

The missing person in this communication of souls that we are watching is her husband. It was his genius that breathed life into her image. Our own age is not rich enough in talents to deny this title to Rossetti. When he first met Miss Siddal, and she became his model, he was not yet twenty-five years old. He was the rebel painter of that day and a more than promising poet. His very Italian energy had gathered together and launched a movement in the arts that was to last until the end of the century, long after his own death. It is not necessary to go into the details of this because its implications are familiar enough to anyone who is likely to read these pages. This excuse absolves us from the

material facts and leaves us free to develop the drama that we are
watching. To begin with, his character is not to be known from
the pictures by his hands. He was an Italian, born in London, of
Southern Italian parents who were political exiles. His Christian
names of Dante Gabriel may be taken for indication of where he
was born and what was expected of him. At twenty years of age
he was already in his maturity and hardly, indeed, developed
beyond that, for as the technique of his pictures improved—
though this never reached to much more than the level of an
amateur—so his inspiration declined. All, then, was in the force
of his character. He was vigorous and robust, in contradiction
to everything that is left to us of his pictures or poems. He had
ribald humor, wrote ribald limericks, and if he saw young women
who took his fancy would resort to such expedients as tugging
their hair in order to get into conversation with them. It was the
higher, more solemn side of his nature that made him fall in love
with Miss Siddal. This was to involve him in as much agony as
it brought pain to her. They fatally injured each other by their
affection. She became his model and his inseparable companion,
living in his studio and sharing his house, but it is almost certain
that her scruples forbade anything but the most fleeting and in-
frequent intimacy. She would become his wife, but only if well
enough, and year after year he was disappointed in this, for she
was little better than an invalid. By the time they were married
she was doomed, and he must have known that he was marrying
a dying woman. For anyone of his ardent temperament this was
an unendurable state of affairs; and, long before this, he had
begun to look for consolation where it could easily be found.
It seems probable that it was because of this, though her health
was so desperate, that she again broached the question of marriage
in the vain hope of saving him from a worse destiny. At the
same time all the force of his old affection for her was revived
from pity, and he let himself be sacrificed, though there was no
possible good that could come of it. And so they were married,
and almost immediately her causes of jealousy were resumed.*
Even now Rossetti was only some thirty-two or three years old,

* They were married at Hastings, on 23 May, 1860.

and was no more capable of becoming a permanent sick nurse than Byron would have been. Whenever he thought of her it will have been with affection, but the symbols of life meant too much to his vigorous spirit. Men will make a vow of eternal love but they are not as much to be believed as women. Even when he said it, Rossetti was more likely than not to be in love with some-one else as well. This was a thing that the gentle spirit of Miss Siddal was incapable of understanding. If he loved anyone else, he no longer loved her; and when he began to go out in the evenings without her, her heart must have shrunk into itself. This was the tarnishing of the immortal bond there was between them. She had been taken out of darkness and silence by him, and taught to write and taught to draw; and now it would have been better if she had been left by herself to make her own meal in the evening, and read, and never go out. This was how she had lived before he met her. She harmed no one and had no enemies. But now her image or spirit had been given life by him, and like his own child it was bound to him and had a physical affinity with him that none except his own hands could spoil. It was now that she began a period of unhappiness to which, we must be afraid, it would be difficult to find a parallel in other lives. As a person she was abnormally sensitive, and had been given a soul which, because it had arrived so mysteriously, could find nothing else to live upon but that other heart out of which it had been born. He was her only affection. She had tried more than once for a child, and failed. Therefore the injury that her affection suffered in him was inconsolable. She was like an orphan, adopted and dependent; or, more still, like a little servant of another race, a little Indian it might be, who could not escape and had no life but that of those who had been kind to her. We must remember her humble origin, coming out of that shop; and somehow the horror of her sadness is immeasurably increased by the beginnings of poetry in her, her stammerings, as it were, in this unknown tongue that she heard spoken around her. In a curious echo, or prophecy, of a great poem that was to be written many years later, it is evident that her thoughts were centered on death:

> How is it in that unknown land?
> Do the dead wander hand in hand?
> Do we clasp dead hands, and quiver
> With endless joy for ever?
>
> .   .   .   .
>
> Hollow hearts are ever near me,
> Soulless eyes have ceased to cheer me.

This is the testimony of her spirit, and the wanderings of that lonely soul are reflected in them in all her misery and unhappiness. We must own, in thinking of them, that the ever-increasing legion of those who wonder why they were ever born must number Miss Siddal among themselves. Why should she be so cruelly bruised when she might have been left at peace living her own life of silence, harming no one and happy in her little room? Her only consolation can have been the thought that this was her destiny and that she could not avoid it. But if this was destiny or fate, the pattern of it was to be discerned coming to an end just before her eyes. She must be true to the direction of that and, indeed, it was no more to be dispelled than the beginnings of her life or that break in it when she was brought out from the shuttered room into the light. The lines of it were inexorable and pointing to the end. This, indeed, was the giving of the poison cup into her hands. The image or glyph of her days is imperfect without that. Every consideration was shaping her into that direction. The unborn child that she was carrying within her she would not allow to be disappointed of dying with her. It was hers and only hers and would stay with her. The little knockings of it upon her heart were when it spoke to her, and this was all the communion they would ever have. She would never see it or hear its voice. They were two prisoners, two living souls in the next cells to each other, who never spoke and never saw each other among the living, but rapped out the rudiments of words and met in this manner halfway in their misery. If she was destined to this end of life, was there not even a distinction in that, another proof that she was set apart from the rest of the living? But then, if this were so, why was it that she had failed? In her husband she knew, by now, the limitations of his talent and that the flower of it, due to their infatuation, was already over and done with. Now he was edging away from her and an excuse was ever on his lips. Their old delight in each other was sullied and soiled, as it were by dirty hands. It was a thing broken and never to be resumed. There were spectators and a crowd who looked upon them. Also, her nature had never been so physical as his. She had been certain that her kind of affection was stronger than that other and could never die. It had been left to him to prove to her that both sorts were mortal. There was, in fact, no reason to live. The purpose for which she had been created—to inspire—had failed miserably within a year or two, and the rest of life had been a dragging along of weary feet. And so, as she began to relinquish life, she began to love death. Earlier on that winter evening, before she went out, the pattern of her life had been more true to itself than ever. It was only necessary now to wait for what would happen when she came in, to lie in bed and hear the same lies and see him go out into the night and know that he was not lecturing but that, if the truth must be said, he was across the river, on the Surrey side of the river, seeing Fanny Hughes. And her he did not even pretend to love. It was not love, then, that took him away from herself and out into the night. It is one of the cruelties of the living that it is the unphysical who suffer most in jealousy, because they cannot forgive and have no willingness for revenge. With Miss Siddal this is more particularly true, who never recovered from the shock of physical discovery, who become disetherealized in the light of that and found that love had lost its spiritual significance. There were some aspects in her nature that made her like the Sleeping Beauty in the fairy book. She was predestined to be awakened from her trance, but she might live or she might die at the approach of her rescuer. It is the irony in her unhappy life that no sleeping maiden could have had, as rescuer, a lover more true to her dreams and imaginings, but she died from the manly roughness of his touch. She was too delicate to respond to him. It was through being his physical inspiration that she would have taken his soul into dominion, though to believe in the lastingness of this is to believe in every promise rashly made. We may think that his experience of his own broken vows was more sad than the experience of most other men. In his poem we can read:

> Along the grass sweet airs are blown
>   Our way this day in Spring.
> Of all the songs that we have known
>   Now which one shall we sing?
>   Not that, my love, ah no!—
>   Not this, my love, why, so!—
> Yet both were ours, but hours will come and go.
>
> .   .   .   .
>
> The branches cross above our eyes,
>   The skies are in a net:
> And what's the thing beneath the skies
>   We two would most forget?
>   Not birth, my love, no, no,—
>   Not death, my love, no, no,—
> The love once ours, but ours long hours ago.

Nothing could be imagined that was more different from this than the serious thoughts of Miss Siddal when she wrote poems. The contrast in their characters could not be better expressed than in the quotations that we have given from them both. Yet, for all this difference, the echo of their affinity is to be found in it. She wrote in that way because he had taught her to do so; but it is a curious thing that it is really her personality that haunts both poems and that, of the two, hers has the sincerity and the strength. She is more surely present in this than in the pictures that he painted of her, and we can see her in it just as clear before our eyes as we see her, sitting here in this restaurant, at the table in the corner. She has closed her eyes once more and is listening; or perhaps she has sunk too deep into her own misery to hear the words.

For now there is this friendship of hers to be accounted for. There is no one else, except Swinburne, with whom she is upon these terms, while we may wonder, after this evening, whether he ever dined again alone with any woman, save Adah Menken. It is difficult, indeed, not to be drawn aside into a consideration of that. The heroine of "Dolores" was his only other woman friend; and while we may be sure that Swinburne will have celebrated such occasions with more than his usual libations of wine, we must remember that she too, like Miss Siddal, was a lost soul and that her love letters, like these few poems by Miss Siddal, are something lasting and permanent left over from an unhappy life. The two women would have recognized each other from their scanty writings and have been reconciled in the friendship of the poet for them both. At the same time there was every difference in their influence upon him. As to the reciprocal side of this, the attitude of Swinburne toward Miss Siddal must have been the fulfillment of exactly what was lacking toward her in Rossetti. Or it was the presence of those things that the physical side of Rossetti obscured. He had been, at the start, too much in love with her, and after that too little concerned with the permanencies of her nature. Swinburne, who did not have it in him to be in love with her, could give her exactly this companionship and sympathy. Also, Swinburne, who was only twenty-five years old, was in the full effulgence of his genius. *Poems and Ballads* was not yet published,* but its best poems were already written, and no friend of Swinburne could complain of never having heard his poetry. On the other hand, the side of his nature that was excessively violent—his idolatry for the Marquis de Sade, for instance—had not yet begun to warp his personality. He was the most extraordinary genius that had appeared in poetry since the already legendary figures of Shelley and Keats; and in the youthful Swinburne genius was coupled with an appearance that allowed no doubt of its presence. In Miss Siddal, Swinburne will have found just the shell, the empty shell that he required the friendship of a woman to be: a lovely shell, huskless, but echoing on its lip just what he would have it say, or, in fact, listening to him. Anything more corporeal than that, for all the frenzy of his talk and behavior, would have interposed itself into

* *Poems and Ballads* was published in 1866.

their friendship. They met together, therefore, in outward admiration of each other, and they had the friendship of the soul and the friendship of the heart. What was missing in them both was that other thing; and of this they were both incapable. His frenzy, and the foaming at his lips whenever he writes of this, betray the difficulty of his approach. This was his abnormality. He required the strongest and most violent stimulants; and, in default of their desired effect, he liked them for themselves. As early in his life as this, he was persuading himself that they were not the cause or the excuse but the indispensable accompaniment to those desires which, in his case, were little more than cravings. But the very peculiarity of his angle toward life must have endeared him to this other person who was, also, outside its limits. His physical personality was in itself an instrument of poetry. He was and could be nothing else than that. But both of them in their different ways were a race apart, coming out of the two opposite ends of the world, for he was an aristocrat and she had come out of the smoke of a northern town and from behind the counter in a milliner's shop. But it made no difference. They met together in poetry and were signed of the same blood in that. They were male and female of the race; few in number, but of the same blood as those others whom they admired in the past. This affinity made one kind of affection impossible between them because of their identity of blood. They were as brother and sister, but without that possibility of one parent's imposing his or her personality to the exclusion of the other. Between such persons as these there is instinctive affection; and perhaps its perfect balance and reciprocity calls for no emphasis or assertion and since it is so entirely natural may pass for being less deep than is really the truth. This is not, in fact, intended to be an account of a passionate emotion, but it is the study of two characters who were outside life and who were linked together because of that. Their disembodied and uncorporeal affection has a pathos which is lacking in the more normal contingencies. Both of them were so ill suited for life. She made her own exit from it; and he became a life prisoner in a shared house, the semidetached "The Pines," on Putney Hill.

If we look more closely at Miss Siddal, sitting in her corner, we may perceive in her three phantoms, corresponding to time's three divisions. She casts her shadow, or it comes back to her, from the appearance that she is trying to copy in her clothes. This is a conscious medievalism; but its effect is to make her not the figure out of an Italian picture, which was her intention, but into the living embodiment of the Romanticism of a previous generation, of "The Eve of St. Agnes" and the poems they had read together years ago, before the waning of their love. It was this thought that always dragged Rossetti back into his real self, or into his youth, for the constrictions placed by her conscience or her illness upon their friendship made it seem like the prolongation of that wonderful period in his adolescence. That had been a harmless but imperishable fever that possessed them. It was going to burn forever. Nothing would extinguish it. The second of those phantoms—or they are a series of superimposed shadows—is her authentic or contemporary self. This is to be typical for us of its own time. That Pre-Raphaelite shadow is the end of the '50s and the early '60s; and for an antidote it is unconvincing to look at Winterhalter, who represented Paris more than London, or at the old-fashioned Surtees, whose novels were only true of the remote shires. The reawakening of the aesthetic conscience needed this effort of the will in order to combat the careless ugliness of industry and the age of smoke. And this brings us immediately to the third of these shadows. It projects far into the future. It is no less than the whole of our aesthetic movement, emanating out of Miss Siddal's languorous poses. In all the nineteenth century, England was the only country which devoted its best energies to the conscious culture of something that was irrevocably dead. Deliberate affectations of speech and dress were the outcome of this striving after the unattainable; and nowhere else have they ever been considered the indispensable accompaniment to intelligence. They are satirized as being of South Kensington, in *Patience;* and they are no less true today, of the squares of Bloomsbury. Out of all this energy, which began in the '40s and is hardly ended yet, we are left with a little of Swinburne, written at an early age, and with perhaps a

like amount of W. B. Yeats. So it may seem now, though when
the enthusiasm of new discoveries, made elsewhere years before,
has worn off, when the addition is to be made of all this total, it
will surely be found that more survives from that distant past
than is true of our exiguous present. A little of Millais, more
particularly his "Blind Girl," most of J. F. Lewis, and an admittedly minor painter like Arthur Hughes—none of these are
of such small account that they can be forgotten for the works of
present-day giants. Whether this be so or not, it is at least certain
that the one great artist involved was Swinburne. We return,
therefore, to the importance of his last meeting with Miss Siddal.
It has already been explained that the sentiment existing between
them must not be exaggerated; but the man and woman who were
most typical of this phase of our literary history (and painting, in
England, is ever the handmaiden of literature) cannot fail to
interest us at their last meeting together. She is the heart of all
the women aesthetes there have ever been, while he is unique and
incontestable. The whole of Pre-Raphaelitism is expressed in
their personalities; and besides that there is the tragedy of their
isolation and of their fruitless and unprofitable affection, of a sort
which must occur somewhere in the experience of every reader of
these pages. In the impossibility of that barrier being broken
down between them, it is almost as if she were so much older
than he that their relationship was something to be looked on
furtively and with shame; or it was as if, for all the consanguinity
that we have mentioned, he had fallen in love with someone of
so far distant a race that they had to stay apart from each other
because of the shame and danger in their progeny. And yet there
is no question of love between them. She was ill enough, and
coming near enough to death, to smile at his proofs of life; while
he admired in her the shell, as it were, or the external ghost of
poetry, and conveniently for him there was no need to make love
behind the mask. Where the relationship is not that of lovers,
nor of brother and sister, there is need of a neuter term to describe its course. Neither of them had the longing for any other
bond to be between them. This was enough; and perhaps for
them both it was as far as they ever traveled in the way of that

happiness. They were not outside its necessity, but only incapable of its achievement. On the contrary, to be left outside the possibility of its enjoyments was their misery in life; but while he struggled furiously not to be deprived, she was resigned from the first. Her fate was implicit in her appearance, the points of which are pathos and an early death. His character, on the other hand, is to be gauged in the violent auburn of his hair and in his jerky and spasmodic movements. On this particular occasion too, he was more than a little drunk, which made for the increase of these phenomena. And poor Miss Siddal, who had taken drops of laudanum before he came to fetch her at Chatham Place, all her craving was to be stilled and not excited. The agony of her consumption and her weakness after her stillborn child of last year*—it was owing to these things that she slept with a bottle of laudanum under her pillow. Without laudanum, by this time, she could neither sleep nor eat. There were times when she had taken a hundred drops of it in order to quiet herself. In the light of this knowledge we can see another reason why she closes her eyes for long moments at a time. The force of the drugs drags her away out of the life that she dreads. Her craving is for a sedative, for an allaying of her pains. With Swinburne, it is just the contrary. Brandy inflames him and gives him the changed focus that is the half of inspiration. The music sings in his ears, and he is seized and shaken by the sacred tremors. He is lifted into life by this fire of intoxication. His normality is when he is drunk, for it is only then that he is free of life and that his thoughts can move in it swiftly and without awkwardness. In fact, the Pindaric mood is upon him whenever he is successfully drunk; and this word is of as much import in poetry as are the names of the classical orders in architecture. Or, in another sphere, it can be compared to that moment when the speedboat suddenly increases her pace and, lifting her prow out of the water, scuds along the surface of the waves, "on the step," as it is called, and no longer concerned with their depths, but flying freely and of her own volition, moment after moment and for as long as need may be, until, upon the whim of a mood, she

* It was born in April or May of 1861.

as quickly comes down upon the sea and in a breath is slow and
ordinary, heading for the harbor. So did the afflatus of drink run
its course in Swinburne, and in the ebb of it he relapsed again
into the person who was awkwardly outside life.

This man and woman with auburn hair are, at least, conscious
of their rarity. And this was a truth which did not admit of
contradiction and could be supported by every proof that was
dear to the hearts of the Romantic age. In this sense Swinburne
was more related to the greater world of the Romantics than was
any other person associated with our own Pre-Raphaelites. He is
to be traced, not in direct influence but in consanguinity of idea,
to such a figure as the poet Alfieri, as red-haired as Swinburne and
of as ancient lineage, who went over Europe, even to Norway,
with his white horses, and in final affirmation of his Romanticism
contracted marriage with the Comtesse d'Albanie, relict of the
Young Pretender. But, more than all, and insuring for this
reason the very recent condescension toward himself of the Sur-
realists who have lately disinterred his prose, if not his poems,
more than to all other forebears of his race of romantics, Swinburne paid homage to the Marquis de Sade. He even boasted
of a distant connection with him through the Grimaldi family,
rulers of Monaco. The importance of this influence upon Swinburne has only lately begun to run the risks of publication, but it
was familiar to all his circle of friends. "Close your ears to the
clatter of bayonets, the yelping of the cannons; turn aside your
gaze from the changing tides of battles lost or won; and then you
will see an immense shining and inexpressible phantom arise
from the shadows; you will see dawning over a whole star-sown
epoch the enormous and sinister figure of the Marquis de Sade."[*]
These are Swinburne's words, and there is no reason to doubt
his sincerity. However, to outward and easier criticism, it was
Keats who was the derivation of the early Swinburne. It is in
this that his personification mates most admirably with Miss
Siddal. Not that something of romance was absent, even from
Miss Siddal's descent. Her family had owned Hope Hall, on the

---

[*] Cf. A History of Surrealism, by David Gascoyne (London: Faber & Faber,
1935).

moors above Sheffield, and had come down in the world from
their medieval knighthood. This distant glamour brought her
more near than ever to "The Eve of St. Agnes." She was most
perfectly appropriate to that background. And, rising out of it,
images of the millstream and the weir, of the long grass and the
blossoming orchard, of the cornfield that was like a sweet honeycomb, uncut, of a dovecote full of white doves, of a dove-gray
crinoline and an upturned face with sad straight hair, looking
with closed eyes into a little bird cage that dangled in the sunlight—these images that mean the Pre-Raphaelites to our minds
owe their creation to the poetry of Swinburne and the personality
of Miss Siddal. This must not blind us to the negative side of
their friendship, which is, indeed, its interest to us. Their
platonic relationship, that neither of them wished to be otherwise,
is one half of the drama, for there are certain people bound
together by ties that are closer than any physical love, who would
seem to be separated forever in this world. It is as if some
previous fault had ordained that they should go through one life,
in perpetual contact, but meeting ever in the heart and never in
the body. This love, though, is more slow in waning, and this is
its reward. The other part of the drama is in the portrayal of a
person who was destined to assert such inspiration on talent and
to have a personality which has so long survived its pathetic possibilities of happiness. It is a study, therefore, of the influence
that a woman can exert on the mind and imagination of men, not
upon their hearts but their souls. This does not occur so frequently in the world that it can be passed by without comment.
The beginnings or stammerings of creation in her make it the
more poignant. On the very rare occasions in history when that
gift of creation has also been present in women, it is due from
those who have witnessed it that they should leave a record of
that flowering. Having lived since early childhood, but now with
lamentable intervals, in the flowering shade of a figure who is not
less remarkable in appearance and in personality than Miss Siddal
and not less talented, at a mild computation, than Christina
Rossetti, the writer of these pages may lay claim to an inborn
comprehension where this part of his subject is concerned. The

discerning reader will know to whom he refers. The invention of another imagery—the houses, white as salt, like the houses of Cadiz, and haunted by the Spanish Captain; the long steel grass and the cat's serenade in the moonlight; a hundred or a thousand metaphors in which old truths find fresh light and there are constant discoveries of new values; the wisdom clashing from an uncommon rhyme; the contradiction, and then the unfastening of symbols; the endless proofs of intuition and observation, things not perceived through the eyes but absorbed into the intelligence; the force and the daring vigor, in boniness of construction—for poems need bones—and the wonder of their subsequent clothing with flesh; the stores of imagery, gathered in richness as they have seldom been; the sparkle and brilliance and *brio,* concealing sadness and bearing investigation and inquiry for as long a time as nearly any fiber of poetry that is left to us—these considerations cannot fail of a peculiar aptitude when we return again to think of Miss Siddal.

For she is still before our eyes, in her long trailing dress of striped silk, leaning her chin upon her hands. She is so present a part of aesthetic experience that it is difficult to believe that this evening on which we see her is nearly seventy-five years ago. The pallor of her skin is heightened by the gas lamps; while her auburn-red hair, that is golden in sunlight, has become darkened and is the color of a bloodstain or of dried blood. The dark length of it is almost threatening, with no light out of its tresses. This is the time of the crinoline, but Miss Siddal will not wear that. Because of this only, she is as different as a Gypsy from other women. Her long, narrow hips, which are her pride, put her apart from fashion. This was the distinguishing mark of the other women of the Pre-Raphaelite circle. A painstaking diarist, Mary Howitt, notes down: "On Friday evening, June 20th, 1861, we went to a great Pre-Raphaelite crush. Their pictures covered the walls and their sketchbooks the tables. The uncrinolined women, with their wild hair which was very beautiful, their picturesque dresses and rich colouring looked like figures out of some Pre-Raphaelite picture. It was very curious. I think of it now like some hot struggling dream in which the gorgeous and fantastic forms moved slowly about. They seemed all so young and so kindred to each other that I felt out of place, though I admired them all."* Anyone of even little experience in the world will know Miss Siddal from her dress and appearance. It is a kind of instinct that attaches people, at sight, to the groups to which they belong; but in no instance could this be more easy than where Swinburne and Miss Siddal are concerned. They are the aesthetic movement in epitome. The green and dove-gray stripes of her dress** only lengthen the straight lines that are her protest against contemporary time. Even so she is young enough, with her slim figure and delicate features, to wear a crinoline with enchanting effect and to look her best in a fashionable bonnet with her soft features framed by the light silks and ribbons of its lining.*** But it is too late for that. Five years ago, perhaps, but not now, when the hand of death is on her. Those are conceits that she has put far away. She has been ill for too long and the laudanum bottle is under her pillow —laudanum that needs brandy or whisky to drown it. Even to feel well again only means more worry and more unhappiness. It is better that things should be as they are: it is not forever. And, thinking thus, she seems to grow into the straightness of her dress: the long thin folds of it are drawn out, like the dank water weeds upon the current, till she is the living Ophelia of the picture.**** In that, she is dead already, having posed for long weeks together as one dead. Nothing could have better suited the beauty of this person who was ever half outside life. The chill of fireless rooms and little meals had entered into her. This had been her childhood; and after that the dark shop with long hours of work and a glass of milk or a cup of tea behind the hat-boxes. It must be remembered that she was always poor. She had worked in a shop and was now a painter's model, while her sisters would have liked posts as governesses. This was the

* *The Wife of Rossetti*, by Violet Hunt (John Lane & Co., 1932), page 272.

** *Ibid.*, page 315. The dress is here described as of brown and black striped silk.

*** *Ibid.*, page 210.

**** "Ophelia," by J. E. Millais, in the National Gallery.

pathos of how she had been born into life, in a family that had
come in a generation or two from Hopedale to Sheffield and then
to the Old Kent Road, where she was born.* At Chatham Place
they had no servants, only a charwoman, and it was a treat to
be taken to dinner at the Sablonnière. Seeing her silence and
her good looks and her love of reading, her family had always
told her that she was to be a genius, and that she was apart from
other people. Only the last part of this prophecy had come true.
The rest of it was unfulfilled. But as to her solitude, this she
was determined to increase. To those who knew her before, the
lines of her face had altered. She had always looked unhappy,
and now she was unhappy. But it was her character that had
really changed. Her gentleness was growing into shrewishness.
She would answer in a bitter, hard voice; and this person in
whom there had never been sign of her slum surroundings would
be full of reproaches, and then—or if she had lived a little
longer—would have been ridiculous in her affected dress and
mannered ways. The one life, that is all we get, had not been
fair to her. She had been predestined to obsess and inspire; and
to some other being upon her own spiritual level, the difficulty
and delays of ill health and the scruples of conscience would but
have sanctified their love. She had to have the love that is half
pity. She had been found by someone whose ardency had inspired every vow, and had caused them all to be broken. Now
when he promised she did not believe him. And they were not
even promises, but only excuses. The time for promises was
over. There was nothing more to be gained by them, nothing to
give and nothing to keep. And as for romance of poetry, what
was there left of that! She had been quicker sullied and quicker
shriveled than she could have believed. Her heart had become
a little tight thing, dried up and giving out nothing. She who was
used to living upon milk and tea now lived on laudanum, and
was ill without it. The fire of the brandy or whisky burned into
her thin body, and then that gnawing stopped. The comfort of
the smoky slums came down and hid everything, so that it was
like beginning life again: and then the horror would dawn once

* See note at end of chapter.

more, and the aching to be lifted out of it. Or, with less trouble, to sink through it into blackness.

Now suddenly the door opens—the door of the Sablonnière. It is still early, only eight o'clock, and the night is young. The noise of Leicester Square comes in, and a cold air of that February night, enough to cause people to turn round and pull their coats about them. With it come footsteps, and the crushing of wide dresses through a narrow door. Two streetwalkers have advanced into the room, shaking out their little umbrellas and adjusting their crinolines. It is necessary to smooth these down and spread them out, as though going round the edges of a little tent, looking, that while, down at the floor and behind them. This gives time for their dresses to be seen and to attract the attention of anyone curious to see their faces as they look up. This long-drawn delay is to advertise their charms. But the artifice fails, for the manager is appalled at them and, as they look round from table to table seeking, or pretending to seek, a friend, he takes them to the door and asks that they should leave. At this they turn impertinent, and had they been given time would have mocked the corner table in broken English, or in their Belgian-French. Hardly is this done when the door turns once more and a man comes in who looks about him and goes straight up to that table, reinforcing, as it might be, the man and woman who had just drawn down that laughter on themselves for their odd dress and remarkable appearance. He must have met the two streetwalkers upon the pavement coming out. It is Rossetti, as we know from his dark Italian swarthiness and from the bow of Michelangelo across his forehead. He sits down with them and drinks a little, talking the while with so much more vitality than his silent wife or the drunken and now comatose poet. He is in lively humor, telling stories in his deep and grand voice and laughing a lot. Perhaps he is only silent when he is alone with her at Chatham Place. But Swinburne wakes up from his trance and stretches out his hand to take the bottle; whereupon Miss Siddal tries to remonstrate with him, and while she does this her own head nods and lolls and she pulls herself together with an effort and is falsely and feverishly bright. Swinburne resents the interference. It is enough for a quarrel to begin. The waiters and some of the other diners have been watching them a long time, for while his condition could never be misunderstood, from the start of the evening her drowsiness and her long spells of silence have turned into this nodding of the head, this mannered and drowsy incapacity. At such moments both of them are oblivious of their surroundings. With the arrival of Rossetti they are merely stirred out of this into a quarrel. And now she is falsely bright and flighty, as if in pretense that her drowsiness was all pose. To Rossetti, even if he was used to this, the pair of them can have been no less peculiar and not normal than to the eyes of those that were watching them, who were accustomed, when they saw drunkenness, that it should be in ordinary revelers and not in this corpselike young woman and this red-haired man. That only emphasized the obvious truth. It was time they left. The bill was brought and paid recklessly, without a scrutiny.

They parted with Swinburne on the pavement and began the long drive home in a four-wheeler along empty, gaslit Pimlico. The poet may be seen walking away with much dignity and indecision down Leicester Square. His tall stovepipe hat, crowning his mass of auburn hair, reminds us of Paderewski in his top hat. Both are of the lion tribe and apart from other men, the puny Swinburne no less than the lithe and agile pianist in his prime. As for Miss Siddal, she was very drowsy in the cold of the cab, and sat still and would not speak. She would not take his hand and it was evident that she was deep in thought, even though this was but the daydream of her drugged mind. For this, it was as if stillness were essential. The leather padding of the cab was icy cold to the touch and the wooden floor had its winter covering of straw which rattled like dead reeds and gave no warmth. The long porticos of Pimlico, all dark but numbered with great letters as if they were mansions of the dead, came past in endless enfilade, street after street, with cross streets that ended in darkness. And then, at last, there was the river, in an icy black gulf of swirling waters, and the long steep breathless stairs, with matches to be struck, and then the crocus gas. There

were lodgers above and below them, and it was early in the evening—not yet nine o'clock. She started to undress, too ill to do
anything but go to bed. He was anxious for this and tried to
hurry her, suspiciously hastening it, so as to be free of her before it was too late. She would be dead asleep, with more laudanum, when he came in. He could not reproach her with
drowsiness, for his own evening depended upon her becoming
more drowsy still. And now, when she was ready, he admitted
that he had to go. It was his evening at the Working Men's
College, and he must go there for an hour or two. At this her
mood changed, not from drowsiness into feverish brightness, but
trying to conquer her ineptitude and to show her strength. She
pleaded with him not to leave her, twisting her necklace round
and round in her hand and saying to him, "Stay with me, Gug,
stay with me."* This moved him not at all. And now clapping
her hand to her side, she threatened him with another mis-
carriage. He was still hard with her, hating the loud pitch to
which she raised her voice—a new trick she had learned and did
not have before—and not believing her. It was her fantasy and
her threat to hold over him. We are told that, half undressed,
she followed him to the landing and stayed hanging over the
banister, shrieking, "Go then, and you'll kill this baby as you
killed the last," to his descending shadow. And after this she
must have set about the business of the night, loading her
tumbler with the laudanum from underneath her pillow, pouring the brandy into it, and looking for or finding more. Soon,
very soon, she will have laid herself down, after finishing. It had
all the impulse of a sudden wave of feeling. Nothing else in the
room was touched or disturbed. The straw from the floor of the
cab was still sticking to the hem of her dress, for she had not
bothered to shake it off. And pinned to her white nightdress
was a piece of paper with the words written on it: "My life is so
miserable I wish for no more of it." It was thus that she was
found, some hours later, with an empty phial by her side, when
Rossetti came back to her.

* All the details of this scene are taken from *The Wife of Rossetti*, cited before.
This book is a mine of information on the Pre-Raphaelites.

She was dead asleep, suspiciously and deadly asleep, and black in the face. Nothing would wake her. And all the time a loud and ominous snoring came from her throat and nose. This is the most terrible of sounds, to those who have heard it, for it suggests that some exterior force has entered and taken possession.* The doctor was called and stayed with her till six o'clock in the morning, trying the stomach pump, but to no avail, and injecting several quarts of water into her stomach. She must have died just before the winter daylight began.

The trancelike state of this Ophelia with the livid face was to continue for several days until her coffin was closed. There were friends of Rossetti who, remembering how he read Edgar Allan Poe aloud, wondered if this were the trance of a Ligeia or a Morella, and ran to the doctor that he should have another look at her. Meanwhile, the sordid details of the inquest dragged to their close: Rossetti was exonerated from all blame, and her death was ascribed, happily enough, to an accidental overdose of laudanum. The time came for the closing of her coffin. One of her white doves, which had escaped and flown away the week before, came back and tapped with its beak upon the window-pane just as the undertakers were at work on her body. The landlady let it in and it died from exhaustion on the window sill. This they placed, with its wings folded, by her side in the coffin; and at the last moment Rossetti, who had not dared to look at her body since that night, came into the room with a green-bound manuscript book of his unpublished poems and, still not looking her in the face, lifted the napkin and laid the book on the left side, between her hair and her cheek. With this, and with the other, she was buried in Highgate Cemetery, in the great hecatomb.

The decline of Rossetti into the chronic victim of chloral began from that day. He was to live for twenty years more, but his genius had left him. He brooded in ever-increasing melan-

---

* The writer remembers Robert Ross describing the appalling death rattle of Oscar Wilde, that continued all through the night as he lay dying at the Hotel d'Alsace in Paris.

choly, and there can be no doubt that he imagined himself to be haunted. There is a curious story of how, staying at Penkhill Castle in Ayrshire, he went for a walk along the cliffs with William Bell Scott, and a little bird hopped along by his side, chirping to him, and made little fluttering flights and came back to him. This he declared to be the spirit of Miss Siddal; and coming back to the house they found that the great bell of the castle had never ceased ringing, by itself and without the touch of any hand, while they were on their walk. There must have been other, and less pitiful, appearances.

Nine years after her death the story of her corpse comes to an end with the indiscretion of taste by which Rossetti, wishing to reclaim his poems and publish them, caused her coffin to be opened. The permission of the Home Office was obtained, and in an early winter morning of 1869 a fire was lighted beside her grave. The gravediggers descended while Rossetti with his friends waited by the warmth above. He dared not look into the coffin—he even left express instructions in his will that on no account was he to be buried in Highgate Cemetery—but the book was given into his hands. Her auburn hair had grown across and entwined its mildewed green binding; but after the stained and discolored pages had been chemically treated, Rossetti transcribed the poems and they were printed. After this Rossetti never painted another good picture nor wrote a good poem. For the rest of his life he was the victim of chloral.

NOTE

It is necessary to point out that had a verdict of willful suicide been brought in at the coroner's inquest, the body of Miss Siddal, according to the laws of that time, could never have been buried in consecrated ground. There was, thus, every inducement to her friends to prove an accidental death. They had also to clear the name of Rossetti, who, for instance, had it become known that he was not in reality lecturing on that evening at the Working Men's College, would have emerged somewhat badly from the case. Even graver implications might have been attached to him; but of this most mercifully there was no word in court, and it is certain that nothing of the kind should be believed. His complete innocence in the matter is beyond question. There is, though, no doubt whatever that some friend had taken away and destroyed the note that was found pinned to Miss Siddal's nightdress. Its discovery and publication would have altered the verdict of accidental death from an overdose of poison. The unhappiness of her life, and its causes, would then have been revealed. Finally, I must plead poetic license; for, in reality, Rossetti was present all the evening at the dinner that I have described. But Swinburne and Miss Siddal had dined alone together often before; and, therefore, historical truth has only been contradicted during that half-hour or hour before I have made Rossetti come in to join them. With that exception, the situation is as accurate as I can make it; and I do not think it possible that I can have injured the feelings of any relatives of those concerned in the story. That has, certainly, been far from my intention.

Before we leave the black purlieus of the Old Kent Road, it is well to recall that the murderer Greenacre, from the horror of whose circumstances we can, perhaps, gather a little strength for our next task, made as recondite and dramatic a quotation from Shakespeare as could be expected of any scholar. Greenacre murdered his wife. He dismembered and burned her body; her head he could not dispose of and threw into a canal, where it floated down, catching in weir after weir with its long hair, while he came back every morning and released it to travel down a little farther between the tall houses on every side. Eventually he came and took it away, wrapped in paper in a bag. He got with it into a horse omnibus, nearly fainting away with horror when the conductor called out "Sixpence a head!" It was Greenacre who kept a little shop in Lambeth, and when Miss Siddal was a child used to carry her across the road in his arms, inspiring in her such a presentiment of horror that her morbid imagination could never forget him in later life. When the condemned sermon was preached to this murderer, on the night before his execution, coming into the chapel and seeing it empty and lighted with candles, he called out: "My God! Hell's on fire."* It is easy to see that Greenacre was an admirable audience for melodrama, even if it is not true that he himself had been an actor. Greenacre was hanged in 1837, when Miss Siddal was about seven years of age.

* Cf. Falstaff in *The Merry Wives of Windsor*. "I think the devil will not have me damned lest the oil that is in me should set hell on fire." This information is drawn from *The Wife of Rossetti*.

AMES DAMNÉES*

This is the story of two human beings, and of what becomes of them. For as long as they are caught up in their mutual passions, they are not an ordinary man and woman. What happens to them is exceptional.

But we will enter immediately into their state of feeling.

She is nineteen and he is twenty-seven.

They had passed each other once or twice upon Sauchiehall Street, the main street of Glasgow, a few months ago during the autumn, and he had persuaded a friend to introduce her. That was the start of it. At once he began writing to her and she answered him. They had one or two meetings in the house of a maiden lady, who was in their confidence. She was moved to allow this by her romantic and kind heart, and could see no harm in it.

By now the ordinary—or extraordinary—has begun to work in them. Already the flame of it is so intense and violent that we can clothe them in our own imagery and find no discrepancy in that. Indeed, their ghosts can take our colors. If the soul be immortal, we wonder in what underworld they hold their converse now.

1. The Woods of Rowaleyn

It is the season when young knights go out riding in the woods. When the cavaliers look up at the castle windows to see the pale wrist and the misty form behind the mullion. All manner of birds are singing. It is the month of May, even in the great city, no less among the merchants than in the villas of the *Decameron*. There are young women whom we would paint or draw for Venus. For the fine weather makes all women seem more beautiful.

* From *Splendours and Miseries*, 1943.

54

And the Venus, the enchantress, has gone out of town. The house in India Street is empty.

You could pace up and down idly on the pavement and not incur suspicion. It is impossible, in fact, not to wait at the corner just opposite and in imagination breathe in the air of that room which has its windows just above the railings. For that is the bower, that is the nest in the lime branches. It permeates and is impregnated with her body. Nothing else matters. The huge city is, in fact, deserted, for all the crowds upon the streets. There is no one in the town. They are supernumeraries, mere persons of no sensibility. Not in the secret; and the secret, in any case, has gone away. So that morning or afternoon is like a holiday, like early closing day. Everyone is in the country. For it is one of the first days of spring.

But for no one else as for this young man in love.

He has only to take the river steamboat in the evening. Then it is a few minutes' walk. There is no boat back that night. But the spring night will not be cold. His heart beats within him as he thinks of this. The hours will go by like moments. And he will return some time in the early morning.

We shall not be so pleased with him as we climb the stairs into his attic. He is a little man, a foreigner, and we are irritated by his combing and curling of his hair and whiskers. By his insistent glances into the square of mirror. By his pulling and tugging at his coat and waistcoat. It is, in fact, a velvet waistcoat, in the fashion of the time, and he has pomaded hair. His hat, lying on a chair, is a Balmoral bonnet; but it has not that implication. For ourselves, owing to what we know of him and of what will happen to him, it is the jeweled cap of some prince or courtier of the Renaissance. Perhaps his pointed shoes and mincing steps bear out this analogy. He is scenting himself, and eating something.

It is the room of a poverty-stricken young man. We may comfort ourselves that in the sixteenth century of philters and pomanders, the most luxuriously furnished bedroom had not his comforts. For he has a gas lamp, and newspapers and medicine bottles. He can take the train, or catch the steamboat. And certainly for a foreigner this Northern city is a happy hunting ground. He is in the latitude of Rizzio.

He has a satchel and a drawerful of letters in different handwritings. He boasts of these and has shown a few of them, or read aloud a sentence here and there, to the other clerks in the office. For that is his livelihood. He is employed by a firm of seedsmen, at a meager wage. But he has ambitions that are above his station. He works with a firm of nurserymen; but in a meaning that we shall reveal later he could be a student of alchemy in a chemist's shop or pharmacy. We infer that he claims to have advantages, or to be possessed of secrets.

It is an elaborate toilet that he is making. Complicated, that is to say, when we consider the small space of room that he has hired. But he is arming for the lists. And the spring air blows in through the attic window. Coming from the woods, from the birches and the mountain ashes. Should it be the cypress or the ilex? But this is a foreigner in an alien land. His successes are because of that. He is working the arid North. His lute hangs on a fir tree. The landscape is of lochs and glens. Though we must transpose it, so that its truth is universal and not particular. The Woods of Rowaleyn become the immortal myrtle groves where wander the youths who died of love.

This young man will be wounded, and will die after the tournament. After much jousting.

In the meantime he is the perfect little gentleman.

He chooses a handkerchief and knots his tie. In the corner of the room there is a dirty-linen basket. No pictures upon the walls, but a likeness or two of himself, a daguerreotype, in the second drawer. That is, indeed, his jewel box, his precious cabinet. It is full of souvenirs. And it contains his diary.

But it is time to get going. And he empties all his money into his pockets. The chevalier, the paladin, comes down the dusty stair. He shuts the front door and makes sure that he has brought the key with him.

No longer an aimless walking to and fro, and an involuntary straying of his steps into the empty square. Instead, he steps out with assurance. The period of waiting is over. Everything has changed. It is as though a bell had rung, and his name been called out for his cue. It is action now. Not preparation or rehearsal. Ah! How much would we give to see him, before our eyes, setting forth to conquer. Perhaps, though, he is better than we imagine him to have been. A little knock-kneed, with finicking walk and a way of putting his feet down and pointing them as if for the first position in dancing. But it will not do to be too scathing. He is to succeed with a very beautiful and spirited young girl. He conquered where many others would have failed.

No one stares at him. It may be that he is little and inconspicuous. Yet it is his story that all women turn round to look at him. In ridicule at first, but he soon alters that. It is a good plan to dress distinctively. Then everyone remembers having noticed you before. You become a personality. People ask each other who you can be. Word goes round from mouth to mouth. Even if no one knows the answer. That is the way to get a reputation.

It is so fine an evening that the streets are paved with gold. Young women who come past walk by on golden pattens. The smoke climbs straight into the sky. The fogs of great Glasgow have been lifted and dissolved into the heavens. The horses that draw the brewers' drays are like proud battle steeds. But it is necessary to board an omnibus. And there, a foreign accent, however slight, is sure to attract attention. It is only a penny ride down to the docks, where the river steamer lies waiting. Two hours' sail to Helensburgh.

Probably it is an advantage that the journey has begun by water. For it is an excursion into another element. And it is all prelude to the supreme adventure. There are ways in which a long walk restores the nerves. We shall see that he thought nothing of coming back from Bridge of Allan, mostly by foot, into golden Glasgow. To keep his tryst. But by that time it was someone setting out on foot to claim what was due to him. To appear on the doorstep, or below the window sill, walking stick in hand. Almost as though he wore her latchkey upon his chain. In a very different state of mind. Not in anticipation. But in full right of possession. Here and now, though, he prefers the gliding on the river. Those who are for execution are often driven to the scaffold. It is the last compliment, the last polite attention, before insult is heaped upon insult and they are kicked and struck into the underworld. And they at least have a priest to comfort them on the way. If you are so fortunate as to believe in that. In fact, his mood is changing. He is losing confidence. After all, he is a poor young man. And she is daughter of a rich family.

But not on this May evening.

How he could ever have doubted her for a moment! Suddenly, wonderfully, he is brought right up against her. There is this fiery, animal communion between them which can annihilate time and space. They comprehend by instinct. They do not need to speak. They understand each other perfectly. The clandestine should be a single flower, like the celandine. It has no need of two tiers of petals. It is singlehearted, contained in itself and self-sufficient. This may be mere play of words, but there must be an analogy for the secret union, the liquefaction of two souls. Besides, the dog rose will soon be hanging in the hedges. And it is the season, or indeed the evening in their lives, when something extraordinary is going to happen. The breaking into blossom, which really will be entirely personal to herself alone. But he is concerned in that, to pluck the flower. He is messenger, participant and secret partner. And how many pubic thorns it has! And what subtle poison in them!

But the voyage continues; and you can see across the Clyde to Greenock. On an early paddle steamer, propelled by the crinoline. No one could fail to know such ships are feminine. This runs, like a woman, along the evening waters. The sun is setting behind the Western islands, over Bute and Arran. But their names do not matter. The soft colors of the hills are feminine too. It would even be romantic to look out of the window of a railway train. This would be the hour to be walking at the edge of a cornfield, quite hidden, and to vanish for a few moments into a little wood. After a little while, to shake yourself and brush the leaves and grasses off your clothes, and both have flushed faces as you come out into the sunset. That is a tramp's life; but a poet's, also. It is not so sordid as an attic. And there is nothing to pay.

A white butterfly wings slowly but unerringly across the ship and flies forth, over the other side, along the water. It knows its direction and does not hesitate. In a moment it is no more than a white sail down the distance, or a white flower blown out to sea.

Meanwhile the ship's wake spreads out like a pair of wings behind it. In the end these must wash up on both shores. For there is not much more time to wait. It becomes like a journey up a river. And it grows dark. Just at the right moment. For it is better not to be recognized. The last few moments are as a voyage in a dream. He steps on shore: not like Othello, for Cassio and Montano have not come to meet him. He is alone. He goes singlehanded into battle. No one knows him. He is a foreigner, an alien with a peculiar accent. And we see him vanish into the darkness.

But now we enter him and go into his flesh and bones. He is no longer the little undersized lover. We do not stumble against him and wonder who he can be. For the shadow of his appalling drama sheds forth from him. He is walking alone, and deliberately, into the flames, and has come all this way on purpose for that. But we need not pity him. For it is his pleasure. It would be cruel to prevent him. Are there not nights when all the dogs of the village are abroad and howling? In the full moon. But who would not feel it on this evening of early spring? It is instinct. He will rush immediately into the fire. And whom has it ever hurt? We shall find that it is not the heat, but the chilling of the flame that kills. For it turns cold and unendurable. A reptilian cold, a chill serpent that cuddles upon the heart. This is the worm that coils out of the fire. It is a bitter pill, and as with the firework in the cracker, when lighted, a shape like a worm's crawls out from it. Later on. Not now. The match is only just put to the tinder. And what a scented bonfire! They are aromatic woods, green saplings, perhaps fir cones that smell of the sweet pine. That is all incense for the sacrifice.

And now the storm blows into his heart and blood. Beginning

with a gentle torment that is mostly pleasure. With pauses of
dread, and moments when he wonders why he was ever born.
When he wishes he were a small babe, but born to this opportunity. For he was destined to this. It is inconceivable that he
should be allowed to miss it. But it could have been arranged
for some other time. When circumstances were more propitious.
When he had more money; and there would be no reason, none
at all, to hesitate. Ah! How many difficulties have been put in
his way. But also how easy it has all been. Like the mingling of
two streams which have almost but not quite joined, which have
found their way together. And then he can shake it and entirely
drop it from his heart. For he blows callous and pitiless, and the
whole romance now is no more than the blooding of a dagger.
Part of a ritual; part of a warrior, or a "toff" and city clerk's
initiation. But more of it than comes in most men's way. Ah!
Yes, it is exceptional. Nothing like it happens to the majority.
In his present mood he could leave her strangled and for dead.
She will be quite alone and at his mercy. That is the way mur-
ders are committed. And the sane and cold-blooded wonder why,
and want to know the motive. As if there could be any reason,
when the whole thing is fiery and unreasonable. But yet, natural. On the other hand he is frightened of her. She is so strong
in character. She has urged him to this. She is to be his partner in the darkening wood. She has chosen him as much as he
has chosen her. He had no option. He could hardly have avoided
it. They are in each other's hands. He also is at her mercy.
Perhaps the shoe will fit the other foot. She may or may not
spare him. That is to say, it may or may not continue afterward.
He may be thrown back forever into the darkness. And never
see her again. That is why he must have some assurance. He
must take steps to tie her down. It is not enough that she is in
love with him. She must fall more madly in love still, and not
be able to get rid of him. He must see to that. He must make
her sign her name, for it comes to that. There are certain things
that she would not be able to go back on, without too much risk.
That is where he can keep her to himself and never let her go.
For she will have to be held firmly. She is even too strong for

him already. She writes to him every day, sometimes twice in the same day, and mostly late at night; but are her letters really for himself alone? Are they not for the person, whoever he may be, who is her lover, and who happens to be himself? But who is a fiction nevertheless, invented by her, though about to become real? A doll, or automaton, about to have life breathed into him. At her lips. And he feels himself drawn along, and depending from her. There has been some extraordinary fatality, some note of doom, of the inevitable, from the first moment that they met. He has been gathered up and whirled along. And it is coming to its climax. What does it mean? Why does she have such power over him? "I cannot tell how I long to see you—it looks such an age since I saw you, my own sweet pet. P—— has been in bed two days. If he should not feel well and come down on Tuesday it shall make no difference, just you come— only, darling, I think if he is in the boat you should get out at Helensburgh. Well, beloved, you shall come to the gate (you know it) and wait till I come. And then, oh happiness, wont I kiss you, my love, my own beloved. . . . I dont think there is any risk. Well, Tuesday, 6th May. The gate, half past ten. You understand."

That is the letter in the casket, in the drawer of the table in the attic, and he has learned it off by heart. Not deliberately, but from reading it so often. And now he stands perfectly still, without moving, while the spring night drenches him with its peculiar sharp feeling, and with the animal, soft imminence of this young girl of nineteen who is waiting for him until her father and mother have gone upstairs to bed. Probably reading some book aloud to them, and drawling her voice so that everyone feels tired and thinks it is getting late. Perhaps yawning herself, so that the others will yawn, too.

How hard it must be not to tremble and grow dizzy! But not for her. No one could tell that tonight is any different from other nights. Her hand is as steady as that of the executioner who has beheaded hundreds and has another, just one more, for instant execution. Who may put it in his diary, like Sanson, under just another date and name. If her lover could see her he would be the one to tremble. For her fire is not flaming, but white hot and hard as ice. It would be apparent that he is not himself, for her, but a form conjured up in her imagination; a fiction that she has determined upon and given life, as much as a woman gives birth to a child that is as she would have it to be, and then she may forget about it, and if true to herself, would desert it and become interested in something else. For how long does the cat love her litter? How soon does she grow indifferent to them? The vixen is more loving and keeps her cubs for longer by her side. The wolf also. And now it might almost seem that she is delaying her father and mother downstairs, on purpose. But it is not yet half past ten. He has come early. She knows that, because she knows what time the boat arrives. She is playing a little game of self-torment, postponing the golden moment. And there comes a long interval, and he sees the lights go out, one by one. And the lamps go up on the upper floor; and he can hear, in his fancy, the shutting of the bedroom doors. One by one. And one after all the others.

But a sudden and curious innocence is in the air. For it is a spring evening in the first week of May. Now, ninety years later, we would say the crescent moon, like a virgin sickle that has not yet cut the corn—as how could it, so many weeks before the harvest?—climbs the sky. The one or two stars are inconceivable in their purity, lights of diamond or hyaline in eternal time. For it is of time that such things speak to us. A time for youth. A time to be young. And you cease to be young, and grow to be middle-aged and old, and there is still this utter and entire youthfulness, which is cruel and irresponsible, and innocent withal, and to which this virginal and sweet-smelling purity of the spring evening is implicit, and speaks in the gentle silence, as though it was and will always be the voice of god, but not of the god who is prayed to in the churches. But another god altogether, whom we remember only at particular moments and in certain seasons. At other times he is forgotten and is no more than the shadow behind you in the wood, or following in the corn, and it is little use to be alone with that shadow running by your side, inviting rest and calling, as tonight, out of the

branches, in the songs of the birds and in the flowers of spring
at the tree foot. Such are feelings that transcend the individual
and are beyond words; but they are in the experience of everyone. It is a sacred trance, no more, nor less, to be remembered
in silence and with a tingling of the skin. That is how the Ancients knew inspiration, and it is the effect of music. This is
how she will write of it in a letter to him: "I shall always remember last night. Shall we not often talk of our evening meetings
. . . for it is a pleasure and no one can deny that. It is but human
nature. Is not everyone who loves of the same mind?" That
will be written at five o'clock of this same morning, after he has
left her. Soon now. For the great change is impending. The
moment is drawing near. And it finds her, we may be certain,
looking in her mirror and making sure that her little sister Janet,
who shares her room and lies in the same bed, is fast asleep. It
would be curious to see her look down at the sleeping child. This
must have happened so often in human relationships. It is a
convention in a play, almost, part of the miming or the pantomime. The mother weeps to lose her daughter; or the angry
father shows himself at the window. But in her case she turns
down the sheet to see that the child's eyes are closed and to listen
to its breathing. It is close and regular. Perhaps her cheeks are
flushed a little in a dream, and she may move and put her head
farther back upon the pillow, and be sound asleep again, all in
a moment. All the time her elder sister has not undressed. She
has taken off her shoes and that is all. Her stockings will be wet
with dew. That she knows. But, in fact, we may wonder if she
has not gone by herself into the garden every night and glided
like a ghost in and under the shadowed branches and come back
sighing, out of the spring evening, looking behind her, and
climbed to her room, like a bather from the moonlit sea who has
been bathing naked, where nothing prevents her, and loves the
feel of the waters and their godlike purity which is as nothing
else but the freshness of the morning sky or of an early summer
night, and as full of mystery as that, of hidden voices and of
movements that are full of meaning.

In a moment the lamp will go out and she will come down

the stairs. There is a wicker cage with a pair of white doves in it that hangs in the doorway. She stands on tiptoe and looks into their cage. They are awake and milk-white in the moonlight, and edge nearer to each other and begin their cooing. But it will disturb no one. Often they are cooing the night through; and if you wake up you wonder if you heard them, and are fast asleep again. But this is the first instant that we can look at her, while she moves so noiselessly with stockinged feet. She wears a dove-gray dress, not exactly a crinoline, but the skirt is long and full in the fashion of the '50s, and appropriate to a young girl. The dress of a beautiful young girl who is provincial, but who has been to school in London, who left school, indeed, little more than a year ago, and has come home and does the house-keeping for her mother. She is of medium height, neither short nor tall; but, as though we are familiar with this country place and know how often she looks on tiptoe into the doves' cage every time she runs in or out of the house and garden, we see her, as though in memory of that same morning, standing there in the sunlight. We notice that her bell-shaped sleeve is transparent, and see the shadowed arm within it, and the hand that will hold the cup of coffee or chocolate and pass it to his lips. It is her left hand; her right will then be smoothing his hair or round his neck, to make him drink and leave no dregs of it. But we will continue with our description of her from that painting which, for ourselves, is identified with her and forever haunted by her. This murderess—if she was that—can become an obsession with all who read about her, and it is literally true that she seems to haunt or inhabit any music heard during that time, and that it will suggest her physical person and her strange history forever-more.* This can never happen to the same degree with char-acters from fiction. We go with Madame Bovary to the opera at

---

* Madeleine Smith is forever associated in my mind with the Liebeslieder Waltzer of Brahms which, as far as my imagination is concerned, she may be said to haunt. In the same fashion, the exquisitely graceful and lovely piano Quartet in G Minor, K. 478, of Mozart was spoiled for me when I most loved it by Hitler's murder of Röhm and his friends on the dreadful June 30, 1934. In differ-ent vein, Chopin's Mazurka in C Sharp Minor, No. 3, played in incredible and supernatural nuance of touch by Horowitz, makes me think of the Talking Mongoose of Cashen's Gap. Most lovers of music will have known similar sensations.

Rouen and see a performance of *Lucia di Lammermoor,* but we do not hear the music. The only music in *Madame Bovary* is the little hurdygurdy air sung by a blind beggar, once before in the novel, and then below the window when she is dying. This is of appalling effect because of its words, which have come down from the century of shepherds and shepherdesses, through the winds and tatters of the Revolution:

> *Souvent la chaleur d'un beau jour*
> *Fait rêver fillette à l'amour . . .*
> *Pour amasser diligemment*
> *Les épis que la faux moissone,*
> *Ma Nanette va s'inclinant*
> *Vers le sillon qui nous le donne . . .*
> *Il souffla bien fort ce jour-là*
> *Et le jupon s'envola.*

A hurdygurdy air. You can hear that wheezing and grinding in it. But the ghost of Madeleine Smith inhabits music and painting; this picture for some reason personal to ourselves, more especially.* In Pre-Raphaelite detail we see the gravel path and the grass borders. Beyond lie the woods of Rowaleyn. She wears, as we have said, a country crinoline, and the bodice which fits so closely to her young figure, with its long sleeves and high neck, gives her the look of a nursemaid or a servant girl. It is because fashions decline, and the bonnet of one generation becomes the mark of the old cottager or housekeeper in the next. But in this picture her white hand, which is to mix the powder, and that other hand which, by coincidence, holds a cup, but only in order to feed the birds, tell that she is daughter of the house. Also, the dress is smart and new and summery. It is lilac in color, more than dove-gray, and this is the month of lilacs. We know immediately that it is intended for the country.

* "Lady Feeding a Bird," by W. H. Deverell, now in the Tate Gallery. Deverell, who was short-lived (1827-1854), and is one of the rarest of the Pre-Raphaelite painters, was the discoverer of Miss Siddal, whom he saw in a milliner's shop in Cranbourn Alley off Leicester Square, and introduced to Rossetti.

It has a white lace collar, and what would appear to be some kind of a silk tie round her neck, which draws attention to her dark hair. And this brings us to her throat, which is drawn out and elongated by her attitude, so that it is a Rossetti neck; and to her rosy and clear profile against the bird cage; and to her hair which is combed down over her ears, with a braided twist of hair, like a coronal, rising from the back of her head up to its crown, glossy and shining, and youthful as her throat and hands. Nothing more than that. It is the simple dress of a girl of nineteen or twenty. Probably the rest of her character, in one who is so young, is determined more in her actions than in her physical appearance, which is not yet mature. We have seen her in the sunshine of that May morning ("Tuesday, 6th May"); and now it burns up golden for the sunset; reddens in the furnace glow, which is full of portent, fades for the twilight, and is now the early summer night, at half past ten.

The hour is come.

He sees a gray form, only her dress and nothing recognizable of her but her shape, gliding toward him along the grass edge of the path, under the trees. And she unlatches the gate for him, which he could have done himself, and takes him in. In that moment they are in each other's arms. The gear of time alters. They are in the shadow of the trees and sitting at the tree foot, where no one can hear or see them. Here their compact was signed—for we will call it that, a compact of tragedy—upon a May night, when blood fell on the anemone and their fates were signed and sealed. When he rises he is dead tired, and she has awakened into life. She will remember this night forever after. What, indeed, can she have thought and remembered five years later, upon her marriage night! Did she think of his dead body, dead but incorruptible—for a reason—and scored or eviscerated by the surgeon's knife? But she never slept on this May night. "I shall always remember last night. Will we not often talk of our evening meetings . . . for it is a pleasure and no one can deny that. It is but human nature. Is not everyone who loves of the same mind? . . . I was happy. It was a pleasure to be with you." The letter is dated "Wednesday morning 5 o'c."

2. *Incognito*

Through that summer and early autumn they must have had many meetings. This is proved in her letters to him. These consist chiefly of the most passionate outpourings of her love for him; but also, owing to the peculiar circumstances in which they met, the letters are full of trivial details that ordinarily would have come out in conversation. In almost the only one of his letters to her that have been preserved, written, we may note, the day after their first meeting in the woods of Rowaleyn, he replies to her question, "Tell me the names of your sisters," by a disjointed sentence interpolated next to a reproach to her for having lost her virginity to him. "Since I saw you I have been wretchedly sad. Would to God we had not met that night. I am sad at what we did, I regret it very much. Why, Mimi, did you give way after your promises? Think of the consequences if I were never to marry you. What reproaches I should have, Mimi. I shall never be happy again. If ever I meet you again, love, it must be as at first. I will never again repeat what I did until we are regularly married. . . . I was not angry at you allowing me, Mimi, but I am sad it happened. You had no resolution. . . . It was very bad indeed. I shall look with regret on that night. . . . If Mary [their spinster confidante] did know it, what should you be in her eyes? My sister's names are Anastasie and Elmire. I cannot help doubting your word about flirting. You promised me the same thing before you left for Edin., and you did nothing else during your stay there. I do trust you will give me no cause to find fault with you again on that score. . . . Oh! Mimi, let your conduct make me happy. Remember when you are good how truly happy it makes Emile——"

Her letters, on the other hand, contain such expressions as: "I adore you with my heart and soul. . . . My love burns for you. It increases daily. Oh! To be with you this night. But I fear I would ask you to *love* me, and that would not do. . . . I thank you so much for these grapes; they were so nice and cool. I do not wear 'crinoline' as you dont like it. It is off today. No one heard you last night. Next night it shall be a different win-

dow. That one is much too small. . . . A fond embrace . . . A
kiss, darling of my soul . . . If M—— and P—— were from
home I could take you in very well—at the front door, just the
same way as I did in India St.—and I wont let a chance pass—
I wont sweet pet of my soul, my only best loved darling. Oh,
Emile, I wish I could throw myself in your arms, and ask you
to *love* me. . . . Oh, Emile, I dote on you, I love and adore you
with my soul. A kiss. I see de M. passing the house. . . . A kiss.
Another . . . I think I heard your stick this evening (pray, do
not make any sound whatever at my window). A kiss, pet love.
Good night. A fond embrace, thy own true Mimi L'Angelier."

By this time her family have returned from Helensburgh and
are living in a house in Blythswood Square. It is the late winter
of 1856. Her father was an architect with a big practice. They
kept a carriage, had several servants and lived in a round of
theaters, balls and dinner parties, with the social life of Edinburgh near at hand. Madeleine was the eldest of the children.
She had a sister Bessie, two brothers Jack and James, and the
little sister Janet who shared her room. The house in Blythswood
Square, which is still standing and is now the offices of the
British Legal Life Assurance Company, is very similar to the well-
built stone houses of Charlotte Square in Edinburgh. They occupied two floors of it, a street floor and a sunk floor. It is the
corner house of Blythswood Street and Blythswood Square, and
the two upper floors formed a separate house, entered by a front
door, round the corner in Blythswood Street and up a separate
staircase. This upper house was occupied by a middle-aged
Glasgow merchant, Mr. William Minnoch.

Madeleine's bedroom—and there can be little doubt she chose
it for herself on purpose—was on the sunk floor and it had two
windows, the second pair of area windows in the side street. It
was next door to the kitchen, and the top of the window was on
a level with the area railings. Mr. Minnoch lived next door.
Indeed, his front door was immediately next to Madeleine's bedroom. That, as we shall know, was not the least astonishing part
of this drama. For by now Madeleine had become engaged to Mr.
Minnoch, with the full approval of her parents. He was a per-

son of fortune and it was most suitable. More extraordinary still, she wished it herself. She accepted him on January 28, and they arranged it more particularly on March 12. The marriage was fixed for June 18. This is stated in his evidence at the trial.

But we come now to some extraordinary contrasts in her correspondence, and it is better to point these by quotation. "I know who it was that saw me walking to Helensburgh, and told you . . . A few minutes before I met them I had been jumping and running with my large Newfoundland dog 'Major.' . . . I have got two dogs now to make pets of, 'Pedro' and 'Sambo,' both of them terriers. They are most affectionate. Their great delight is killing rats, and I assure you I gratify them in their desire. . . . My own beloved husband, my sweet, dear Pet, my darling, I love you with my soul and heart. Kiss me, my fond one, a dear, sweet embrace, sweet, ever sweet Emile. If P——and M—— go, will you not, sweet love, come to your own Mimi? Do you think I would ask you if I saw danger in the house? No, love, I would not. I shall let you in; no one shall see you. We can make it late—12 if you please. You have no long walk. . . . Were you in Helensburgh one day about ten days ago? I thought it was like you, but I could not say. . . . I do wonder if you are in Helensburgh tonight. I fancy no—something says you are not. . . . I promise I shall not go about the sts., Emile, more than you have said. We went about too much. I shall not go about much. But one you must promise me is this, that if you should meet me at a time in B——St. or S—— St. you will not look at me crossly. For it almost made me weep on the St. last winter, sometimes, when you hardly looked at me. . . . Nay more—one day I met you in Glasgow; you looked so cross at me that when I went home I wrote you a note taking farewell of you. I went to bed, I dreamt of you, I fancied you still loved me, and in the morning all my love for you returned. . . . Emile, darling, I think I can promise that I shall not be in S—— St. on Saturday. I shall go out in the forenoon, come in about half past one o'c., and not go out again; it will please you if I do so, so I shall do it, sweet love. A kiss, a fond embrace . . . Well, my dear Emile, you did look cross at your Mimi, the other day. Why, my pet, you cannot expect I am never to go on S—— St. Sometimes I must. It is not quite fair of you. I have kept off that St. so well this winter, and yet when you meet me, and the first time you have bowed to me this season, that you should have looked so cross. When I saw you, my little pet, coming, I felt frightened even to bow to you. . . . Did you go to the concert? I did. I looked at everyone, but could not see my husband. . . . I have not been out since Wednesday, when I was in a cab, and I thought I saw you in St. Vincent Street, but I was not sure."*

What do we gather from this composite of her utterances? That they never met in public, but only at her window or when she let him into the house. That if they met on the street they did not dare show recognition. She had no means even of knowing if he was in Helensburgh. The most subsidiary matters, which they had no time for on their rare meetings, are mentioned in her correspondence. Her childishness comes out in the references to her dogs. She is a young girl of twenty in that part of her letter; but we should not forget the sentence about her terriers killing rats. A moment or two later, in the same breath almost, she is putting irresistible temptation in his way. While her parents slept, she admitted this foreigner into the house; and we know from the evidence at the trial that these interviews took place generally in the drawing room, but on at least one occasion, also, in the servants' bedroom downstairs, and also in a lane or area at the back. The maid, Christina Haggart, stated: "In the Blythswood Square house there was a back door leading to an area and into a lane. She asked me once to open it for her. I don't know when that was. It was a good time before Miss Smith was apprehended—weeks before, and maybe two months. It was at night—I think past ten—that she asked me to open the door. I was in her room when she asked me. . . . I opened the back gate into the lane. I saw no person there. I left it open and returned to the house, leaving the back door

---

* In a letter dated "18th day of April"—and obviously written at her father's dictation—saying she will never see him again, she adds this extraordinary remark, over the page: "But as the song says, 'There is a good time coming only wait a little longer.'"

open, and went into the kitchen. Miss Smith met me in the passage; she was going toward the back door. I heard footsteps coming through the gate. I went into the kitchen. I did not hear where Miss Smith went to. I did not hear the door of my room shut. I don't remember how long I remained in the kitchen. I think more than half an hour. . . . I think I remained longer than usual in the kitchen that night. Miss Smith had told me to stay in the kitchen. She asked if I would open the back door and stay in the kitchen a little, because she was to see her friend. She did not say where she was to see her friend. While I stayed in the kitchen I did not know where Miss Smith was. I did not know she was in my bedroom. I had no doubt she was there, but I did not know it. When we heard Miss Smith go to her room I left the kitchen. We heard the door of her room shut; I did not hear the door of our room open. I did not hear the back door of our house shut. . . . I never saw any rats in the house in Blythswood Square. We were not troubled with rats. . . . I had charge of cleaning out Miss Smith's bedroom. During February or March I never observed that the water in her basin was colored peculiarly black or peculiarly blue."

The bedrooms in which the other members of the family slept were on the floor above, and at the back of the house. Her father and her sister Bessie had, it is true, bedrooms that looked out at the back, above the lane, but to this adept in silent movement and dissimulation this presented no difficulties. She writes in one letter: "If I cannot get you in at the back door I will take you in at the front door." Emile L'Angelier had lived in Paris and joined the *Garde Nationale* during the Revolution of 1848. We may think that this night intruder had enjoyed experiences in the French capital that were unknown, or unattainable, to the staid citizens of Glasgow, but which made him the more interesting to this young girl whom he was debauching. And if he had not had such experiences, we may feel certain, nonetheless, that he will have boasted of them: for such was his character. At other times, to his men friends and the clerks in the office, he spoke of his broken heart, and threatened suicide. He talked of drowning himself, and took up knives as though to stab himself. One witness said of L'Angelier: "I saw quite enough of him to enable me to form an opinion of his character and disposition. I formed anything but a good opinion of him. I considered him a vain, lying fellow. He was very boastful of his personal appearance, and parties admiring him, ladies particularly. . . . He said ladies admired him very often. . . . He told me he had met a lady in Princes Street with another lady, and she had remarked to her companion what pretty little feet he had. I had said he was rather a pretty little person, and he had gone out and concocted the story of the lady's remark. I never believed anything he said afterwards. . . . It was a common thing for him to speak of ladies admiring him on the street." As against this, his spinster friend, Miss Perry, who had encouraged the romance and was the confidante of both of them, said of him: "I had a warm affection for M. L'Angelier, and corresponded with him frequently. I thought him a strictly moral and religious man. He was a regular attender at church. . . . We attended the same chapel, St. Jude's."

The reader will by now be aware of what is coming. Emile L'Angelier is in possession of her incriminating letters and refuses to give them up. He threatens, indeed, to show them to her father, for he is determined at all costs to marry her. She asks for her letters back. It is obvious that she has become tired and sated with him, appalled perhaps also by the dangers of this secret intrigue, and having recovered her senses realizes the impossibility of marrying this clerk with a salary of only a hundred pounds a year, whom she no longer loves and who has been objected to most strongly by her family. For six months and more she has been the mistress of L'Angelier; while, a year before that, her father and mother who had intercepted his first letters forbade any further communication between them. Immediately after that she had begun admitting him at night, after the family had gone to bed, into the house in India Street. Her seduction by L'Angelier in the woods of Rowaleyn was the next step. That, as we know, was in May, and all through the summer and autumn they carried on their intrigue. By early January she is tiring of him, though she continues seeing him after her engagement to Mr. Minnoch. But she has made up her mind to be respectable and marry Mr. Minnoch. And L'Angelier will not give her back her letters.

3. *The Painted Cheek*

She writes to him upon a day in February: "I felt truly astonished to have my last letter returned to me. But it will be the last you shall have the opportunity of returning to me. When you are not pleased with the letters I send you, then our correspondence shall be at an end, and as there is coolness on both sides our engagement had better be broken. . . . And you also annoyed me much on Saturday by your conduct in coming so near to me. . . . I trust to your honor as a Gentleman that you will not reveal anything that may have passed between us."

The next letter, bearing an illegible postmark on the tenth of a month in the year 1857, reads: "Emile, for the love you once had for me do nothing till I see you." It ends: "Do nothing till I see you, for the love of heaven do nothing. I am mad, I am ill." A further letter, unposted but found among his papers, so that she must have handed it to him, says: "But Oh, will you not keep my secret from the world? Oh will you not for Christ's sake, denounce me? I shall be undone. I shall be ruined. . . . If you will never reveal what has passed. Oh, for God's sake, for the love of heaven, hear me. I grow mad. I have been ill, very ill, all day. I have had what has given me a false spirit. I had to resort to what I should not have taken, but my brain is on fire. . . . P.S. I cannot get to the back stair. I never could see the way to it. I will take you within in the door. The area gate will be open. I shall see you from my window, 12 o'c. I will wait till 1 o'c."

But Emile would not bring the letters back.

At some date in the second week of February, Madeleine sent the page boy to try and buy some prussic acid for her. She said she wanted an ounce of it for her hands, and the chemist refused to give it to her.

On February 21 she herself bought sixpennyworth of arsenic and signed the chemist's book. In what is presumed to be her next letter she says: "You did look bad Sunday night and Monday morning. I think you got sick with walking home so late—and the long want of food, so the next time we meet I shall make you eat a loaf of bread before you go out. . . . My head aches so, and I am looking so bad that I cannot sit up as I used to do—but I am taking some stuff to bring back the color."

What does this mean?

Madeleine made a second purchase of arsenic on March 18, saying she needed it for the rats in the house in Blythswood Square, and going into the chemist's openly with a friend in order to buy it.

But here we come to the greatest mystery of all. L'Angelier was taken violently ill, with every symptom of arsenical poisoning, for the first time on the night of February 19, two days before she first bought arsenic. This is proved in the evidence of his landlady, and from a diary kept by him which was produced in court but not admitted in evidence. The part of his diary in question reads: "Thurs: 19 Feb.—saw Mimi a few moments. Was very ill during the night." "Frid. 20 Feb.—passed two pleasant hour with M. in the Drawing Room." "Sat. 21 Feb.—don't feel well." "Sun. 22 Feb.—saw Mimi in Drawing Room. Promised me French Bible. Taken very ill." His diary ends on "Sat.—14 March," a week before the last act in this drama. It was not admitted in evidence because the judges argued that: "It was quite conceivable that vanity might lead to statements being made wholly imaginary, with a view to the subsequent exhibition of the book. . . . A man might have threatened another, he might have hatred against him and be determined to revenge himself, and what entries might he not make in a diary for this purpose?"

L'Angelier had made some curious comments to his friends. To Miss Perry, the spinster confidante, he remarked, "It is a perfect fascination my attachment to that girl; if she were to poison me, I would forgive her." Miss Perry said, "You ought not to allow such thoughts to pass through your mind; what motive could she have in giving you anything to hurt you?" L'Angelier replied, "I don't know that; perhaps she might not be sorry to be rid of me." He said also, "I can't think why I was so unwell after

getting that coffee and chocolate from her." Miss Perry understood he referred to two different occasions; "her" meant Miss
Smith. He was talking about her at the time. A Frenchman,
Amédée Thuau, who lodged in the same house as L'Angelier and
took his meals in the same room with him, stated: "I knew that
L'Angelier was to marry a young lady. . . . L'Angelier was sometimes in the habit of going out at night. I knew that he went on
these occasions to his intended's house. I recollect one morning
finding that L'Angelier had been out, and very ill in the night.
I saw him that morning. I asked whether he had seen the lady;
he said that he saw her the night before. I asked if he had been
unwell after seeing her. He said that he was unwell in her
presence."

This would seem to refer to Madeleine's letter saying: "You
did look bad Sunday night and Monday morning. I think you
got sick with walking home so late—and the long want of food,
so the next time we meet I shall make you eat a loaf of bread
before you go out." The Lord Advocate remarked of this letter at
the trial: "It proves that he was sick at the time, and looking very
bad. . . . It proves that she was thinking about giving him food;
that she was laying a foundation for seeing him; that she was
taking stuff to bring back her color. It proves that she was holding
out a kind of explanation of the symptoms which he had, because
she says she is ill herself; and it proves that all this took place the
day after she bought the arsenic at Murdoch's."

After L'Angelier's second attack of illness there is a pause in
the correspondence. It looks as though Madeleine, if she were
trying to poison him, had relented somewhat. Soon she begins
persuading him to go away. She wants him to go for ten days to
the Isle of Wight. He replies to this: "The doctor says I must go
to Bridge of Allan. I cannot travel 500 miles to the Isle of Wight
and 500 back. What is your object in wishing me so very much
to go south?" In the meantime she sets off herself with her family
for Bridge of Allan, and Mr. Minnoch visited her while she was
there. But before she left Glasgow she made that second purchase
of arsenic, in case, the prosecution argued, L'Angelier insisted
upon seeing her. She bought the arsenic on March 6 and went,

that day apparently, to Bridge of Allan. On March 17 she returned with her family to Glasgow. The next day she made a third purchase of arsenic, saying that the first lot had been so effectual—she having found eight or nine large rats lying dead—that she had come back to get the dose renewed. What had she done with the unused second purchase of the poison? It was contended at her trial that, having no use for it for the moment, she must have thrown it on the fire.

In her written declaration to the court this is what she said: "I have bought arsenic on various occasions. The last I bought was a sixpenceworth, which I bought in Currie's, and the other in Murdoch the apothecary's shop in Sauchiehall Street. I used it all as a cosmetic, and applied it to the face, neck and arms, diluted with water. The arsenic I got in Currie's shop I got there on Wednesday, 18th March, and I used it all on one occasion, having put it all in the basin where I was to wash myself. I had been advised to the use of the arsenic in the way I have mentioned by a young lady, the daughter of an actress, and I had also seen the use of it recommended in the newspapers. The young lady's name was Giubelei, and I had met her at school at Clapton, near London. I did not wish any of my father's family to be aware that I was using the arsenic and therefore never mentioned it to any of them; and I don't suppose they or any of the servants ever noticed any of it in the basin. When I bought the arsenic in Murdoch's I am not sure whether I was asked or not what it was for, but I think I said it was for a gardener to kill rats or destroy vermin about flowers, and I only said this because I did not wish them to know that I was going to use it as a cosmetic. . . . M. L'Angelier was very unwell for some time, and had gone to Bridge of Allan for his health; and he complained of sickness, but I have no idea what was the cause of it. I remember giving him some cocoa from my window one night sometime ago, but I cannot specify the time particularly. He took the cup in his hand and barely tasted the contents; and I gave him no bread to it. I was taking some cocoa myself at the time, and had prepared it myself. It was between 10:00 and 11:00 P.M. when I gave it to him. . . . As I had attributed his sickness to want of food, I proposed, as stated in the note, to give him a loaf of bread, but I said that merely in a joke and, in point of fact, I never gave him any bread. . . . On the occasion that I gave M. L'Angelier the cocoa, as formerly mentioned, I think that I used, it must have been known to the servants and members of my father's family, as the package containing the cocoa was lying on the mantelpiece in my room, but no one of the family used it except myself, as they did not seem to like it. The water which I used I got hot from the servants. On the night of the eighteenth, when I used the arsenic last, I was going to a dinner party at Mr. Minnoch's house. I never administered, or caused to be administered, to M. L'Angelier arsenic or anything injurious. And this I declare to be the truth.

(Signed) "MADELEINE SMITH."

L'Angelier went to Bridge of Allan the day after Madeleine and her family had returned to Glasgow. He had previously been away for a week or so to Edinburgh. Before he left, he asked for his letters to be sent on to him, saying that he would not be home till Wednesday night or Thursday morning of the following week. But he suddenly appeared back at eight o'clock on Sunday night, saying that he had walked for fifteen miles. His landlady asked him why he came back, and he answered: "The letter you forwarded brought me home." He asked to be called early next morning, said he was much better and went out at nine o'clock, after having changed his coat, and before going out made this request: "If you please, give me the pass-key. I am not sure, but I may be late." Half an hour later he called on a friend, who was out, as though he had some time to waste; but the rest of his movements will never be known.

At half past two in the morning the front doorbell rang with great violence. The landlady came down to open it, and L'Angelier was standing there with his arms closed across his stomach. He said he thought he would never get home, he was so bad on the road. After much delay the doctor came, but L'Angelier grew worse. He asked, "Can you do anything, doctor?" and said later, "I am far worse than the doctor thinks."

Before he died he said, "Oh, if I could get five minutes' sleep, I think I would get better." The landlady asked if there was no one he would like to see, and he asked for Miss Perry to be brought. She came too late. L'Angelier, who said nothing more, turned his face to the wall and died.

A letter was found in the pocket of his topcoat. It was the letter which had brought him back from Bridge of Allan. "Why my beloved did you not come to me. Oh beloved are you ill. Come to me sweet one. I waited and waited for you, but you came not. I shall wait again tomorrow night same hour and arrangement. Come beloved and clasp me to your heart. Come and we shall be happy. A kiss fond love. Adieu with tender embraces ever believe me to be your own ever dear fond Mini."*

In view of his two previous illnesses, which had been accompanied by the same symptoms, and his death, the friends and employers of L'Angelier asked for a post-mortem examination to be held. Eighty-two grains of arsenic were found in him; and a search of his room and of his desk at the office revealed all Madeleine's letters to him, in consequence of which she was arrested by the police just a week after his death. Her movements during the intervening days are curious to think of. On the very day L'Angelier died, Miss Perry and a Frenchman, De Mean, called separately upon Madeleine's father and mother to acquaint them of what had happened, and to warn Madeleine that her letters had been found. She denied all knowledge of his death, and said she had not seen him for three weeks previously. Two evenings later she was taken out to dinner by Mr. Minnoch at the house of Mr. Middleton, who was Presbyterian minister at the church attended by her family. On the following morning she was missing from the house in Blythswood Square; Mr. Minnoch and her brother Jack found her upon the Helensburgh boat. They accompanied her to Rowaleyn, and drove her in a carriage back to Glasgow. The purpose of her flight is a mystery. It may have been in order to persuade the gardener to stand by her statement that she had bought arsenic to destroy rats and vermin in the

* Madeleine Smith, in her letters to her lover, writes her name arbitrarily as "Mimi" or "Mini," according to her mood.

garden. Or it may be she had gone to fetch back some incriminating letter. In any case, this is the one movement on her part
that appears to acknowledge her own guiltiness. They stayed
three quarters of an hour at Rowaleyn, long enough for her to
find—or destroy—something that she might have wanted. One
of the maids stated, in evidence: "On the morning of the Thursday, when it was found that Miss Smith had left the house, I
don't know if it was found that she had taken any of her clothes
with her. I saw her on her return; a small carpet bag, containing
things of hers, was brought back with her. The bag was not very
small. It was such as a lady might carry her night things in."
Mr. Minnoch continued to call at the house every day, believing
that some old love affair was causing her pain and distress. On
the morning of the day she was arrested, he called to see her at
half past nine and she spoke to him of her own accord of
L'Angelier's death, and of the rumors that he had been poisoned
with arsenic. She said that she had bought arsenic herself, as she
had learned at Clapton School that it was good for the complexion.
Mr. Minnoch also had heard this rumor of his death by poison.
But he did not know L'Angelier himself, and was not aware that
she was acquainted with him.

During her trial Madeleine Smith behaved with the most absolute calmness and composure. She was not, of course, put in the
witness box, for that was not allowed in the usage of the time.
Had she been put to examination in the searching modern manner, it may be thought almost impossible that she would not
have revealed her secret. But she was asked no questions at all.
There are various other most obvious omissions in her trial. Her
parents made no statement, were not in court, and appear to have
been asked no questions. They were protected, it would seem,
by the Victorian delicacy of sentiment. Neither L'Angelier's
mother, who lived in Jersey, nor his two sisters appeared in court.
Yet it is certain that they must have had letters from him containing mention of Madeleine.

The verdict of the jury was "Not guilty" as regards the accusation of administering poison on the first occasion, and the Scottish
verdict of "Not proven" was returned in answer to the accusation

of administering it on the other two occasions. Madeleine was taken below, where she changed her dress, and was escorted by her brother Jack to a side door and a waiting carriage. They caught a train to a station near Glasgow, whence another carriage drove them back to Rowaleyn, where they arrived at ten o'clock at night.

4. *Poison Cup*

It must have been a curious homecoming, an odd unlocking of that wicket gate. The family, it would seem, were too horrified to keep her with them, relapsing, we may think, into a stony Scottish silence. At any rate, she soon left them and went with her brother Jack to London. It is not known how she employed her time there; but five years later, in August 1861, from an address in Sloane Street, she was married in St. Paul's, Knightsbridge, to Mr. Wardell, her father so far relenting as to be present at the ceremony. The family by now lived under another name, and her younger sisters were brought up in ignorance of what had happened. Her husband, Wardell, was a designer and craftsman who was much employed by William Morris, and who drew the flowers and plants in the foregrounds of the Merton Abbey tapestries. Her marriage brought Madeleine Smith into contact with many members of the Pre-Raphaelite circle, and she was drawn by Rossetti more than once as the Magdalene. Rossetti, with his morbid taste in crime, will have been particularly interested in this romantic and beautiful young woman. There is a story that for her dinner parties she was the first person to introduce the fashion of dining without a tablecloth; while another legend, which could be true, relates to the consternation of some of those present when, at that very dinner table, thirty years after her notoriety, conversation turned to the case of Mrs. Maybrick, at that moment on trial for poisoning her husband. Rossetti and his friends were, of course, aware of her identity. On the death of her husband, Madeleine Smith went to live in a cottage at Leek, near Macclesfield in Staffordshire, on an allowance from her late husband's brother, who was in the silk trade. After a few years she is described as living in poor circumstances; and in

1913 she crossed to the United States, where in 1914 she married
an American. He died, and she continued in increasing poverty,
but apparently not too reticent of her past history to consider, for
a moment, the possibility of making an appearance in a film about
herself. And in the United States, in 1927, at the great age
of ninety-two, this astonishing—or only completely natural—
woman died, taking her secret with her into the grave.

But, if we return for a moment to this drama, it is to examine
an extraordinary plea that was put forward. This was to the
effect that Emile L'Angelier was an arsenic eater. The evidence
for this was of a curious nature. It was advanced that he had
acted, for a time, as courier to a family who were traveling on
the continent, having charge of the horses, and it was alleged that
he had spoken to acquaintances and fellow employees in his firm
of the practice of giving small portions of arsenic to the horses in
order to improve their wind. Articles on arsenic eating had appeared, at about this time, in various journals, some by coincidence before his death, and others owing to the notoriety
caused by the trial. Miss Giubelei, who was at school at Clapton
with Madeleine Smith and who was part pupil and part teacher
at the establishment, denied in her evidence having ever mentioned arsenic as an aid to the complexion. But Madeleline
Smith, in her statement at the trial, alleged that she had read of
it in newspapers, and it has been argued that, if she had knowledge of these, it was because she had been given them to read by
L'Angelier. From the evidence given, there can be no doubt whatever that L'Angelier had toyed with the idea of eating arsenic,
even if he was not an adept. Also, he was seen on one occasion
in the seedsmen's office where he worked to gather up handfuls
of poppy seed and eat them, at the end of a conversation in which
arsenic eating had been mentioned. In other instances he spoke
of it, and said he took it for his complexion, and also, we may
surmise, for more intimate, other purposes, of which a person
of his temperament would not hesitate to tell his friends. He is,
indeed, described by those who knew him as a little rosy-cheeked
individual, with a blooming complexion and with exceptionally
glossy hair, this applying also, no doubt, to his mustache and

whiskers. In fact, a little pretty fellow, but with false aids out of the bottle marked "POISON."

The practice of eating arsenic had originated, in innocence, in Styria, a province of Austria, among the peasants. So much we learn from the published articles in question, and from an essay in particular in *Chambers's Journal*. This may have been the article put into the hands of Madeleine Smith by her lover. It is in description of the province of the Styrian waltz or *ländler,* a village dance of the turning, turning kind, of familiar sound because a Styrian waltz appears sometimes as the trio to the minuet of a Haydn symphony. Whenever, in Haydn, we hear a primitive slow peasant waltz it comes from Styria; and we may be reminded, too, of Schubert's *ländler.* The background for the eaters of arsenic is that of the colored prints of peasant costumes. Wooden châlets with carved eaves and balconies, with flowering window boxes; or peasant interiors with the tiled stove in the corner and carved wooden furniture, peasant pottery, and the aged grandparents, the young lover with a sprig of flowers in his slouch hat, and the young girl in her dirndl.

We are in a subalpine valley. Beyond the mountains are the cretins of Courmayeur and Aosta, limestone valleys of the goiter. Those were villages where, at the time of which we write, every fourth person was goitrous and had the hideous appendage hanging at the neck, swelling slowly until it choked him or her. On the other side of the mountains, far from this land of pears and apples, of cherry orchards and wood-strawberries in their season, but a subalpine condition, nonetheless. Here, there was not such poverty nor hard circumstance. It is a land of cheeses. The cornemuse plays upon the summer evenings.

But we may find a particular valley in which the young peasants are like prize animals, primely fattened. Waxed and glossy in appearance, with rosy cheeks and eyes that glisten, but like eyes of glass, like the eyes in the head of a doll. Open or shut, but always with the same expression. It is as though their skin, their exterior, were of another texture from that of other beings. And, in fact, their flesh is incorruptible. One of the horrors attached to poisoning by arsenic is that the criminal, by his own handiwork, preserves the dead body of his victim. It is always noticed, when the grave is opened, that the corpse has not experienced the usual processes of decay. The skin is blooming; but the body is more like a waxwork figure than a living person. How much more must this be the case when arsenic eating has been indulged in, of free will and on purpose, over a period of years, during the long protractions of a peasant courtship! With no evil consequence, but only in order to conform to the ideal. To the waxwork standard. For it is impossible not to be reminded of the waxwork figures of peasants in local museums, wearing the costume of the region. Those are haunted interiors. The very objects and utensils of peasant life by which they are surrounded become like the souvenirs of crime and are repellant to the touch.

If it is possible that Madeleine Smith, under the influence and at the instigation of L'Angelier, had dabbled with arsenic and, in order to please him, had taken it in small quantities and used it as a cosmetic on her person, then the whole affair between them takes on another and more lurid light. No evidence was ever given of L'Angelier's having purchased arsenic, although it was to the advantage of the prosecution to prove that he had done so. Only a small quantity, though, would have lasted him for many months, for as long as a woman can keep a bottle of her favorite scent. He may have bought arsenic in Paris; it is possible that he procured a quantity in London. One thing is certain: It cannot be mere coincidence that he had spoken of arsenic eating to his friends, and that Madeleine Smith, his mistress, a young girl of nineteen who had just left school, should have known of its uses and its potential danger.

Obviously he must have told her of it, and perhaps given her a pinch of it to swallow, or persuaded her to use a dilution of arsenic as a cosmetic on her face and neck and arms. There is even an argument, heard only in whisper, but surviving from persons who were contemporary with the case, that it was by an extension of this cosmetic practice that he met his death. Not, then, from the poison in the cup of cocoa; unless she handed that to him, also, from the window at the end of their last meeting. But, also—for nothing in human relationship is too extraordinary to be true—it may be that he drank deliberately, knowing it was poisoned. It has even been thought that he may have poisoned himself, wishing that the blame should fall on her, and having made those entries in his diary on purpose so that she should be suspected. Suicide by arsenic might be considered to be out of the question, owing to the appalling agonies of dying by arsenical poisoning; but yet there have been cases of it. Again, there is the possibility that he accepted the cup of cocoa from her hand and dropped arsenic into it, with or without her knowledge. He may have determined to kill himself on leaving her for the last time; or it may have been a sudden impulse. He may have told her what he was doing. And she may have known, and not prevented him. Indeed it is almost too easy to think that she administered the poison. But there are other possibilities. Why did L'Angelier, on his deathbed, ask to see Miss Perry? He never asked for his mistress. He never spoke of her, although he must have known that he was dying. "It is a perfect fascination my attachment to that girl; if she were to poison me, I would forgive her. . . . I can't think why I was so unwell after getting that coffee and chocolate from her." Those had been his words to Miss Perry. Had he sent for her now, when he was dying, in order to tell her that his suspicions were confirmed and that his mistress had given arsenic to him? Or had he made those two remarks for the reason only that his planned suicide, or his frequent suicidal impulses when crossed in love (of which there was much evidence brought forward at the trial), should be laid at her door, and that she should be charged with it? In any case he wished to tell Miss Perry something before he died. That Madeleine Smith had poisoned him? That once more, once and forever, it had been in the cup of cocoa?

Or there is another explanation. That he knew there was poison in it. That, after enjoying the favors of his mistress for the last time on earth (this part of it a secret of which Miss Perry had been told nothing), refusing to give her back her letters, but accepting the pretense in her last letter that she still loved him, words had been spoken which meant that they could never meet again. She then handed him the cup of cocoa and, knowing his

fate, he drank of it. He accepted the sentence of death and made
no resistance. He took it in his hand willingly and drank down
the poison. Was it to tell Miss Perry that he had forgiven her?
That he knew, before he took the cocoa from her, what was intended when his mistress went to the mantelpiece and took the
packet, and fetched boiling water, and mixed it with a spoon?

What would we not give, for its romantic interest, to have seen
this last interview between them! Did he go to it believing the
sentiments in her last letter? " . . . Come to me sweet one. . . .
Come beloved and clasp me to your heart. . . . Why my beloved
did you not come to me. Oh beloved are you ill?" Why the last
two sentences? Because she was not certain if he was still living?
Whether the poison had slowly done its work, and that was the
reason why he had not come? And, in view of their next meeting,
to which she was beguiling him, in order to disarm him and allay
his suspicions, by mentioning that she knew he had not been
well? For she had to see him once again. There must be one
more meeting. She would give herself to her lover, and then
poison him. Or we may suspect that L'Angelier was not deceived
by her letter. That he knew its falseness. But could not resist
the promise held out in it. "It is a perfect fascination my attachment to that girl; if she were to poison me, I would forgive her."
Then he knew about it all the time. Upon two occasions before,
he had been very ill after coffee and chocolate taken from her.
There was the evidence, as well, of Amédée Thuau, that he had
been unwell after seeing her, that he was unwell in her presence.
And, contradicting all of this, more evidence, of L'Angelier's suffering from another attack, with all the symptoms of arsenical
poisoning, long before when he had not even met his future
mistress.

We find it, however, more easy to believe the story as it reads.
He had been unsuccessfully poisoned twice, and made a note of
it in his diary upon each occasion. "Thurs: 19 Feb.—saw Mimi
a few moments. Was very ill during the night." "Sun.—22 Feb.
—saw Mimi in Drawing Room. Promised me French Bible.
Taken very ill." And a month later he was dead. He suspected
what she was doing to him. For he had told her of the properties

of arsenic, and perhaps given her some. It is curious that he should have made that first entry in his diary in such concise words. "Saw Mimi . . . Was very ill during the night." It was almost as though she had attempted it before and he had realized. Had begun his diary only in order to record their meetings, and whether he felt ill afterward. For there is nothing else, practically, in his journal. But then he only kept it during the last few weeks of his life. Or it could be that the only purpose of the diary was to throw suspicion on her. But no! We must take it, surely, for true evidence. The purchases of arsenic from chemists' shops were proved in her case, and she was proved to be in possession of the poison. L'Angelier would not go away. He would not give her back her letters. She tried twice to poison him and failed. And now must try again. She wrote that last letter in order to get him back, and get him into her room. An angry letter would not bring him. It must be loving and hold out the promise. She would take him in, "same hour and arrangement," at the front or back door or at the window. With her family, as always, only a few feet away and the maids in the next room; and Mr. Minnoch in the other part of the same house, just above. And her little sister Janet sleeping in the bed.

We are to imagine L'Angelier, then, standing at her window and directed to the door, which she opens with a white hand, holding a lighted candle in the other, but moving back with it into the shadow. He enters. And what can their first words have been? I believe we can guess from the phrases in her last letter, which was in his pocket. "You have come, sweet one. I waited and waited for you. Oh, Emile!" What is she to pretend? That she still loves him? That she longs to see him, only to lie once more in his arms? She is in her nightgown, like the young girl of St. Agnes' Night, lighted taper in hand, who stands on the stair and looks out upon the frosty night. That is in Millais' woodcut, and we are reminded of her. But she leads the way into the drawing room. Puts the candle down upon the mantelpiece and lies wearily upon the sofa, pretending she feels ill. Is her hand trembling? Is it fiery hot, burning, burning, we wonder, or icy cold? She pretends that she is ill with longing. That she is his again, altogether, and has broken her engagement? Then why must she have her letters back? Or what other argument? That there can be some arrangement, if only he will return the letters to her? That she can put off her marriage? That she can continue living with him? That she will not be married till the summer, and there is much time till then? For if she says that she is being forced into marrying Mr. Minnoch, then L'Angelier has said that he will send her letters to her father. Letters which she signed "Mimi L'Angelier," and that leave no doubt, from their language, of the intimacy between them. Better, far better, that she should send him reeling into his garret. Or to die in the street on the way home. For the poison takes some minutes, or half an hour, to work in him. She thinks that he will say nothing. He suspects nothing. He was ill before, but only thought the coffee or chocolate had upset him. After the nervous excitement, after the liquefaction of soul and body. After he had kissed her face and neck and arms.

If he dies in his lodgings they will burn his letters and belongings. What does it matter if someone ignorant finds his letters? Also, under the strain and worry, there were certain contingencies of which she could not think. Certain blank spaces in her mind. Certain possibilities that must take care of themselves, for she was too ill to consider them. It would be better to give herself to him once again and ask him for the letters afterward. The best pretense for her would be that she was tired out with the worry and could not think of the future. They would meet again in two days' time. But, in fact, his death sentence was already signed; and we may think that she hardly bothered him about the letters. It was more important that he should drink the cup of cocoa.

How long were they together? Only a month ago he had "passed two pleasant hour with M. in the Drawing Room," the night following her first halfhearted poisoning of him. He was "very ill during the night." After this night in question the entry in his diary reads "don't feel well." But on the next night he saw her again, when she promised him the French Bible, and that entry ends "taken very ill." So we feel the interview may have been a long one. We are not to suppose that anything in the nature of a quarrel took place between them. He will have scolded and reproached her, and held the letters over her. Had they quarreled outright, and not had another lovers' parting, she could not have handed him the death potion. She could not have persuaded him to turn back for the cup of cocoa. So we may think that she soothes him with gentle words, and lets him tire himself. The more tired the better. And takes his head upon her breast and tells him he is exhausted. He has been ill lately. Why is it? Had it done him no good staying at Bridge of Allan? Ought he not to go away again, and stay away for longer? But no, for she would miss him. But circumstances had altered. There was no point now in her urging him to go away. It was too late. He must be gone for good and all. We may think, though, that if she contrived to effect her purpose, which was to make him drink poison, there must have been promises of further meetings. Perhaps he was by then in the state in which he did not bother much, but only insisted that they should meet tomorrow. They must have talked together in low tones, with long intervals of silence, and in imagination we can hear their voices. She gets up once and goes into her bedroom to see if Janet is asleep.

But time is drawing on. It is growing late and cold. The fire dies down. She fetches boiling water in a kettle from the kitchen. And brings a cup out of the cupboard, and sitting on the end of the sofa near the fire, puts up her hand and takes the paper package from the mantelpiece. Puts the cocoa powder into the cup and pours water directly upon it. Then goes with the cup in her hand to look for some sugar in her bedroom, and comes back stirring with a spoon, and gives it him to drink. And that is all we see. She had left the drawing room for that one moment. He takes the cup in his hand and barely tastes the contents. But there is enough in a spoonful to kill a dozen men. Does it not taste bitter? No, he takes the cup from her as though he is under some spell. Or does he know the truth all the time? Does it, familiarly, as twice or more before, burn and parch his throat as he swallows? For he says nothing. He drinks it down; only a little, but it is enough.

How can he get down the liquid arsenic without coughing?

He is going out into the street, and will fall in agony upon the
way home, but meet not a living soul in the great city. And now
she must make him go at once. She hands him into his overcoat,
because he is looking cold. She tells him he must be cold. She
asks him if his teeth are chattering. She puts her hand upon
his hand and leads him to the door. At the door they do not kiss.
They stand for a moment, and she holds him with his head
against her breast, and perhaps feels his forehead with her hand.
Then he turns to go, and not looking after him, she shuts the door.

Madeleine will have lain awake beside her sister Janet, and
then, with sleep working in her, turned upon her side. But
L'Angelier knew by now the fate that was in store for him. It
took him with full force in a few moments. Not a drunken man
staggering home, but a young man dying for love, and knowing
in his heart that he is to die. He has been poisoned; and next
morning, when with dying breath he asks for his confidante to
come to him, what was it to say to her? That his mistress had
poisoned him, and he had forgiven her? No one will ever know.
He must have literally dragged himself toward his lodging. Why
did he not turn back and hammer at her door? But he said
nothing. He kept his secret. As he lay in agony he must have
turned it over and over in his mind until he felt quite certain.

But, if the soul be immortal, they will have met again. Forever,
in deception and concealment. This young girl, who lived to be
so old, lies restless and gets up continually to see if her little
sister is asleep beside her. She does not haunt us with the cup
and spoon, as she stirs the poison. But she dissimulates, and is
awake while all are sleeping. Listening for the tap of his stick
upon the railing outside her window; and coming to the door to
open it. A ghost in the big city; and in the woods of Rowaleyn.
Upon a May evening, when blood fell on the anemone and the
compact of tragedy was sealed and signed.

LONDON CHARIVARI *

For the lightening of our thoughts here are two pairs of figures. All four of them are embryonic, in the sense that the butterfly is foreshadowed in the chrysalis. That is to say, they contain a prophecy the span of which has just been reached. Their lengthening shadow touched ourselves and then receded. We have all seen persons who resembled them.

It is the dude in coat and trousers. The nineteenth-century man. The fop, or masher, or any other name for him. This was man's livery for a hundred years and more. Upon occasion he wore it for his coffin. It is outmoded. The boots, with their long toes, strap into the trousers. None of our four tyros has seen a steamboat or set foot inside a train. It is not their fault, for this is just before that time. All the same, they are ghosts of a hundred summers, of a hundred seasons, whom we have before us in this evil hour. They are Monstrosities of 1816 and 1821. And we must give that word its true significance, for in a hundred years it has changed its meaning. To be called a monster was a half-endearment. It meant something excessive and without restraint; or a person whose attentions were flattering, or even welcomed. At the same time an extravagance, an absurdity. The feminine Monstrosities were not so favored by the artist. Perhaps the eighteenth century was not quite dead, when men had been the peacocks and women were the hens. This male ascendancy had lingered on. It was men who wore colors; and on the part of women, anything but simplicity was a presumption. Their attempts at fashion are a mere absurdity. The men of the Monstrosities are more directly funny, though their vanity is not attacked. They are drawn half mocking, half in admiration.

But we must come nearer. We must feel and touch their

* From Sacred and Profane Love, 1940. Begun on the 13th June, 1940, the day the German armies entered Paris.

clothes, and hear their voices. First of all, to the Monstrosities of 1816. Two young men who are encased in overcoats and braiding. In this respect they are rivals, and yet in partnership together. They must go to the same tailor. Or could it be that each has his own particular tradesman who will devote all his labors to this living and walking pattern of his skill? Persons, it may be, who are a little subservient, and of foreign blood. Who knows? Jews, or Italians, or perhaps a Frenchman. Persons who love gilding, and in its glitter betray a warmer sun. In their back parlors, in the gilt mirrors of their shops. But it is more than gold frogging or the application of black braid. It is a question also of fur collars and fur linings. There are astrakhan and Persian lamb. Astrakhan especially, which is curled like a French poodle. An invaluable discovery. No other material can match or, indeed, rival the talents of the hairdresser. And he of course must be, or should be, French, or carry a French name. But what is the idea behind this pair of strange appearances?

In their attempts at the ideal they have contrived to look the same. They have reached an identity together. It is the difference between your right foot and your left. As to the trend of their ambition, that is another matter. For it is most peculiar that two young men of fashion, self-appointed, should appear quilted from top to toe, and so stiffly tailored that it is an agony to move or turn the head. Looking closely at them, we remember that it is only a couple of years after the peace of 1814, when the Allied armies entered Paris after Napoleon had gone to Elba. The Parisians stared in wonder at the Highlanders in their kilts and feathered bonnets, at Uhlans and Lancers, at the dolmans and fur pellises of the Puszta. The Russians especially were a subject for astonishment. Cossacks had set up their bivouacs along the Champs Élysées. In the next year, and after Waterloo, London also went cosmopolitan. This pair of young men could be compared to the wildest of Hussars, but on foot. Cossacks we might call them, of the retreat from Moscow, padded for the cold, with an augmentation from their horses' cloths as well, but all come forth again from the crucible of fashion. Cossacks of the mode, in the latest style of hairdressing. They have put themselves into uniform. But look at it more closely and you will see it is not for war. It is a walking-out dress.

What it presupposes is sempiternal snow. You could not expect these officers, these men of fashion from a legendary North, to have made provision for a London summer. For in their fantasy Russia was always cold. Yet it is but fantasy. They are, in fact, the Monstrosities of Hyde Park Corner, near the statue of Achilles, but before that bronze figure was offered by the women of England in honor of Wellington. So do not demand of them that they should be true Russians. It is allowed that the beaux may be influenced in their ideas by the notions of a foreign clime. The Russians and their Czar Alexander had impressed the world. This was a tribute to them, and an attempt to introduce that novelty into the streets and drawing rooms of London.

But this is in exaggeration. For are these the real beaux? Come a little nearer still and listen to them. We hear an unfashionable accent, a drawling language full of slang and turns of phrase. The speech of greenroom and hairdresser's salon, hints of the cockpit and the boxing ring. They are not bucks of the first water. Or can it be we are mistaken? Who could be more far-fetched, more fantastic than Alvanley or Petersham, more redundant than the Regent? None of them had the good taste, the refinement of Beau Brummel. We know the wasp waist and striped trousers of Lord Petersham, his goatee and whiskers, and the odd or boat-shaped hat which, together with his features, gave him something of a Jewish air. There were Sefton, and Worcester, dressed in black, and walking with his poodle. All of them—we know this—had their peculiar voices. Some spoke like their own grooms, or imitated, if unconsciously, a huntsman or a jockey. Others had a family accent, come down to them from generations of country houses in great parks. We do not feel certain our two tyros are of these. The great beaux of the Regency never dressed alike. It was their pride to be different. Our pair of heroes is standing in the wings; not either upon the stage and playing to the world, nor among its workers. Onlookers, gorgeously uniformed, in fact dressed to kill, but a little unsure of their background.

And what has brought them into this close identity together?
Do they share the same lodgings? Never for one moment could we
take them for two brothers. Everyone who reads this must have
among his own acquaintance characters like these, who from similarity of circumstance and condition have become alike. They
are comrades in arms. Both are drawn together, as if by a magnet.
One enhances, or completes, the other. They are inseparable, in
appointed places and at certain hours. And there are others like
them or, it may be, themselves, who in a sense resent this near
facsimile and avoid each other, delighting their public, therefore,
whenever they are seen together. Such could be this moment.
And were it the truth, they would be forced into pretending a
friendship which is not genuine. They are, however, too young
in years to have endured a lifetime of such competition. It is of
course the genius of George Cruikshank that depicts for us these
possibilities. And he may have emphasized their likeness to each
other. Did they ever, then, exist at all? Or are they his creation?
It does not matter. But of all the Monstrosities among whom
they figure, they are most closely studied, and for ourselves it is
impossible not to believe in them.

They are our mirror of fashion and we would look into it. Do
not, however, expect their images to be imprisoned there. We
find them at one moment in mean streets, in Clerkenwell or
Islington, and the next, before a muslined dressing table. This
is because we alter in our opinion of them. And it is, as well, our
opportunity. A fine morning came when it was time to put on
those coats, newly arrived last evening after many fittings from
the tailor. A great parcel, with much soft paper round the cuffs
and collar. In those days there were no cardboard boxes. The
boy who brought the parcel passed so many brightly painted iron
railings. These were newly treated every spring and had gone
black by winter. If one of our beaux lives in Clerkenwell, and
the other in a terrace near Hyde Park, there are these railings just
the same. They were, and are, in sign manual of London. But
we must be careful in our chronology, for this was before Nash's
rebuilding and the age of stucco. It may be even that the fantastic
nature of those postwar fashions was due in part to the absence of

their proper background. Little or nothing had been built for twenty years. They were capricious and conjectural, completely "in the air," and unrelated to the scene. It will be noticed that this series of skits by Cruikshank continues, as though in proof of our contention, until the late '20s, by which time the stucco streets and terraces were ready. After that the fashions become sober and coherent. They take a direction that has nothing to do with the cold, mass classicism of the Regency, but they do not lose control again. Their development is logical, not sporadic and without plan.*

This person—for we take them separately, attend to them one at a time following our military comparison—has camped out in his rooms. He has hung the walls with draperies of which the straight folds resemble the temporary decorations of a pavilion or marquee. His bed has a canopy in the form of a tent. The chairs, like those in the bedroom of Talma, the tragedian, may be shaped like drums. His sitting room has a flock paper on the walls. There are elaborate pelmets to the curtains. In every detail it is suggested that quick and drastic steps have had to be taken in order to bring such old-fashioned premises into conformity with modern taste. The permanent frame is not yet ready. This is a mere temporary expedient. It is—this is the reason—the beginning of a new century.

We shall find in his dressing room a long cheval mirror and a dummy for his clothes. The dummy, indeed, is already dressed like him. It is as though a lay figure were wearing the model's clothes. The dummy, a limbless, featureless fetish, is made exactly in his image, to his precise measurement, but without resemblance, as if it were the work of primitive sculptors who could

* We would draw attention to the fashion plates issued by B. Read, 12 Hart Street, Bloomsbury Square, and Broadway, New York. These show the epitome of masculine fashion from 1830 to about 1846. Most of them would seem to be colored aquatints after Robert Cruikshank, elder brother to the more famous George. They show scenes in the Surrey Zoo, a skating scene on the lake in Regent's Park with the new stucco terraces in the background; a delightful print with William IV riding in the foreground past the bow windows of the Steyne at Brighton, and so forth. A few of the original *gouache* drawings by Robert Cruikshank are in the Bethnal Green Museum. His fashion plates are the masterworks of this neglected artist. The whole series, which is very rare, comprises some twelve or fifteen plates.

not catch a likeness and so left it formal, the mere convention for a man. And yet it is his fetish, his statue made in his own image. In extreme cases of the Regency infection we would find a wig put out upon a barber's block. That this was not endemic only in Great Britain could be proved in a multitude of instances. Of this the composer Rossini is most typical. His rooms in Paris, in his famous apartment in the Boulevard des Italiens, where he lived until late in the '60s, had a number of wigs upon stands, often visible through an open door into his bedroom, and connecting him in the imagination of all who visited him with those far-off days of the Regency or Restoration. Much earlier, when he came to London in the winter of 1823, he lodged at No. 90 Regent Street and, if not ill in bed with nerves, took a pet parrot and sat on top of Nash's then existent colonnade, looking down on the traffic and the passers-by. Beau Brummel too had usually a cockatoo or parrot in his rooms. Even in his decline at Calais his drawing room was enlivened by a fine macaw. We place then, perhaps without anomaly, a parrot in this house that we are visiting. Its home is a cage shaped like a pavilion. The bright feathers of its chest and wings shine in the spring sunlight, or in the dark days put to shame the fire in the grate.

This parrot of the Amazon came, so the beau might like to think, from close to the lands of snuff, an exotic paradise confused in no certainty with the hills of green Pekoe and the coffee groves, all products of the Indies. In the names of the different kinds of snuff there is preserved, indeed, a particular poetry that cannot have been less potent when the kegs or casks were new. "A fine old rappee of San Domingo, just arrived," the tobacconist's advertisement would run. The earlier sorts, become old-fashioned by this time, were Bergamota, Jessamina, Orangery and Neroly, named from the scents from which they were compounded and dating, it is evident, from late in the seventeenth century. There had been, among the foreign snuffs sold in London, Carotte; Palillio, which was Portuguese in origin; Étrenne, offered every year to Louis XV on his birthday by the different snuff manufacturers of Paris, from which the best was chosen and called by the number of that year; and Bureau, of which the history was somewhat similar. Violet Strasbourg, made in the city of that name, of powdered rappee and bitter almonds mixed with ambergris and attarjul, was the favorite snuff of Queen Charlotte and every morning she added to it a spoonful of green tea. There was Bolangaro's Hollanda and St. Vincent, Bolangaro being an Italian snuff manufacturer who lived near Frankfurt and retired to Italy with a large fortune. Other kinds were the various sorts of Kendal, called after the brown cloth of that capital of Westmorland, made there by descendants of an old colony of Flemish weavers, with in all probability a green snuff, scented, after the green cloth of Kendal for which that town was famed. There were Scholten's best rappee; Gillespie's Scotch snuff, in whose memory the wooden Highlanders still stand on the pavement at the door of the tobacconist; Prince's, made for the Regent and to be bought even now in London, in the Haymarket; plain and scented St. Domingo; Dutch and Strasbourg, Hoxton and all other sorts of rappee, Spanish, Seville and Havannah, Brazil, Portugal and Bergamot. Others were Macauba, highly scented, from Martinique; Princeza, from Lisbon; Cuba; Latakia, made from the light tobacco of Persia; Masulipatam, dark, moist, richly scented, brought from the coast of Coromandel; and Penalvar, a mixture of tobacco and red earth, coming from Havana, of great pungency and used also as a dentifrice. Such, in brief, is the geography of snuff. All or most of these the beau could buy. But we will return later to his other shopping.

For the Charivari takes us to the mean street where himself or his companion or rival might be living. Shall we say it is Pentonville, near to the home of Cruikshank, and observed by him. In one of the long terraces where the mist hangs in the autumn mornings, every house alike, so that there might be this beau, this "Burlington Bertie," living in each one. In a street perhaps not far from Sadlers' Wells. There is no cheval mirror, no parrot in his lodging. Oh! To breathe for a moment this apartment air of more than a hundred years ago! To hear their voices on the narrow stairs, to choose a day—it does not matter when or in what month—and see and touch and listen to them!

A more wonderful experience than to enter Pharaoh's tomb, where everything is only dead, in catalepsis, and air or light will crumble it to dust. One could not ask for anything more humble, a mere metropolitan instance, with naught of history or romance to it. How like a ghost he is, with his thin trousers and his pointed shoes! We see it too in his cravat and in the way his hair is cut! The ghost of the modern man; and his clothes, in some manner, are as the clothes we have cast off. Our chrysalis, and black and withered as that rejected skin would be. Perhaps every generation in the form and style of its clothing is midwife, or funeral mute, to those that follow after it. Certainly this person whom we visit is the devil, the man in black, of the old story.

And we begin, in the light of this, to look at more of the Monstrosities. We mentioned in our beginning another pair of figures. Here they are, one the exact facsimile in little of his bigger brother. Both are drawn alike, even to the smallest detail. But it is peculiar how their difference in height brings out dissimilarities in their expression. The elder or taller of the pair is all inaneness and vacuity. In the smaller of the pair this is translated only by the dwarfing or compression into a blind and mole-like acquiescence. He does everything his elder tells him, and it is as though his eyes were not yet opened. Hand held in hand, he is led along like a little homunculus. We feel that he cannot speak and cannot think, being in all things subordinate and dependent on his brother. This pair of figures is near to being a masterpiece of caricature. You may almost measure the scale of their exaggeration. For they are not, they never could be a father and his son. It is a case quite simply of two absurd young men. The elder is a dude, a zany, hopelessly in debt and forever laughed at behind his back. He will have, inexplicably, some success with women. The other is a diminuendo of his brother, but will never achieve it and is not even seriously in debt. Everyone has known these two brothers, and we meet them here as though standardized for a hundred years and more to come.

Other Monstrosities from those curious years could be described as being more annual than perennial. Their importance, that is to say, is for their year, not for the future. We choose the two beaux, at the foot of the statue of Achilles, who are ogling two women. Their dress is still that worn in the Napoleonic wars. They have breeches, not trousers, their coats have wide collars, they wear top hats—the top hat of Thurtell, and of Bellingham, who murdered Mr. Perceval. These are the roisterers of Real Life in London, of Alken and Pierce Egan, of the brothers Cruikshank. One of them has his monocle, or quizzing glass, in the handle of his cane. Both men have wide hips, from the fashion of their clothes, and this gives to them an overbearing, a truculent or rather bullying appearance. The bulk of them together, walking arm in arm, is like a gust of wind. They seem to be blown or inflated in our direction, about to topple over. We must think of them, in analogy, as nautical sportsmen, leaning upon the wind of their own half-drunken impulses. The two women on whom they bear down advance toward them holding up the hem of their dresses in order to show their ankles and their petticoats. This was an affectation of the time, for in the background of the print other women, always two by two, walk away in the same manner. The unfreshness of these women is most wonderfully expressed, and to such point that they are faintly sickening to look upon. There is a frowsiness in the dot and stipple of their line. From this point, indeed, the Monstrosities become like figures in a nightmare. It is the cloaca, the abscondita, of Hogarth and Gillray, a dwelling upon the sinister and sordid which is akin to madness, the pabulum, the common or daily meal of the satirist, when his powers are in their full flow of creation but, in their effect, it is as the dropping of the mask. Every living figure is tainted by their madness. Not a face but is pitted or pockmarked; all bodies are too fat or thin. In Hogarth and in Gillray the very dogs are deformed and starving.

Such of course is not the case at the foot of the statue of Achilles. The Charivari of Cruikshank, under which name we might assemble all such various satires upon fashion, could not include the hungry. They are his early ephemera drawn under the influence of Gillray, being in part the comments of an inhabitant of Islington or Pentonville upon the absurdities of Hyde Park. There is another of these prints, portraying the fashions of a particular year, in which the women wear ugly, barrel-shaped and hunchbacked dresses, with ridiculously short skirts, hats like a shovel or a coal scuttle, nearly exposed bosoms, and are impelled by some vagary, some contagion of their senses, to walk leaning forward as though in great pain and agony. The immense hats of the later '20s are drawn with tiresome and exaggerated repetition, being depicted as huge straw platters tied with ribbons and heaped with fruits and flowers. This is the weakness of these caricatures. And they come toward the end of a long series. Let us look, though, at their strength. There was the epoch of the *"chapeau de paille"* with wide, flopping brims. Cruikshank has drawn a group of children completely hidden under these great mushrooms they are wearing. The whole of this print billows and flops with the wide shapes. We are nearly in the land of Bosch and Brueghel. In other prints we see strange apparitions. A man dressed like a naval officer, but it is his own fantasy. He has designed it for himself. His coat has the braiding of a commander or an admiral; he wears the cocked hat, and his trousers might be the white duck trousers of the fleet worn in summer or in southern waters. But it is his copious whiskers which are the mystery. For at that time only Ernest Augustus, Duke of Cumberland and later King of Hanover, with the officers of Hussar regiments wore those whiskers. It is this fact, and not only the scandalous incidents connected with his life, that make the Duke of Cumberland so conspicuous and sinister a figure in the prints or caricatures of his day. This crypto-naval officer, however, projects forward to the epoch of Lord Dundreary. He forecasts the fashion of the '60s. The ranks serving under him would even wear the beard of the naval rating within the lifebelt upon a packet of Player's cigarettes. Another figure to attract attention must be a portrait. It is a man thirty to forty years old, with most decided or emphatic features. He is stout and broad-shouldered, and wears his top hat on the back of his head at an angle which must have been characteristic of him. He is, in fact, so accustomed to his top hat that we cannot conceive him without it. He will have worn it indoors, in his own library, and in the dining room of his club. In watching him, and at the thought of him without his hat, we must remember that men had worn short hair only for a very few years by then. Before that their hair was powdered; they wore wigs or periwigs or the long locks of the cavaliers. He is cleanshaven, we remark, and this carries him from 1826 to nearly a hundred years ahead, to the epoch that we have seen and known ourselves. In his left hand he holds the purse or bag of the woman with whom he is walking arm in arm. This is shaped somewhat like a peer's coronet and is, at the same time, a money bag. The symbolism of this is too evident not to have a meaning.

Across the background, in his high curricle with a groom at the back, drives the phantom shade of Lord Petersham wearing his pink and white striped trousers, his brown coat and his boat-shaped Jewish hat, and we are to think of him—though indeed he is but suggested or hinted at more than drawn in full—as muttering his continual exclamations.* They come forth in a cloud from his mouth, with a line drawn round them by the pen of the caricaturist. Some of the words are always spelled

---

* Viscount Petersham, born 1780, succeeded his father as fourth Earl of Harrington in 1829, and died in 1851. He married in 1831 Maria, daughter of Samual Foote, the famous actor. Lord Petersham was a great devotee of snuff. He must have possessed, indeed, all and more than those different varieties mentioned in our geography of snuff. One room in Harrington House, the old family mansion off Whitehall, was filled with shelves bearing Chinese jars of great beauty, which held the various kinds of snuff. He had too a collection of snuff boxes, and it was said that he used a different box on every day of the year. Lord Petersham was also a great connoisseur of tea. In the same room that contained the jars of snuff were arranged tea canisters containing Congou, Pekoe, Souchong, Gun-powder, Russian and many others. This sacred room was presided over by an eccentric individual who blended the teas and prepared the snuffs for their noble owner; in fact, a sort of dispensary of tea and snuff, a private emporium into which it would be a delight to enter. The character of Lord Fitzbooby, in Disraeli's *Coningsby*, was founded on Lord Petersham. We are told elsewhere that he never ventured out until after 6:00 P.M., that his manners were decidedly affected, and that he spoke with a kind of lisp. The style of his equipages and liveries (snuff-colored) was formed on the model of the old French noblesse. He prided himself, furthermore, on his resemblance to Henri IV, his goatee and peculiar hat being in evidence of this. The Petersham snuff mixture and Peter-sham overcoat were his inventions. After his death two thousand pounds of snuff from his collection realized about one thousand pounds at a sale in London in July 1851.

wrong and are difficult to read. In another print, not one of the
Monstrosities, we see the same person attended by his groom on
foot. His appearance in this is almost too fantastic to be believed.
The groom is obviously his mirror, his little idol whom he con-
sults and who takes messages for him. And yet an absolutely im-
personal relationship—that of someone who must argue, even
if it is a monologue, before he can make up his mind. The caricaturist has built on his eccentricity until he is so extreme a case
that it is difficult to believe he has a friend. We begin to wonder
if his idiosyncrasies, which are as fantastic as those of any character in Italian comedy, are not done unconsciously to please
himself alone. Something—it may be in the shaping of his
shoulders—makes him birdlike. He is one of the family of
bucerotidae, or hornbills. In looking through the plates of the
monograph of that genus by D. G. Elliott, 1882, we are continually reminded of Lord Petersham. The colored lithographs
of Keulemans (for this is one of the most superb publications of
its kind, apart from Gould) time after time are reminiscent of
him. It is because these most eccentric-looking of all the race
of birds have developed in their Bornean or Sumatran jungles
a physiognomy that has its parallel in the aggressive whiskers and
hooked nose of this beau of the Regency, crowned or surmounted
by the horned or bony excrescence of their skulls, which has its
equivalent in the cocked hat of Lord Petersham, so inveterately
a part of him that he is not to be recognized without it. He is a
person who, like some curious or exotic bird, could be studied a
long time together in his every movement. Such specimens are
the bird-actors. There is something hieratic in their resemblance
to mankind. For this reason the ibis was a god in ancient Egypt.
Other birds are like actors in the masks of comedy. For the mask
of the comedian is never funny. It is always sinister and frightening. In the same way the bird-actors are bird-headed men. Lord
Petersham is a flightless hornbill. He has lost the power of
flight. This makes him, as a bird, more like a man. His staccato
sentences are like a bird's. They are no longer in context than the
chattering of the beak. Birdlike too is the thinness of his waist,
though it becomes at once unpleasant but to mention anything

physical in a bird. It must have no beauty, nothing handsome but the color of its plumes. It is two-footed; it walks upright, and in that it has resemblance to men. In more, it is evil and anthropomorphic.

The Monstrosities of Cruikshank are not all absurdity. We would suggest that the summer glitter of Hyde Park during the first half of the English or nineteenth century, in those years after the fall of Napoleon, is our only equivalent to the Prater of Vienna, to the Chiája, the Alameda, or the gondola. Could we but follow those crowds back into their homes, there would be material for many lifetimes. It will be remarked that, apart from Lord Petersham, the Monstrosities are all on foot. We are given no equestrians, no amazons. There are none of the fashionable equipages, though the art of the carriage builder was a prerogative of London. We do not see a britzka, a light phaeton, or landaulet, nor a single curricle nor chariot. We miss their brilliant colors and appurtenances; the yellow, scarlet lake or green bodies of the carriages; the coats of arms and family mottoes; the glitter of the spokes; the harness and rosettes; waistcoats with blue and yellow stripes; driving coats of white drab cloth with fifteen capes; bouquets of myrtle and pink and yellow geraniums; "cattle," so went the phrase, "of a bright bay color." We cannot, for there is no space, pursue these noble or plebeian origins. But at least we may walk in the streets and look into the shop windows.

In accordance with a part of the theory of these writings, where we deal with perfection in little, one of the first things noticed would be the bakers' or the butchers' handcarts, or indeed the delivery vans of haberdasher, glove seller or any other shop, because of the style in which they were painted, and the gilt scrolls and lettering on their sides. In point of spacing and lettering, that was one of the finest epochs of the printed book, and its influence can be seen in the firm but imaginative lettering and in the forgotten art of flourishing. That was an art of contrasts. There were ways of leaving bare of ornament the most important word in such inscriptions, and embellishing the rest. Or this principle could work by opposites, giving emphasis by means of every prolongation and intertwining of the calligrapher. Such metropolitan or urban art, the exact opposite to peasant arts and crafts, has not yet been treated with the care that it deserves. It is one of the contradictions of history that it was the aesthetic movement of the latter part of that century which brought it to destruction. In tradition, it went back to Cheapside of the time of Chaucer, had reached to perfection, we might imagine, at the end of the seventeenth century, and was in its last phase in the rebuilding of London after Waterloo. The art of the shop sign; but in its hundred divisions and ramifications it has proceeded much further than that name suggests and, in the neatness of the bakers' carts, where we first meet with it, we are only at the beginning of its possibilities. That it did not advertise or pride itself as art is perhaps its most conspicuous charm. At the time we are speaking of, it took advantage, as we have said, of a golden age in printing. There was the fine lettering above the shop window, while it descended to small details as in the printed wrapper. A delightful instance, which is still in commerce, is the paper wrapping of the flat sixpenny packets of Parkinson's Doncaster butterscotch. This could not be improved on for the spacing and set up of its lettering. We would expect to find such trifles at their best in Brighton or Cheltenham, centers, self-styled, of elegance and refinement. But they had reached as well to older towns, to Bath or Scarborough; while there was hardly a market or a posting town without the bow window of the chemist or the grocer with square panes and shutters, and the fanlight placed above the door.

Evidence is to be found in tradesmen's cards and billheads of the time. There were firms of engravers who specialized in these, sending around travelers to collect their orders. This was in the great age of the steel engravers, and these little vignettes, which approximate to the beautiful engravings on old writing paper of the '30s and '40s, had died out soon after the middle of the century. Often they show the particular shop, sometimes a whole block of Regent Street with its new buildings. Or they depict the objects sold, arranged in a trophy and, upon occasion, engraved singly in great detail and precision. There was a specialty even

in the engraving of the Royal arms, often with an array of banners
and lances, of trumpets, drums and mortars shown behind them,
and the lion and unicorn, enraged or in defiance. Two billheads
from Scarborough have the Spa bridge and the castle drawn almost as though it were the Bay of Naples. The wine and spirit
merchant, even in an inland country town, has a wharf with a
sailing ship tied up beside it and a top-hatted overseer who checks
the list of casks and barrels. Or it is the port of embarkation;
Negroes roll the hogsheads of rum and take the planters' orders.
Tea merchants have their particular style. Often it is an engraving of their premises. The firm of J. H. Tibbs (late Ireson) of
Oxford Street, has sugar loaves shown in the window and an
assistant in top hat and apron, with a case of tea upon his
shoulder and others standing in a pile, with the Chinese characters visible upon their sides. The Tea Exchange of Upper
Parade, Leamington, is a place of enchantment. A corner shop,
with a tall lamppost at the corner. The dado is an open balus-
trade; the cornice, below the name of the firm, a long inscription
in golden Chinese characters; beneath that, high in the windows,
a row of Chinese paintings, mandarins and ladies; four windows,
shared between two pairs of hanging gaslights with glass shades
shaped like tulips; and, for the stock in trade, tall vases of porcelain and chests and cases of the different teas. Banbury and
Towcester, my two local towns, had tea merchants who took
their customers abroad with them. Their billheads have little
chinoiserie scenes engraved beside the title. In one, a pair of
Celestials is upon a flowering shore. Strange palm trees wave
about them and in the distance stands a pagoda. Kegs and bales
marked Fine Hyson, coffee and tobacco and snuff, surround
them. In the background is the ocean, and a distant sailing ship.
The other billhead is a double scene; to one side a coffee mill
worked by a European; and beside it a group of Celestials in a
kiosk, underneath a parasol. Below, in fading ink, is written
"two pounds of Congou tea."

The trophies of the Royal arms, above the shops of the Royal
warrant holders, were in the prime then of their manufacture.
Those few specimens that are left us now are in reproach for

that. It was a minor art, to itself, in which great imagination was displayed. This too has its obvious descent from medieval times, with its affinities to tournament and chessboard. Many of them were masterworks of carver and gilder, subtly differenced, for instance, for the Queen-Dowager Adelaide, the Royal dukes and duchesses, or the kings of Hanover or Belgium. The heraldic animals of country inns, the white or red lions, the white harts or swans belong to the same tradition, and may have been carved and painted in the same workshops. A walk down Oxford or Regent Street in the '20s or '30s of last century would have shown the lion and unicorn in greater number than ever before or since. The low buildings of Regent Street in their bright stucco, still fronted by Nash's colonnades, following the gentle curve along from Piccadilly Circus to Oxford Street, were enlivened by these carved animals and their shields of arms. In particular there were corner buildings, at the turn of Conduit Street or Maddox Street, where Nash had employed his favorite device of a low, domed pavilion. Here the Royal arms were set above the door, as though on guard, and in toy fantasy the eyes could travel but a few yards along the painted cornice to the next lion and unicorn above the near-by shop. Their wooden medievalism, that of the painted playing card or the sham tournament, was not at variance with Nash's bastard classicism. He too had made his experiments in Gothic; and the sudden birth of these animals of wood and stucco, bastard descendants of the gargoyles, or of the heraldic supporters upon the pinnacles of such buildings as St. George's Chapel, Windsor Castle, was as though Gog and Magog, or the figureheads of shipbuilding yards, had brought their progeny and mounted them along the cornice. We could make out, too, an analogy to the canal barge, the Gypsy caravan, the roundabout of the fairground. In every weather, in the fog and rain, these heraldic animals were part of the Charivari of the streets of London.

The passing of time, which extolled the buildings of Regent Street, grew indifferent and then condemned them, is illustrated in the facility with which our eyes would seek out these details that many persons might not notice. They may be there for the eyes to see and yet not be seen. These are questions of emphasis, omission or incorporation. They can be given their importance, pass unnoticed or be compounded in the painter's or the writer's presentation. An instance is in the lithographs of Thomas Shotter Boys. There is no better-known topographer of London. And Boys is more than that. He is in the tradition of Bonington. In his lithographs the whole material is worked up into the finished surface, as though, that is to say, each lithograph of the whole series had to be examined and passed for its color, its detail and its figures, before publication. If found unworthy, it would have been rejected. Where this painter excels is in porches and steeples of white Portland stone. His crowds too are in tact and harmony with his buildings. But already he is early Victorian. His pleasure lay in the play of light upon the architecture. It may not be too fanciful to see the white chalk hills of Kent and Surrey in the predominant candor of his scenes. The majority, in tone, are as white as the whitecoats of the old Hapsburg army. White Portland stone and white chalk hills. Even his stucco buildings are more white than yellow.

But there is an artist, less well known than Boys, who gives to us the exact conspectus that we need. He follows with fidelity the every detail. And their accumulation tells us the factual truth. In his water-color drawings we see how a London street appeared if we would study it as a traveler might look, again and again, upon a row of Oriental booths or shops. With eyes, that is to say, alive to every strangeness and unfamiliarity. All of this is set down by him because of his engagement with the truth. A person therefore who is without imagination; but, in the result, his surprise at every brick and stone is not less interesting than the lithographs of Boys. The painter in question is George Scharf, who was born near Munich in 1788 and died in London in 1860. He studied in Antwerp and Paris and accompanied the Allied armies in their final campaigns against Napoleon, being occupied chiefly in painting portraits in miniature of the British officers. He arrived in London in 1816. His scrupulous draftsmanship recommended itself to the authors of scientific and, more especially, geological works, with the result that his illustrations are to be found in many of the books by Professor Owen and other scientific writers of the time. In this way he delineated the skulls and skeletons of many extinct animals found embedded in the soil or rocks, and numerous plates from his hand are to be found in the annals of the Old Geological Society. Besides this, he made large water-color drawings, on commission, of such subjects as a sitting of Parliament and the Lord Mayor's banquet. So far a pedestrian, more than an inspired, career. But it is precisely as a pedestrian that Scharf is of value to us. His private hobby seems to have consisted in making water-color drawings of old London, with particular regard for beadles, night watchmen and other vanishing figures of the past, and a special enthusiasm for old shop fronts and for the little details of costume and street architecture which would appeal to someone of foreign origin as being characteristic of his adopted capital. An enormous mass of these small drawings, amounting to several hundreds in number, were deposited by his heirs, a year or two after he had died, at the British Museum, and are to be studied in the Print Room. As documents, but in point more of painstaking detail than of character, they compare with the collection of drawings given by Constantin Guys in his old age, just before his fatal accident, to the Carnavalet Museum in Paris. Those, of course, are works of a great artist; these are topographical illustrations, but their meticulous detail amounts in the aggregate to something as typical of London as the Monstrosities of Cruikshank. His drawings of provincial towns could not, it is obvious, be as important as his rendering of the Strand. They could but be subsidiary to the great street of London. And it so happens that one of his finest drawings is a view along the Strand.

To look at this drawing, and contemplate the possibility of walking down that Strand, is a prospect to make the mouth water. For as far as the eyes can see there are shop fronts, bow windows, every enticement that painted lettering and a pane of glass can offer. There is more to buy than in the bazaars of Damascus or Grand Cairo, under the arcades of the Palais Royal, or in the toyshops of old Nuremberg. So let us start from Charing Cross and walk along the Strand. In the distance hangs the white dome of St. Paul's. Straight in front is Gibb's steeple of St. Mary-le-Strand, a little masterpiece of elegance and good manners, paying tribute in its pagoda or pepper-castor form to this mart for foreign lands, and recalling in every detail works of the silversmiths in the reigns of Charles II or Queen Anne. Behind it must be the other church of St. Clement Danes; and were we to climb upon a roof or mount that very tower, we would see seventy or a hundred white steeples, all of Portland stone, curving away in the distance, past St. Paul's to Greenwich, as in Canaletto's paintings, where as a foreigner again he seized upon this feature of old London. They are London's minarets, in form and variety not less capricious than that name suggests. Works of an earlier age; for the Strand, as we see it this fine morning of a hundred and twenty years ago, is nearly contemporary. With few exceptions the shops and houses date from not later than the beginning of the century. They must be modern enough to suit the requirements of business and trade. Many of them are gilded and painted to look new. But for ourselves they have the newness of any medieval town, of any place intangible because of physical impossibility, be it Antioch or Ephesus, Byzantium or ancient Rome, made a living reality and known and touched by us.

We pass by the shop of an ivory and hard-wood turner and carver. He advertises chessmen and billiard, pool and bagatelle balls supplied; his sign, which we should find again upon his billhead, is the figure of an elephant standing in a forest clearing, with a pair of ivory tusks lying like crossed swords at his feet. Next door, a grocer or fancy warehouseman has in his window English, French and Spanish chocolates, Westmorland and Westphalian hams, Parmesan, Gruyère and Chapzugar cheeses, Dutch beef for grating, Russian and reindeer tongues, Vermicelli and Cagliari pastes for soups. A curious mingling of past and present, for among so much else that is familiar, what are Spanish chocolates, Chapzugar cheeses, Dutch beef for grating? After this comes an ordinary or eating house. The slate reads: "Giblet soup, roast ribs of beef, Cheddar or red Leices-

ter cheese, cheap oysters, Colchester or Whitstable, Cornish or
Dutch Zeeland, jellied or smoked eels." Inside there are high
wooden pews and top hats everywhere, as in an Eton classroom.
For we begin now to take notice of the crowd. Figures in black
and drab and bottle green, with nankeen breeches, dressed with
that contradiction which turns the townsmen of one decade into
countrymen of the next. Outside a chemist's window it would
be impossible not to linger. We read announcements of Sim's
only genuine white and musk brown Windsor soap, mottled and
Naples soaps, Rowland's Macassar oil, in an older packing;
notices, respectfully worded, addressed to the nobility, gentry
and the clergy, calling attention to the advantages of certain preparations, composed, as it were, in a particular language, the jar-
gon of elocutionist or dancing master. Authentic eau de Cologne,
guaranteed against imposture and pleading vociferously its
address—"Gegenüber dem Julichs Platz"—with fulmination and
threat of action against all other persons who called themselves
Farina, took up the center of one window. It is plainly the wrap-
pings and labels that are the fascination.

In another window, Hannay and Dietrichsen's fragrant
essence of Rondeletia, for the toilet or handkerchief, prepared
expressly for the use of the Royal family.* We read: "The lovers
of elegant perfumes are solicited to call and try this article on
their Handkerchief, for which purpose a Bottle is always open
free, to which Handkerchief, so perfumed, the combined fragrance of the choicest conservatory must yield precedence. . . .
Perfumers, whose appearance of respectability would induce a
belief that they would not sell a counterfeit article, are even
guilty of this." And we come to Hannay & Co.'s Oriental Oil:
"A pure limpid white vegetable substance. . . . The great care
is proverbial, that is paid to the cultivation of the luxuriant
tresses of the fair Captives of the Harem, and Art is there well
known to succeed in outrivalling even the far-famed beauties of

* According to The Art of Perfumery, by G. W. Septimus Piesse (London,
1855), essence of Rondeletia was composed of cloves, lavender, musk and vanilla.
He suggests that its inventor took the name of this perfume from the Rondeletia,
the Chyn-len of the Chinese, or from the R. Odorata of the West Indies, which
has a sweet odor.

Circassia. The Oriental Oil, as prepared by Messrs. Hannay & Co. has been employed for the purpose during the period of three centuries." Close to it is Gowland's Lotion: "Distinguished as a safe and congenial appendage of the toilet during a period of nearly eighty years. A copy of that popular work, 'The Theory of Beauty,' is enclosed with every bottle." And there is also Shaw's Mindora Oil, known too from 1750. By its side, goods and an advertisement of Brewster's: "Haircutter and Manufacturer of Ornamental Hair to the Royal Family. Makes Ladies' Headdresses, Gentlemen's Perruques, Scalps, etc., of the finest natural curl. Hair distinguished from all others for their lightness, durability, and exactness in fitting. W. B. most scrupulously excludes all common hair from his house, and being the greatest buyer of that of the first quality, he can always ensure such a supply as cannot be had in any other house. Brewster's Almond and Honey Soap, combining the emollient and balsamic properties of the honey with the finest Almond Oil soap. Sold in squares, at a shilling each. The only house in London where Chardan Houbigant's Pâté d'Amandes au Miel can be had as imported." And in a corner next to Rowland's Kalydor, Rowland's Essence of Tyre, for changing red and gray whiskers to black or brown. We pass on and come to the *Maison de Deuil:* "Mourning Furnisher by appointment to the King, H.R.H. the Duchess of Gloucester, H.R.H. the Duchess of Kent, H.R.H. the Duchess of Cambridge, and the Grand Duchess of Mecklenburgh-Strelitz." "Mr. Pugh," we read, "takes pleasure in introducing to his numerous patrons and the public his highly approved materials for Family Mourning, the Royal Bombazin Cloth, and Amphomoion or Widow's silk, to be had only at his house. Widow's Mourning in a hitherbefore unknown variety. Mourning costume, Pelisses, Paletots, Polish Mantles and Cloaks, in velvet, satin, glacé, gros royal, moiré, and other silks, in every variety." And close to this, the next window has a label, "Mock Turtle always ready."

This prospect of the Strand, seen not in detail but in all its length, is a wonderful and a characteristic vision. We would like the enlargement of it on the curtain or back cloth of a

theater. So many dramas could be played in front of it; Dan
Leno or Little Tich equally with Shakespeare or Ben Jonson.
For many reasons. Because anything so exactly dated is true to
all time, and for the vast human history of this thoroughfare
and parallel to old Thames. It is East to West of London and
includes it all. But looked upon without regard to this, simply
for its appearance to the eyes, with no thought for its purpose or
its meaning, the shops and houses are in simile the bows or
stern galleys of many ships tied side by side; an endless collection
of bow windows looking upon the sea, ghosts, therefore, of seaside terraces and parades; temples of Aesculapius, with magic
waters of the alchemist in great glass jars and cruchons in the
windows; altars of the green turtle, where it was brought alive
and slain; counters loaded with the golden saps of sugar canes;
the white sugar loaf, in sign and emblem, in reminder of gaiters
and pipe clay and the moustachioed grenadiers; Tegg's print-
shop and the colorists at work; a tea and coffee warehouse, ter-
minus of the green tea hills; the seedsman with a window of
bright seed packets; the painted carnation and the picotee; a
baker's shop with, at back, the dusty clowns or scullions of the
oven; mercers and haberdashers who had slaves of the needle
working for them in the slums; elegant establishments where
there was not heard the weeping of the children; the clockshop
and its traps for time; the funeral furnisher; sugar cakes for
weddings and baptisms; the tallow chandler; the shop of the
East Indiaman, with clothes to take out to India and Madeira
and curries for the traveler returned; on and on, until we get to
Ludgate Hill and, climbing that, see the spire of St. Martin's,
Ludgate giving measure and proportion to the dome of St. Paul's.
We are in Fleet Street, in Grub Street, and it is before the stamping of the presses. No one's ruin is called out on the hoardings.
It has not come to this: the balloons of the barrage have not
risen over greater London. And we come back along the Strand
of shops and warehouses.

The curious part of this perambulation, if we would have the
experience with our own eyes and senses and not surrender into
another time, has the effect precisely of poverty among so many

riches. We may go where we will and look into the windows, but we have no money in our pockets. We are as the children who gnaw a crust of bread and pass along the gutter. Our translation from this time into that other could be effected no more simply than by making a purchase and having it handed, wrapped or in a parcel, across the counter. There would be a touch of hands, a communion or sacrament, and such contact, perfunctory and superficial, would be all we needed. We long even for a thing so trivial as the folding of the paper and the knotting of the string. To watch the packet being sealed, and the sealing wax held into the flame. To ask the shopkeeper for a simple direction and be told how many doors away, up or down the Strand. And stepping down into the street, to have living persons brush against us, hear their voices and stand still for a moment at a corner to listen to the hurdygurdy.

No! We cannot buy: we are penniless and wandering. We can look into the shopwindows, but we dare not enter. Another street musician is standing in the gutter. A little Savoyard, with an old barrel organ strapped round him, of which he grinds and grinds the handle: a dwarf, or an ugly child with nothing of the child about him, with a mouth that only gnaws or snarls, never his mother's darling, but kicked into the world to bring back half-pennies with a hired organ. He wears a little peaked hat, the hat of a Calabrian brigand, of Masaniello, and boots and trousers that are too big for him. This child has known the secrets of his parents since the day he was born. There has been no privacy for him. He has the cleverness of a little mongrel cur, to pick up crusts and dodge the traffic. We wonder to what dark den he creeps to sleep. As for the hurdygurdy, it is played by a pigtailed sailor with a wooden stump. His trousers, bell-bottomed, are of white canvas, and he has a wide-brimmed hat; he is swarthy and bearded and cannot read or write. His heavy build is that of a picador, who rides out to the bull upon a starving nag and is lifted, horse and all, and thrown back against the barrier. Here there is no bull ring; but there is much of the bull about this burly hurdygurdy man. Such are the persons with whom our lot would be thrown were we to stay here until the gaslit dark. There are

so many beggars and ragged children with frayed ends to their
trousers like a torn and ragged cuff. Who has ever seen a beggar
in a top hat? We shall know presently that he may not be the
strangest of his brethren. For in an age when all men were top-
hatted, there is nothing peculiar in this. It is not his top hat; what
is frightful is the condition of it, as though it had been found
floating face downward in the river Styx after being worn at
many funerals in fog and rain. The women beggars are perhaps
more fearful still; but if the finery of one generation becomes the
garb of old landladies and charwomen in the next, in example
of which are to be noticed even now the black mantles and
bonnets of the '60s worn in the back streets of great cities, it may
be imagined how the beggar women wore the rags and tatters of
the age of coal. We hear cracked voices singing and watch the
slow walk that we know so well, looking up from the gutter into
the windows of the houses and listening for the falling of a
copper coin. We might think, with a swarming population, that
this was but the beginning of their miseries which were to last
for another hundred years until the age of coal was dead. That
has happened. But now the sky above the cities is black again
with clouds.

The shopkeepers, meanwhile, would be in their back parlors
drinking sherry. It is the arts of the shipbuilder and the fairground that have raised them to comfort. Or we see in those
arts, still living, as to the merry-go-round, their descent or perversion into special purposes. And we pass at that moment by a toyshop. It is their world in little, not in literal copy, but for the
flight and fantasy of their imaginations. The faces of the dolls
have a special horror and repulsion; and there are musical boxes
with dancing or moving figures that are part of them. One in
particular has a little dining table set with little dishes, with
little figures sitting in their chairs round the table, their heads
being formed like mice—or could they be real mice?—who move
their hands and roll their beady eyes to music. They make a
clatter, too, and lift their knives and forks. They are dressed in
shawls and bonnets, or wear tail coats. One indeed is a soldier,
and another a mouse notary. What can their bodies be under-

neath their clothes? An ordinary doll's body, wired and articulated in order to improve it from a mere image into an automaton that moves. For not only do they raise their knives and forks but they turn from side to side as though dancing in their chairs, becoming more staccato as the music finishes, and the mouse notary is left looking up, with his knife and fork held high into the air. Their heads are certainly the heads of mice, treated by the taxidermist and given back their beady eyes, then sewed on to the doll's body—a little mouse homunculus, a little mouseheaded man or woman with mouse hair brushed and treated and mouse whiskers glued on one by one. Somebody will buy this and years later it will be found in the lumber room, where the hands that played with it will scarce dare to touch it. The dolls' heads made of china are repellent too, never the right size, but with the horror of nanization, the midget freakishness, even in proportion to their build. They have the cretinous, the goitrous stare, dolts of the mountains from Aosta or Courmayeur. There are also, of course, painted hoops and painted carts, toy soldiers, glass ships in bottles, windmills, model shops, even a toyshop. It is the land of red cheeks, marionettes in wood, wax dolls and wooden dolls, bells and hearts and cradles.

Just around the corner there is the cat's-meat shop. The peculiarity of this shop is the lowness of its ceiling. It is necessary for a person of medium height to stand upon the pavement outside and lower his head in order to look down into it. The beams are then upon a level with his shoulders. It might have been built, in fact, especially for its purpose. The inscription reads: "Cats and Dogs meat supplied daily at the lowest prices." Other painted sentences are nearly, if not quite, illegible, for no fresh paint has touched this dwarfish building. The interior walls are pasted with cheap prints of pugilists, as though this low den was a resort of the "fancy." But after all it is a meat shop, and meat means flesh and blood. Kept, therefore, by someone with a masculine taste, with a taste, we mean, in men, for these are boxers —they are not actresses or ballet dancers. Nor is it mere sport. There are no horses and no jockeys. It is flesh and blood and bloodletting: the "tapping of the claret," as they would say them-

selves. Someone who likes muscle and is not put off by bruises.
A meat eater theirself, of course, who does not want the meat
too browned. Someone who knows the slang and knows the diet
and training, who can make poultices and put raw beef upon
black eyes. At the same time a friendly little den with something of the oyster bar; somewhere to drop into, shaking the raindrops off your coat, and sit upon a stool close up to the rail.
Somewhere to find warmth and congenial company. Often we
have passed outside the cat's-meat shop and once, only once, seen
the owner. For in spite of the invitation, no squeamish person
would step inside. The proprietress is a fat woman of sixty or
sixty-five, dressed in seedy and stained black, with a gray woolen
shawl and a man's flat cap upon her head. A woman who might
be a midwife, a costerwife, or huckstress, owner of a fish stall,
who sells jellied eels. But the oil-cloth counter has on it piles
of offal, as to the nature of which, or the internal geography, we
are not competent to tell. Soiled newspapers are there for
wrapping; and there are strips and scraps that have been cooked
but are green as though with mildew, or have a milky iridescence
shining from them. They must be horseflesh from a slum stable,
slaughtered before the mare falls down dead between the shafts.
Close to this is a battered pair of scales, for fair measure to the
purchaser. And there is fish for the cat. A tin plate of cods'
heads and bits of fish with the black skin clinging to them for
dainty.

At six o'clock in the morning, or late at night, this woman goes
to the slaughterhouse door and to the fish stalls. She buys a few
pennyworth of offal and in the fish stalls, from long custom, is
allowed to look into the pails and buckets, hand-picking what
she wants to take away with her. We have walked past her shop
and seen another woman on her hands and knees swabbing the
soiled floor. A thin woman dressed in black whose face we did
not see, the servant or charwoman of the establishment, living,
we might think, on dregs of beer and cups of tea in the back
room, for even she could not eat the cooked meat on the counter. Whence comes then the sporting atmosphere and the prints
of boxers? It is a mystery. Had the owner's husband been a

pugilist? A butcher whose hobby was blood sports? A slaughter-man with strong arms from wielding the poleax? Every butcher's shop has the butcher's cat to it. And there is a cat in every fish shop. It was, perhaps, in this way that she became familiar with cats. For it is cat's meat more than dog's meat. And to some persons it will be more unpleasant for that reason. It is the lean cat's-meat shop; but that does not explain the prints of boxers. No more perhaps than the fantasy of a mind that could not write or read: the same spirit that loves window boxes and will grow red geraniums at a window in a slum street; that would have pictures of the sea on land, and in a cabin, pictures of the green fields and the harvest. Yet there must be a more direct link than this. Is she a widow with an only son who died and was a pugilist? Did the "fancy" set her up and buy the cat's-meat shop for her? And at this moment a slum woman goes into the shop and comes out, after a time, with a penny bundle wrapped in newspaper. She is taking home meat for her cat. Twice a week she comes to buy it.

Now there is no one to whom the thought of a cat drinking milk could be horrible; but it is different with meat. If a cat licks your hand, is not your hair inclined to stand on end? Its tongue is warm and prickly: you must look down to be sure of what is happening. For it is something serpentine or reptilian. It is not friendly, like a dog's tongue when it licks your face or hand. It is unpleasant and insinuating: not warm-blooded, neither hot nor cold, but apt to cause a shiver, indeed intent on that, for it will take advantage. It knows by instinct those persons it can terrorize. And if it be affectionate, we know the cat's amours end in pain and wailing. The thought then of when a cat eats meat is horrible, not only because of the vile offal that is given to it, but also by reason of some feline creepiness in its approach to meat, some link with the tiger and the panther. The man-eating tiger poisons with its fangs. You get blood poisoning from its teeth and claws. And when a cat eats meat, we must think of the mouse. The caresses of the cat's tongue might lull it into sleep. As a toy, it has such a gentle child to play with it. Never a broken bone, and scarce a scratch, but

always the sharp points of the claws. Mouse and sparrow are as
though loved by it. They are silky balls playing with that velvet
hand. There is always the parable of a drowned cat whenever
a cat is eating fish, for the fish was safe once in its element. This
is its degradation; but the tyrant too can be humiliated, can
float like a knotted rag upon the river or in the harbor. The
slum cats that are fed from the cat's-meat shop, and are lucky
in that, we are bound to think more horrible than the Persian or
Angora. Is the slum mouse more horrid than the mouse of
church or palace? We would answer that no sight in London is
more sordid than the cat's-meat shop. It is worse than the charnel house, for its purpose is to feed an animal that is alive, that
lives in our rooms with us and is our plaything. When a town
has been destroyed by earthquake or by bombardment, when the
plague is rife in it, starving cats are the only creatures stirring
in the streets. But if they devoured what they could find, it
would not be more horrible than the dainties on this counter.

We come back again to the painted shops and houses. For of
all the inventions of England, there is none with more character
than the bow window. It has the build of the figures in a Row-
landson drawing, whether nymphs or wagoners, the alehouse
keeper or the Wapping sailor. The great bow window of the
Ship Inn at Greenwich, the whole width of the room from floor
to ceiling, like a bow window in Venice, the palace of white
Portland stone, as white as the Istrian, but a foot or two away,
confounding the Adriatic with the estuary of Thames. This bow
window could be the stern galley of a vessel tied up to the quay,
if it were not for the white walls and white ceiling on which the
reflections play. On rainy days it is the river of Dickens. Who
is there who has not eaten whitebait in this dining room? For
here the fish dinners of Greenwich were served, and now it is
the studio of a painter. The bow windows of Clovelly or of
Robin Hood's Bay; the one hung with fuchsias, the other giving
on the cliff where jet was found. The bow window of a village
shop, in any village, under a thatched roof, where jasmine and
honeysuckle are entwined and lilies and clematis are growing.
The bow window of Mr. Pollock's Juvenile and Theatrical Toy

Warehouse, down in Hoxton, with spangled prints and miniature theaters hanging in the window. The bow windows of
parades and terraces, each whole house bow-windowed with
that odd effect, as in the squares of Brighton, that each building
is a microcosm of the human race, that the garden in the square
may be yellow with laburnum, and that the fourth or open end
of this enclosure is the ocean with its limitless horizon. The bow
windows upon the cliffs, where the air smells of clover in the
summer, looking down on the sea; but all the winter there is the
rattling of window panes. Bow windows of the Monstrosities,
taking us into the homes of every one of them. An art which
we should have studied at Weymouth or at Brighton, and that
has its culmination in the seaside pier. It has no equivalent in
other lands, but like the parade or the circus is found only in
England. The one exception is the town of Hanover, owing to
its connecting links with England, and here an architect whose
name I have forgotten built houses, between 1820 and 1840,
overlooking a public garden and near the long avenue that led
to Herrenhausen, with bow windows and caryatids in a classical version of the English style. We may think there that the
Duke of Cumberland drove past, become Ernst-August and King
of Hanover on the death of his brother William IV, his equipage
being one of the splendid carriages from Herrenhausen, perhaps the closed Berlin painted maroon with the royal arms on
it, his outriders wearing the royal livery of England, and drawn
by the cream Hanoverian ponies. We see his red face and
choleric whiskers and his blank blue eyes of race. That same
Duke of Cumberland who is familiar from the London caricatures. The bow window in intention and origin was a sun parlor.
It was to trap the sunlight. A purpose that gives it pathos in the
pall of smoke.

For let that now descend and we have the London fog. In
looking at Scharf's drawing of the Strand, which has inspired us,
we must realize on how many days and nights we would see no
more than a house or two at a time. No other phenomenon
could give the size of London. And on a foggy evening let us
stop outside the back door of a theater. Near the Strand off

Drury Lane, near Covent Garden, names called out by the bus
conductor and known to the hundred million in a hundred years.
Come, stand at the door and look inside! It is a huge black pit or
cavern with its height nearly hidden in the fog. Its walls are
of sooty brick, the brick of backyards and dark alleys. You must
not touch them, for they will stain the hands. There are ladders
and stairways that lead to upper dungeons. For this, in one
sense, is a nightmare prison, the Carceri of Piranesi, but without his chains and fetters. The nightmare of the prenatal, the
imprisonment in the womb, in some mine or cavern deep into
the earth.

The stage of the theater is invisible. It corresponds, in this
vision, to birth into the world. At present there is no sign of
that. It is only the arrival of new scenery, for a new play is in
rehearsal. The paint is still wet on the canvas. But this is our
opportunity, the moment of our flight or levitation, for it is the
transformation scene. In fact, the Christmas pantomime, and
the month of December, near the shortest day. Having begun
the Charivari upon a day of dark depression, mingling in this
false summer with those summer crowds, we have walked in
search of character to the end of the seasons and to the far end
of the town. Harlequin must touch us with his wand and the
transformation will begin. Were there wings on his heels and
a pair of wings on his hat he would be Mercury, the winged
messenger. Mercury, or Hermes, which you will, was presented
by the King of Heaven with a winged cap called *petasus,* and
with wings for his feet called *talaria.* With these he was en-
abled to go into whatever part of the universe he pleased with
the greatest celerity, and besides he was permitted to make himself invisible, and to assume whatever shape he pleased. Thus
far, Dr. Lemprière;* but we will go much further.

For a moment, though, let us come on the stage. And whom
do we find leaning with her back against the scene? This is the
farewell, and we will never see her form again. Balancing on one
foot, she puts the point of the other into a tray of sand and rubs
and preens it on the wooden boards. And for an instant of time

* From Pembroke College, Oxford, in November 1788.

we see her in a different light, that of the evil-smelling acetylene flare. It is midnight. The performance is just over. There is a table on trestles, and the chairs are drums, or the corners of packing cases. In fact, we see them sitting at their supper. And when a comedian takes off his mask his hair is ruffled. They have shorter hair than the fashion of their day, and it falls upon their foreheads in Napoleonic locks, as though the winds of revolution had blown upon them. Their whole character has been in ferocious fantasy or satire, and now in repose and in a life that is so poor that it has no privacy, this is a meeting of demagogues who are resting from the crowd. In no sense are they entertainers of the public. It is not entertainment but a whipping up of hostility and hatred. Such comedy was never invented for the affections of its audience. They are always sinister, or avaricious, or peculiar in brain.

Take a last look at them! Where is Francischina's goose's wing, that she should sweep the floor before us? Who, then, are Cucurucu and Razzullo, Capitan Bombardon and Capitan Zerbino? They have their identity. Or are they but actors? And if actors, they are painters, poets or musicians: all who are tired by creation and have no life of their own. Such dancers as Capitan Bombardon and Capitan Grillo have never danced again. Look at their hands and feet, and the pointed noses of their masks! The draggled feathers in the cap of Capitan Grillo are his person and his movements, mimicked. This extraordinary pair is executing a dance which somehow is decidedly obscene in effect. It is a dance of two nightmare dogs, in one of those rare dreams in which the exact resemblance is forgotten and cannot be requisitioned out of memory, and a sort of substitute or parody appears for it. In this dream a dog, yes! even the form of a dog cannot be called to mind. Instead, there is this terrible invention in duplicate, or rather in alternation. They are human in shape but doglike in movement, trained to their hind legs and dancing in horrible courtship, diseased and degraded like dogs of the gutter. It is a frenzy of hopping and scratching, with those quick turns that give the only comedy of the scene. It is the theater and the dance in an inch or two of

space. That is why Capitan Bombardon and Capitan Grillo
have never danced again. They are still dancing, like the others
of their company.

We would continue. Here is the din of market stalls. High
walls of white, or staining stucco, with doorways that smell of
wine and olive oil and salami. We may see, if we would imagine
it, the slanting sun upon the yellow streets. Milk-white oxen,
their horns garlanded with flowers; blue grapes in their tumbrils;
the forms of amphora, of fiasco, and of wine jar; the trellised
vine. For the season is autumn. The harvest has been taken in.
Now the turn of the grapes has come.

They are dancing, we see at once, to practically no music.
And, in fact, at that time, the primitive age of music, there could
be no airs quick or sinuous enough to accompany their dances.
All they could achieve was a rhythm, which they doubled or increased in time, music of the fanfare or the drum roll, no different from that of the mountebank, the herald or the public
execution. It called the citizens into the piazza, and may have
had little that was appropriate or fantastic in its sound. Yet we
remember that trumpet call in the winter streets, and at the
Castillo de Bibataubín, and cannot be so sure of this. When we
think of the Italian genius, then falling from its prime, there can
be no certainty. By the simplest of methods, the musicians of
the streets may have produced just those effects that would seem
impossible. Who, indeed, can have any doubt of this? As we
look at each pair of dancers their tunes are in our heads. And
not always tunes, but the strumming of guitars, the crashing of
the tambourine, drum taps that give the notation, the pattern of
their steps, while each sequence by endless repetition brought
its ghost alive. Sometimes there are other figures dancing far
away, at the other end, as it might be, of the piazza; men are
walking upon stilts while they play their mandolins; or tumblers
and acrobats are performing. Spectators are watching them, with
a gallant or two wearing the Spanish cloak of the day; peasants go
past with their loaded mules; and the houses are those of Empoli
or Prato, or any Tuscan town. It is the same place, same time,
same company.

There are the *Balli di Sfessania* by Jacques Callot, 1621, in a little oblong volume no larger than a diary or a notebook, but bound in old red leather. The Balli di Sfessania meaning dances of Fescennia, Fescennine dances, a name deriving from the town in ancient Etruria where dances were performed that in the end were proscribed by Augustus as being of immoral tendency. Their season was the harvest homing. Callot had first come to Italy from Lorraine with a company of Gypsies, when thirteen or fourteen years old. He was sent back to his family in Nancy, but returned again when nineteen years old, leaving Italy for good ten years later. His Italian experiences were all before his thirtieth year. He will have done such drawings under the immediate excitement of what he saw before him. And this thought will bring us nearer to the Italian comedians than we could ever have dreamed. This was his process. It can be known from first sketches that are still preserved. The artist made a great number of preliminary studies, many figures to one sheet of paper, drawn with the reed pen, even smaller in scale than the finished woodcuts, not higher, indeed, than the proverbial thumbnail, and reduced for this to the simplest outlines. They have nearly the character of little stencils and could, upon a larger scale, be cut out for manipulation, like puppets of the shadow plays. Arranged in their rows upon the sheet of paper they are like the ranks of toy soldiers in a cardboard box, each one pinned down at regular interval from the other. There is the feeling that each could be taken out, turned round, put back again. But their special fascination lies in the skill with which they have been drawn for translation into woodcut. The line exactly corresponds to the hatching of the graver. They are executed in broad strokes that are precisely the incision of a knife blade upon wood. The cuts of the knife even are closed up, but with slightly swollen edges. It would be possible to open and thicken them again with the sharp point of the blade. Because of this, like the original sketches, they give the effect of speed and inspiration. No long time, a few weeks or a month or two, can have elapsed between the first thought of these and their finished form. The drawings had, as we have explained, to be somewhat magnified in size when they were cut upon the wood, doubled, in fact, or even trebled in scale. Also, the background was put in; and this in itself is unlike nearly all else in the art of the theater, for these were comedies of the open air. Coming just before the greatest age of scene painting and scenic construction, the age of the Bibiena, these had no scenery at all. Callot knew the character of the little towns and their inhabitants. He shows the penny theater in a penny print. The place in these woodcuts is nowhere in particular, just any Tuscan town.

Scaramuccia and Fracasso, who have been sitting at a table, begin their evening preparations. The pair who are fastening their masks are Scapino and Capitan Zerbino. Gian Farina is slowly and with difficulty writing out a letter. Cucurucu and Razullo are finishing their supper. Capitan Bombardon and Capitan Grillo, leaders of the troupe, seem to be talking of their plans. Isabella, or Francischina, comes down from her lodging. When Callot drew these comedians, it was in the lifetime of Shakespeare. This knowledge must always come as an extraordinary surprise, so forward are the shadows they cast. They will have been at work before *Hamlet* or *Macbeth* were written. They could have performed in any play of Shakespeare in which there were interludes of music or of dancing. And yet their shadow falls forward to the immortal Gilles of Watteau!

Who is this that sweeps the floor before us? It is Isabella, Francischina, Cinderella with her goose's wing. That comes into her play or pantomime, and meanwhile she leans with her back against the painted scene. In a white ballet skirt, and with her hair hidden in a net or turban. It is a pause or interlude in the rehearsal, but her face is already painted for the lights. This gives her a hieratic air, like a painted priestess or an idol, contradicted in a fantastic manner when she smiles.

It is Colombina, the Columbine of the poets; the ghost of the wellhead; the circus acrobat; the little bayadère. Also, the person of the convent and the boarding school. Cinderella, holding the point of her shoe into the tray of sand. Cinderella dressed for the glass coach and the ballroom. How neuter and how curious, and how much the dancer, with her hair screwed up and hidden in that black bandana, with a black woolen pull-over, and only her white skirt and her painted face to show! Also, her dancer's dress reveals all the grace and lightness that is hers, made more human by the handkerchief or turban that she is wearing, in place of a ballerina's diadem or tiara. Our last sight of her is in the light of all the lamps, like a goddess in a nimbus, but smiling as though we were to meet upon the morrow.

But where is Mercury, or Harlequin? Did I not feel the touch of his wand, or bat, upon my shoulder? Did he not tell me that we could make ourselves invisible, that we could travel into whatever part of the universe we pleased? It is our farewell to her in the half-world of the theater. The end of the Charivari, and the curtain falls.

FERIA OF SEVILLE *

A light gray rain was falling on the day we left Madrid, not so much falling perhaps as implicit or suspended in the lead-gray air. It had been tropically hot for the time of year, hot enough to have luncheon and dinner out of doors in the garden of the hotel, a little oasis of white columns, of palms and pine trees, surrounded on three sides by trams, but where an owl hooted late at night when the trams were intermittent and the jazz band had done. The road out of Madrid starts from the Puente de Toledo, one of the most fantastic and magnificent creations of decadent architecture, a bridge that is splendid and Spanish in scale but positively Aztec in ornament, and that could lead over the lagoons, the *chinampas* or floating gardens, to the stepped pyramids and to Montezuma's palace. But instead it traverses a dreary slum of new tenements and shacks built out of petrol tins. Later comes Aranjuez and its green groves, its splashing waters and its nightingales. The treeless plain resumes, and presently, under a bluer sky, we reach the deep red soil and the vineyards of Manzanares, where, in the words of Richard Ford, "the red blood of the vine issues from this valley of stones." We are in the midst of La Mancha, among the bare hills and windmills of Cervantes. Next comes Valdepeñas, with more vineyards and a still redder soil. There follow a rocky gorge and the mountains of the Sierra Morena. The rockrose is in flower upon the hillside, first one and then hundreds of white rockroses, as far as the eyes can see, and the rarer crimson pinks, or it may be magenta. Lower down, as we near the plain, there are asphodels and soon dwarf palm (palmetto), the acanthus and the aspidistra. A huge peony, alone of its kind, is in flower down in the valley. The first cactuses and prickly pears appear. This is Andalusia. Is it only imagination that there seems to be a mist

* From *Spain*, 1950.

125

or haze out of Africa hanging over the plain? But the heat is deep and tremendous. The sky is unfathomable and of intense blue. When we stop late in the afternoon at the Albergue de Bailén, and the blue flags are in flower, the sun awnings are let down to shade the whitewashed pillars and the semicircular dining room is cool though full of travelers bound, like ourselves, for *las fiestas de Sevilla.*

Some hours later we are in the suburbs of Córdoba, and, coming to the Moorish bridge over the Guadalquivir, turn aside up the little hill to the battlemented walls of the cathedral or, we would have it, the mosque, *la Mezquita,* as it is still known today. It is late, nearly dark, and the doors are locked; but one gate is yet open into the court of orange trees, and the lovely, spicy, drowsy smell of the orange blossom, after all that has happened during these many years of war, is an intoxication and a draft of magic. In that moment one felt that one might not have lived to know that scent again. Impossible not to stand quite still and motionless and breathe it in. A pyramid of the red-gold fruit lies heaped in a corner under a Moorish archway. It was worth while coming all the way from London in order to breathe for this one instant in the orange grove. And the mosque was opened for us, which looked, in that darkening hour, even more beautiful and mysterious than I had remembered it. But a mosque that is ten centuries old must not be hurried. We leave its forest of columns and horseshoe arches, the Moorish stalactites and honey cells for another time, and after crossing the bridge with its many arches, stop for petrol by an age-old water well, a fountain to which the women come with their pitchers, where horses and mules are watered now that dark has fallen, where not so long ago, when the women were veiled, there must have been men in gowns and turbans, and long strings of camels. For that is the secret of the orange blossom. Those are the perfumes of Arabia. And for a couple of hours more, through the night, there came that breath of orange blossom from time to time and the deep croaking of the frogs. The "dew-dropping South" of Mercutio was eternal and unaltered; and so it continued, balmy and spice-laden out of the dark leaves, until the red glare of a distant town announced

Seville; and after inquiry in the dusty suburbs we drove past the fairground, with its high masts and arc lamps, and along the flank of the famous Tobacco Factory, now become a barracks, to where the hotel, with innumerable motorcars drawing up and departing, stood enmeshed, as it were, in a perfect cocoon of tramlines.

To awaken in Seville is in itself something of a sensation, as though the syllables of that magical name had been ringing in one's ears through all the other noises all night long. And coming out of the hotel how hot it was! How narrow the pavement! How shrill the motor horns and the clanging of the trams. But here was the cathedral, its golden parapets stained with lichen or even nodding with weeds in that cloudless sky. And in a moment or two we are in the Plaza de San Fernando, where formerly in the cloisters of the Franciscan convent stood the Roman statue of the *Comendador* in his toga—in fact the statue of the supper scene in *Don Giovanni.* Since last I saw Seville this square of San Fernando has been converted into the most beautiful of rose gardens. The rosebushes in the middle of April were in full bloom, a most wonderful vision after the long and pitiless winter, roses high and low and in every variety of form and color, some few of them, no doubt, new triumphs of Señor Pedro Dot and the rosarians of Catalonia, and many of the them more scented than the new English roses. They were beautiful in full sun and not less lovely when the rose beds were in shade under the tall palms.

But, continuing on our way, where is there a street of shops more fascinating than the Sierpes, as narrow as the Mercería in Venice and, like that, motorless, without wheeled traffic, but so much more interesting than the Mercería owing to the goods in the shop windows: the high tortoise-shell combs and mantillas, and fans painted with scenes of bullfights and serenades or the processions of Holy Week, with farther on the posters of bullfights and colored postcards of matadors in the tobacconists' shops, the confectioner at the far end of the Sierpes with the bonbon boxes in his window formed in the shape of the cowled figures of the different *cofradías* of the Semana Santa; at about which spot in the Sierpes, toward noon, are gathered the *aficionados* of the bull ring in their short jackets, stiff-brimmed Córdoban hats, black or gray, and carrying their long, thin sticks or wands, sticks which are peeled of their bark in alternate rings of black and white, tapering to a point, and with a forked end where they rest their thumbs! The *majos,* or most of them, are countrymen come into Seville for the bullfights, and they are meeting their friends at the wine shops in the Sierpes, a sign that it is midday and that soon the shop shutters will be noisily let down.

At the hotel a mule carriage and pair was waiting at the door, for its owner had come to call on us, and it was in this same carriage, with its coachman and footman on the box in gray Córdoban hats and liveries of gray cloth with brown facings, that later in the evening, after a long and necessary siesta, we drove through the Parque de Maria Luisa and down the Paseo de las Delicias, names that breathe or whisper of the tall acacias, the roses, camellias and orange trees, of what must be the most beautiful public park in Europe. Indeed, this drive becomes in memory one of the most lovely experiences I have had for many years, not least because of the anachronism of the mule team— not an anachronism really, because there were few other vehicles but mule or horse-drawn carriages—but there was an indescribable air of excitement even down the languorous and scented avenues, a hurrying in one direction; and here we saw the first of the many horsemen of the Feria, but forbear to describe them because, as warned at the time, they will appear in all their finery tomorrow. The Paseo de las Delicias, which lies along the bank of the Guadalquivir, now comes out from the shade of its trees into a huge plain, known appropriately as the Tablada, and we see the scene toward which all this concourse of persons has been riding or driving, the whitewashed walls and enclosures of the Venta.

For it is the eve of the Feria of Seville and the great festivities will begin tomorrow. The fighting bulls have been driven in this morning, or the night before, from the *ganaderías* and are now penned or paddocked, each enclosure bearing the breeder's name above it. Thirty or forty bulls, enough for a week's entertainment, are in the three or four enclosures, each with a bullock or two, a cowbell round its neck, to simulate feminine company and the familiar sounds of home. The huge beasts are colored either black or brown and seem hardly conscious of the great crowd come to watch them. To the stranger they may look alike, but the *aficionados* can discuss their heredity not only in physical appearance but in movement and action. The strains of the different breeders have their qualities and peculiarities and are known for the particular temperaments and methods of attack, in light of which they are being examined by the onlookers for their physical condition, while the ignorant majority are come only to look at one another and at the animals that are doomed to die.

It is the Venta, in a sense the first of the ceremonies of the Feria, and the grandstand above the pens is crowded with the rank and fashion of Madrid and Seville, drinking sherry or eating ices to the strains of a band. Young men and women on horseback, in Andalusian costume—but it is even painful to stare at them in the direct rays of the setting sun—are pressing their way through the crowd. Many will stay and dine here, and look down on the bulls that are lying out like shadows in a false moonlight; but we drive back along the Paseo de las Delicias into Seville behind the jangling mule team. The sun is setting, the church bells are ringing; tomorrow will be the Feria.

It has been settled that at midday we are to drive round the fairground. The mule carriage is at the door, but today both grooms and mules are in their splendor: blue and yellow cords and cockades (the colors of the Duke of Alba), rosettes of blue and yellow on the trappings and the harness, blue and yellow hammercloths; the duke himself has put on a gray Córdoban hat for the occasion. And so, along the length of the Tobacco Factory, with its baroque statues trumpeting fame upon the sky line, to the Feria. The fairground is near by, on the Prado de San Sebastián, but "it is not so much a fair as an outing or festival," lasting three days, in which the entire population, high and low, participate. A huge cattle fair is the immediate excuse for the Feria, and the present year (1947) being the centenary, the celebrations have been doubled and extended to six days, with a bullfight every afternoon. Passing the fountains, which will be illuminated this

evening, the scene of the Feria is a quadruple avenue, three or
four hundred yards long and bordered on both sides of its four
lengths with *casetas,* which are pavilions or open summerhouses,
"the origin of which is to be traced to the tents put up by the
cattle dealers, long ago, in order to sleep beside their herds."
No motorcars are allowed on the two middle avenues, which are
open only for carriages and persons on horseback.

Within a moment our mule carriage is moving no quicker than
at walking pace. The heat is tremendous, such as it may have
been seventy or eighty years ago in Hyde Park or the Champs
Élysées during the age of the carriage and the crinoline at the
height of summer, and such as I do not remember, of its kind,
since childhood, since in fact I last drove among the other
carriages on Sunday morning along the Esplanade. I believe this
must be the sensation of all persons who see the Feria for the
first time, as we did, at midday, when the great concourse of
persons is driving or riding round. We shall discover that it is
due, principally, to the Gypsy dresses worn by the young women.
It is this that makes the scene like a vision of the early or middle
part of the last century, though it is only necessary to be reminded
of the riders or the mule carriages to know that it has nothing to
do with the dead world of the Bois de Boulogne or Rotten Row.
For this is a sight that is to be seen nowhere else in the world
today; and it must be described slowly and, as it were, at
walking pace.

There are many different sorts of dresses. All are not dressed
alike. The young women of the sidewalks are wearing flounced
skirts that touch the ground, of blue or pink or red cotton, patterned with different sizes of white dots. All day yesterday we
had noticed such dresses being carried home from the dress-
makers', over one arm of an owner or dressmaker, and had
stopped and tried to examine them. It was a revelation of how
many effects can be made with a white ring or circle. But there
are dresses of white flounces too, edged with a blue or red cord-
ing, like the moonlit equivalent to those patterns of mock suns.
And, as well, there are the different shapes and forms of flounces
—crinolines, if we call them that—of three or four or five or

more tiers or stories. The young women in these full skirts walk bareheaded, with a scarf or handkerchief at their necks, their glossy hair kept well in place, always with the traditional flower behind the ear. There are little girls of three or four years old dressed in even more detail than their cousins or elder sisters, sometimes with a long train behind that sweeps the ground. And we are looking continually, delighted at every turn, for fresh ideas and colors, as for instance to see a green dress or one of saffron yellow, which did not happen till the third morning of the Feria, when a flowered crinoline of daffodil yellow made an appearance, was lost in the crowd, but quickly recognized again.

At this hour of the morning the *casetas* are half empty. The crowd is on foot or on horseback. On the pair of outer avenues, where it is allowed, we even pass motorcars carrying three or four young girls draped in their full skirts upon the bonnet and the mudguards. But this is in bad taste. It is one of the few faults of the Feria, and is corrected quickly by much jangling and a mule carriage of more substantial make, drawn by a "six-in-hand," with a middle-aged man in short black coat and Córdoban hat holding the reins. This beautiful equipage seems to sail forward upon the admiring glances of the onlookers. But after rounding the corner, we are on the outer side of our avenue and can see in every detail the splendid cavaliers and their ladies as they ride toward us and pass by. Taking the young women first, there are the two sorts—those who go pillion and those who ride alone. The pillion riders, perched precariously with an arm round their partner's waist or holding to the horse's tail, wear the flounced skirts of the pedestrians. Their brothers or lovers ride generally one arm akimbo, which accentuates their thin waists. Many are wearing elaborate and fanciful leather trousers, in which we can see the origin of the cowboys' leggings and of the Mexican *charro* costume. The young women ride pillion with an amazing grace, the beauty of their bare heads and arms in that violent sunlight being as animal as the steeds they share. Every young woman is beautiful to look at, some of the girls being real visions of Spanish beauty with their camellia skins and black hair and eyes. But not all are dark, and there are young girls riding pillion in green and white crinolines, with fair hair, bareheaded like the rest and glowing in the midday sun.

It is wonderful to watch a cavalier, arm akimbo, riding toward us, Spanish-fashion, and then to wait and admire the young woman on the crupper holding lightly to his waist. But the other sort of riders, the true amazons, are yet more enthralling, those who ride by themselves astride, not hatless, and wearing more than one type of costume; in fact, one form of dress is worn the first day of the Feria, and we are told that tomorrow they will be wearing another costume and a different form of headdress. The first—for we will take both together as they are to be seen on later mornings—consists of a leather apron and divided skirt, a white shirt like a man's, a short jacket, and one of the hard-brimmed Córdoban hats. It is a feminine version of what the men are wearing, with the addition perhaps of a rose behind the ear. The thin waist, the level shoulders and hard outline of the hat, worn at a charming angle above a rounded face—such are the attractions of this riding dress, which is infinitely varied in detail and which suits the Spanish type of good looks to perfection.

The other form of costume belongs, as it were, to another tradition; the skirt or trousers, it matters not which, are not so aggressively in imitation of the masculine; the jacket is short, and without the leather apron or leggings reveals more of the figure; the hair is worn at the back in a snood or *chignon*, while the hat is a round black one, resembling the crown, without the wings, of the matador's three-cornered cap or tricorn. This must un-doubtedly be its inspiration, and nothing more in the popular tradition of Spain could be imagined than a young woman on horseback in one of these round black hats, particularly if she be wearing, instead of a snood, a *mantilla de madroños,* which is a scarlet or magenta net with wide meshes worked with bobbles. The soft complexions of the young girls are ravishing to behold, and to compare with the carnation or camellia behind the ear, to which we must add the peculiar beauties of the Spanish horse-manship that allow of so graceful a seat and, where the women riders are concerned, could have been conceived especially in order to be admired.

But the heat is such that the leather and the painted woodwork feel by now like fire. The mules are halted, and after a drink of sherry we drive back to the hotel for luncheon and to take a siesta for the greater part of the afternoon. But at that hour there is nothing else to do in Seville—nothing until about half past five, when you hear people starting off for the bullfight. Then it is quieter still, and the air is more languorous and somnolent than ever. Perhaps I enjoyed as much as anything else in Seville those hours when the noisier part of the population was at the bullfight. In the shuttered room one's mind filled so easily with nostalgic longings. I would lie there thinking of many things, for another hour or more, until, from all over the town, there would come the sound of castanets, snapping and crackling, hundreds of pairs of them, some fast, some slow; and on going to the window I would see the pavements and even the street itself full of a great crowd of persons all converging in this one direction, toward the Feria, a multitude mainly of young women and children, and all playing their castanets as they walk along.

This would be the signal to begin moving toward the colored fountains and the lights, which go off as we come near them at the same moment that there is a flicker of lightning and that people standing at the cheap jewelry stalls, close by, look up for rain. But it is better to see the Feria in the sunset—leave it when the lights go on—and come back again. For it is a marvelous sight at this hour. The *casetas* are filling up; dancing has begun, but we will not listen to the music till tonight. We are only aware of it, and of the growing and increasing sparkle on the air. Instead, we turn down one of the side avenues to the *barracas,* which are the roundabouts and merry-go-rounds of the fair. Here is a stall where they are selling an extraordinary spun concoction, of the consistency of cotton wool, dipping a stick or straw into the frothing, churning mass, drawing it forth with a shock or head of the sugary cotton wool attached, and handing it out as quickly as made, like a sweet cocoon. The sellers of prawns or *langostinos* are doing a quick trade. There are stalls, too, where colored drinks, *agraz* and *horchata de chufa,* are sold. But the merry-go-rounds and mountain railways, the miniature motorcars and "witching waves" are no different from those of any other fair. Not so the mountebanks, the like of whom may be extinct in every other country, and who maintain the centuries-old tradition of the actor coming in front of the curtain to advertise the play, with a cracked voice this evening, and through a megaphone. His speech is interminable, and the heat in the crowd such that it is impossible to stand still and listen.

Besides, this is only a few feet away from the open-air restaurants or eating places of the Gitanas. They have established themselves and put up their booths along one entire side of the pavement. The setting is a line of cabins or small *casetas,* a half or a quarter the size of those upon the main avenues, and with chairs and tables arranged in front of them. Unexpectedly, there are white linen cloths on the tables, but the Gitanas are awarded a prize every year for the cleanest and prettiest arranged of their *casetas.* Even in this noisiest part of the Feria, next to loudspeakers and steam organs, they manage to assert themselves above the din. It has, in fact, spurred them into frenzy.

The younger and more alluring of the Gitanas have come right forward in front of their own tables, into the edges of the crowd, where they stand like bathers in a heavy surf, nearly carried away, and having to struggle in order to get back to the thresholds of their flowering caves or grots. They will come out and pursue you, and be borne along for a little, smiling and cajoling with all the battery of their bright glances, with red lips and fingernails, even and superb white teeth, and smoothed black hair. They are small in height, with the crowns of their heads well below your shoulder, probably no more than fourteen or fifteen years old, and with the rounded faces of their race. In fact, their tawny darkness is extraordinary; and in the background, as if this is not enough, the older women with their snakelike locks—could serpents be as ebony and glossy as a raven's wing—stand in the open doorways, lifting the caldron lids or stirring, half hidden in the steam. They have turned this corner of the fair into a nomad encampment, and their unbelievably dark skins at this hour of the evening in the fading light betray the Indian origin of their nation. The old women are in a fury too, and the whole scene of these booths or cabins decorated with flowers and branches is something entirely and absolutely of the Gypsies. There is no other race who has the power to create a nationality and a nomad background by merely cooking something and standing in a door. They have only to do this and it becomes at once the fortuneteller's tent and the cave of the sorceress.

There is the savor of their world apart in the fumes of their cooking, which has the Oriental pungency and is, at once, an enticement and an alarm. They are frying things in oil and can be seen cooking as though frenzied. Excellent their food is said to be, but not suited to this hot night and to the noise and hubbub. It is to be noticed, moreover, that here they have the entire air of Gypsies, but that they have nearly lost it in their Gypsy suburb of Triana. It must fire their blood to be once more in the smoke and uproar of the encampment. At Roumanian cattle fairs there are these identical open-air restaurants, with roofs of leaves and branches, which are the pleasure gardens of the fair, and that evoke some of the imagery of Rimbaud's *Les Illuminations.* On a particular occasion, upon the plain between Sinaia and Bucharest, they lined both sides of an alleyway, and held some hundreds of persons sitting in the shade, eating their midday meal; the meat was grilling on the charcoal embers, while here and there among the diners musicians wandered, violin in hand, playing popular tunes. There was the same Eastern pungency in the air that I recognized at the Feria, and I now wish more than ever that I had seen the great horse fairs in Moldavia, that last for as long as three days, and had walked late at night by the open-air eating booths. Neither fair, it is true, would allow much time for thinking of the other. Here in Seville the cries of the mountebanks, the din of the roundabouts, above all the blare of the steam organs, make the night low-hung and lurid, for all the lights are now switched on, the lines of lamps and lighted fountains, and we leave the Feria for an hour or two in order to have our dinner.

It was always midnight or after when we returned, a phrase that holds in itself the sensation of the Feria, by which I mean the memory and feeling of the six days it lasted, for it seemed to be a world or experience apart and to go on forever. At half past twelve or one o'clock, then, we return by the changing fountains, down the floodlighted avenues, under the festooned arches. A great crowd is still arriving, playing castanets as they walk along, and when we stop in front of the *casetas* there is music coming from nearly every one of them. There are *casetas* belonging to clubs or associations, others that are shared by groups of families or owned by individuals. They can be of all sizes—as large as a restaurant or quite small—but most are on the scale of the pierrot's booths upon the sands, with room, that is to say, for a piano and a row of chairs. The chairs are pushed back against the walls, and in the middle is the dancing floor. Many of the *casetas* have had climbing rose trees or flowering creepers trained on their walls; they have been decorated with posters of bullfights or hung with paintings and family photographs, and furnished so as to give them the semblance of little rooms. One of the fascinations of the Feria is to pass by such a *caseta* at a moment when an entire family in all its generations—but it may well be two or three families and their friends, one whole side of a little street, or all the inhabitants of some whitewashed court—are resting, exhausted, the older ones staring in front of them, with the smaller children crawling at their feet or asleep upon their knees, awkward on their chairs as are housewives and small shop-keepers who have to stand all day and, as it were, caught or imprisoned in this cell or interior of their own choice with the enlarged photographs upon the walls and the family piano in the middle of the floor. It is one o'clock in the morning, but not one of the smallest children has been put to bed. There is no one left in the house to look after them and they must stay at the Feria till the whole family goes home.

Meanwhile the crackle and fire of the castanets is continual and strains of music come from every direction for as far as the lights glitter and the night sky is lighted from the fair. There is this accompaniment of the castanets playing in the crowd as they walk up and down, and the music of the *casetas* as you stand and watch for a moment and move on. There are mechanical pianos which are too loud and drown the music from next door, but at least the music, or nine tenths of it, is Spanish. There is no "jazz" or "swing." It is mainly clapping of hands, and the guitar, *Flamenco* music, good or bad, but on a night like this such is the intoxication from light and sound that the whole body of music becomes lifted and inspired. They are dancing the *seguidilla* to an accompaniment of castanets and clicking fingers, to the clapping of hands and the grinding of a guitar, perhaps six or eight young women dancing at once, the older teaching the younger, even little girls of five or six years old in their long-trained crinoline skirts joining in, and one of the younger men of the family standing up without warning and taking up the rigid posture of the dance. The *seguidilla* is admired largely for the gracefulness of arms and hands, for the feet do not move much; it is the lascivious grace of the upper part of the body that it is judged by, and by the languorous movements of the wrists. If we would search for an image for the hand and fingers of a dancer in the *seguidilla* it would be that her hands resemble the head of a cobra, or of some other serpent, as it sways its head to hypnotize and prepares to strike; or that it is like a peacock's head and crest upon that long neck, when the peacock is displaying and makes the snakelike movements of its dance. As a spectacle to watch upon a hot night, and as an expression of the heat, the *seguidilla* is an invention of genius. In which other city of the world or upon what occasion is it possible to watch fifty or a hundred *seguidillas* being danced at one time, and without pause? Only in Seville, and only during the Feria. There is no other population born to this dance, as are the Sevillanas, no other inhabitants who fall naturally into those attitudes or who can wear those flounced dresses so becomingly, being heirs and descendants of the Gaditanian dancers, who "were known" in antiquity "for their agility of body," and Dr. Lemprière of the *Classical Dictionary*, delighting at the shock, adds "their incontinency"; but, in fact, the evidence of early Greek travelers points to the inhabitants of Andalusia as running great herds of bulls upon the swamps and plains and to their women as excelling in the dance. The castanets, we are to suppose, come down directly from antiquity, from pre-Roman antiquity, and were borrowed in all probability from the temple dancers of the Carthaginians, who in their turn had taken them from their ancestors in Tyre and Sidon. This Phoenician heredity or influence is to be seen in so many things that are typically Spanish: in the dance of the Seises before the high altar of Seville cathedral and, contrasting the sacred and profane, in the high combs and mantillas of the Spanish ladies, after the bullfight, as they move about in the American bar of the hotel.

In order the better to appreciate the marvelous spectacle of the Feria it was a good plan to go away from it for half an hour, and so on one of the last nights we went to walk in the Barrio de Santa Cruz, a whitewashed labyrinth of narrow alleys lying in a sempiternal moonlight of its own, with doorways, hidden patios, iron wellheads, and some of the oldest palaces of Seville. At one end of this there is a garden, touching upon the lovely gardens of the Alcázar, and like those breathing of the orange blossom, and here —it was between one and two o'clock in the morning, in that moonlight begotten of so many whitewashed walls—we heard the sound of voices, and in the tiled space around a fountain found a group of young men and two young women; one unslung his guitar, the others clapped hands rhythmically, there was the crackle of castanets, and the younger of the two girls began to dance the *seguidilla*. This done, they talked excitedly, and she danced again, another form of *seguidilla* with ballet steps, to no tune, only the clapping of hands and the strumming of the guitar. Once again, and yet once more, she danced; a cool air moved along the overhanging branches; the loveliness of this ancient city, the soft and balmy breath of the orange blossom— something I had not known for so many years since the jasmine-laden airs of the Tunisian gardens; airs so pungent and redolent of jasmine that they amounted almost to a jasmine civilization, made this scented early hour of the morning, this music and this dancing into an unbelievably beautiful experience; and all the time, not far away, the night sky was lighted with the Feria, and you could hear a continuous, distant roaring, now and then individual voices or strains of music, and the crackling fire and rattle of perhaps ten thousand pairs of castanets. It produced an excitement and a beauty that were indescribable. The Feria was beckoning, and we must return.

The *casetas* are numbered. They are referred to by their numbers, and it was to one particular *caseta* that we were on our way, where the dancing was known never to begin till two o'clock in the morning. It belonged to a young lady who bore one of the most famous names in Spain, heiress of one branch of the Borjas and descendant of the Borgia Pope Alexander VI, collaterally related to his bastard Cesare Borgia, and to Lucrezia Borgia; a race more proud now of San Francisco Borja and of their descent, on two sides, from the Gothic kings of León, represented in more modern times by the Duke of Osuna, who was ambassador to the Court of the Czars and was notorious for his extravagance during the years of the Second Empire, and since the extinction of that name living mostly on their Andalusian properties. The Duquésa di Gandia was, in fact, married a year or two ago to a young man of an old family of Seville, and we saw photographs in the newspapers of her wedding procession in the golden coach with footmen and halberdiers wearing the old family liveries. She is herself, we were told, a most graceful and accomplished *Flamenco* dancer, but unfortunately did not dance on the night we were invited to her *caseta*. With her mother, she was receiving the guests when we arrived, and if we did not see her dance, were able at least to agree that she must be, in addition, one of the most beautiful young women in Spain.

Flamenco, in spite of its ever-increasing popularity, is a dying art, comparing in this with Russian ballet, which became the rage in England and then in America just after the last generation of great Russian dancers had ceased to dance. The great period of *Flamenco* music, it is probable, was between 1880 and 1910, at a time, therefore, when no one paid any attention to it, and it flourished in its natural setting of the wine shop and the boarded dancing floor. It is not suited either to the houses of the rich or to the theater. We had been warned that the *Flamenco* singing would be bad in Seville, and the bullfights also, for although the greatest living masters of the latter art—Manolete (since killed in

the bull ring), Arruza and the girl matador Conchita Cintrón
—were present in Seville, were even staying in our hotel, they
were prevented from fighting by the other matadors, who accused
them of staying too long and making too much money in Mexico
and Peru. All the older critics were agreed that *Flamenco* was
not what it had been in their youth and that Niña de los Peiñes,
or her like, had no successors in this generation.

The *caseta* was full of persons and there was at first some singing in a high, falsetto voice after much preluding upon the
guitar by a male singer who had been famous, but found it difficult to compete with the strains of a mechanical piano from next
door. It was a problem that found its own solution, for after a
time the occupants of the next *caseta* fell asleep where they were,
or more prosaically went home to bed. Not that the noise and
clamor of the Feria were in the least abated. The din was if anything louder than ever, and it was only our good fortune that
this particular family or group of friends had tired themselves out
on this third or fourth night of the fair. At one end of the row
of chairs, in front, a woman some sixty years old was sitting, and
it was impossible not to be struck by her upright bearing, the
carriage of her neck and shoulders, and the confident and alert
way that she glanced about her with her extraordinary green eyes.
Swarthy-skinned, but with something of the air of another Yvette
Guilbert and a definite and marked touch of that period, of the
'90s and of the drawings and posters of Toulouse-Lautrec, about
her. It was whispered to me that this was the famous Pastora
Imperio, who had been the most renowned Gypsy singer of her
day; and for a long time we waited on, hoping that she
would sing.

She applauded every other singer and showed no inclination
to perform, but at last, and without any visible urging, rose to her
feet, spoke to the guitarist, and draped her shawl round her,
taking care to leave her hands and arms unencumbered. The
first chords of the guitar sounded; she seemed to reflect for a
moment with closed eyes, the rhythm quickened, she opened her
eyes with the alert green fire in them, and her hands and arms
became like the hooded cobra or the crested peacock's head while

she stamped her feet and achieved the subtle and alternately thunderous rhythms that are to be heard only when the Hindu musicians rattle or strike their drums with their fingers or with the palms of their hands. I have never known so strong a proof of the Indian in the Gypsy. She glided forward like the cobra, erect and gliding on its tail, a movement accomplished with an incessant, quick tapping of her feet, her body held quite stiff, clapping or fluttering her palms together, while she leaned her head as though listening to the incantation. She glided in this manner, in succession, to the four corners of the stage, returned to the center, stamped her feet in another rhythm altogether, like a roll of drums, and started the long-held wavering cry of the Gypsy singer. Pastora Imperio is the most controlled singer of *Flamenco* music that I have ever heard; and, as her physical appearance would suggest, she is an artist comparable to Yvette Guilbert, but of the period before that great *diseuse* had forsworn her birthright and turned to little ballads of swains and shepherdesses, to the epoch therefore, as I said, of Toulouse-Lautrec. The great period of *Flamenco* music is present again in all its glory whenever Pastora Imperio is performing, and hers is a mastery which puts all her younger competitors to shame. It is to be imagined on this evidence what the masters of *Flamenco* must have been before they appeared in drawing room and music hall. There can be but one or two living singers and dancers of her caliber.

It had been a wonderful sensation to watch this great exponent of the Gypsy art, who must herself during so many decades have had such wild, barbaric strains of music running in her head, have seen in her life so much of the stuff of romantic fiction— being married, we were told, to a famous matador—and have spent her life in scenes and circumstances so remote from the norm of European or American experience. We could have seen her ourselves in no more ideal setting than in this *caseta*, belonging to the last scion of the Borgias. But a still more extraordinary adventure had befallen some persons whom we knew. They had been leaving the Feria very early on the previous morning. It was already light, the sun was rising; and as they walked past the *caseta* they saw that the curtains had been drawn wide and that someone, whom they knew immediately for Pastora Imperio, was dancing in the pale dawn before a small crowd on the sidewalk who were looking on. Our friends watched this great Gypsy dancer for a few moments and walked on.

And we must end our account of this marvelous festival of the Feria. There is nothing like it in our contemporary world, no such scene of popular and spontaneous enjoyment. Music as an art of pleasure and excitement plays here, night and day, unspoiled. Beautiful costumes in the Gypsy idiom give sparkle and color and the illusion of crinolines, but without the whalebone cages. The young women on horseback and their cavaliers form a spectacle without equal as they ride slowly round and round the Feria in the midday heat. To drive among them in a mule carriage while the sidewalks are crowded with Sevillanas in their spotted crinolines is an excitement that is nearly indescribable; then, late in the afternoon, comes that extraordinary moment when from all over Seville, in every direction, you hear the rattle and crackle of castanets. The crowd is making for the Feria and the women are playing their castanets idly and in anticipation as they walk along.

Soon they are dancing the *seguidilla* in a hundred different booths at once. All the lights of the fair go on at one and the same time. The fountains change color. Under the electric lights the crowd is thicker than ever and moves up and down, watching the dancing, to the crackling of its own castanets, which breaks the rhythm; and young girls are dancing in little groups upon the sidewalks. Round midnight the entire Feria is alive with music. Till three o'clock or after the dancing is general. It is a marvelous and never-to-be-forgotten feast of sight and sound. As you walk home and look back for the last time, leaving the lights and music behind you, your breath will be caught with the orange blossom, and falling asleep, forgetful of the hour, you may think, as I do, that the Feria of Seville must be the most beautiful public spectacle in the world today.

DJEMAA EL FNA *

The dawn in Marrakesh must be unlike any other experience this side of India or Peking. No other town in the black continent is comparable for this sensation, for there is no other town like Marrakesh. But the morning is immediately African. It has the colors of a bird's breast. To awake on the first morning in Marrakesh is to know another world, another creation. A blue of a dove's breast, misting into white, touches on a rose-red crater's edge. It is the African night and, under it, touching it, the new-born morning. This quickens, even while you look at it.

But near and familiar things are not less strange. The shapes of olive or of orange tree are of a tufted richness never known before. The palms are taller and more rich in fronds. And in the air, high in the air, are gigantic snow mountains, running from end to end of the horizon, right across the sky. Near by—for in Marrakesh it is always in view—there is the minaret of the Koutoubia. At its summit the flag flies from the gallows post and the muezzin calls down to the world. This is the acknowledgment of morning, announcing it is day. But the solid bulk of the Koutoubia calls to mind its sister tower, the Giralda of Seville. Marrakesh was the winter capital of the great builder, Yakoub El Mansour. If it is, by some strength of affinity, the Seville of all Africa, it is hotter than ever Seville could aspire to, while its snowy mountains are whiter and more magnificent than the Sierra Nevada at Granada, seen from the Alhambra hill or from the hill of the Albaicín. And yet there is a certain breath of Andalusia in this scented air. It is Seville without the gypsies or the castanets, more serious and solemn, with less shade and fewer fountains. The rose-red colors and the green or blue of the sky merge into each other, like walls of flame. And there is fire, or white-hot heat, behind them. Of a sudden it is high daylight.

* From *Mauretania*, 1940.

143

But the town of all Africa, with its flat roofs stretching out of sight, still lies sleeping.

In a few moments the firmament will be of that immeasurable, unutterable blueness which calls for whitewashed walls. Any building seen against that sky has the fact, the importance of an island in the blue main. The blue ocean plays against its shores, and somehow the very whiteness of the walls is equivalent in simile to bathing in that sea. The whitewash is like salt, or snow. It stings against the sky. By now there is movement in every house and hidden court. But the southern day, which has its pattern, can be left to take its course. Midday appears to last two hours or more. The languors of the shade are as a net from which it is impossible to escape. There is nothing to be done until four o'clock. Then a cool wind begins. It is possible to go to the waters of the Aguedal.

At five o'clock, over most of the town, if you listen for it, there is a confused murmuring. It is mysterious, like a stirring of the waters or like something glittering out of a cloud of dust. The noise of it travels on the wind or, in the lull of that, is deep down in the distance. But it never stops. It is gathering and insistent. It has that kind of excitement toward which it is only natural to hurry your steps. Any moment of delay may be something missed and gone.

At every corner the noise comes louder. Now it is a beating and a stamping of many feet—the roar of an enormous multitude. It cannot be much farther. It was round that corner and now is still a block away. This is it. A huge square with, in the middle, as it were, a circus ring. A crowd of thousands moves round it, while its inner side, toward the center, has circle after circle watching, moving on. Over all hangs a haze of dust. The noise is such you cannot hear a person speak. In a moment you are lost in it.

This is the Djemaa El Fna, and there is nothing like it in the world. To begin with, it has no shape. This square—which is to Africa and to the Orient what the Piazza of St. Mark's was to the Venetian Republic, La Serenissima, and to all that is implied in that most magnificent of memories—is without any architecture. It has nothing but low buildings, most of them dating from the French occupation of thirty years ago. They are European stores and countinghouses, a post office and a café, no more than that. Into the middle of it juts an incongruous market building, used by the grain merchants. No square could have fewer advantages of architecture or be less suited by nature to its purposes. There is, indeed, no reason why this unlikely open space should present the most astonishing spectacle of its kind in the contemporary world. Yet there are to be seen here, in this close area, sights that are not to be found in all the towns of Asia, or in the few of Africa. This is, in its humanity, the old Orient of a thousand years ago. Nothing has changed. The cigarettes that are being smoked, and for which there is insistent begging, are no more incongruous to the scene than are those celestial cigars for which Sir Oliver Lodge produced evidence in the next world. They are even convincing, as proof that all these sights are true and alive, that they are not creatures of the imagination. Without their cigarettes, or the occasional motorcar or bicycle, the living truth would be diminished. As it is, these sights are here before our eyes, and in their acceptance of some of the evils of our civilization it is not improbable that they may continue.

The Djemaa El Fna is in itself a sinister memory. Its meaning is the place of death, or the place where the dead are collected and exposed—in fact, the execution ground. The public executioner wielded his sword in midst of terrifying crowds, and the heads were exhibited here in the memory of many persons still living. Such a square as this can contain an enormous population. We know that, at moments of public excitement or pleasure, but in later centuries more especially during carnival, the square of St. Mark's could hold the major or most characteristic proportion of the inhabitants of Venice. In the same way the Djemaa El Fna, which may not be more than one hundred yards in breadth by one hundred and fifty yards in length, has the entire character of this town of two hundred thousand people. And it is apparent from this that the interest of Marrakesh will consist more in its persons than in its architecture. For it is better to go to the Djemaa El Fna before you see anything else in

Marrakesh. If there is one point in Morocco to which it would be best to go immediately on arrival and without touching, were this possible, on any other place or scene, it would be this. And without further delay we are lost among the crowd.

The first sensation is not a little frightening. It comes from the dirtiness of the burnooses, and from the guttural sound of Arabic or Berber, which is almost the gobbling of a turkey cock in the excitement of all this noise. It is impossible not to shrink from being touched. The beggars are appalling. Their dramatic appeal is such that they outplay, at first, the real actors and dancers of the square. Since most of them are in regular attendance, day after day, in the Djemaa El Fna, one or two of their leading players may be so briefly indicated that their identity can be recognized. They form—this is certain—fit subjects for a Callot or a Brueghel. One old man in particular—but so low is he in the human scale that he is no longer old, not a man and hardly human any more—has a really terrifying method of pursuit which is peculiar to himself. He is led along by a nondescript attendant whom there is no time to notice, the ghost, we might think, of one of the executioner's assistants of old, someone of no importance to the scene, who merely removes the bodies and the limbs or heads, the chulo of this bull ring, who drives in the team of mules and drags out the dead horses and the dead bull. His only purpose in his present embodiment is no more than to supply the velocity of the attack. For it is a speed which has to be maintained. It consists in a rapid shuffling of the feet, like a child imitating a train. His bare feet are never lifted from the ground, so that it is as if his paralysis or palsy chained him to the dust in which, at the same time, he has every liberty to wander. This fearful creature can follow you at high speed all over the square, reappearing continually, unable to stop himself, and accompanying his own gait with a most unpleasant shaking and trembling of the head and with a steady convulsion of his lips and chin productive of a dry quacking noise, like the quacking of a duck. He appears never to rest, never to be, for a moment, still.

Perhaps the other most insidious frequenters of this square

are a group of blind boys, about eighteen or twenty years of age. They come toward you in traditional manner, each with a hand on another's shoulder. Their instinct takes them immediately to you, even if it is to the closed window of a motor. They will put in their hands, blind hands, if another window is open, and leave them there till, perhaps, the motor moves on, dragging them for a step or two, when a shade of hopelessness passes over their blank faces and they turn about, holding themselves still for a moment, out of the way of the car, until their hidden senses find a new direction for them. Their words, *"Donnez-moi un sou, monsieur,"* are not the least dreadful thing about them when we think that, being blind, they can have no visual picture of the foreigner in their minds. Why do they keep in a band of three or four? Is it that, alone and individual, they could not move so quickly and would not have the whole square under the control of this mysterious intelligence? Or that the massed effect of their misery produces alms and that, alone, with nothing to share, there would not be enough to give them strength to move? For these blind men, and their rivals and companions in want, are nearer to true starvation than any but the victims of a famine. What is to be done with them? They are hopeless; and is it right that they should be spared?

Fifteen years ago, in the court of the mezquita at Córdoba, under the orange trees, there were two such brothers, fifteen, perhaps, and eighteen years old, in ragged coats and trousers, with bloodshot weeping eyes, or at least eye sockets, for their eyes were gone. This pair of spectral children had some air of Picasso's child harlequins. They had never seen the living world, and their entire lives were to be want and misery. They walked hand in hand, as inseparable in misfortune as the freak twins of the fair. There is a probability at least that in origin they were not so far distant in Córdoba from their equivalent in the Djemaa El Fna. What has become of them now, one may wonder. Have they been killed, wantonly and carelessly; or is it possible that, from mere misery, they may have had a better chance of survival than many other men of their race? The thought of them, though, carried with it the image of their whimpering somewhere, in some shadow, in the terror of sounds which they could neither understand nor see, trapped, in fact, by the twentieth-century civilization as dispensed by rifle and bomb. The poor white must be always more pitiful than poor Arab or poor Negro. And there is this much, if no more, of comfort in the spectacle of their unhappy brothers who haunt the Djemaa El Fna.

And now, with them following at our heels, we begin to move about the square. The noise and animation are extraordinary. As for the excitement, this is only made more intense by the nauseating odors, some of which are so dense as really to halt or impede all progress. The first public performer to take our attention may be a fire-eater. He has an orchestra of two men who bang upon tins, and is himself an immensely tall man with long black hair in snakelike coils reaching to his shoulders. He has a thick, black candle made of horrible wax, as though of a black bull's fat, and kneeling down he plays with this candle as if worshiping it, shouting aloud some code of prayer. Seeing some strangers in the crowd, he will address himself particularly to them, in tones that are half exultant and half threatening, all the time with one hand lifting loose and shaking down his hair. This elaboration of gesture, this perpetual playing with his long hair, is in preparation for his act. In Morocco it is the actors or acrobats who pursue careers of danger who wear their hair long. This fire-eater, who has come up from the Sous, is of the blood of Liszt or Paderewski, the two great protagonists in music of this cult of danger. The dramatics of showmanship in art show no two other such examples. Both, it will be admitted, had some qualities of the fakir in them. It is through this that they are related to the fire-eater, who now, throwing back his hair for the last time, lifts the horrible candle to his face and with final imprecations puts the flaming stump into his mouth. While it continues there, he never ceases to preen and stroke his hair. His head held right back, the fire pours forth from his lips, till with a neat, quick movement, holding the candle stump with both hands, he takes it from his mouth. Smoke comes from his lips, and it is with the appearance of someone awakening from a momentary trance or hypnosis that his head jerks up, his eyes open wide, and with a movement of the mouth and throat that are those of a man swallowing something that is too big for his gullet, he regains full consciousness and in a moment is begging for money.

After a few repetitions of his act, the fire-eater seats himself on the ground and takes a rest. For it is, in fact, not only a feat of concentration, of absorption, but also so limited in scope and brief in performance that it cannot be practiced all the time. He is content, therefore, to let his rivals attract the public to themselves.

This art, or profession, of fire-eating is strictly hereditary. If we knew enough of his history we should find that he came from some village, some subsection of a tribe, among whom it has been taught for many hundreds of years. This is nothing unusual in Morocco, as we hope to show later on. It is certainly true that the fire-eaters are impervious to pain when they swallow the flame. This is no trickery, but a secret taught in childhood and of the nature of the Indian yoga, a mastery of the body by some portion of the brain. When he begins again, the fire-eater will quickly collect a circle round him. His performance is impressive enough, now that it grows darker and he is his own torch to light the scene.

Near him are the snake charmers. They also are the long-haired virtuosos, and have a more numerous orchestra of flutes and drums, for it is the serpents and not only the public who require music. The home of the serpents is a wooden box. They are lifted out of it after many preliminaries, one by one, and with the hooded cobra last. The snake charmer must both exaggerate his danger and also stress his friendliness with the pythoness, being both slave and lover of the snake goddess. He cajoles her and calls to her. It is entreaty one moment, abuse of her, glorification of his own danger, soft persuasion, sudden assurance, despair. He reminds the serpent that he is her master, that she is his mistress, his slave, his paramour; or the Naga king, if it is the male python, that he is his servitor. He puts the tail of the serpent in his mouth, allowing it to coil up and strike at him. Its forked tongue dashes at his eyes or temples, recovering, and again darting in attack. As for the cobra, his is the kingly caste. It must always be a wonderful moment when his head is raised straight up and his hood stiffens like a mane, or like a peacock's tail. This is the lion among the serpents, the maned warrior. There is majesty and terror in every movement that he makes.

It has been said, and often repeated, that the fangs of the snakes are removed so that their bite is harmless. This is, on the contrary, very seldom done, and only a year or two ago an American visitor who took up one of the snakes in the belief that it could not harm her was mortally bitten. Snake charming must be one of the oldest of professions in the East. This, again, where Morocco is concerned, is a strictly hereditary craft or profession. They come, like the fire-eaters, from the Sous, from certain recognized districts. Their snakes are procured in large part from the forest of Admim, in the Chtouka country, between Tiznit and Taroudant, in the South. When caught, the serpents are kept in reservoirs or wells, rather like our fresh-water tanks for trout, and the snake charmers replenish their supplies from this source. There must be curious scenes, which the taste of another time would have said to be worthy of Salvator Rosa, when the long-haired adepts gather together and one serpent after another is taken out of its darkness for them to handle. But the forest of Admim, as we have said, is far to the South. It is near to the borders of Ifni, that enclave of Spanish territory which is nearly as unknown as the legendary Rio de Oro. No one seems to have been to Admim. Its mysteries are mere conjecture and nothing more. But the snake charmers at least have this background in which the *chiaroscuro* is not less picturesque and romantic than their extravagant gestures and their long wild hair. The shrill tones of their voices carry into the distance, even in this pandemonium of noise. They have always a crowd round them, although they perform day after day and everyone has seen them. But even in the circle that attends them—and this is most typical of the Djemaa El Fna—lying under the feet of those persons who are on the fringe of their audience, on the thick dust of the square, is a group or huddle of three or four Negro children, their nakedness hardly covered by a rag between them. They are fast asleep, a litter of small Negroes born, so it would seem, at one birth, now three or four years old, living by what they can beg, and with no better home, unless it be the corner of some wall, than this inferno of noise. If you look for them, coming back later, they will be moving round, begging under a common impulse or instinct, but they have, of course, a mother, whose misery lies in another part of the town and who has discovered the profit in leaving them to beg, as though motherless, for themselves.

A part of this degradation of humanity lies in its music. It is enough for them to bang upon a tin, to strike a wedge of metal with an iron ring. Later on we shall know what lovely music there is in Marrakesh; but here it is a bestial clowning, personified by a dwarf in the circle next to the snake charmers, who wears the peaked hat of the jester, of the Roi d'Yvetôt, who is bearded, which makes more gnomelike his appearance when he walks, and who earns his bread by clanging an iron file against an iron circle. A baboon could do this. Sometimes he will walk away. He is not even needed in the orchestra. It is only his freakishness that brings the public. When he hobbles back again the crowd opens for him, but the music is no different. His is the low, doltish Negro in whom no improvement is possible.

The tumult of shouting only a few feet away comes from a troupe of acrobats. They have asked their audience to intercede for them. Everyone is praying aloud before a dangerous turn is begun, while the leader, his long locks dangling in the wind, goes into pretended ecstasy from their support and steels himself for the attempt, of which the success is known for certain in advance. The storytellers also we may pass by quickly, for their tales go on forever and would not be interesting even if we understood them.

The whole square—for it is now six o'clock—is in the full beat of its life, sending up a noise and clamor which are indescribable. The setting sun makes the dust to be blood red, the red of a blood orange, or of a pomegranate, but gilding the corners of the mean buildings while it tinges the dirty white of the sempiternal burnoose. But it is not everyone who wears white. There are more soldiers in varied uniforms than on the operatic stage. The Spahis, in their Algerian turbans and their magnificent cloaks, red for the Algerian regiments and blue for Moroccan, wander in the crowd. The officer who first designed the Spahi uniform, a hundred years ago in the reign of Louis Philippe, deserves the title of artist. The special form of the Algerian turban in itself has something formidable about it and, as an invention, is not less effective than the bearskin. In a world from which all or nearly all of military glory has gone, these uniforms of Northern Africa may remind us of what has been lost, and it is Constantin Guys in particular that they recall. There are many more military subjects. The Zouaves, to one who remembers them in France, as a child, before the first war, are a little of a disappointment. Those persons who, like the writer, knew of the Papal Zouaves and the Zouaves of Don Carlos must be sorry to see how much of character has been taken from them. They are no more the Zouaves of the baggy red trousers and the immensely long skewerlike or file-shaped bayonets, distant descendants, as I used to think to myself when a child, of the more glorified Zouaves of the Garde Impériale of Napoleon III. But the Tirailleurs Marocains give, in pictures-queness, what has gone with the Zouaves. They are almost an altered or improved Spahi. There are also military police and a corps of watchmen, or constables, put into a new blue uniform designed only a year or two ago by the Pacha. Senegalese sol-diers, porphyry in color, or so entirely, utterly black that it can-not be believed, are here in numbers. They are, moreover, absolutely unrecognizable one from another, to the extent that the officers in some of their regiments know their men only by number and not by name. One hundred thousand new Senegal-ese troops are said to have been trained by the French authori-ties during the last six months (March 1939), which, added to the large number already existing, should amount to a most effective deterrent in the cause of peace. Here and there in the crowd can be seen as well the white-banded caps of the Foreign Legion, representing a few of their number who have come to Marrakesh from distant posts on a few days of leave. And there are as well the light blue burnoose of the Mokhazni, native police recruited from the Irregulars, or Goumi, their cloaks and white headdresses giving to them a particularity which will, from this moment, be noticed all over Morocco.

And now for the crowds themselves. Their costume is the
white burnoose, worn more often threadbare, and stained and
yellow with age. It may be nothing more than a piece of old
sacking or a dirty white linen sheet of the sort that beggars
might use if they were to masquerade in their workhouses as
ghosts. Of the richer sort there would seem to be three varieties
of the white burnoose, but differing not in material but in the
manner in which it is worn. There is a kind that resembles the
Roman toga, so that its wearer seems to be in descent from the
base classical age, as though there were really some living connection between the Roman Africa of Djemila or Timgad and the
Moors of today. Another way of wearing the burnoose is so that
it becomes the white robe of the Carthusian monk, an order
founded in the twelfth century and still wearing the dress of
the poor at that time. The third manner, but with only minor
differences, is the complete Moor, as we may imagine him for
Othello. This is the Moor who is entirely distinct in dress and
appearance from the Algerian or Tunisian. Sometimes it will
be a person of importance, a *cherif,* a *caid,* or a *cadi,* his feet
shod in fine yellow babouches, and with the hood on his back
ending in a silken tassel. He is followed by a slave and walks
slowly and impressively with the aid of a walking stick. As we
look at him, he is saluted by another Moor who stoops and takes
his hand, at the same time kissing the hem of his sleeve or
shoulder, a procedure which was in use in England and France
during the seventeenth century and can be seen in prints of the
time, but more especially among the small figures in the foreground of views of towns or palaces. But the aristocratic Moor
is not often seen in Marrakesh. It is in Fez that he rides past
on his mule with its red housings, led by a slave through the
crowded alleys. There are, as rarely in Marrakesh, burnooses
of another color, of an almond or pistachio green, and of its
equivalent again in gray; sometimes, also, of the same tonality,
off-red. Burnooses of camel's hair, striped black and white or
brown and white in their straight lines, are worn by the tribesmen, who carry a curved dagger in a silver scabbard at their
waists, this being the invariable rule for all the tribes who come
from south of Marrakesh.

The dress of the richer Moors and of the tribesmen is that of our fourteenth century, but there are other and discordant notes in time. Another sort of street Arab, not starving like those blind beggars, or as the Negro children sleeping in the dust, but spiritually much poorer still, although advanced out of rags and nakedness into European coat and trousers, represents the true century in which we live. He has bare feet, or a pair of tattered and loathsome slippers, and wears in badge of his inferior blood the tarboosh or chechoua, but it appears to have grown to his head, to be irremovable and hiding something worse beneath. His sort, of whom there appear to be dozens or even hundreds, is closely related in degradation to the Spanish bootblack, any person who has seen the one sort being in instant knowledge of the other. They are like the worst slum children of a hundred years ago, immortalized by Cruikshank in Fagin's den. And, as well, always with time to stop and stare, are those little apprentices, from tailor or leather shop, out of the souks, their shaven heads closely powdered or greased, and covered with unmentionable sores. It has not, at least, affected their vitality nor, since they are in such number, has it given them any sense of shame. The Jew, in black or white caftan and black close-fitting cap, forbidden to wear the babouches of the Arab, goes past. Something in his manner of walking tells of his unpopularity, though there are no less than twenty thousand of his race in Marrakesh, and were they but possessed of different qualities, their position would not be one of such cringing, shaming humility. The Jewish women would seem to be superior to their men. They are to be known at once by the mere fact of their having their faces exposed, as also by the silk handkerchiefs worn on their heads and the silk shawls on their shoulders, a costume which gives them the air of peasants, or *contadini*, in an early Victorian engraving. They have, indeed, something southern Italian or Maltese in their appearance. All other women, of course, are veiled, even the beggar women. This is highly romantic, but it is something lost and missing from the scene.

This is the still hour of sunset, when smoke climbs straight and slow into the air. And from all over the town, not less than from the square itself, come those scents and smells which are the Orient to all who have known that. They derive, in the pleasanter sense, from the pieces of wood that are burning and that include, most probably, some cedar. Walking round any village at sunset, you can get this magical evocation, however rudely it may be removed the next moment by the dirt and squalor. But in few places can the sunset hour have the strength, the living reality, of Marrakesh. Here in the square so many braziers must have something scented burning in them. And at this moment you may see spread out on the dust the whole stock in trade of a doctor or medicine man, being in real truth the abracadabra of old witchcraft, as though a painting of black magic had its contents, its philters and potions, its nameless horrors, poured out on the ground. There are trays of disgusting objects, concoctions of bat or frog, it can readily be believed, with the carcass of a raven looking like a body which has been dragged through a town at the horse's tail, a body in black armor from some Gothic tragedy, half-Negroid, half-Macbeth:

> Light thickens, and the crow
> Makes wing to the rooky wood;
> Good things of day begin to droop and drowse,
> While night's black agents to their preys do rouse.

At hand there are dead adders, dead vipers, an owl's wing. The pharmacopoeia is made up of matted, horrid fragments, the disjecta of the owl's nest, of the vulture's lair, things spurned by bat or spider.

Here is music. The dancers of Senegal, so black that scratches on their arms or legs are like abrasions on a pillar of porphyry, all old men, some with whitening hair and white, Negroid beards, dance furiously to the drums and bells. They carry a jester's staff or wand, strung with bells, and wear caps of beads, black, white and red. Their dancing has the ugly Negroid rhythm. They stamp and jump, clapping their hands in the air above their heads, giving the utmost of energy with but little of effect. The mere volume of noise that they make and the length of time during which they can sustain it are remarkable, more especially when it is considered that most if not all the per-

formers are old men, this profession being, we may think, one
which has no appeal to the young.

The Chleuh dancers, always one of the sights of the Djemaa
El Fna, are close by. Nothing could be more different from the
Negro dances than their subtle, oversubtle nuances, their un-
derstatements and the emphasis put on hidden things which are
themselves concealed. A large band of musicians, perhaps a
dozen players, is already performing while the boy dancers wait
to begin. They wear long white caftans, exaggeratedly laundered
and pressed, have painted faces and painted eyes and eyelashes,
and are viciously demure, like satanic choirboys. This com-
placency is accentuated, as it were, in the precise folds of their
Chleuh turbans, which are of a plaited form peculiar to that
people. As they stand there with confident but downcast expressions, their long surplice dresses with sashes at the waist give
to them that heterosexual air which is contradicted almost comi-
cally by the tribesmen's daggers worn at their waists in sign of
their origin from the Kasbahs of the South, but is confirmed again
by the guitars or mandolins they hold, to whose twanging they
now start to sing with shrill but elaborately trained modulation.
We must notice also their hennaed hands and painted feet.
Where all women except the prostitutes are veiled, this is a kind
of substitution or contortion, as though, in a land of music, the
voices of women were forbidden and only boys' voices, their
transient equivalent, were allowed of nature, bound to pass and,
in itself, unnatural and temporary, a passing condition like the
change-over from the chrysalis. But, as well, there is the Oriental psychology to consider, which sees nothing unnatural in this
perversion. It is there, in fact, because they want it, not as an
alternative to something else, but in itself, as a desideratum. The
dancing of the Chleuhs at least is not the dancing of barbarians.
This is not the Congo nor the Niger. These are refined pleasures
of Tabriz or Isfahan, where there is no companionship with
women, where women only bear children and are not vessels of
romance or pleasure. But also it is the viciousness of a race with
whom debauchery is difficult if not impossible, given the absence of strong drink and ordinary dissipation. It is sordid but
not vulgar. Perhaps it is even more sinister than sordid. And

the interminable verses of their song continue, each verse being apparently the same and the whole performance being characterized by a reticence which has never been the convention of the modern cinema.

If the Chleuh dancers are most notorious of the sights of the Djemaa El Fna, its real interest from the picturesque lies in the center of the square, and in what lies behind that. For the whole middle of it has become, by this torchlight, an encampment of tents. But they are only canvas shelters. They consist of little more than a sheet of sackcloth propped upon two sticks, like the tents of nomads sheltering from the wind. One side lies open, and the brazier burns within. Many of these tents are some six to eight feet in height, giving the true effect of some Tartar encampment, which is borne out in the nearly Kalmuck features of some of the tribesmen, and by children with their usual head sores but whose pigtails, or the curious long locks on their shaven heads, confirm that Tartar appearance which must strike anyone who notices them in the cities of Morocco, but more especially, we would say, because they are more numerous, in Fez. There is something wonderful in the sight of these tents, particularly so later at night, near ten o'clock, when the noise of the square has died down and it becomes a real encampment.

But the marvel of the Djemaa El Fna is beyond the tents, at the other side of the square, on the pavement of that corn or grain market which juts forward, spoiling all possible symmetry in this overcrowded square. There is a thing to be seen here which is unique. This is Cairo, or Bagdad, of the twelfth century, of that date when those domes were built which are the authentic East, such as we behold in the tombs of the Caliphs on the edge of the desert, outside Cairo, and that we have to imagine for the rest if we want to have a picture in our minds of the age of the Fatimides, of the golden age, in fact, of all the Moslems.

This thing is the row of women bakers who sit side by side along the edge of the pavement. Each has her loaves of bread upon a tray before her. In the light of the flares or torches it can be seen that all of these women—and they may be some thirty or forty in number—are veiled, but their veils are thin

and transparent, making no pretense to cover the eyes or anything but the mouth and the lower part of the nose. There is
an irrepressible coquetry about them. Most are young and exceedingly pretty, with thin figures and eyes that have nearly the
power of speaking, even though this be drowned in the gale of
their laughter. Many have already their lovers sitting beside
them, for they are, of course, not actual prostitutes but courtesans, as is proved both by the thinness of their veils and by the
fact that they are veiled at all. Whether they bake the bread
themselves I was unable to discover. They may be hired to sell
it, or may buy for themselves and use the selling of it as an
approach to their real livelihood. At any rate there should be a
tradition in Marrakesh concerning them, for the practice must
be an old one, dating back, it is probable, to the great Arab civilization, as we know of that in tales and legends.

No living sight that I have ever seen can evoke to such a
degree the Arab world of the Caliphate of a thousand years ago,
for this is the very material of legend and of storytelling. No
subject could be more fertile to the imagination than a walk along
this row of bread wives. For they are in a sense professional
entertainers, the hetaerae, the courtesans of the busy souks, but
without their evil premises. At their back the Djemaa El Fna
degenerates into the African city, the metropolis of the tribes;
this in spite of the fine Negresses who are at every third or fourth
place along the row. But there were black slaves, perhaps the
only women to come out into the world, in every Eastern city.
Color nor race meant little to the Moslem. That again is proved
in the Djemaa El Fna. Here the Negress bread wives, veiled as
in Damascus or in Isfahan, are of the purest legend. From their
white dresses and the thin lawn of their veils comes all the illusion of a thousand years ago. We must hope no rule or bylaw
will forbid them to stay here.

NUNS OF THE FONDOUK*

In the first instance we have a blue sky and walls as white as salt. Some of the whitewashed alleys are roofed with trellises of vines. In the distance you could see the snowy mountains. You pass a dark archway and, coming back to it, step down into its black and fetid vaults. The floor is a quagmire of mud and water. There are mules and donkeys, many men and a blind beggar or two, their long staffs in their hands, mumbling in the darkness. Beyond this, blue sky and an open courtyard. This has an arcade round it, with little rooms like cells and, above, a wide balcony with the doorways of other dens or habitations. It is the Fondouk.

The countrymen come in here with their merchandise. They stay a night, two nights, in some cell along the corridors. Their mules and donkeys are tied up in the courtyard. There is even a camel tethered to a stone. It is an inn, a place of business and a haunt of pleasure. Some Fondouks have pierced balconies or lattices of many stories. This is more simple. Its only luxury is the heat and light, and there can be satiety of both. But this is enough description of the Fondouk and the Moors. We are in this brilliant courtyard, but its importance to our narrative lies in the association of images linked together because of their interdependence and as part of their poetical system. This is, in terms of astronomy, the nucleus of these moods or fancies. They spring from sights or sounds, though inspired always by the inner feelings, so that in the mere difference of Fondouk or Fonduk there could be a chapter written. So let us play, in the first place, with the music of that name. Fondouk, heyduck— such words are not of our world; their smell and sound are of the Orient. But we will forget heyduck, although it started us upon this journey in the sun. And now we see that there are

* From Sacred and Profane Love, 1940.

159

not only Moors in the courtyard of the Fondouk. There are a number of women in bright-colored dresses. Some look down from the wide balcony; others come out through the arches. What we notice are the yellows, pinks or greens they are wearing. They have necklaces of coins, long silver earrings and bangles on their wrists. While they move there is a noise and clink of metal. Their dresses have long sleeves and full skirts. They walk barefoot, and their heads are bound up in a cotton handkerchief tied into a cap or turban. They are the women of the Fondouk, at the disposal of the men who come here.

It is a beautiful sight to see them in the bright sunlight looking down from above the arches. They sit on the whitewashed parapet and some of them are combing their black hair. Others come out from their cells and stretch themselves as if they have just awakened, although it is late morning. It is as though their whole lives were spent on that terrace or in the dark dens behind it. Their freedom of movement, right before our eyes, is the more remarkable in this Moslem land where the women are all veiled. Down below here, in the court, they are laughing and chattering and looking at the strangers. When they walk they have the stride of Gypsies. They come near to us, and we observe that they have tribal tattoo marks on their foreheads and sometimes at the corners of their lips. Moreover, their eyelashes are painted and it may or may not be a touch of rouge on their cheeks. For they are young, most of them from fourteen to twenty years old, while certain old and withered hags who are in control of them may be thirty, but no more.

Not one of the young girls is a Negress. Even those upon the terrace can be seen to have the round faces of country villages. They are Berbers from the mountain tribes, probably Chleuh, who have sold themselves and come down to the town. Their price is a few centimes. In color they are dark or burnt olive, which shows itself in their hands and wrists, that are always well shaped. And we see that the soles of their bare feet are painted red with henna. It is a new population in this land of hooded women. There was no sign nor sight of it until we came out from the archway into this sunny cloister.

What is characteristic in the nuns of the Fondouk is their solemnity, or laughter. For there are no moods in between. They cannot be vulgar. They are grave and dignified, or laughing. Most of them smoke cigarettes, a conspicuous clue to their moral character, and walk about hand-in-hand with a friend, like schoolgirls, or the common soldiers in a company of amazons. They are off duty, out of lessons; but at any moment or for any individual, their services may be needed. Yet this is the rest hour, the long and hot siesta of the South. Their duties begin in the afternoon and last into the morning.

Not a flower, not a tree, not a palm grows in the court. It is bare, of no tints but the whitewash and the colors of the air. The rooms or cells have no furniture—at most a mattress or a heap of rags. These are their homes, who have had little better in their mountain villages. They live here for a few months or a year or two, fall ill, improve themselves or go back home and marry. But they leave it as they found it, like the dove her wooden cage or the dog his kennel. They are mere animals. They leave no soul behind them. Their ghosts would not haunt the cells. Or if they did, a living replica of no difference would be dwelling there, and would come out of that darkness into the sunlight of the terrace, join her sisters in their bright colors and walk in the court below among the mules and donkeys and the bales of merchandise. The Fondouk has no age. It has stood there forever. For five years or for fifty or for five hundred years. It has always been the same. And if for the Moors it is an inn, a Fondouk, this school or convent is no prison for its women, although they never go outside the walls. They have no medicine. No doctor ever comes to visit them. One of the older women buys their food and markets for them. If they fall ill, they die or are disfigured. So we see them in health and not in sickness, whatever may be hidden, or may lurk within their blood.

They have come down from their mountains to the metropolis, to the typhus town. Every winter there is typhus. It comes up from the South, and is brought here by the countrymen. And from this interior court they can see nothing. There are no other buildings in the sky, not a house nor minaret, though the voice calls down to them in the dawn and at midday, when everyone is sleeping stretched upon the ground. But it is a faith, in any case, for men and not for women. We need have no sentiment for them. They have none themselves. They are mere animals, the lowest of their low profession. And yet, in these sad lands where all the women are veiled, it is some compensation, some gift of liberty, to see the round faces of these self-sold slaves. At least this is love without its cares and agonies. It can kill by disease, but it cannot still the heart. Nor quicken it. The dirt and squalor of the Fondouk cannot, though, destroy its beauty for the eyes. And it has more than that. We hear, from some hidden place among the arches, a snatch of one of the songs that are heard all over the town, though it is, doubly, in a language that we do not understand, for it is impossible to remember its turns and modulations. The more you think of it, the quicker it goes from you. It is as elusive as if you were in love with it. You can remember other music heard but once, and many years ago, while this, which has just ended and may begin again, dies from overcare, from too much thinking of it.

This is Atlantic Africa. You may miss the fountains and guitars of Spain. This is more solemn and more silent, though the voices are like turkey cocks. Their speech is a gobbling, gobbling, never far from anger. The muleteers are ever quarreling, night and day, in this court of the Fondouk. But it is so distant, so remote, even in its noisy town. We are reminded of Mercutio's speech:

> True, I talke of dreames,
> Which are the children of an idle braine,
> Begot of nothing, but vaine phantasie
> Which is as thin of substance as the ayre,
> And more inconstant than the wind, who wooes
> Even now the frozen bosome of the North:
> And being anger'd, puffes away from thence,
> Turning his face to the dew dropping South.

How, we may wonder, could a man have written this who had never been to the South, for the last line of our quotation can-

not be mistaken in its light and sound, though his South is more
lyrical. This is the bare bones of the South. His are the halcyon
valley, the hill of cypresses; this is no more than whitewashed
walls and the colors of the air. But it is more Southern than
the Mediterranean; Andalusia and Sicily are but legends; this
is close upon the sands. So the beauty of the Fondouk, for ourselves, must lie in how near its sordidness or misery are to the
last flowers or fountains, the ultimate shade of the dew-dropping
South.

Look again at those bright dresses, those cotton turbans! The
mere fact that these women are not veiled puts them into another sex from the hooded women of the streets and alleys. And
this we must feel whenever we see women on the flat roofs of
the houses at sunset when they take the air, or whenever we can
look down into a court and see them, barefoot and unveiled, at
their household duties. This is the hour of the Alameda, of the
mantilla, "where the vanilla-colored ladies ride"; here they can
only climb up to the terraces and talk from roof to roof. Those are
the veiled ones, but the women of the Fondouk are unveiled at
any hour, and this gives to them the audacity of a troupe of
strolling players, of a tribe of Gypsies. They are beyond the rules
of life, and this liberty speaks in their every movement. We see
it in their limbered walk and in their brazen attitude before the
stranger, even if it is belied in their grave expression. They are
priestess or sorceress; and the person who only comes for a few
moments into their cloister will take away with him the memory
of their dignity and their wild, untrammeled walk.

Vain fantasy would have us ask further of their origin and see
them, in fancy, by the last flowers of the dew-dropping South.
Their turbans and colored dresses have the Gitana and, as well,
the touch of Tartary or Persia; but it is only because Islam, from
end to end, has an affinity and the breath of its old past. For
this is Africa and the Atlantic. The white ibis flies above the
court and, if you listen, there is a clacking, as of reed or quill,
which is the stork on her nest who makes this marsh music with
the clattering of her beak. A blue shadow of a fig tree strikes
upon the wall, leafless but with the gnarling of its branches.

Aromatic wood burns in a brazier. The scented charcoal breathes on the air, neither noxious nor perfumed, but peculiarly scented, of Orient Africa, though Western as Galway or as the stones of Carnac. You cannot, farther to the west, nor south. This is the end of two dimensions. It is the Atlantic to one side, and on the other nothingness, the sea of sand. There is nothing beyond it. What lies there is no more the South. It belongs to another world and is the black man's land, the naked Negro Africa.

In this town of the Fondouk there are courts of honeycomb and stalactite, the hand of Andalusia from Córdoba and Granada. There are groves of orange trees; the magnolia would open its waxy flowers and exhale their scented breath, lemon-throated, creamy-petaled, from among the broad and shining leaves. In summer the whole court would breathe of jasmine. That is for the dog days; now, in the early year, the blue or purple bougainvillea colors the whitewashed walls. The wistaria trellis makes a cage or lattice of its honeyed blue fires. There will be the blue paulownia; and the jacaranda that is tall as a branched chestnut tree with candles of blue flame. All these and many more could flower in the Fondouk. Or we can build it, in fancy, on the blue seashore, open to the winds, in a white pirate town. The fishing boats, curved like a sickle or a scimitar, pitch and toss on the back of the blue monster. So vast is the Atlantic Ocean that even its midday calm is troubled. And at sunset the white sails blow in like swallows, cutting and tacking below the eaves of the white houses.

The rest of the town, if it be Sallee, has its hooded women who show no more than one eye, like daughters of the Cyclops. Their white-wrapped forms, hooded in their burnooses, are ghosts or shadows along the whitewashed alleys. They walk so slowly and so silently, the folds of the burnoose held closely with one hand. There is only that one eye showing, and a pair of hands. And so they go like ghosts, into the shadows of their houses. It is a town of fanatics and religious zealots. But all this is changed within the Fondouk. And we allow our fancy to play upon their turbans and bright colors. We take away that court again to the hottest of the South. Here, too, we build it in luxury, giving silks for cottons. They have silken turbans and silken dresses. They walk barefoot, with hennaed feet, or on pattens, the chopines of Hamlet. Their fingertips, and not their fingernails, are hennaed. And we can have music and dancing. But it is still the Fondouk. They are imprisoned by the freedom of their morals, forever priestess or sorceress, human but not like other human beings, a race apart, the Gitanas or bayadères of the town. Where do they come from? The mysterious and unknown South. From little red-walled towns with flat-roofed houses of one story where they live, or are brought down by tribesmen from the mountains. They are trained in schools of music and of dancing, or go to the bare Fondouk to earn their living from the whitewashed walls and wooden floors. These, however, have silken gowns down to their feet, a mandolin in their hands or little bells on their fingers. They are a company, a troupe of dancers, and we would see them coming out from the arches into the moonlight, or bowing their heads and stooping to pass below the orange trees. They are sitting cross-legged, or one of them dances as if chained to the ground, never lifting her feet.

It is a dress which flatters darkness and a smooth or tawny skin. And it darkens, darkens. Here are no blonde maidens from under the lime trees or the lindens. It darkens, yet lightens, for it must not be too dark. It can be coffee-colored, in deeper or lighter shades, of eggshell smoothness. There is beauty in the cutting of the eyelids, in the straight nose, small lips, and in the dressing of the hair, which can have a classical mode, in descent from old Egypt. Beautiful, too, are the thin wrists and ankles. They are the daughters of slaves; or come from the pastoral lands of the Negro, between the Crab and Capricorn, from kingdoms not of Nile, but Niger. There, in the meadows, they wear dresses of bright dyes, and in a long line go down to the river and carry up the water jars. They walk back slowly with the pitchers on their heads, as straight and firm as peasant girls at the Roman fountain. It is a pastoral land of wide-horned cattle, a land of milk and honey. They have been stolen from its riches and brought here in their misery, but that was in another generation, in the old slave wars. They have forgotten that, while the others are their guests, for they are here but in our imagination. We will pass the long hours of light with them in that interior life, knowing that never again shall we come here or spend an afternoon like this. It is a court of orange trees, with empty rooms that lead off it and have no furniture, nothing but rugs and divans. But the quality of it lies in the heat and light, in the blue sky and the fanning of the dove's white wings, in the scented blossom, in the strange and unfamiliar beauty.

Some of the young girls—not the Negresses—have round spots of vermilion upon their cheeks, below their painted eyes, upon which little shapes like frost flowers have been traced in gold. This does not make them look like dolls, for they turn so quickly, and because of the movements of their dark wrists and hands. They have the air of little painted brides, for they have been dressed and painted so elaborately. The secret is that they have nothing else to do. They will spend whole days at this, and weeks or months at their embroidery. Even so, their painted cheeks are a thing that we have never seen before. They have round, smooth faces, and foreheads which are bare below their turbans. Their long silken dresses fall below their knees, and they have wide silken trousers to the ankle, and feet with hennaed soles. They have nothing to do but sit or lie about like animals in cages. Perhaps it is their foreheads and smooth faces, the concealment of their limbs, that give to them a heterosexual air, neither girl nor boy, and the hint of a Persian miniature, though their faces have not the joined eyebrows that were loved in Persia. We would rather look at them in an exotic light, in kiosks of porcelain, near to the flowered tiles, for the lights of china would be holding up a mirror to the matt smoothness of their faces, but it must be blue and white Delft china, like a Vermeer interior, and not any more the arabesque and intricacy of the Orient. The light can be thrown through shutters, or through the boughs outside, or they can stand in the falling light and we will watch their shadows on the wall. It is wonderful, in imagination, to have them standing in the golden sun motes, while we see what of the Orient answers from the whitewashed wall in this tawny light of Africa, all golden from the sands.

But the sable, or the jetty shadows come. First of all as serving maids. There is a young Negress in a pink cotton dress, who has folded a yellow cloth for her turban. Her trousers are rolled up to the knees, for she has been working, and they are looped again, or tied up, in a manner that is all the inner Orient, all its hidden life, expressed. She has the clear, bell-like voice of the Negress, and that pathos which makes it hard to understand how they have ever been ill treated. Her wrists and ankles have heavy silver bangles. If not most grave and sad, she is laughing with animal white teeth. This is the first Negress, but there are many more, and we comprehend why the Moors find them more amusing and more companionable than their own women. With no education, they are not so ignorant. They have more vitality and higher spirits, though easily dejected and, like pet animals, taking their mood from their masters. They are, indeed, just animals, but in the same breath are more human than the Moors. It is their temperament, which is that of a child, while they are not cruel and ruthless.

The black Sultanas have come up from the South to luxury and indolence. To them it is a paradise of silks and snows, while the red-gold orange bough is still a wonder. We should find among them many graces and subtleties that are new or unknown, and of which the poetry is in the past and in the future. That is to say, such dark beauties in old Morocco, or indeed in all the lands of Islam, would have made subjects for our greatest painters, could they but have seen them. And, in the distant future, West Africa, where lies the Negro promise for the whole of their dark continent, may have its sculptors, its poets and musicians, when once more their unfamiliar beauty may enchant a world. But here it moves before our eyes. It must be confined, interior, deeply claustral, like a sight of the nuns in their *clausura*.

What beauty in a smooth black wrist holding but a cup of water! The long thin fingers, the delicate jointing of the arm and hand, though the palm of the hand is ever simian, it is true. The whites of the eyes, too, are like the blackamoor's of pantomime, as if the face had been blacked and would rub off with a sponge. There are Negresses like that, and with the clumsy movements of that stage convention, mere slaves of the plantation, but this is of the black men who are aristocrats or kings. Such Negresses are always tall and thin. Their ancestry is of the shepherd or the warrior. They have small heads and long thin necks. Their backs are straight, and their figures not of the Praxitelean canon but in a mold and proportion that belong to another world, another hue of nudity, not the Pentelic or the Parian marble with its lights of snow or honey. Like a column of smoke, and the nymph or goddess moving in that pillar, is the discovery of their bodies, for it is a different creation. It is thin and clear as smoke, and its line is of a smoke stem, with straight edges curving and bending in the shadeless evening. Their hair need not be the lamb's back with its short, close curls. It can be combed into tight ridges, or plaited like Pharaoh's wife. It can be formal like a dancer's wig, when they wear blond wigs, but this is dark as a raven's wing and glossy as jet. The chocolate or eggshell smoothness of their cheeks descends, with no difference, into their necks and shoulders. Their greatest beauty is in their backs, which are valleyed or channeled by the backbone between the twin shoulder blades, that could in their movements be a pair of flightless wings, down to the thinness of their maiden waists, then swelling below that like the statue of Venus Callipyge. One Negress can wear a net or snood of silver on her hair. Another, with feather headdress, can be the Indian slave or attendant in a tapestry. There can be coral necklaces and, at wrists and shoulders, ambergris from coasts where the whale spouts and where he casts ashore, in dead and empty Mauretania. A Negress holds a golden orange in her hand. Others, with bouquets or wands of jasmine at their ears, or held in the fingers of the ebon face like a toy of ivory, or scented pomander, ensnare our fancy. They can wear sandals or gilded cothurns with the thongs crisscrossing on their sable calves, like black huntresses who will bring home lion cubs; or, barefoot and hennaed, be the black slaves of the harem. Look again at the slender and thin wrists! Their movements are as a language that we cannot understand. But open their hands and they will have simian palms. They are but animals. This is their beauty and their pathos. It is animal or sensual pleasure, and a feasting

of the eyes. Here is nothing for the mind. It is only for the
senses. But music, poetry, painting, dwell here. Who would
impute more things than this to the movements of a sable wrist
and hand?

But the Fondouk sleeps, at last, behind its heavy wooden doors.
And soon, too soon, we would know the smell of dawn, a cold or
wetness, like rain upon the dust, and a freshening of the sky. It
is another white-hot day. Long ago the white ibis has winged
away to hills and plains of marigold, and the stork stands sentinel
upon her nest. The snowy mountains float like clouds upon the
air. Soon it will be the hot Africa, and one more long and
timeless noon.

THE GOLDEN REIGN OF SATURN *

Look! And you will behold the pressing of the grapes. It is a morning and evening in the golden reign of Saturn. For the god has been made partner on the throne and teaches mankind agriculture and the useful and liberal arts.

It is, at the same time, Noah's vintage, but not the drunkenness of Noah. We shall hear silvery, captivating laughter.

Dawn comes with the face of an angel in the doorway.

Wooden shutters are wide open and the upper rooms are full of light. It has already touched the towers or little walled towns upon the hills. Certain houses, too, here and there in the landscape, that must be farms, and have walls of pink or white or blue, and near by long granaries or wine cellars. It is so early that the wagons are still in their sheds. The milk-white oxen are in their stalls. In the distance it could be moonlight in the wooded valleys. For there is shade everywhere, and the trees are the cypress and stone pine.

A woman passes the doorway in a long gown that flutters to her bare feet, holding an amphora upon her head and leading by the hand a child, like Tobias, with round face and a golden head of curls. Noiselessly they go down an outside staircase into the flowers.

When you put your hand on the window sill it is already warm, but the nightingales are still singing in the little wood.

Ah! That was the wind among the cypress stems.

It is the ninth month. Purses of gold hang on the fig tree, under heavy leaves. Not the early small fruits, but luscious figs of autumn, green or purple, with split sides of gum or honey, where the striped wasp works among the golden grains of seed. The shadow of the loaded fig tree is the first shadow of the morning. On a white wall where, like the ghost of a pastoral god, there

* From *Splendours and Miseries*, 1943.

170

hang a pair of reed slippers and a wide-brimmed hat of straw.

Or is it a scarecrow to put among the vines? A straw figure to carry there, that will keep the birds from pecking at the grapes? A god of the corn straws, plaited from rye or barley or the rougher oats, but, now so many grapes are picked, humiliated and thrown away? We shall see women in those wide-brimmed hats treading in the wine press.

We could call it, to this moment, the honeysuckle morning, for it smells of wild honeysuckle where the doves are calling.

Tobias and his mother are in the flowering meadow, for in this innocence of the world the autumn morning is as fresh as spring. He holds a blue cornflower in his infant hand. We watch them from the window, while we hear water coming up from the cold well, see the virgins at the fountain who fill an amphora, lift it to their heads and walk away.

There are light movements of the morning clouds, it is so early yet. The regent Saturn must lie still abed.

Vesta, the evening star, sleeps low down in the heavens above the western hills. She is his wife, goddess of fire and patroness of the virgins.

But she reigns on earth too, and is awake and gives her orders.

Linen is spread out to dry on the cypress hedges, which are still warm from yesterday. You can smell the cypress wood. Other women are carrying armfuls of hay into the mangers, and watering the oxen. The geese are cackling and someone must be feeding them.

There are always geese where there are virgins, and ever a goosegirl.

With bright wings the painted doves come down. Tobias feeds a pretty bullfinch, but holds to his mother by the other hand.

It is the hour to eat, now that the creatures have been fed. Figs and pomegranates of the night's ripening, and a pitcher of spring water, in a long room with a high ceiling and noble doors, like the doorways of temples, and ornamented in that manner with cupids and medallions. The walls are left bare and there is no other furniture than an enormous table. In a few moments the meal is done.

A toad, with hidden ruby in its head, jumps from a leaf into the snapdragons and is lost among their mouths of flame. Nothing in this lovely morning is too little or humble to be noticed. The firefly in a dark corner of the wall that lights and extinguishes her lantern, oblivious of the day. Not contented like the evening star. After a summer night there are always one or two such— foolish virgins, stragglers from the dark. The lichen on the outside walls grows in parhelions, in leopard markings, upon the stone. Feel it, and you will know how hot it is to be! The lizard already crawls on the plaster.

Tobias comes past with a baby rabbit in his arms.

The god is awake and dresses in his bedroom. They bring him a calendar of all the husbandmen. A moth flutters its wings behind the wooden shutters. His Molossian hound laps milk up from a saucer and licks his master's hand.

The serious work of the morning is to begin. But the kingdom of Saturn is this valley and one to either hand, for as far as the eyes can see and no farther. Wherever we chance to be. So that, in a sense, it is universal, but it is as though he visits one part of the world after another, in rotation of the seasons, and in this way it is timeless, and the centuries go by.

Old men can remember the beginning of this golden age. How slow their lives have gone! The dandelion has come up again. His, too, is a kind of golden reign, though we shall all live to see his hair and beard go white. Saturn? No! His is a timeless, measureless middle age, and he will grow no older. But he comes down the stair with the same step that he will tread into the sapphire evening. For, in fact, he has come down among the flowers.

Now the slow progress begins, and men and women climb into the wagons. On both sides of the street there are houses with stone doors and carved windows. A peacock on a window ledge calls out with Indian cry, and there are butterflies that hover on the flowering weeds that grow out of the walls.

It is a pastoral triumph to move at this slow pace with the milk-white oxen by the houses into the deep fields of September. We advance with the milky dewlap through this hush or lull of early morning. There is a haze of heat, and no other sound but the cry of the cicadas and the creaking of the wheels.

The god is in a blue gown tucked up above his knees, and his face is shaded by a wide-brimmed hat.

Down lanes between the olive trees more wagons are coming. Wherever we look a milky dewlap breasts the flowers, and horns of plenty, hung with garlands, point the way. To Noah's wine press. It is not even the reign of two different religions, ruling side by side, but the old men of the wine press have such long white beards. They are patriarchs, husbandmen of the Pentateuch, in enjoyment of the promised land. A pair of them have come back carrying a bunch of grapes from a pole across their shoulders. It weighed heavier than the head of Holofernes. They could scarcely lift it.

All these are but nicknames. The only truth is in the golden reign of Saturn.

The wine press is in a well-known place. There is an arcade or trellis of three pairs of wooden columns, with a wooden beam connecting them, and beams along each side in order to complete the framework. As simple as that. The wood is grained and squared as it would be used to lay the roofs of houses. But the timbers are festooned with vines. It is an open building with a roof of vines. The stems climb up the pillars and the grapes hang down from the rafters, but not so as to interrupt the view.

For it is open to the landscape in all directions, except to one side where there stands a group of buildings, the summer pavilion of Noah in a light and fanciful architecture. But, in fact, houses and little palaces of this character stand on all the tufted hills. It is the whole kingdom at a glance. The capital cities can be seen between the pillars of this pergola, and castles and distant villages where you might lean your arm upon a pillar. Look at the cypress spire beside the window!

The god and his court get down from the wagons and tuck up their dresses and begin to tread. The grapes are handed down to them in baskets, and it is the men who stand upon the ladders and reach up to the grapes and break them from their stems.

It is a morning of summer intimacy with the god who is a

husbandman. Not more than six or seven persons are working
with him. A pair of maidens on the left, in long fluttering dresses,
have the baskets heaped with grapes upon their heads, but they
differ in their attitudes and in the color of their gowns, which
are all of one piece in ribs and folds, or have a peasant apron
round the waist and a skirt which is lighter in color than the
bodice. One girl, moreover, is not ready yet for her journey to
the wine press. Her basket is not quite full. It is being loaded by
the man upon the ladder; and she looks up at him, so that she is
standing still, while the other maiden dances toward the sea of
grapes. This in allegory, for she is the outer of the pair of
virgins, but she will dance to the edge of it and empty her basket
into the wine press.

The god is stained purple up to his thighs. And now a maiden,
lifting her skirt in order to fold it halfway above her knees, climbs
into the wine press with him. It is as though a virgin climbed
into the marriage bed, but the rites are pagan or wanton because
of her smile. There is no weeping. An action which we see, behind her figure, is a corroboration that this is a morning and
evening of laughter under the vines. For, standing under the
far ladder, an old woman in a peasant dress holds up her apron
for the grapes, while a young man who must be her son plucks
the fruit in such an attitude that he could be one of the figures
from the Deposition, about to lower the body of one of the two
thieves from the cross. It is a familiar or sacred reminiscence, but
no more than that. What she is receiving in her apron is the body
of the grapes. She has not to turn back the sheets and stand at
the bed foot and urge the maiden forward into the bridegroom's
arms. Instead, we hear laughter and the treading into wine.

She climbs out and another maiden jumps into the grapes.
The wine press is fed continually as they come and pour their
baskets into it and go for more. The juice has splashed on the
earth. It is not as when the yew tree stems are red after the rain.
That is the red of flesh. This is the blood of grapes, and the grape
skins are trodden into it. Their torn integument must be drained
or filtered to the bottom of the wine press, where it will form the
lees or dregs of wine.

They lift their feet high in order to stamp on the grapes. This is not the treading of damp linen in the river bed, when the washing is spread out on the rocks to dry and the arbutus and the oleander are in flower. It is a miracle, a liquefaction. It is generous, and it stains or dyes with much frothing. It is the grapes' blood, troubled and whipped up into a foam; but it does not spill like blood. For it is a flowering and not an agony. The train of ants wades in and out of it; the wasps drink, too, and know the holy stupor; only the butterfly, that has no work to do and is mistress of her hours, pauses a moment and passes by. So that, in nature, it is the industrious that know the intoxication of the grape.

All the morning the treading of the wine goes on. There are persons standing in the windows who call down to them and bring, from time to time, well water in a pitcher with which they slake their thirst. The god himself, in grapes up to his thighs, takes the amphora in both hands and leans back his head to drink. The others drink too, in the shadow of the vines. It draws near to noon.

Then you would find Saturn sleeping with his back against a wall. Ah! To see a god asleep in the sun, like any husbandman, still holding a crust of bread in his hand! To see the shadow of a god slant down the wall and break upon the ground and reach to the foot of the vine! This person who is sleeping in the middle of the day is one of the lights of the heavens, meaning all or nothing. The others lie round him, but the maidens are too young to be asleep during the day. They whisper together and tell stories to Tobias. All of nature sleeps except the dragonfly.

But the god awakes and sleepily, sleepily, joins in their talk. He comes back to earth out of the heavens.

Now the maidens wrap their skirts round their legs, and work begins. They measure how much wine has been pressed and step down into the grapes. But the afternoon goes more quickly than the morning. It is not long before a wind—but you could hardly call it that—blows down into this airy architecture. Clouds are ascending and descending upon the hills and their effect is like the stops of an organ or distant scales of music, for this pillared building has been designed in the manner of those sea shells that keep the noise of the sea in them. Its purpose is coolness. A gentle wind blows round the pillars and upon the pergola of vines. It is a wind from the sea. But in the late afternoon it is lifted away as suddenly as it began.

And the treading of the grapes is nearly done. The women now take their turn upon the ladders, climbing a rung or two higher than did the men and reaching for the difficult bunches high up, hidden in the topmost leaves. It is a ravishment to watch a pair of grape pickers, carried, each on her ladder, by two husbandmen, for they recover their balance and come down the rungs, holding each bunch as though it were a lovely head held up by its hair, and give it into the hands of the vintagers, and go up again for more. It is in parallel to the ascending and descending of the clouds upon the hills; while the lifting of them, as though they were dancers, and the repetition of their attitudes, only in another place of light and shadow under the leaves, makes the human beauty of the grape harvest. They ascend and descend their ladders under the eyes of Saturn, who is watching. Or it is, at the same time, Noah's vintage.

The evening is at its most lovely moment. All the towns on the hills are to be seen in detail. There are even, in the distance, other wine presses, but without the god. Yet we hear voices and laughter. Their maidens are as though dancing. We even see the air fluttering through their pleated dresses as they carry the full baskets upon their heads and pour the grapes into the wine press. We can apprehend the rhythm as they stamp the grapes, lifting their feet and treading the ripe clusters into wine. Into young wine, which has to ferment and gather strength. It would be no exaggeration to say that there is this ceremonial dance through all the landscape, wherever we see a vineyard, while somehow the adolescence of the world and its cruel innocence are inherent in the architecture of the little towns and castles that stand upon the hills. There is no decay. The buildings are entirely new. They portray, nevertheless, a golden age within a golden age. That is to say, there are classical columns and porticos, domes of

Halicarnassus, the fantasies of a child of fifteen who reads Virgil
and Livy under the pomegranates and stone pines.

But we come to the tasting of the wine. They dip their
pitchers into the wine press and lift them, brimming over, to
their lips. The maidens but taste it, and Tobias is given a sip of
it; but the husbandmen slake their throats and talk of last year's
vintage and the year before. For their wine does not keep long.
Enough is pressed for their needs, and they drink it at a year old,
storing it in wooden casks below the pillared granary, in the next
cellar to the oil press where they crush the olives. Next door to
the stable of the milk-white oxen.

How beautiful to stand in the doorway of travertine, which is
warm to touch, and look down the valley to the blue mountains in
the distance! There is always snow upon them, even in the summer. Down the valley, with ten thousand poplars along the river
bed and no towns or castles in this direction, but innumerable
little farms and houses all the way to the foothills. It is lovely in
the month of the blue iris, in the month of roses, in the season of
oleanders, through high August when it thunders, and now in the
month of grapes. The wheels of the ox wagons are stained purple;
not flashing wet, as though at the fording of a stream among the
banks of pebbles, but a musty, dark discoloration which is the dye
of the grape skin. The floors and sides of the wagons are dyed
purple with it, for these are the tumbrils of the wine press. They
bring home the body of the god who has been sacrificed. At this
moment they are yoking the white oxen.

Old women sit at the doors of their houses, plaiting straw.
The creaking of wheels can be heard on the ridge of the hill,
among the olive trees, and they turn the corner and come down
the road. How lazily the oxen move! It is slower than a walking
pace. Two by two, they plod down past the cypresses. Men and
women all wear the wide-brimmed hats of straw, for the setting
sun is in their eyes. The blue gown of Saturn is stained a deeper
color, but he still wears the fillet in his hair. Here they get down
from the tumbrils; here the landscape and what happens are of
our own inspiration.

They are lost in the labyrinth. For it deepens into a starlit night under the constellations, fixed or moving. Silvery, captivating laughter comes from the maidens. Of golden innocence, before the golden bowl is broken. Or they are the rings of Saturn, who dance round him in the fields of heaven. Of no more substance than the rainbow in a flashing fountain? Or are they fugal bands and choirs, for they move to their appointed measures. In our ears it is innocent laughter. The maidens at the wine press are the youth and beauty of the *quattrocento,* of a time when we are persuaded the painter's hand could not go wrong.

What we have been describing are the frescoes of Benozzo Gozzoli (1420-1497), in the Camp Santo at Pisa. It has been a morning and evening in the manner of Benozzo. Noah's Vintage, or, rather, the Golden Reign of Saturn, for it has been an experiment in his manner, but beyond his boundaries, though not in intention, for Benozzo meant his buildings to be pagan; but his landscape and architecture are of the age of innocence. No picture of the innocence of the world is complete without them. Just as no vision of the heavens is perfect that does not mention Fra Angelico, his master.

What are we to think of this primitive world of the Italians? When they had broken the shackles of the golden background? Or were half emerged from it? We hear silvery laughter, high up, under the tower. They are playing on early instruments. An archaic music. It is a mime upon the legend of the Virgin and the snowballs. The Virgin had appeared upon the same night to Johannes, a Roman patrician, and to Pope Liberius, commanding them to build a church to her upon the spot where they should find snow on the next morning, August 5. Hence, the Roman basilica of Santa Maria Maggiore, and the little chapel of Santa Maria delle Nevi in Siena, with its altar painting by Matteo di Giovanni. The Madonna is enthroned with saints at her side, and angels who hold snowballs in their hands. Now, indeed, we hear silvery, captivating laughter.

We could make a study of the mannerisms of the Sienese painters. Of Vecchietta, who might have lived among the

Buddhist monks of Nara; of Sassetta, who in his paintings of the Franciscan legends hints at a world in which worship of St. Francis had supplanted that of Christ; of Giovanni di Paolo, with his fish-maidens in long gowns that touch the flowers, clasping each other's hands in a paradise of fruit trees. A whole study, even, could be devoted to the Tavolette, which are the covers of the municipal tax registers of Siena. They are painted with heraldry, with portraits, and with episodes from sacred or profane history, by Matteo di Giovanni, Francesco di Giorgio, Giovanni di Paolo and, above all, Sano di Pietro.

We could write of the miracles of San Bernardino, after the manner of Fiorenzo di Lorenzo. There are eight panels in Perugia of his young popinjays strutting in fantastic, rocky landscapes. Pinnacles of rock and rocky arches, as artificial as though cast in lava, with a lake—perhaps Lake Trasimene—seen in the distance, and many poplars. Or it is possible that these panels, which are so personal in style, are a composite work by Fiorenzo, Pinturicchio, Perugino and Francesco di Giorgio.

But, in fact, it would be necessary to have different days or years for Francesco di Giorgio, who was painter, architect and engineer, expert in the Italian military science of the fifteenth century. Brand-new fortifications stand upon the hilltops, and the plain brick or stone, cut in diamonds, is background for men dressed in steel by the armorers of Brescia or Milan. The entrance to the fort is through a classical archway, which is incongruous; but the heat and glare are that of a red-brick town in August, with the site prepared for an equestrian statue in the square. Noise is incessant, and it is impossible to get to sleep. Because of this, dawn is exaggerated, as though it pains the eyes to look at it.

The lifting of the shadows is like a lesson in geometry. It follows the laws of perspective down the colonnades. The red ball of fire comes up out of the Lombard plain and plays a game with the long rows of arches, with the star bastions and deep-dug moats. Every tree has been cut down so as to make a clear field for the artillery, and the only shadows are those of buildings or of persons. But some of the fortifications are in false perspective. Down at the far end the arches do not diminish but grow bigger.

And there are dummies, like tailors' models, seated in the square, with hands on their laps and no head at all, or a stuffed globe that is inclined to one side as though in thought. Mere schemes for statuary, but the dummies are more mysterious in personality than the finished statue, and brood upon the architecture as though its strict geometry has meaning for them. Instead of features, curious dotted lines are drawn on their faces, as though they are the globes of a phrenologist, which are blank and expressionless but have the areas of thought and emotion marked upon them. One is covered, except the head, with sacking, and would seem to be a priest or neuter being in contemplation.

We see a fortified bridge, like that of Verona across the Adige. It is a battlemented, brick tunnel over the swift-flowing river. Or we could paint the Adriatic Sea between the columns for a fourth wall. We are anywhere, in the red-brick tyrannies, under a despot or *condottiere*. Like wasps, his men come out of their hives and pick up their halberds. The pawns are directed, as in a game of chess, from square to square of black and white. It makes a hundred shadows along the empty piazza. A piebald stallion is led out of an archway, and a wooden hobbyhorse is dragged into the sun. In a corner they practice the swirling of the banners. There are stone cannon balls heaped into pyramids, and the tambour and the drum.

How hot it has grown upon this shadeless hill! The clouds have become pagan goddesses. Look down into the sea, and you will behold the leaping of the dolphin! After a while the evening begins, with the same laws of geometry in cancrizans or retrogression, for the shadows point backward, in the opposite direction. The goddess of night shows in the heavens; and, could we stay till then, we should hear the changing of the guard at midnight, and the challenge of the partisans in a square of moonlight.

We know, too, that we could write of a morning and an evening in many other manners. In the style of the frescoes of the Schifanoia by Francesco Cossa of Ferrara, giving the employment of the months and the life of Borso d'Este. Above are the gods of the months in triumphal chariots. Below are the signs of the zodiac. We could recreate the frescoes of Cosima Tura that have

been destroyed. His dolphin curves; or the burning, dry desert
rocks of Erole de' Roberti can become an obsession with those who
are addicted to him.

Dawn in the manner of Paolo Uccello would be no less
dramatic than his battle of Sant' Egidio. Dawn when the sun and
moon are both shining in the sky, as their beams mingle and
interpenetrate in the fragrant pinewoods, and the land is tilled
in long stripes and in terraces. Or there is the landscape of
Alessio Baldovinetti with the hills and little trees that are peculiar
to him.

We could write of the great paintings in the Spanish chapel of
Santa Maria Novella at Florence. It is a place familiar to ourselves since early childhood. We have stood there on wet days,
with the sound of the rain pouring down into the cloister, and
looked up at the painted walls and the four triangular frescoes
of the vaulted ceiling in all the disappointment of a rainy day in
Florence with nowhere else to go except the soaking streets.
During empty August it is not less tremendous, and in a sense
anonymous. This frescoed chapter house is the work of Andrea
da Firenze, painted about 1370. The two greatest of the wall
paintings depict the "Church Militant and Triumphant," and the
"Glorification of the Dominican St. Thomas Aquinas," for the
church and monastery of Santa Maria Novella are Dominican.
In the "Church Militant and Triumphant" the Pope and the Emperor are enthroned side by side, with priests and monks and
hermits round them. In another corner of this crowded fresco
some young men and women are wasting the hours in an orange
grove. A full account of the paintings, in detail, would be impossible in these pages. We can only note the strange currents of
fanaticism. The black and white dogs, *Domini canes,* for the
Dominicans; the hermits, particularly, in the "Church Militant
and Triumphant"; or the strange figure, listening, in the ceiling
fresco of the Pentecost. Below the feet of St. Thomas Aquinas, in
his "Glorification," are the three heretics, Arius, Sabellius and
Averrhoes; below them a row of fourteen women, who are the
arts and sciences, seated upon thrones that are like choir stalls,
and at their feet as many male figures chosen from among those

who were famous in science or theology. These are most
curious. Practical theology with Peter Lombard; speculative
theology with Dionysius the Areopagite; demonstrative theology
with Boethius; mystic and scholastic theologies with St. Augustine
and St. John Damascene; grammar with Priscian; but, above all,
music with Tubalcain. This fanatic with his dark beard could be
a Gypsy blacksmith without his anvil, listening to music and in a
rhapsodic trance. Where can Andrea da Firenze have met with
his prototype? It is a figure that haunts the memory and is for-
evermore a symbol for one half of music. Behind him his muse
plays a stringed instrument, and he is listening to her. Yes! It is,
perhaps, more wonderful to stand here in hot August than on a
rainy day, for it is cool and empty in the great chapter house and
we can pick out the figures of fanatics and heretics. We see
Averrhoes in his turban, and Tubalcain like a wild animal entranced by music. These paintings were beautiful once: they are
still beautiful: but they have been sullied. The foul breath of
politics has smirched them. It is not enough that the tramlines
run in the street outside, that every door has been numbered,
that the custodian sits there like Charon upon the shores of the
dead. When it is done the hour will be late. And they are fading
fast on their plaster. No one will be interested. But few will
know these names. There will be different problems: another
future and another past. An old music-hall song will have more
importance than an early painting. For there will be no more
aesthetes. Those who can travel will not go to Italy. And the
ghosts have fled from Paris.

Yet we cannot let it die as easily as that. What was that? It is
dying, dying: dead already. Here is the "Triumph of Death,"
painted six hundred years ago. Who has not seen lords and ladies
in their green hoods growing in the woods? And now we can
make out on the plaster the hunting party riding to the chase.
Ten of them, knights and countesses, or princesses, with fine
sleeves and hats of different forms that take one back through the
centuries. We see their pointed shoes in the stirrups, and from
steed to steed, hats that rise like crowns from a coronet, that are
wrapped or folded, with a long edge falling nearly to the shoulder;

an older man with a beard, a guest from the Orient, who is staying
in the castle, with a high hat of fur like that worn by the boyars;
next to him, a felt hat shaped like that of the Eastern Basileus,
with crown and brim of different colors, worn by a young knight;
behind, a pair of ladies in peaked hats and wimples, which show
their youthful faces; then another beauty who turns in her saddle
to talk to the last knight of all, riding out of the wood. Below, a
huntsman on foot, in striped dress, with long hair, in a peaked
hat of long dead fashion, holding back a hound.

But the whole party have reined in their horses. And the
horses are rearing back, arching their necks, except one which
cranes forward with its head nearly to the ground so that its
rider has to stand back in his stirrups. The young knight behind
him leans forward in his saddle and looks down. He is the youngest and most handsome of the knights, and suddenly he comes
face to face with death. In that moment it is upon them all.
The smell of death. A corruption, a sickly sweetness, worse than
the rotting stinkball in the damp place in the woods. All living
creatures know, by instinct, what it means. One of the long-
gowned princesses leans her head and weeps; but her knight, who
has fought in battles, is more curious and looks down, but holds
his nose. What they see are three bodies of kings, in open coffins,
in different stages of decay. One is still recognizable, fearfully
swollen, but still in the pose of its last agony which no skill could
alter. Another has sunk down in viscous, furry sleep, lying in a
film or blurr or efflorescence of corruption, having gone back to
the ape in its white shroud. The last is but a skeleton, but with
one hand to its skull. The long bony shanks of it are knock-kneed
and bare of any covering. Its bony head looks not at the hunting
party, but on ourselves, in warning. All are horrified, for a moment, but pass on.

A path, which is a rocky ledge, winds upward and the hermit
Macarius, old and bowed, stands in their way with a long scroll
of writing that is a written warning. Above is the chapel of the
anchorites, and a deer and a rabbit and a cock pheasant run in
safety from the huntsmen. The other hermits have come out
upon the mountain.

The far side of this huge composition is another orange grove with cupids, or they could be angels, flying among the boughs. Music and poetry and love are to be seen, but the pestilence is coming. Death must have the smell of the orange wood in her nostrils. She is an old woman with long, straight hair, winged and clawed like a harpy, wearing a robe of wire, and with her scythe held in both hands. Death comes down on them like the plague, while the heavens are full with wings of demons and angels making off with the souls of the wicked and the saved, all in the form of infants that are issuing from a heap of corpses. In this pile of bodies thrown down helter-skelter in the charnel pit there are kings and queens, bishops and cardinals, court ladies with the linen wimple tying up their jaws, young persons of both sexes who died in youth. It has come to them, and gone past them.

But in the middle there are those who want to die. Many blind or crippled beggars, and those in mortal pain. Their hands are outstretched toward her, and they are whining or muttering to be allowed to die. A horrid, crouching figure of a man in a black cap, with lank hair, leaning on a stick, with his beggar's purse hanging from his belt, leaning forward and pointing with his hand as though it is his habit. Someone behind him, with contorted features, swathed and swathed in dirty bandages. A sitting figure, who cannot walk or stand, with a deformed and twisted foot. In front, one of the blind beggars with mutilated limbs, who can only crawl forward by means of a wooden imple- ment in each hand, shaped like a wooden flatiron. He comes, *clapper clapper,* along the dust. Behind him a terrible creature blind from birth makes no gesture, but grips his ragged staff. All are cursing as they hear the wings go over them. We can smell their beggars' gowns, living and fetid, not like dead men's clothes. But Death does not heed them. They are to continue in their living purgatory.

No one knows who was the master of this painting. Vasari ascribes it to Andrea Orcagna; other authorities to the brothers Lorenzetti, or to Francesco Traini, a Pisan painter. It is anony- mous, like the frescoes in the Spanish chapel of Santa Maria

Novella, but more tremendous still. And, because it is anonymous, it is abstracted from all other association that comes from any knowledge of the painter or his works, and it exists in a corner of its cloister where the hunting party riding to the chase, night and day for six hundred years, comes suddenly face to face with death. Death is in front of them and behind them, having passed the beggars by. All who have seen this terrific relic from the Middle Ages must be affected by it in the same way as though they had been brought face to face with a fearful motor accident on the road. The ladies and cavaliers are spectators too. It is an experience which we share with them. They will return home to the castle in the evening. The horses will be stabled, and they will climb up the winding stair into their rooms. A maid will lift off the ladies' hats and unfold their wimples. Water will be poured over their hands out of a metal ewer. We should see a cupboard full of pointed shoes, and hear one lady speak to another in a language that we scarcely understand. They are princesses, and you must hold the door open for them, and bow as they go past. Here they come again, riding to the hunt. It is a perpetual courting between these cavaliers and their ladies. They have been spared by death.

ORPHEUS AND HIS LYRE *

I. Fugue

There has been demonstration of the universal truth by fugue, and it may be that more wisdom is to be found in that than in the religions and religious books of all the world together.

Only the one genius, Johann Sebastian Bach, was master of the fugue. Even in his hands the form was not always obedient. It might take a direction that, mathematically, was imposed on it; be deflected, by new material, from the argument; or become redundant. But his was the supreme intellect in music. He had most, but not all, of the other wisdoms. Therefore, at times a purely musical virtuosity creeps in. Technical skill in surmounting difficulties becomes an end in itself; or, even, he celebrates his faith by that, as though he had come to believe that the ordering of his giant ingenuity was expected of him by his god.

Nevertheless, he is the huge grammarian. No other genius stands beside him. He frames the laws. His language is of a majesty that none other can approach. He is, all things considered, probably the greatest artist there has ever been. There is only Shakespeare to compare with him. Shakespeare, indeed, is so extraordinary a phenomenon that we are hardly interested in his person, and accept the obscurity of his history as part of the miracle. He was a poor actor who wrote immortal plays. But the personality of Johann Sebastian Bach is of another sort. It is physical, in the sense that he inhabits, physically, his music, and however little we may know of him, we feel his presence in it. This is a question, more than anything else, of his characteristic weight, solemn and serious from his first tread, but moving, when it suits him, in every mood of the heart or soul.

We are concerned here only with his organ music. Not with the

* From *Splendours and Miseries*, 1943.

186

Chorale Preludes—only with Toccata, or Fantasia and Fugue, Prelude and Fugue, and Passacaglia. In these we hear the full flood of his genius in its architectural forms—not interpreting the sacred text, as in his Cantatas; nor in the role of primitive, as in the orchestral Suites or Overtures and the Brandenburg Concertos, where the germ of symphonic shape is not yet developed, and these limitations leave him on a par with his contemporary Handel in the Grand Concertos. The giant hand of Bach and his divine intellect are to be heard in the Forty-Eight Preludes and Fugues, as much in the second set as in the first, in the Goldberg Variations, in the Chaconne for violin solo, in the Chromatic Fantasia and Fugue, in the Cantatas, and in the Mass in B minor. But more than anywhere else, it may be, in his organ music. That is because on that instrument the performance depended on himself alone. Until the coming, in fact, of the great pianists, and the emergence of conductors who were virtuosi, the organ was the vehicle for the greatest triumphs of instrumental music, and this was true until the time of Mendelssohn. The clavichord and harpsichord on which Handel and Domenico Scarlatti were rivals to Bach were not suited by their nature to be heard by an audience of more than a roomful of persons. But in Northern Germany, where attendance in church was nearly compulsory, there could be a public of many hundreds or more. That this music, owing to its intellectual content, can have meaning to but few persons makes an empty, or nearly empty, Gothic church with Renaissance monuments the setting in which we would listen to Bach's organ music. So it begins; but soon, very soon, it lifts us from the cold stone vessel into eternal time and space.

The Fantasia and Fugue in G minor can be our first experience of these wonders. Its rhapsodical opening puts it among the bravura pieces. Indeed, it starts after the manner of an improvisation, like a flourish to impose silence and impel attention. The Fantasia is some three or four minutes in length and the huge personality, the giant hand are apparent in it. Like so much of Bach, its eternity is achieved by retrogression. This is, in fact, not music of the eighteenth century at all. It belongs to an older and more serious epoch, though its content is musical and only musical. Religious thought does not enter into it, still less into the Fugue that follows. The scope is only for musical display, but of the ancient or Northern school of Hamburg, where music was still influenced by the Netherlands composers of the sixteenth century. According to tradition, Bach composed the G minor Fantasia and Fugue for a particular occasion, his visit to Hamburg in 1720, when he played to the organist Reinken, who was ninety-seven years old at the time. The old man is supposed to have remarked that he did not know such players still existed. It was, therefore, not a revelation of something new in music, but the survival of the old which Reinken considered must have died away.

The story may be apocryphal, but nonetheless it tells the truth, for inspiration came to Bach often enough from dried-up and disused sources. To the detriment of his eyesight he was, all through his days, an inveterate copyist of the works of lesser men, of small musical stature, necessarily when compared with himself, but it was as though he had a particular affection for the old grammarians. They were his quarry in which he found unworked or forgotten seams. We know too from personal testimony that in his own home he would always go to his instrument and play some piece of music by another composer, as though that released in him the springs of inspiration, before he played any music of his own. This is an indication of his character and method and it proves that, like other great artists, he would turn to advantage anything and everything that came to hand. He needed, also, to be put into the mood or trance, the fixed focus, or the "step" on which the speedboat moves across the waves. That must be the nearest physical analogy to the act of inspiration and it requires, in every instance, an auxiliary, a vehicle for the intoxication, for the spontaneous flowing of the numbers. It was provided, in this supreme example of the mystery, by the playing of some small piece of music from another hand.

But the Fantasia continues on its way. There are passages of meekness or humility, developed out of the texture, which could be interpreted as deprecation of what is to follow; or are they no more than incidental, part of the musical pattern, as it were?

For this is not yet the mighty and supreme genius of music. That is to come. And soon. The Fantasia ends with a thunderous and martial decision, a formal termination which tells plainly that it is done and ended. This is so different, too, in phrase or architecture, from the Handelian termination which is a magnificent conclusion. That also expresses itself in full-blooded architecture, shall we say of the Venetian order, of Venetian door and window and mounting stair, more splendid, indeed, than any buildings in that floating city, but this decision in the Fantasia implies that more is coming, that we have reached the Fugue, that what has gone before has been but Prelude.

The fugal subject plays itself, for the first time, like a story or a narrative that has to be listened to in full. It must, and can only be, a moral tale, some sentence full of meaning, the titles of God, it may be, as they might be called down from a high tower, not by human voice but by a peal of bells on a clear morning. The material, or the tune, has been said to be an improved version of a passage from a sonata by the nonagenarian Reinken; and again it is claimed as a Dutch folk tune, being probably the one and the other combined and altered into its present form. But the effect, as we listen to it, could well be that of a Dutch popular song of the seventeenth century or earlier, played upon the carillon. It has the substance of a carillon, as though arranged for that in the foundry when the bells were cast, while suitable tunes to exploit their possibilities were discussed.

At first hearing it is like a rustic merrymaking, a kermesse among the canals and water meadows, not in the opening phrase of the Fugue, which we have said sounds like the names of God, but in the second half only of its first line or sentence, after which, with the miraculous changes of which music disposes, the answer or remainder of the whole theme comes back, bound in and staved for treatment so that it is obvious the fugal voices will begin. It turns then, at once and immediately, abstract and not pictorial, as it divides. The second time the theme is played it has changed again, wondrously, in meaning, and is organ music pure and simple, sounding high up among the rafters of the ceiling, played clearly and conspicuously by the person in the organ loft. In silvery and piping tones, and we shall find that it differs in suggestion and meaning each time we hear it; now less energetic and less dulcet than before, but adapted to endless variation in the hands of genius.

The derivatives of the theme seem to grow organically out of the stem as though this was natural to them and not the fruits of his abnormal skill. It is because the theme has been tried and tested in every possible way until it has been shaped into the long melody of the *andamento,* from the Italian *andare,* to move forward or go on, for that is the type to which this Fugue belongs. There can be *andamenti* which have been built purposely so that they divide into a pair of sections in order to give the composer every opportunity for full development and the complete exhibition of his powers. Shorter themes, not complete as tunes, were termed *soggetti,* meaning subjects; while, in the grammar of the fugue, a theme which was so brief that it consisted merely of a musical figure was given the name of *attaco,* from the Italian *attacare,* to tie or bind together, or combine.

The G minor Fugue, then, is an *andamento.* It is not of that type which is just a subject suited by its nature for fugal treatment, as in Bach's Art of Fugue, where an apparently dull or simple theme was chosen deliberately because it was capable of so much development. Nor does it belong to that order of themes, dating from the last period of his organ compositions, written at Leipzig, when he was in the full maturity of his intellect, the feature of which is that their content is that of an aphorism or an epigram. This is definitely a tune, so much so that no one who hears it can forget it.

From its sparkle and liveliness a popular origin is quite probable, while, though Northern and not Italian in phrasing, it is not specifically Teutonic in feeling, but could easily be Dutch, a burgher or folk contemporary of Sweelinck, a Dutch tune that had been heard in Hamburg, which is nothing unlikely. Perhaps the ancestry of this tune or its connections is to be traced by analogy with the career of the great English composer of the previous century, John Bull, who, when he left the service of James I in 1617 and took up the post of organist at Antwerp

Cathedral, not only formed a friendship with the Dutch composer Sweelinck and wrote a fantasy on one of Sweelinck's Fugues, but wrote also a "Dutch Daunce" and folk-song variations upon the Flemish or Dutch airs *"Ein Kindeken ist uns geboren"* and *"Den Lustijken Mey"* (The Merry May). We would imply that the Dutch folk tunes on which John Bull wrote his variations were of the same character and origins as that which served as theme for Bach's Fugue in G minor, and that perhaps the presence of such tunes in Holland was as much a tribute to the importance of Sweelinck as it could be argued, in a parallel sense, that Italian melody and the beauty of Italian singing in the streets was due to the great Italian schools of music and singers in the past. These were, in fact, relics of a golden age of music in the North, of which the organists, Reinken at Hamburg and Buxtehude at Lübeck, were the living survivals.

When the tune or song comes back again it is played reflectively, and in a kind of purposeful solitude, which gives to it, once more, another and a different meaning. More silvery and piping yet, while this particular register isolates the melody and we hear it up near the ceiling, breaking from the flutes; the treble pipes of the organ, one after another, are brought into play as though the strict harmony was a game among them, while the air climbs in and out and wreathes itself upon the pipes. The pace, even, is slow and rambling, for this setting forth of the tune is deliberate so that we can listen to its message. If such there be? Or is it music, pure and simple? Certainly, unlike the other fugal music that we would examine, this has no theory of creation. It does not breathe terror. The huge rolling figures of the organ Toccata and Fugue in F major are not present. Nor the lightnings and thunder of the Toccata and Fugue in D minor. This is more purely musical in meaning because of the long melody of which it is born, and which is treated objectively by Bach, in the sense that the voices of the Fugue are derived or developed from out of it, and not imposed with superhuman ingenuity upon it. But now the voices of the Fugue begin to turn in upon themselves, and alter in intent by doing so. There is an analogy in this to the animal that rolls on its back and shows its belly. The great hounds of the chase do this in play; so does the spaniel and all other dogs. It is with them a gesture of surrender, an offering of their vital parts so that they may die quickly, but it has become a convention in their play, as much so as when they bite the hand but do not close their teeth. In proof of which the humble rabbit turns on his back to let the fox or greyhound kill him. By some humanity, or animal feeling, that inhabits the cold numbers or the architecture of the Fugue, this is what happens. Or it is some gesture of the composer's mind, as though he looked down in that moment from the organ loft while the huge fabric of the Fugue slows down and steadies, and is done.

The organ Fantasia and Fugue in G minor of Bach is of an immortality that never tires, although it is among the most familiar of all his works. It is so cheerful and good-humored that we would listen to it as humanity or human feeling. It never makes the skin tingle or the hair stand on end, in that way which only Bach and Berlioz and Beethoven, in their different individualities, can achieve. Each time we hear the Fantasia ending and the beginning of the Fugue, we hear the shadow of the giant in that formal clension, as though he showed his huge hand, and his powers, for the moment. It is a bravura ending, though less so than another that we shall remember; and after a moment's pause we hear the tune in its wonderful components, interlocking and returning in its phrases, chiming like a peal of bells, compact and fitting, made perfect in shape by the hand of the supreme master, so that its descending phrases are exact in cadence with the opening and it is set forth as a living entity with breath and animation of its own. The perfect balance of its syllables is so mysterious. What does it mean? What is its intention? This is no accident, like the pearl in the oyster shell, like the lump of amber borne to land in the floating seaweed after a high wind, while the strand rider patrols the lonely Baltic shore, nor any other of the happy freaks of nature. This is deliberate: not found by chance, but made by skill. Invented in the one place, and then made anew, like the turning or polishing of that drop of amber. And, in fact, it could be, in substance, a gathering or coagulation of good will or sweetness. Its burden is of benevolence, set forth in an ingot

that is imperishable and, like amber, warm to the touch; that is
no bigger than the one breath only, and then divides or sheds its
sweetness, which is diffused among the various voices and
gathered up into the whole body of the fabric, so that it informs
the argument and points the message.

But immediately, and with only a pause of a moment in between, we hear the organ Prelude and Fugue in G major of Bach.
This is of another character altogether, being one of his lesser
masterpieces, and not to be numbered among the huge and
triumphant demonstrations of his intellectual beliefs, though he
believed with heart and soul as well, but it was his intellect that
proved it to him. In the opening of this Prelude and Fugue,
which are not so little in length, he does not tend the vine; he
does not reap the golden field; there are no voices of God, nor
rushing winds; instead, he is domestic and genial; and in the
Prelude it could be that he is watering a window box, in his
dressing gown, with a painted can. It is a demonstration, from
trivial and little things, of the wonders of the world. We would
number this with his domestic music, which exists in quantity.
Not in scale, for necessarily this is bigger in scope than his
Sonatas for a solo instrument, violin or violoncello, his flute and
harpsichord Sonatas, lovely though they be, or the vast body of
his keyboard compositions, but this organ Prelude and Fugue is
domestic, surely, in its content. It breathes domestic or family
contentment, and in the Prelude sets out to prove nothing, but is
happy in its surroundings.

The opening is a set of brilliant and gay flourishes, not of
triumph but of contentment, with a rocking or rolling upward
rhythm, ending like the notes of a fanfare almost, but this is only
imitated or suggested; the pipes breathe neither defiance nor
exultation; it is no more than the climbing of the fingers, one over
another, on the keyboard. After these flourishes the main theme
appears, which is no more than a rising sequence, something
which by its fluency can be suggested and hinted at and even
imitated indirectly, like its own echo or shadow, so that the pattern or message is repeated, but in outline only. There comes a
moment when this theme proclaims itself four times over on the

manual, given out in ascension, after which it disappears and yields place to ghostly suggestions of itself in harmony and rhythm. But the capping of the theme, which is equivalent to an answer to the riddle or question which it poses, is a marching or a treading of the grapes, for the structure of the Prelude has changed in mood and becomes positive. It enunciates the truth in this marching rhythm, which ends the first section, when the whole form is recapitulated for further argument, but ends with a most lovely phrase of exit or termination, through which the melody is led, to open again in fresh and tireless discussion of moral principles. It would be beyond our powers to enter into technical details of its structure, but a mind which has dwelt for long among the other arts, and lived in music as an amateur, may make a contribution that lies beyond and outside the absolute musical analysis, and yet brings other lights to bear on this miracle of mortal origin.

Indeed, the particular miracle consists in the animation of an inanimate structure, if it is conceded that any piece of music— for instance this organ Prelude and Fugue—has one existence, on the paper on which it is written, in however many copies, and another which comes into being only in performance, and is therefore intermittent. But this latter is its true life. Beneath the rules and complications of its formal structure a heart is beating and a mind is working, as though we could impute this same possession of the human faculties to the elaborate mechanism of a clock, to some mathematical calculation, or other co-ordination of minute and lifeless parts. The utmost endeavors of human craftsmanship are nowhere stricter or more exact than in the Fugue. But those others effect no more than their purpose. They have no ulterior meaning. They advance no argument and pursue it to the end. Their life is intrinsic and not independent. Bach is the only master who can animate the Fugue. The subject, on this occasion, comes from the opening chorus of his Cantata "My spirit was in heaviness," but the theme has been transposed from minor to major and lengthened in the process. It has been suggested by Dr. Sanford Terry that the Fugue was written ten years after the completion of the Cantata, which was an early work. In form it belongs to that type of theme which was called in Italian musical language a *soggetto,* shorter therefore, and less of a tune than the subject of the Fugue to the Fantasia in G minor. In meaning it would appear to be an ecclesiastical reiteration. Some inevitable truth, which does not dull by repetition but even, as the sacred formulas of the Buddhist church, confers immunity. At first hearing there is certainly a threat in it, an allusion, it may be, to death, which is unavoidable, and a state which was as important, in the mind of Bach, as the living world. But the theme coils in upon itself. It is not a melody but a sacred formula. It has a pushing rhythm, which pulls its conclusion after it, and begins again. Belonging in spirit to an earlier century, to a hundred years at least before the period of its composition. It has, in this beginning, a grimness which appears nowhere else in its own time. But soon relieved, and as though that threat was no longer necessary, turning to a gaiety in the exhibition of its own powers, but little and unimportant in locality, as if this was a morning spent happily with Bach during years when he was unconcerned with the world and living outside it in some small contented place.

The liturgical voices have become secular. We are in the pastoral or idyllic world; and it would have many parallels, we do not doubt, did we but know his Cantatas, where it is certain more beauties lie concealed than in the whole body of music that is unfamiliar and but seldom given. There is, indeed, the same feeling in the Cantatas as in this organ Prelude and Fugue, that the music does not care whether it is performed or not. This is not the case with an unfamiliar work by Berlioz. On such rare occasions as those are given, they call aloud to be repeated. But the Cantatas of Bach were composed in the routine of his duties, and would seem content, as it were, with the date of their original performance. This makes them immortal but ephemeral. A series of masques, but without action and played without scene or dresses—such are the Cantatas of Bach. In many of them the splendors and miseries of the world are not the theme. So it is with this Prelude and Fugue. It is concerned with quite other things. We hear that in the opening flourish of the Prelude, and it continues within the Fugue. For the burden of this music is affection. And by what miracle is that expressed in fugue? Not the lifting of pain, as in *"Es ist vollbracht"* from the St. John Passion; not the broad flowing Arcadian vale of "Sheep May Safely Graze," both of which breathe thankfulness and peace, in their kind; nor is it the reflective picture, complete in itself, that Bach could evoke from the three words *Et in Unum,* in the Mass in B minor, which is among the most lovely of his inspirations. If we are to imagine these, for a moment only, as though their idiom expressed itself in painting, they are revealed as timeless in their greatness, but old-fashioned in their time. The design is as copious as in a tapestry or picture of the Middle Ages. Let us name no names of painters, but affirm that in these he is a master of before the date of Rubens, untouched by the Renaissance and drawing most of his imagery from the Bible. In the particular works that we have mentioned there is nothing, as painting, that is later than the time of Luther, and it is, in fact, that contemporary vernacular in music that he has extended and made into his own. It is possible, therefore, to be timeless and two hundred years behind your time. And, if as great as Bach, to be appreciated only in part after two more centuries have gone by. The curious isolation of this Prelude and Fugue in G minor in space and time, and what we have called its happy indifference to its fate, are confirmed in the odd modulations of the ending, which are even Oriental in sound, in the sense that all early music, and most early works of art, have an Eastern accent. It can be no more than an accident, unless the imagery in which it deals comes from the Bible. It is suddenly wafted away from the landscape into contemplation, or into prayer. Without doubt it is a religious ending, and it seems to express some mystery which it does not understand, but which must be accepted implicitly by a world which is not old enough to comprehend. What has gone before has been childlike in confidence and serenity. What follows is certain, but must not be argued. There is much, in fact, that cannot be explained. And the Fugue ends on that mystery.

The melody of Bach, when it is idyllic, must be based upon

the visual surroundings, which will include the books and music that his eyes had seen. In another instance, it is impossible to believe that Handel, in spite of his notorious indifference and apathy toward the other arts, does not reflect the Roman and Venetian travels of his youth. Handel composed in the grand or classical manner, not because of his robust physical frame only, or because of his Gargantuan appetite, but for the reason that he was a cosmopolitan, imbued with the urbanity and humor of a world that we have lost. His music is the mirror of that civilization, just as the beauties of his musical structures, composed in England, are as though Brunelleschi, Bramante, Sansovino had built upon English soil. *"Ombre mai fu"* depicts ilex or cypress, the shade of Soracte or of Vallombrosa, not the wood of Dunsinane. His *Water Music* comes from a gilded barge moored at Hampton, where the Thames flows past villas and soft lawns. What an era of visual perfection is to be perceived in the organ concertos of Handel, where all around is new and splendid! And the rolling organ leads the eye to new statuary and painted ceiling.

But the melody of Bach goes deeper and concerns the whole of life, in an older world apart, where the values are more permanent and there are no coats of gilding. In order that this should not be transitory, it has been fixed in time. That is to say, it is eternal because it deals with things that do not alter. But it speaks a ritual language, not in modern speech but in a universal language which is at once old and new. With no grand buildings or classical façades, but of timber-frame houses out of which you can step directly and look up into the sky. Because he needed nothing more, but was contented. The musical facility had been developed in him through all the generations of his family. They had been peasants and artisans, organists and town musicians throughout Thuringia. The names of more than sixty members of the Bach family who were connected with music have been preserved. He spoke, musically, in a vocabulary that was their own. There was no need for him to invent an idiom. It was born in him. Perhaps there may even be some obscure natural reason for his genius in that the father of Johann Sebastian, Johann

Ambrosius Bach, was twin brother to Johann Christoph Bach, and that they were identical twins, both of them violinists, alike in thought and speech and so similar in appearance that their own wives were unable to distinguish between them. It would seem, in Johann Sebastian, to be equivalent to a double transference of talent, resulting in an endless multiplication of the family abilities. A phenomenon which has appeared, perhaps, but this one time in history. By a freak of nature, or a rule which we do not understand, the uncle had a greater talent than the father. But, again, the sons of the uncle in their turn became the one an obscure violinist, while the other abandoned music and went into the grocery business. The balance of genius righted itself and regained its level of normality. Of the twenty-four children of Johann Sebastian, three or four were remarkable for their musical talents, but if positive genius had appeared again we should expect to find it not among his offspring but in the descendants of his brothers Johann Christoph or Johann Jacob. With so many known individuals of the one family it could be possible to draw up a graph or chart showing the direction taken by their talents, and even what would be, from conjecture, the path of probability. But this excessive blossoming was not to come again. Nevertheless, its reasons are apparent. It flowered, as we should expect, on one of the least likely of the stems. The seedlings showed promise, but Philipp Emanuel, Wilhelm Friedemann, Johann Christian never approached their parent in his genius, and the phenomenon expired among them.

We are now to hear this greatest of all artists at his fiercest and most tremendous fire of mind. What has gone before has been by comparison but the gentle warmth. This particular work is the organ Prelude and Fugue in C major, one of the five great organ compositions of his Leipzig period, written probably about 1735, when Bach was nearly fifty years old. This is important to remember, while we listen, because the reader who is not professionally interested may not realize that the bulk of Bach's organ music, which in any case represents a much smaller part of his output than the layman might imagine, was written during his early life, chiefly at Weimar. This Prelude and Fugue in C major represents Bach, then, in mental and physical maturity. It is, in fact, an extraordinary work, as physically exciting as any music ever written, and to which belong many implications. The theme of the Prelude, and of another figure that occurs in it, are closely related to the opening chorus of his Epiphany Cantata *The Sages of Sheba,* No. 65, written ten years previously in 1724 and having, perhaps, some special association for his mind. Certainly the character of this Prelude suggests that the theme has not been chosen just because of its musical possibilities, because it was so hard a core or germ of melody, nor for the converse reason that, being superficially meaningless or like a riddle, it lent itself readily and pliantly to his designs. On the contrary, from the opening bar of the Prelude its soaring and ascending energy is apparent. It has been described by one writer as pastoral in character; while another critic interprets the Prelude as the vociferous welcome of the population to a reigning prince. Probably it is nearer the truth to point out again that it is an Epiphany Cantata from which the theme, in reminiscence, has been adapted and that, therefore, it is more likely to have a Pentecostal meaning. Bach felt so powerfully the power of words, and gave to them so literal and pictorial a setting, that the clue to the meaning of this Prelude is probably to be found in the exact words of that first chorus of the Cantata, and again in the precise mood of that other coincidental figure which immediately precedes, so it is said, the entrance of the voices and concludes the movement when they have done.

The prevailing tone of the Prelude is harsh and strident, to the point nearly of being frightening. In effect it is a whirling and spiral climbing, which it is impossible not to associate with the Pentecostal winds and fires. This is expressed, so to speak, upon the trumpets. None of the dulcet shades of the organ are required. Nor is it a rolling figure, for the sake of rolling, as in the organ Toccata and Fugue in F major, where it is the play of a mighty strength, an infant strength, even, as though it were possible to conceive of a youthful creator who is making order out of chaos, and whose intentions and movements are depicted

in this rolling figure and in its constant clensions, which are as
though things had been put to rights, and then he sets out again
and with more tasks to do. But in this Prelude the flames do not
catch instantly or consume entirely. They return again and
again. The succeeding subject, that comes after the soaring and
ascending fire, seems like an expression of pious wonder at the
miracle, not in surprise, for it is implicit that it is expected.
Definitely, this calm and thankful return which prepares for
the fire and the fearful winds to come back again can mean
nothing else, if music has a meaning. And, in fact, the ground
is set and ready. It returns. The succeeding stages of the miracle, or just its repetition, are depicted in the music. The second
reappearance is more terrifying still, accepted once more with
pious and deprecating confidence, which is nothing else than a
message that all is believed in and credible, but the tones of the
organ thereby suggest in some way the empty vessel of a church
with all the ornaments of devotion. And then, when all is ready,
the winds and fires begin for the last time. But for this occasion
they catch; and their whirling, soaring fury makes the hair stand
on end. There can be nothing else like this in music for its
terror. It gets right away, with the ground cleared for it, in a
manner of physical excitement or inspiration that can only be
compared to the enormous acceleration of some engine, or the
drop from the minor into the major key, as when, in that simile
we used before, the speedboat rises on its "step" and roars away,
or the airplane alters its note of menace to die down in the distance behind a cloud. This concluding part of the Prelude becomes more and more like the cranking of some gigantic engine.
It is to be more formidable still. But there is one more return
of the subject in a changed tone, as though in worship of the
power that sent it, almost as though the flames were bowing
low, or kneeling at the altar stone. And they are lifted, suddenly,
dying or diminishing. The gigantic engine beats its flails and
plowshares into trumpets. The flames are quenched. The giant
power intervenes and orders. There comes the tremendous ending, in three phrases, like words of two syllables upon the trumpets, so peremptory that it is not credible this should be the

triumphant proving of the problem. They are, in fact, three blasts of the trumpets, at sound of which the whole world falls down, in the name of the Holy Ghost who worked this miracle of the tongues of fire. It is the voice of God, and no more is said.

The Fugue which follows is built upon a theme so short that it is a phrase or little more and occupies only one bar. By nature, therefore, it belongs in fugal language to the type of Italian *attacco,* a subject which in the literal meaning has needs to be combined or bound together. This is a Fugue in five voices, and the mysterious subject is repeated so constantly in different forms that, in effect, it is never absent from the structure. An unfortunate resemblance between this figure and the Prelude to *Die Meistersinger* is no fault of Bach, and probably an accident on the part of Richard Wagner. But the coincidence is soon forgotten. At first hearing, this phrase or theme of the Fugue, as is so often the case with Bach, comes out of the remote past. It is archaic; and if superficially it has some resemblance to the Prelude to *Die Meistersinger* it could, as well, be said to be nearer in spirit to the opening notes of *Le Sacre du Printemps.* But the voices of the Fugue, one after another, break in on its ritual phrases, and in a curious way they are so suited to a fugue that each entrance sounds like the introduction of new material. That is to say, the figure in itself is little more than an entrance. It exactly suggests that and no more; and for a while the Fugue employs itself with the accumulation of its parts, until all have entered. To this point the Fugue has but little other meaning beyond the ancient liturgy of the phrase itself. But there comes an augmentation of the subject, on the pedals, by which it is altered in character, at which time the whole complex machinery of the Fugue is set in motion, and that figure has become menacing, and as it were, proved in action and not awaiting contradiction. In reedy tones and with a gathering speed it enunciates the sacred apothegm, and states it again, more positive still. The entire Fugue moves with assurance to a foregone conclusion. It is as though this were some Euclidean problem to be solved, which will be proved by logic, without argument. But now the parts are quickened, and the turning, whirling of the Prelude comes back, with less intensity, it is true, more resembling a cloud of incense as that seethes and swirls up from the censer, and conceals, it may be, some miracle or transformation that is taking place, that occurs regularly and is part of the ritual. Or the ritual itself, the Communion, the miracle of transubstantiation, it could be. Whatever that thing may be, it has happened and is over. The ending of the Fugue is concerned only with the conventional dying of its voices, while the music lifts up its eyes, as it were, toward the heavens. And when the voices have stated once more what they have to say, the Fugue slows down and dies in full diapason against the mortal walls and ceiling.

In this organ Prelude and Fugue in C major, in particular, Johann Sebastian Bach is the greatest of the Ancients. Of none other of the great artists is this so true. It is because his concern is with the ancient truths. He does not belong to his own century at all, but, being rooted in eternity, has a meaning for all times and speaks, therefore, in an ancient voice out of the universal and omnipresent past. Probably in order to be numbered among the Ancients it is necessary to be peculiar or uncomprehended in your time. Johann Sebastian Bach is not the last of that race. Beethoven, obscured but happy in his deafness, and William Blake are two others. They are approached by Cézanne; and there have been no more. These are not of the race of Watteau, Chopin, Keats, of whom, down perpetuity or in purgatory, the youthful ghosts wander among the myrtle groves.

But Bach is most Ancient of them all, before, in his old age, he withdrew into the mazes of the Fugue and concealed himself where few could follow. That technical obsession betrays the Teuton in him, of which, despite their separable beauties, the *Musicalische Opfer* and *Die Kunst der Fuge* are the exemplars. Probably, also, another work unfortunately inaccessible to us, the Canonic Variations for organ on the Chorale *Von Himmel hoch, da Komm' ich hier,* composed in the last years of his life. Sir Hubert Parry, in his account of this work, describes how in the last of the eleven variations the canons come tumbling out one after another, close upon each other's heels. It may be that these variations in canon are more readily appreciable than the many difficulties of the Musical Offering or the Art of Fugue. They were handed in by Bach as an exercise on join- ing the Mizler Association for Musical Science in Leipzig, and were composed in 1747, only three years before he died. In thinking of his final contrapuntal masterpieces, of which this is to be numbered as the third, we must express gratitude, in our admiration for him, that he lived too early to become involved in the arguments for symphonic form. Too much of his Ger- manic energy and thoroughness might have been wasted on the orchestra. The Suites or Overtures and the Brandenburg Con- certos are sufficient. Those are enough to show that the orchestra of the eighteenth century was not suited to his genius. That he was too big for it. That, in fact, its restrictions, into which he could not fit himself except in a string of dances and *galantieren*, impeded his greatness and brought him inferior, in this respect, to Handel. The orchestral music of Bach is even provincial when it is compared with that of Handel, if we except such a masterpiece as his Concerto for two violins. Where his forms had room for their natural growth he is supreme. That is why he is to be preferred on the organ to with the orchestra. That is why, not the Forty-Eight Preludes and Fugues only, but the six French and the six English Suites, which are heavier in texture, the seven Partitas, more lengthy and important still, the Italian Concerto, the Chromatic Fantasia and Fugue are so imperishable as works of art. That is why the stray Fugues and Fughettas, the Six Little Preludes, the Twelve Little Preludes and Fugues are so individual in experience. That is why short pieces, such as the Fantasia in C minor (with an unfinished Fugue), written in Italian style and so purposely bringing in the crossed hands that it is meant, evidently, as a *pasticcio* of Domenico Scarlatti, or the little Marches and Polonaises found in the notebook of his second wife, Anna Magdalena Bach, are so perfect as small works of art.

The drums and banners of one of the little Marches in par- ticular and its turkey step are realized in so small a space that it is as simple as a folk song, and yet is the epitome of parade and pipe clay. We see the parterre of soldiers in their red coats, white leggings and high half-sugar-loaf caps, planted like flaunt-ing tulips in rows, flamed scarlet and white; and after a little maneuvering they dismiss, but for another moment the drum taps on. Bach brought as much skill and workmanship to these miniature pieces as to the greatest works of his intellect.

But upon clavichord or harpsichord Bach has one rival, Dom-enico Scarlatti. For it might be possible, after a lifetime at this music, to prefer Scarlatti. That much must be admitted. Dom-enico Scarlatti was a supreme artist and a specialist. His physical energy and vitality were given to this one task only. His intellect was not quicker than that of Bach, but it was more human, in the sense that he was more sophisticated and of the world. He had elegancies of manner that were below the contemplation of this other, with his provincial background in a small North German town. At the same time, what might have been super-ficial in Domenico Scarlatti was redeemed by his exquisite taste and sense of poetry, having been brought up, too, in music, in the strict school of his great father. Domenico Scarlatti had in him the virtues of Italy, while it is difficult to find in him an Italian fault. Bach had in him the German virtues, a humanity and genius which belong to all time and to the whole world, but the German prolixity and, on occasion only, the faults of their thick speech. At the back of him there was the shade of Veit Bach, his ancestor, who was a miller and baker, and there were the shades of the Thuringian town musicians.

But few persons are privileged to know in entirety Bach's organ music, while those who have written on it are concerned, naturally, with its technical analysis. Thus it comes about that some of the supreme works of the human intellect and imagina-tion have to depend on occasional performance and have been left unrelated, in asthetics. Even Dr. Schweitzer, who can ex-plain the musical imagery of the Cantatas, being an organist himself, seems to consider that the organ works are accessible and makes little or no attempt to group them according to their form and meaning. When removed from their purpose in a transcription, these pieces take on lesser and diverted values. Their ancient language is translated into that of the concert hall or drawing room. But of Bach, at least, there need never be an end. He has ever something new to say. His old and familiar music is reborn with a different meaning; or some tremendous work by him is heard for the first time. This could happen until the end of a long life, so that it becomes a positive benefit that so much is hidden. The organ compositions are the great works of Bach as a solo player and his only opportunity to appear in that character to a big audience, and above all to himself, for they were written, we may be sure of it, for his own pleasure.

In the result we have such works as the Passacaglia, which take their place with the most superb creations of the human spirit, with the greatest poetry in any language, and with the most sublime in painting or in architecture, but which, hardly yet, have been judged along those parallels. The Passacaglia, because it is the unique work by Bach which bears that name, is even in a favored situation for discussion. What can be done, though, if only for purposes of identity, among the three Fantasias and Fugues, five Toccatas and Fugues, six Trio-Sonatas, seven Fugues without introduction, and twenty-six Preludes and Fugues? The six Trio-Sonatas can be reserved, at least, as chamber music, for they can be played on the harpsichord or pedal piano. Of the Preludes and Fugues there are those which are early works and can be set aside; and again there are, among the rest, the eight Short Preludes and Fugues, leaving, in all, some twelve organ Preludes and Fugues to rank with the Passacaglia and the best of the Fantasias and Toccatas. This is an opus which, given the opportunity, it would not be difficult to discuss in the manner which we should wish for it. Their basic principles, not technically but in imagery and aesthetics, could be assembled and compared. We could class them according to their moods of pleading, rolling, dancing, gliding, soaring, marching, according to the architecture of their entrances and terminations, according to the mingling and intonation of their voices. There is that step which, in the words of Dr. Schweitzer, is like the treading of the grapes; and another which depicts a heavenly exultation, or indeed the footsteps of Creation, for life springs up where it has trodden. The Passacaglia would seem to consist of many poses or arrangements of a pleading figure, in which affection is touchingly portrayed, and the acceptance, also, of whatever may be coming. But the phrase or figure is in double profile, as it were, for, as well, it expresses infinite love and compassion on the part of the Creator. The same figure, with a little difference, conveys the one or other. In the form of the Passacaglia this is all clothed in springtime beauty as are the personalities in an Italian painting of the *quattrocento:* that is to say, the exquisite pathos and loveliness of the phrasing and the modulations make the wild flowers of the foreground, so that the forms are advancing through a flowering meadow and the repeats and interweavings of the shape confine the valley and carpet it with flowers. Are they the living or the dead? They have their children with them, and they are holding flowers in their hands. The form sways and dances, slowly. It is almost a Sicilienne. But the intonation is always on the pleading. And the Passacaglia is followed by a Fugue in which the authentic voice of God is heard, in linked or joined syllables, in the form of a chorale with which the strains of pleading are combined, conveying the answer of assurance. This fugal portion of the Passacaglia is inexorable, and even terrifying. It mounts to a climax, though the voices of pleading and of pity are still heard in it, and the whole passionate and gigantic structure maneuvers for its ending, throwing out buttresses, tying itself with ropes, moving bodily forward and dying away in pious wonder. No musician, besides Bach, has been able to build up these formal shapes with so full and fiery an intensity, to render them so completely the vehicle of creation. His Chaconne for solo violin is a parallel instance. Again, its close-knit form, without the returns and shackles of the Sonata, allows him to build up a drama that is nearly unbearable in poignancy and depth of feeling, and which is so miraculous in conception and so gigantic in scale, of such mortal meaning, moreover, that it is utterly incredible, and makes all other music whatever, except, perhaps, that of the passing moment, sound trivial and false. We have called attention already to the rolling figure of the organ Toccata and Fugue in F major; and we would compare the opening of another organ

Toccata and Fugue in C major, an effect which is strong and magnificent, almost beyond credibility, in its expression of masculine force, like the sudden view of some fantastic architectural frontispiece approached by processional staircases and flanked by towers, so high and old that the weeds and flowers grow from them, the western façade or El Obradoiro, as it is called, of the Cathedral of Santiago de Compostella, shall we say, seen suddenly in the sun after a shower of rain in all its ancient and quasi-Indian magnificence, to which succeeds a flowing melody that depicts the laughing valley and the loaded vines. Or again, the organ Prelude and Fugue in E flat major, another late work of the Leipzig period, which opens didactically, like a lesson in the catechism to a small boy,* until, after a bar or two, wonder and astonishment supervene at the length and breadth of the divine exposition, and it comes to its masculine conclusion and begins once more. It has completed the argument, and now gives proof as it progresses on its way. If you listen you will be convinced. Of what? That there are purpose and design. That there is benevolent intention; but that humanity must help itself. That the masculine will can bring order into the world. And the argument is repeated with overwhelming emphasis, and is indisputable, at the end. The Fugue that follows is of a primal simplicity, it would seem, until its tremendous nature becomes apparent. It is concerned with dogma, as though setting forth to give theological proof by mathematics: that is to say, it is one of the deepest, musically, of all the Fugues of Bach and at first hearing, therefore, dry and, we have said so, dogmatic in effect, until the passionate ending and the problem proved. Such is this tremendous and cataclysmic work, for it is no less than that. As serious as the paintings of Michelangelo in the Sistine Chapel, as tremendous in scope as Dante's *Purgatorio,* but devoted, as it were, to the spreading of light, to the diffusion of day, of logic, into the primal darkness.

---

* I may not be believed when I state that my clue to the meaning and import of this Prelude in E flat major was written before reading in *The Art of Bach,* by A. E. F. Dickinson (1936), that this Prelude introduces the Catechism Preludes. Nevertheless it is true, and perhaps some more of my imagery may be confirmed by such an instance of intuition on my part.

But we have kept till last what would seem to be the greatest
wonder of the whole. We intend the organ Prelude and Fugue in
E minor, again a Leipzig work. This begins, impressively, as any
organ prelude of Bach, and probably of intention, or in order to
give itself the time to climb into its dizzy height, relaxes somewhat its hold on our interest, until it has prepared its place of
advantage and is ready. This wonderful work of art has no less
than five themes that rise spontaneously, as it were, from the
structure and rhythm of the Prelude, two of them being more
important than the others, although it is true to say that all five
are not audible to the amateur at every hearing. But the visual
knowledge that they are there must add something to the enjoyment of the professional musician. The structure seems to
rise up or lift itself into the immortal air with much evident
soaring of wings, and on a series of steps or paired notes, infinitely varied but recurring continually, sometimes in a marching or a dancing rhythm, and at other times like the coupling of
a pair of pillars or columns, when, in fact, these are the props or
stays of this universe, for it is too great in scale to be mere architecture. They are more comparable, then, to the parts of some
immense engine, being certainly the means or machinery of its
propulsion. And it circles in the distance. It is climbing steadily,
and will come back.

The sensation is as though some enormous subject was bank-
ing out of the clouds above our heads. It is only to be indicated in
terms of the aeronaut; in fact, of those who gaze into the heavens.
It comes steep down from a sheer height, and like in sound to
those organ pipes of Spanish cathedrals that point out hori-
zontally over the heads of the congregation, ending sometimes in
the carved head of a Moor in his turban, as though they were the
medieval artillery or culverins, comes down with cannon blazing, and having reached the bottom of its trajectory, just over
our heads, soars up again into the empyrean. This process is
accompanied by the steps or paired notes which now are definitely the scale motifs that commentators have identified in Bach
as being associated in his mind with ideas of rejoicing. After
this climax there comes another period of preparation, an inter-

val which is filled with religious contemplation, almost as though in excuse for the unearthly excitement of what has gone before. But it comes back again. The return is more thrilling still. From a steeper height, and still more tremendous in its dive down above our heads. Once more the process is repeated. The religious interval; and then the terrific descent or entrance of the theme, which steadies now for the conclusion, and like the great white cumulus, cloudlike sails levelly away.

The Fugue begins at once, seeming by some illusion in space to come after with scarce a pause at all. Its theme is a handful of notes, indeed a scale passage for the fingers, up and down, like "Chopsticks," of little significance in itself but leading to a stupendous countersubject, the irruption of which can only be compared in simile to the descent of an angelic Michelangelesque figure with knit brows, employed upon some process of thought which has become action, a young male angel, or, more properly, the face of Creation itself, and therefore the countenance of God. This revelation comes again, and more than once; but now the Fugue sets off at a tangent, in a new direction, a thing for which it is condemned by the purists, as also because this middle portion of the Fugue continues on its way for a hundred and twenty bars, which is as long as the beginning and end of the Fugue put together. It consists in a huge treading or skirting, or a system of maneuvering for play, into which that magnificent countersubject breaks with superb utterance, while the ascending scale passages prepare its entrances. After each appearance the rhythm steadies itself a little, and a quiet or pause comes in the measure, to allow time for the mind to wonder and prepare for more. The whole of this section, allowing for those intervals, is miraculous in its energetic strength, rising to tremendous climaxes that are foreshadowed when the onward march of the entire structure is broken by the fluttering of great wings, as the force of creation, fearful but benevolent, comes down again on the Pentecostal gales. A huge agitation or churning of the air precedes each appearance, while, if we study its successive entrances, they are accomplished like a tour de force with manifest difficulty, which enhances the miracle; or it comes down triumphant, like the lightning of the storm, in a splendor and terror that take the breath away. After this tremendous passage, whatever it presages, the strict Fugue returns again, and having stated the argument, dies away in wonder, and the Fugue is ended.

The fugal subject of this terrific work has been characterized as meaning nothing in itself. It is not a tune at all, nor yet an epigram, but more accurately a rhythm merely, balanced by a trill. But it is enough; being as indefinite, for a germ of creation, as the faces and figures seen by Michelangelo on the plaster of the wall. It would not sound, even, to have particular musical possibilities. There has merely to be a beginning. No mental message is attached to it. But inspiration comes so closely after it that it could almost be that Bach, having devised the wonderful figure which follows, prefaced it on purpose with this nondescript opening, which is no more than the grinding of the engine's wheels as it begins to move. A fugal subject, just as short as this, but, for contrast, full of meaning, is that of the Fugue following on the E flat Catechism Prelude, for again this is quite obviously of purely religious significance. That is proved, if tunes mean anything at all, by its chance resemblance to the hymn tune of "O God, our help in ages past," from which circumstance it is known in England as the St. Anne Fugue. There can be no doubt, then, as to its meaning. A tune, needless to say, can be parodied or distorted. A hymn tune, for instance, can be played in waltz time; but when identity is so close as this, the meaning must be as though we had the same text in a different translation. That must be the limit of divergence. The only changed sense is in the ending, which with Bach portends not sturdy defense but abstract meditation. In the beginning the invocation is the same, that is to say. The identical God is addressed in it, but the melodic line is inward-looking and falls back on itself. As to the meaning of the phrase in music, there could be no more clear example than the organ Chorale *"Ein feste Burg."* We need not to be told that this is a setting of Luther's anthem; or that the same melody is to be heard again in the Chorale Cantata (No. 80) written by Bach for the Reformation festival of 1730, which was the bicentenary, as well, of the Augsburg confession, for the tune is Teutonic, of the century of Dürer and Lucas Cranach, as much as the "sea tunes," "Rule Britannia," or even "Hearts of Oak" are Britannic, of the age of Nelson, breathing as they do the salt airs of Trafalgar, Greenwich, Portsmouth, Plymouth or The Nore. It was Wagner who said that the national character of the English was portrayed in the opening bars of "Rule Britannia." To a like extent the German Reformation is apparent in *"Ein feste Burg."* The Chorale Cantata, with accompanying drums and trumpets, is overwhelming in grandeur of effect, with alternating chorus, strophe and antistrophe, given forth and answered by the voices, culminating in the open, foursquare rendering of the Chorale hymn in four parts.

The Cantata *Wachet auf* (No. 140), known to the English audience as *Sleepers wake,* which is another great masterpiece in the old German mode, the tune having been composed by a priest, Philip Nicolai, in 1599 after a plague in his parish, should be heard sung by the Catalan choir of Barcelona, because the nasal Spanish voices of the boys add still further to the ceaseless and imperturbable surging of the sacred rhythm. It goes on its way supported, as in some great procession that is spiritual and not physical, by the phrases of the chorale. Never, indeed, can there have been such rhythm. And the voices surge up into it in a manner that stills the blood but rubs its hands on our hearts to bring the life back. Voices cry down from the watchtower till the whole heavenly city of parable is awake. We may use our own discretion as to whether we hear in the opening, with Dr. Schweitzer, the virgins starting up from sleep to wake one another, and the preparation for the coming of the Heavenly Bridegroom; later a dance of the virgins who strew flowers before His way; or, in the end, where the Chorale is sung in plain chant, unadorned, the music of the Heavenly wedding feast. The images cannot be decided in precise terms. All that is certain is the surpassing wonder of the music.

The Easter Cantata *Christ lag in Todesbanden* (No. 4) should be heard, also, sung by the Catalan choir, for it is unforgettable in majesty, proceeding at the same slow pace of ceremony to the wonderful and solemn plainness of its end. Here again the Spanish voices, with their addition of Latinity, increase the warmth and fervency of the music so that the starched ruff and plain dress of the Lutheran pastor are not present, and we are in the Middle Ages. Particularly, we say, when it is performed by Spaniards. For it is interesting to compare with this any good rendering of the Cantata *Gottlob! nun geht das Jahr zu Ende* (No. 28), in which comes the Chorale written by Kugelmann about 1540 and known in this country as the *Old Hundredth,* phrase by phrase, verse by verse, delivered, commented on and then resumed, by strings, oboes, trombones and organ. Old German melodies by Martin Luther and his contemporaries form, of course, the basis for Bach's Chorale Preludes for organ, and supply the material for many of the great choral movements in his Cantatas. Of that incredible total of a hundred and forty-three Chorale Preludes for organ in their three different modes, plain and reflective in the style derived from Pachelbel, the decorated or coloratura in the style of Böhm, or treated in fantasia fashion in the manner of Buxtehude; of the three hundred and nineteen Chorales harmonized by Bach; and among the two hundred and eight Cantatas, and the hundred or more additional Cantatas that are lost, making three hundred, perhaps, in all; as to two thirds, it may be, of this total, Bach was working in the old German manner. Among the incunabula. For that is how we would consider it. These are the incunabula of Northern music, corresponding to the woodcut pictures of the Reformation period. But the music is greater than the draftsmen. Or is it that we only hear it through the mind of Johann Sebastian Bach?

The early German masters in music, those we mentioned together with Heinrich Schütz and Samuel Scheidt, were men of the seventeenth century, spread over three human generations, but all born after the Reformation. They invented the art form of the Chorale Preludes, but mostly did not compose the Chorale tunes. The greatest name among them, and the foremost German composer before Bach, was Heinrich Schütz (1585-1672). Closer knowledge should enable us at once to recognize the in-

fluence of Böhm or Pachelbel, of Scheidt or Schütz or Buxtehude, Reinken, or indeed of others who have been long forgotten.
Not that the Chorale Preludes of Bach are consciously archaic,
but he takes in them the current pabulum, tunes which were a
hundred or two hundred years old and known to all the population, and gives to them their Germanic setting. In this way, and
in part through his own forebears of the same name, was the
old German style of Bach invented.

Bach is computed to have written the Cantatas at the rate of
one a month for twenty or thirty years of his life. In spite of
their sacred purpose there can be no doubt that he regarded
them as music of occasion, for passing performance, and felt
no scruple in detaching portions of them or otherwise altering
and incorporating where it suited him. The Secular Cantatas,
few in number (there are only twenty-three), could on the same
principle be convertible, from Profane to Sacred. The Dresden
Court Cantata *Die Wahl des Hercules,* the giant being an
Electoral Prince who was eleven years old, had most of its music
embodied a year later in the Christmas Oratorio. Another of the
Secular Cantatas was used, as well, for the same purpose, while
a chorus from yet another Cantata was employed by Bach for
the Osanna of his Mass in B minor. But it so happens that two
of the most lovely and well known of all his melodies occur in a
Secular Cantata, afterward to become immortal in their sacred
setting. One of these, moreover, is in the pastoral style and the
other in the old German manner.

Their occasion was in the "Hunting" Cantata, *Was mir
behagt.* The year was 1716, so that it is the first and earliest of
these secular compositions. Bach went with his master, Duke
Wilhelm-Ernst of Saxe-Weimar, on a birthday visit to Duke
Christian of Saxe-Weissenfels-Querfurt, whose remote capital
lay a day's ride of thirty-five miles away, through the Thuringian
forest. A great hunt was to be held. The Duke's birthday was
February 23, when the deciduous trees would be leafless, but
the hunt will have been chiefly in the pinewoods. In the landscape, as it might be, of Dürer or Altdorfer, passing through the
magpie villages of black and white. Near Weissenfels the coun-

try becomes more hilly and, according to an old guide book, "the vine is cultivated with some success." It is this contrast that we find in these two airs, one romantic and the other pastoral. The Cantata was given, we suppose, on the birthday evening, and the musicians presumably had been brought from Weimar. Salomo Franck, of whom the name is the most poetical part, had written the libretto. The characters are Diana and Endymion, Pan and Pales. Dr. Lemprière, whom we have consulted, tells us in his *Classical Dictionary* that Pales was the goddess of sheepfolds and of pastures. Her festivals were called Palilia. The ceremony consisted in burning heaps of straw and in leaping over them. No sacrifices were offered, but the purifications were made with the smoke of horse's blood. The purification of the flocks was done with the smoke of sulphur, of the olive, the pine, the laurel and the rosemary. Offerings of mild cheese, boiled wine and cakes of millet were made to the goddess, and it was during the original festival that Romulus first began to build the town of Rome. Such was the curious occasion for these two immortal airs, for the two songs of the goddess Pales were that known, in translation, as "The sheep may safely graze," or "Flocks in pastures green abiding," and that which, twenty years later, in 1735, reappeared in the Sacred Cantata *Also hab Gott die Welt geliebt* (No. 68), from which it is familiar as "My heart ever faithful."

No description could exaggerate the beauty of this pair of melodies. When we remember their occasion it may remind us of the immortal tunes in *Figaro,* were it not that those are tainted with the theater. We have to recall again the hunting party for the prince's birthday, and the bucolic setting. At the palace of Herrenhausen, outside Hanover, in an upper room there are paintings by a Dutch or Flemish painter that depict Ernst-August the first Elector and father of our George I, with his hawks and huntsmen. They are probably the most detailed pictures of this subject that were ever done, in large cartoons that call for tapestry, and that could be illustrations for a treatise on falconry. The hawks are on the wrist, in their hoods and chains, and there is much delight to be had, besides, from the horses, the liveries of the huntsmen, their horns and equipment, and the curious portraits. It could be, with little difference, the hunt of Weissen-fels, and it should be in this spirit that we listen to "The sheep may safely graze" and its companion air "My heart ever faithful." Behind that, with only the subtle change of Sacred to Profane, there is the hunting party. The first mentioned of these tunes is broad and flowing, with all the physical healthiness of Handel, preceded by a recitative of heavenly beauty, to which the lapping rhythms of the pastoral succeed, vale on vale, among the wattle fences of Virgilian calmness and serenity, tinged, though, by the radiant clouds and rounded shades of trees, till we are reminded perforce of "Opening the Fold," "The Bright Cloud," "The Rising Moon" and the pastorals of Samuel Palmer, painted at Shoreham when he was under the influence of Blake, and the lovely melody becomes English in this association.

The other tune, which has been more familiar for many years, is more pointed and angular in its beauty. There is more in it of the German primitive. This is great music because of the world of purity and faithfulness in which it moves. By some miracle it is musically the whole expression of its text, so much so that it is spiritually a tune that could be offended against and that, in certain circumstances, we would not dare to remember or to sing to ourselves. Of no other music could this be true, except of some simple tune remembered from childhood with poignant or particular association. It is the answer given in the second half of the first phrase of "My heart ever faithful" that lays bare the humanity of this faraway but ever-youthful tune. It repeats again, and then lifting itself on what has been said and settled, carries the mood a little further, and stating it once more until we are in that landscape of long ago with the steep houses, up the stair into the many-windowed attic where the red apples lie, gives to us the little village or Thuringian town, it does not matter where; for it could be in Hungary when Veit Bach lived there as miller and baker, or in one of the Saxon towns in Transylvania. Certainly there is a winding street of steep houses that leads up a hill. This is an instance, in analysis, of the rising figure in Bach's music that Dr. Schweitzer interprets to mean the lifting of the human heart. We are in that world of musical images that he describes, and of which he was the first serious interpreter. He remarks the notes in repetition that mean spiritual crisis; the toll of funeral bells, in warning but sometimes welcomed, and even, in the Cantata *Christus der ist mein Leben* (No. 95), insisted on, in a tenor aria that calls repeatedly for the bells of death, which are imitated in the bass.

There are the sounds, as well, of knocking or hammering, like the midnight knocking at the door which awakes the porter in *Macbeth* and brings him to the gate; or less intermittent, with quicker blows, it means divine judgment; or, with a figure of wild trembling, the last dread day of all. There are the rhythms, again according to Dr. Schweitzer, of running and following. Paired notes can mean a heavy, dragging walk, while a weary, limping rhythm portrays fatigue and the approach of death. Running is closely echoed by a running figure, and following by an imitation in two or more voices. The marching rhythms can be grouped according to their different meanings—in degree of pride and confidence, exultant or in triumph. There is that measure which Dr. Schweitzer identifies as the treading of the wine press, according to an image from the Old Testament; pictures of storm, and of the calm of evening; the coiling of the serpent, portraying evil; or the silvery, captivating laughter of the angels. Paired notes, in a light and dancing rhythm, intend running water; while quick scales, ascending or descending, mean clouds or waves.

If such be the musical language of the Cantatas, first translated and described by Dr. Schweitzer, who had the curiosity also to follow it out among the Chorale Preludes by tracing and comparing the same figures as they occur in both, then there must be meaning elsewhere, when there is occasion for it. Not in the dances and *galantieren* of the French or English Suites; not in the Brandenburg Concertos; for their frame and purpose do not allow of that. But this incredible genius was the master of all styles. In this respect there is only Shakespeare to compare with him. What is the intent of the Chromatic Fantasia and Fugue? The Italian Concerto, on the other hand, has no need for any further meaning. Its late date (1735) infers, in all probability, that Bach had come across the Sonatas of Domenico Scarlatti.

Certainly it is identical in manner with the Fantasia and unfinished Fugue in C minor for harpsichord, in which the crossing
of the hands betokens the Italian influence, and which was a late
work composed in 1738. We could call them Venetian or Neapolitan according to our mood, not in the shallow effects of
Italian opera, but they are Italian by their light and shade, of
deep cornice and pediment, as though in a dramatic lighting that
never was in the little Thuringian towns. This Concerto in the
"Italian style" has an opening theme derived from Georg Muffat,
one of the many forgotten composers of whom Bach made a
study, but the answer to it is so skillful in construction and so
perfect in idiom that the work is in a category by itself. This is not
in the Italian style of Vivaldi, but of a different character altogether. Bach knew the music of Vivaldi very well indeed, to
the extent of arranging sixteen of his violin Concertos for harpsichord. But there is no evidence that he had come across more
than a stray Sonata or two by Domenico Scarlatti, and we are left
to infer that the Italian Concerto of Bach is, therefore, "Italian"
in an ideal sense, but that by intuition it approached the style and
mannerisms of Scarlatti, who was by turn Venetian, Neapolitan,
Portuguese or Spanish, according to the vicissitudes of his career;
but, in fact, in all things Mediterranean or Southern. The slow
movement of the Concerto, though beautiful in itself, is of another identity, not Italian in texture or sentiment, but the mood
returns and we come too soon to the last cadences of the sparkling,
exhilarating Italian scene. We would attach no other meaning
to it than that of light and color.

Very different in intention is the Chromatic Fantasia and
Fugue, gigantic in scale within its compass, and descending to
the very depths of feeling. We feel not that it is one of many
works by Bach, but that it is the entire creation of a great master
in itself, as though there was no need of anything further from
his hand and all he had to say is expressed in it. The Italian Concerto, by contrast, is an extra work, or something added, as when
we discover with delight some picture by a favorite painter, and
its size and importance come as a revelation of a fresh side of his
genius. One of the chief pleasures of painting is derived in this

manner, since few but the expert will keep in mind the printed measurements in books and catalogues. How often have we known this to happen: in Venetian and Toledan churches, in Italian palaces, in the picture galleries of Europe, mostly dispersed now in precaution against bombing! The Italian Concerto is the master working directly under Italian influence; but the Chromatic Fantasia and Fugue are in no Italian convention, however lightly worn. In some three or four of the wonderful Goldberg Variations we detect the Italian hand, for its late date, 1742, makes it more than ever likely that Bach had seen Sonatas by Scarlatti, or, by that alchemy of human instinct, through long reflection had approximated to the unknown truth. By these three works alone—the Goldberg Variations, the Chromatic Fantasia and Fugue, the Italian Concerto—Bach is evident in his stupendous greatness. But when we think, as well, of the Forty-Eight Preludes and Fugues, of the eighteen Suites for harpsichord, other Preludes, Fugues, Fantasias and Toccatas, realizing that this is but Bach's clavier music, and not even the main ocean of his genius, which was for choirs of voices and for organ, then it is to know in him the master of all masters, and, with Shakespeare, the greatest light of the West, dimming the Latin glitter of the Mediterranean. All other composers, compared with him, are like lesser poets of the Elizabethan age. They worked in the same medium but can but be mentioned with him. Their whole universe is music, but this is its fountain. He is past, future and recurring present. Beethoven not always, only now and then; Handel at his most superb; and Chopin, always Chopin, are all that are left beside him. And that natural music which is anonymous, the airs or folk tunes which are the emanation of the soil and that, even if their authorship be known, remain no less a mystery. The wild flower can be as beautiful and as richly scented as that to which humanity has put all its pains. In no other music but that of Bach can a portentous complexity wear a calm and smiling face. The Goldberg Variations are in proof of this, for their beauty can be appreciated in ignorance of the canons at every interval from the unison to the ninth, and twice in contrary motion, which is to say, the subject is answered by its inversion. Most perfect instance of all is the *quodlibet* that forms the thirtieth and last of the set of variations, for the four popular songs which it presents in combination at one and the same time coalesce in their fragments into a miniature that, in its robust manliness, is an epitome of the burgher tunes that it conceals. The enormous hand of Bach has, in this, descended into microscopic detail. He is the master of all proportion, as in the little Marches and Polonaises copied into the notebook of Anna Magdalena Bach. The surface melody, so to speak, of the *quodlibet* is equivalent to those. The *quodlibet* could be four of the little Marches wrought together into one.

But the mighty hand of this Ancient intones the language of the Fugue. In the words of one who heard him at the organ: "His fist was gigantic . . . his hand was never weary and lasted out through a whole day's organ playing. The comic style was just as familiar to him as the earnest." That phrase may be puzzling until we remember the Fugue subject of the organ Fantasia and Fugue in G minor; or again, the Fugue *alla gigue* in G major. "Comic" is intended in the lofty style, and in the sense that figures from the Italian comedy appear in Watteau's paintings. Those are not less serious because comedians form their subject. There can be little doubt that both theme and treatment in the two organ works that we have mentioned are in the "comic style." Not the light *badinerie* or *galantieren* for harpsichord, but in the manner of the greatest architecture, as though Vignola or Palladio had been called on for buildings in the "comic style." This is conceivable at Caprarola or Villa Lante, or in the villas of the Venetian terra firma. The comic vein of Bach was, by nature, Northern and old-fashioned, if things that are eternal need not be ephemeral and absolutely of their day. Let us think of this as Dutch or Hanseatic humor, lying from the North Sea to the Baltic and not influenced by Italian skies, but characteristic of the high-gabled buildings of the Northern Renaissance, anywhere from Brussels or Antwerp, across Germany, to Danzig or beyond. The Fantasia and Fugue in G minor, we suggest, might be called, architecturally, a work of the Netherlandish Renaissance, coincident with late Elizabethan or with James I, and therefore about a hundred years earlier than its actual time. Not medieval, nor having lost, altogether, the effects of that, but older, certainly, by a century than the date at which it was composed.

The other organ works, or a few of them at least, are too gigantic to be classified. They are only to be listened to and wondered at. Such, truly, are works of a huge fist. This is the Ancient of all time, and musical genius has no existence by the side of him. He is the only one. The others have but little meaning. Compared with his solid sculpture they are but arabesques in stucco. It is because he, only, speaks the fugal language and moves freely in it. No other can manipulate its difficulties and make sense of them. It is too old and formidable; but in his hands it is the secret language of the soul and mind. It expresses what has never been expressed again. It improves at every hearing, and it never stales. At the end of a lifetime all has not been said. There is ever something new, and so much of it that no one living can have heard it all.

His giant form emerges out of the Biblical past, quickening the shades of old polyphony. His sources are forgotten men. The Biblical Sonatas of Johann Kuhnau; the organ works of Frescobaldi; the Toccatas of Froberger and Merulo; Pachelbel, of whom the name, for an organist, is as suited as Thomas Tompion to be a clockmaker, for it suggests the syrinx and the dulcet tones of the organ; Schütz and Böhm and Buxtehude—such are his origins. They are his primitives. It happens, therefore, that the supreme genius of music springs from a forgotten soil; and, in view of his family history, an exceptional flowering or a hybrid that has never come again. Perhaps this analogy is not applied enough in explanation. But, possessed of it, many mysteries in the arts may yield their secret. We see the *Nozze di Figaro* as all comedy and music resumed in one, and even the side comments of farcical situation given the line of beauty. But there are artists like Chopin who cannot be explained at all; whom no one could prophesy unless we consider that the invention of the new instrument, the pianoforte, made it certain that he would appear.

In the case of Bach there are almost too many reasons why he should have been. He had all the past behind him. We hear that in the pleading phrases of the Passacaglia. For the rest, it is a language and an architecture for all time. But the true secret is his Christianity. It is on that assurance that his rolling phrases mount into the heavens. Such are the truths that his Fugues set out to prove. And there is more wisdom in him than in religion; more of truth and beauty than in all the prayers and aspirations. Many faiths, but only one true Ancient, of whom we hear the huge fist when the formal language of the Fugue begins.

ORPHEUS AND HIS LYRE *

II. Hurdygurdy

This is to be a musical experience without parallel. All who would listen must come with us to a town consisting of a wretched street, a mile long, unpaved and very wide. A Jewish town entirely, to judge by the inhabitants. We will give its name. It is Mohilev, in White Russia, on the far or left bank of the Dniester.

There are no roads or railways. It is 1835, and all countrymen over a certain age still think and talk of Napoleon and his pride and fall. The gentry look upon him as their savior.** The Russians recall only the barbarity of their own sufferings, and how the Cossacks slew with sword and lance and set fire to buildings where the French wounded lay. That was twenty years ago. What everyone remembers is the cold and hunger.

Meanwhile the past has slipped back again. That means, for many of those concerned, a subsistence that is little better than starvation. It is as if—and there may be comfort for us in this parallel—the tyrant, or hero, had struck a sudden and murderous blow without warning and been driven reeling back into the snows. But, in fact, it is again as it used to be. Only with burned villages, where the war has been, and many men maimed.

But come, walk into the town. It is an October evening. We have passed a row of windmills. For the wind blows here out of China and Tibet. There is nothing to prevent it. Much else besides comes out of that limitless distance. We meet great wagons driven by men in long gowns with long beards. Shall we say the snow is falling? No! The sky is the color of the cheeks of green apples.

* From *Splendours and Miseries*, 1943.

** The landowners, who were Poles, expected that Napoleon would deliver them from the Russian yoke and restore Poland.

222

The houses are one-storied and like the shacks of mining towns. But old and dilapidated when new built. Of gray wood and plaster brightened with flat paints. Each house is a shop and has its goods for sale. In some the oil lamp is already burning in the dark back room. But the peasant population cannot read or write. For their sakes there are shop signs all along the street. A great jack boot of rusty iron, a long shirt or caftan made of tin, the barber's cup for bleeding, a golden bowl or pestle for the apothecary, a gilded fish, a gilded goose, all tarnished—how they must crank and rattle upon a windy night! If you walked here under a stormy moon you might imagine these to be the creaking trumpets of the rag fair. For, in fact, there is little for sale that is not secondhand.

But it is the busiest hour. There has been rain, and the street has big puddles that reflect the sky. Nevertheless, men dash from one side to the other, ankle deep in mud, holding live chickens, but half starved, or mended garments. If a coin were dropped it would sink into the mire. No one could find it. But they are so poor they live by barter. A peasant brings a few eggs or a dried fish and, in return, takes away a cup or plate or printed handkerchief. The traders or peddlers are all dressed in black, with high boots and fur caps, but their gabardine is soiled and green with age. For the number of its houses the town is swarming with inhabitants. The children are their parents in little, dressed no differently, and the boys wear the same black curls below their ears. Some, though, are red-haired, and show the Tartar in their cheekbones. The red-bearded Jews, who are always tall and thin, are like the magician in a fairy tale. Or like the wicked uncle in the pantomime.

This enormous population is so miserable that it longs to move. Not that it has ever known a settled home. Is it the Tartar strain in them that makes them nomads, only wandering from town to town? They are swarming, like the ants. When they are ready, and when the barriers are down, they will migrate to Vienna, to Berlin, to Whitechapel, to New York. If we could see this town toward the end of the nineteenth century, a particular horror might attach in our minds to some of the Jews, red-bearded ones

among them, who, above their top boots and tattered coats, wear
a tall silk hat, tilted back above their ritual curls. It is the top hat
of the age of prosperity, of the bank and stock exchange, worn
jauntily—could we forget the fox, the showman, the wizard in
the children's story—and implying no more than that the wearer
looked forward and saw himself on Broadway or in the Mile
End Road.

No sign of that, this evening. The secret police will but herd
them toward the Austrian or Polish frontiers. And leave them
there to starve, or pick a living out of the gutter. Where were
their ancestors a hundred or two hundred years before? We do
not know. Spread everywhere from Lithuania to the Crimea.
The red ants driven before the swarming black ants, that is all.
Swarming, and then migrating, like the lemmings. Driven on by
their misery, and in the end into the emigrant ship. But not yet.
Not for another human generation. Some of these children
whom we see this evening will take their families to America.
But, until middle age, they will live on as serfs and pick up their
living secondhand.

Down to the left, beyond the houses, flows the Dniester.
Through the empty plain. This is so huge that in the distance it
is another color. Here it is like mud, desiccated, but bleaching
gray for winter. Far off, as though from every weed on its surface, it is a velvety or mossy green, rubbed thin. Deep down runs
the river, very broad and slow. I have seen it sixty miles higher,
at Hotin, which is a slum, not a town of Jews, in Roumania, on
the other or near bank of the Dniester; and at Mohilev it will be
no different. It flows quietly, for it is very deep. Suddenly the
town ends, there is a steep drop, and the river flows below.

We pass soldiers in their long gray coats wandering stupidly,
in amazement, even in Mohilev, for they are moujiks out of the
northern birch forests and have known only the wooden towns.
They are conscripts and may never get back to their homes. It
must be a market day. The peasants are spending their money.
But the black-gowned Jews outnumber them. And it is the Jews
who go hungry. The peasants are well fed. But it is as though
the whole town is too poor to afford a light. And it has grown

darker. You can catch the sunset in the pools of rain. Lamps are lighted at last, and they must be naphtha flares; here and there, when the light can shine on tin or china or cheap enamel. Where obscurity helps business, there is no light at all.

We have the feeling that we are many miles from home. It would be a nightmare to have to sleep here on a filthy floor, and we are to imagine that we shall return, before it is too late, to a small manor or country house a few miles away where we shall sup on beetroot soup, thick with cream, on partridges from the October woods, and the sharp berries of the season, and afterward, round the wood stove, listen to music and talk of our extraordinary experience. We do not live here, but are foreigners, traveling perhaps to Kiev or the new city of Odessa, handed on from country house to country house in the manner of that day; journeying like Lamartine, who had the same adventure as ourselves, and described it. Perhaps the confidence of that safe comfort at the end of the day helps us to exaggerate the squalor of the scene. Were we forced to spend the night in it, we must shut our eyes to the shades and undertones of this remote and miserable slum.

Was anyone happy or contented? We see characters who could be Jewish comedians, and many others from the Yiddish theater where, it could be said, genius is often hidden under grease paint. Here and now, in embryo, for their opportunity has not dawned. Remember, this is a hundred years ago! Probably, in any such community of black-gowned men, there must be those who can mimic, or create character. For they never come out of it into the fields. It is as far as they go if they are seen at the edge of the beet fields, bargaining, where the black raven hops. Where the magpie flies off. They are never to be seen digging, harvesting, nor herding. You will see a black-gowned man riding on a peasant's wagon, and it means that he has possession of the peasant's holding. They are, eternally, the middlemen. They buy up the eggs; they do not set the hens. A Jewish child is never goosegirl. Rather, they are the sparrows, the mice, the rodents of the town. In big cities they congregate in dark cellars where mushrooms might grow. They do not spend money on the exterior of their houses. For, in fact, in this town they are so miserably poor they have nothing to spend at all.

The children of the Jews are curiously birdlike in their similarity. Palely precocious, and at the age when their features alter, it is to be felt of them that they are only growing into the plumage and physiognomy that is natural to them. The lamb turns into the sheep, or the squab with its huge beak and scraggy neck becomes the painted pigeon. But in their early youth it is as though they might turn into something different. And so it is with the ringleted children of the Jews.

Mohilev is a town in which to search for musical or dramatic talent. A town of many towns, for their frontier extends from Wilno to the Golden Chersonese. It is enough if, in one place, there should be an Anton Rubinstein, a Menuhin. Yet how could there be a chance of that? At this moment they are imprisoned in the ghettos. They are fermenting, seething, boiling in their slums. For where this race dwells, there are always slums. There are never the carved and painted wooden houses of the peasants. Those rustic houses are like wooden boxes. Their eaves are carved with the fret saw and then painted. The peasants walk like peacocks in their embroidery. Could we see a village on a wedding day, the headdresses of the young girls would be like the crowns of princesses in a fairy story. Their *kakochniks* or bridal crowns are in a hundred patterns according to locality; a northern Orient in which the women go unveiled. But the Jews, by comparison, never beautify their houses nor their persons. They are nomads of the unpaved streets. Of the back rooms. And, in big towns, of the basements. As middlemen and sellers of secondhand clothing their trade is drabness. Their racial instinct is the quick return. They move from one town to another town, but it becomes the same. Yet it is impossible not to pity them. Deep in themselves they are discontented, dreaming of New York or Johannesburg, of Broadway or the Rand. As yet unheard of, but they feel that in their bones.

But Mohilev, or Hotin, a hundred years ago! The carriage wheels sink up to their axles in the mud and filth. It could not properly be described as mud. For mud is formed from soil or

humus. It should have clay or chalk in it. But this is the dust
made liquid and coagulated. The accumulation, down the years,
of animal and vegetable detritus. Gray with poverty, and swollen
with cabbage stalks, with garbage, and the nameless refuse of the
drains and sewers. Which, in Mohilev, are the gutters and the
whole width of the slimy, pullulating street that seems to flow
with mucus, with expectoration. There is the knowledge here
which it is impossible to suppress in our minds, that their food is
slaughtered in another way. It is the sign of their religion. Perhaps the Kosher slaughterhouse may be more merciful than the
poleax of the peasant, but we think of the Jews, in imagination,
sitting down to milk-white veal, bled white and pale, according to
their ritual. There are tanneries in Mohilev, and we smell the
hides and skins. But the carriage step is put down and we must
walk across that open sewer. For a little time it is impossible to
look up, until we are so muddied that it does not matter. Then
the swarming misery takes possession. And we hear the shop
signs swinging in the wind. Idly, idly, like men hung in irons
upon the gallows tree.

What can be the average of life in Mohilev? Many children
and little babes must die. There are many old men, who have
flourished like the weeds. In stony places. Or rather, in between
the stones. Except that here are no stones. The shacks are built
of wood and plaster. But there are fungi that grow on old bits of
wood, and there is the mildew that spreads on the plaster. How
else could they live? They have crept in between the bricks.
They have sprouted in the crevices. They crawl forth into the
gray light of Mohilev, and go back again.

For all its vitality this town is inanimate and imprisoned in
the past. The Jews are so orthodox and conservative. Tonight,
as we see them, it is a medieval ghetto. The barriers are still up.
The world is not yet open. There are no hospitals. What happens to the sick and ill? For an answer, come into the crowded
cemeteries. Count the Jewish headstones. There are many here,
with more room space than they had in life. They lie at last in
their own beds, and have not to seek their living. In the distance
there are the golden domes of the Russian churches. Not in

Mohilev, but in the villages on the plain. This flowerless mud is neighbor to the orchard and the grove of birch trees. The priest and the rabbi pass by on the street. The one is an ignorant and drunken peasant; the other, bred for generations in the slums. But his roots are in the earth; while the Jewish rabbi is like the weed on the wall. His community are of their own planting, without invitations, and can be uprooted. But, like the weeds, they seed themselves anew. They spring up in waste places, and choke the sunflowers near the peasants' cabins.

Nor weed nor sunflower has any color, here and now. It is autumn, and the sunflower rattles its dead leaves. The plant is withered to an iron skeleton; an iron standard which has been hit and twisted, scorched even, and the tin head droops, for it is like a head of painted tin until you touch it. Here and there the heads have fallen, burned out by their own flames in the summer. The yellow corolla has gone black. By that curious alteration in dead things, if you pick up a dead sunflower it is flat and heavy, a wadded or stuffed disk, that is all, and then the seeds drop from their cells and we have that analogy which we noticed in another place with the dead flies of the window casement, with the smoked-out wasps' nest, or, in our time, with the radiator of the wrecked motorcar, or the shattered airplane of modern wars. So much for the dead sunflowers of the backyard. They are the roses of the Ukrainian gardens.

A child comes by holding a bunch of weeds, like groundsel. Probably he has a linnet in a little cage. Another may feed a crust of rye bread to a whiskered mouse. Children's games go on. But the mud is too thick to trundle a hoop or spin a top. They have to be games of guessing, or little riddles. You would not find the wooden hobbyhorse. But the children are starlings if their elders are the crows. They gather, we mean, in the branches of a tree. You hear a hundred voices chirping all together. Or so it seems. They are collected together at the corner of the street. And they dart off with a movement of a hundred pairs of wings, and dipping all together, cut another angle and are gone. They are round the corner, out of sight, or but a few steps in front of us; and then are gone again. So it is in autumn fields, and in the hedges. Soon they will be gone altogether, to another clime.

But it is a hundred years ago. The old evening darkens. Down toward the sunset it fades like a sheet of red-hot metal. Tighter, tighter, into darkness, like the turnings of a screw. That is how it fades. We will not have it that it is quite dark. The huge plain is so empty that the dark will come up, all at once. The wind, blowing toward the sunset in the west, comes from unknown lands in the utter distance. Here are no safe woods and covers. It is because of this such cruel things have happened in their history. We have not had the Tartars on the plains, or the winds out of the north and east. From the tundra, where mammoths are found in the cold cliffs of the river. Or listen to it! Blowing from all imaginable Orients, in semitones and quarter tones beaten with the palm of the hand upon the sheepskin drum.

Could it be music that we hear? Ah! It must be ancient music of the dulcimer, and a thrilling and strange excitement seizes us because of the sunset and the fever in the air. It is not the mouth organ, nor the street violin. There could not be pavement music in this far-off town, so long ago. Yet they must be street musicians. It sounds like a little band of instruments that accompany peculiar and special tones. Ah! It is nothing. Do not listen so intently! But we have known a hurdygurdy to bring magic into a London slum. We cannot help but listen who are the slaves of music. This does not turn and grind. It is not music of the handle. It is not mechanical. What can it be? For it begins again. Now harsh and vibrant, and then melting. That is the mystery of music, for this is of the sort that suddenly intoxicates. It steals upon the senses. It does not work immediately and at once, though that can happen, but not here and now. For we heard it in the distance. We must come nearer in order to be entranced. To the next street corner, hurrying, reluctant, for the dread of disappointment. But it begins to assert itself. Oh! Stop still and listen. It is a peculiar instrument we have never heard before, or not played in this manner. For those are the hands of genius. There is no faltering. The notes break or impact in their peculiar way because it is an instrument, half harmonica, half

dulcimer, akin to the cymbalom, and its special qualities are de-
scribed in the word *claquebois*. Listen! Listen! The like of it
will be heard no more. For this is the transcendental player.
Probably the greatest untaught musician there has ever been.
Upon an ancient, rough instrument of which he is the virtuoso.
He is, in fact, playing in the street.

What we see is a bearded man in a long black caftan, seated at
his instrument in the middle of a crowd. His fox-skin cap is on
the ground. Behind him four men, much alike, as though they
are his brothers or near relations, hold their violins and basses
ready. When we come up he is sitting with half-closed eyes, waiting for inspiration. Then he looks down at his dulcimer, and
tests it by preluding upon the strings. During the course of this
we feel that he has seen us. He draws us, by that, into the orbit
of his hypnotism, although it was not a direct glance, but he has
taken notice of the strangers, and allows time for the drug to
work. A moment, also, for us to stare at the extraordinary appearance of this man of genius. He lifts his head and gazes into
the air again; then with a sudden movement raises both arms, and
looking down at the dulcimer, brings down both hands in unison,
and strikes with the pair of hammers together. The four musicians take their cue from him, and follow.*

This Jewish musician is Michael Joseph Gusikov, but, before
we remove him into a room (his own bedroom), a concert hall,
an opera house, or to anywhere else that we should like to hear
him, and attempt to explain his untutored genius and the extraordinary effect it had on his listeners, we should look at him again.
He wore, always, the clothes of the wandering Jewish musician
of his land. Because he was that, by profession. The fact of the
many distinguished persons he had met made no difference to
him. He wore the beard of the Russian Jew, looked poor and,
indeed, was very poor. He has the sunken cheeks and high cheekbones of the Slav, and is very pale. In fact, he is dying of
consumption.

* Bihary or Czermak were alternative in my mind to Gusikov for this study of
illiterate or instinctive music. But the material and background of the Hungarian
Tzigane are well known by now; and also, even from the meager accounts that
are left of him, it will be apparent that the Russian Jew was the greater player.
Probably, indeed, the most wonderful genius of his kind there has ever been.

This is his history. He was born at Sklot, a little town near Mohilev, where his family had been musicians for upward of a hundred years. His father played the cymbalom, or dulcimer, an instrument with cords of metal which were struck with a pair of hammers, and which was in use among the Jews of Russia and Poland. At the age of seventeen he was married, according to Jewish custom. He could not read a note of music, but learned several instruments, and played at weddings and village dances, and made occasional short journeys to Moscow. Soon after he was twenty years old he could play the flute, his chief instrument, no more because of his consumption, which gave him fearful fits of coughing and made it painful for him to draw in his breath. This disaster plunged his family into misery and starvation.

But in this mortal predicament Gusikov, who was formed by nature to be a great musician, set to work to make a musical career possible for himself. For this purpose he chose a musical instrument of the street or village fair, and resolved to introduce such improvements into its tone and range as would make it capable of the most subtle shades of execution and interpretation. This instrument, called *Jerova I Salomo* by the Jewish peoples, was of most ancient origin and may have come from classical China and India and their schools of music, but the use of it had spread in medieval times among the Tartars, the Cossacks, the Russians, the Lithuanians, and as far as Poland. It was formed somewhat after the manner of a marimba, out of a number of slats or strips of pine wood on a bed of straws, struck, we would imagine, as though it were a clavichord, but capable of a deeper and louder tone than that because it was a bigger instrument and, in any case, played with a pair of hammers like a cymbalom. Originally this instrument was tuned upon the major or Chinese scale.

Gusikov increased the number of the strips of pine wood to two and a half octaves, disposed chromatically, not in the order, alternatively, of semitones, but arranged in a particular way in order to facilitate his execution. He contrived to isolate the vibrations of the wooden notes and make them more powerful in tone. Three years were spent by Gusikov, from 1831, in perfecting his instrument. But at length his preparations were complete,

and in July 1834 he set forth with his four brothers or relatives to
Kiev and to Odessa, where he performed in the opera house and
was heard by the violinist Lipinski, who has left an account of
him. At this time he was heard also by Lamartine, who was
traveling through Southern Russia. It was due in large part to
the encouragement of Lipinski that Gusikov undertook his journey to Western Europe, appearing with wild success in Vienna,
in Milan, in Germany, in Paris and in Brussels, where his health
completely broke down and it was evident that he was dying.
And he died at Aix-la-Chapelle in 1837, at thirty years of age,
when about to start upon his journey home.

The repertoire of this transcendental player consisted entirely
of Russian, Polish and Jewish popular melodies and folk tunes.
Further accounts of his genius are given by Mendelssohn, who
heard him play in Germany; and by Fétis, the musical biogra-
pher, who made friends with him, saw him continually during
the four months that he was ill in bed in Brussels and dying, and
took down from him, personally, the facts and details of his life.
Fétis gives a warning that his description of Gusikov, short
though it be, is genuine and authentic, and will be found different in some respects from others. He must be referring to the
Biographie Universelle of Michaud, which claims personal knowledge of Gusikov but gives a ridiculous account of him, and is responsible for the sensational story according to which Gusikov
died in the concert room at Aix-la-Chapelle, on the platform, in
the act of finishing his recital. He claims, also, that Gusikov
could read music, that he was well known in Italy as a virtuoso,
and that a concerto written by him for clarionet was given with
great success in the San Carlo Theater at Naples. The truth is
that Gusikov was entirely obscure and had never performed outside his native Russia until he came to Western Europe a year or
two before he died. In the end, Michaud describes the instrument of his invention, or perfection, as being of the nature of a
harmonica or xylophone. Michaud, it is evident, was unmusical
and insensitive. It is better to trust to the musician Fétis, to
Lipinski, to Mendelssohn, to Lamartine. All these are agreed on
his genius. According to them, Gusikov was of the sort that appears once, and for ever, and is gone.

We are in the presence of probably the greatest untaught or impromptu musician there has ever been. But, in fact, this description is not accurate. For he was a musician by heredity; while no one who could play on his variety of instruments, and could devote three years of his life to the perfecting of so special and subtle an instrument as that on which he made his fame, could be called unskilled. Gusikov was a musician in the medieval or Oriental meaning of the word. He could not read music, and it was not necessary. Indeed, it was not written down. The music he played was composed by instinct and instilled by ear. It would never be charged against the poets of the sagas, of the old epics or the ballads, that they could not read or write. It was their particular poetry, and it even gained because of its special conditions or restrictions. The poems lost nothing in beauty or subtlety because they had to be got by ear. In the same way, folk music, epical or lyrical, in its hundred sorts, loses nothing because it has not the sophistication of print and paper. Rather the opposite. It loses when it is written down. Many of its nuances may be impossible to transcribe; while performance from the printed copy, in the concert hall or music room, must lack the fire and vitality of the original. Street music, if divinely inspired, or the music of the fair—indeed, all popular music when it bears the marks of genius—spoils and tarnishes at the hands of those who have been trained in schools.

Circumstances of race and environment brought it about that the airs played by Gusikov were music of the street, more than of the mountains or the plain. Hurdygurdy tunes, coming out of nowhere, such as would be heard in little towns, together with the grand or epical embodiments of nationality, for this is one of the regions of the world where folk music is part of the history of the land. The focus for these tunes was the fair of Nijni-Novgorod, six hundred miles to the east, on the Volga. Most of them anonymous, of unknown origin. But Gusikov will have brought back with him, too, the popular airs of Moscow. He will have gone to hear the Gypsies who made their living by singing and dancing in the *guingettes* and *cafés-chantants* of the suburbs, and who sang both in their own language and in Russian. He will play the germs, or first ideas, of many tunes we know, together with airs of Tartar or even Mongol origin. Polish and Jewish tunes from the fairs of Poland and Lithuania. Some, also, which approach the Hungarian, and could be mistaken for Hungarian airs. The true historical analogy of Gusikov is, of course, to the bards or rhapsodists of Russia in the Middle Ages, and he represents a survival of this into modern times, but in conditions made exceptional by his peculiar genius, by his special instrument, and by the flowering of his talent due to the consumption that killed him young.

But enough of this.

We watch him putting his instrument together, in public, before his audience. He does this in order to show how simple are the means from which he draws such great effects. In the same way a magician demonstrates how much he can do with nothing. For his instrument is only a dulcimer of wooden slats or notes lying on ropes of straw. But they are strung or balanced with the extreme of care, almost as though the instrument is made anew each time he plays on it.

His black caftan is like a primitive form of the frock coat of the virtuoso. It accentuates his thinness. We notice the pallor of his face, and the habitual cast of melancholy on his features. He never smiles. We wonder, having heard him in the distance, and by rumor, what the character of his music will be. For his face is utterly impassive. And, according to the nature of the airs he plays, we shall hear him in the street at Mohilev, or in the humble bedroom where he died.

Now he begins to tune the notes and strike them with his fingers, listening in rapt attention, and then again, as though disdainful or indifferent. Those are moods of creation. He takes up the hammers, and now he plays a prelude, but only to test his instrument. It is a sip or taste of the intoxicating liquor. There comes another preluding, this time for display of speed and power, a sweep of all the notes at full force, dying away pianissimo, so that the whole of his magical world lies open in its strangeness from end to end, as it were, from masculine to feminine, in tones that we have never heard before, deep and angry, but fading into enchantment among the strands of straw.

But he breaks off suddenly, and lifts both hammers into the air. It is the beginning. He brings down his hands together and strikes with both hammers, this time in a tremendous shake or rattle. It is the typical opening with the cymbalom, a sort of throbbing or quivering like the swaying of the python, a shivering from head to foot, even as when the priestess of the oracle, who has bathed her body and her hair in the waters of the Castalian fountain, shakes the sacred laurel tree and eats the leaves with which she crowns herself. In fact, it is to give a moment for the narcotic to get to work, and it is succeeded by a pause which is indescribable in excitement while he waits again, with uplifted hands, and then begins, softly, to play one of the tunes of the Balagani.

A little, early, hurdygurdy waltz.

They are the tunes belonging to the painted wooden booths that were set up, on public holidays and festivals, for the performance of strolling players. The booths used to spring up in a night in the square of the Admiralty, at St. Petersburg, for the Mid-Lent Fair. During the rest of the year the actors toured the country. There were Balagani, too, in Moscow. And they came to every small provincial town. But the fascination of the Balagani consisted in the prodigious talent of its performers. There were Italian and French dancers who were in actual descent from the *Commedia dell' Arte;* and families, like the forebears of the Legat brothers, who were to become famous in the Russian ballet. But the French or Italian genius had become acclimatized. We can trace its origins only in the skill with which the wooden booths are painted, and in some of the characters of the pantomime. Also, in the music. For that is in the Russian idiom, but now and then, as in this little waltz, taking on a foreign form. It is, indeed, not far removed from the simple waltzes or *ländler* of Haydn, such a tune as sometimes forms the trio in the minuet of a symphony, but composed on this occasion for a musical clock, shall we say, and taken from that, or the mechanical organ, to the Russian fairground. Then born anew, and become the waltz of the Balagani, on the hurdygurdy.

Shrill notes are mingled with it, as when the ballerina dances while she plays a bugle. It is not so much that the tune is mechanical as that it is a primitive waltz, in wooden or archaic form, turning, turning, within a little space. Written where, and by whom? No one knows where they make the hurdygurdies. But it has been altered a little in order to fit it to that wooden box upon a stick, and the changed notes have given it the Russian nationality and idiom. Is it our imagination? Can it be but the creaking music of the hurdygurdy that is identical in every slum? How appropriate on the *straufiedel* or cymbalom! Listen! Listen! It is the Balagani in every wooden bone. It plays in slums and below the painted palaces. Young persons walk here with their governesses, and carriages come by, painted green, with outriders and postillions in scarlet cloaks. They halt for a few moments, and drive on. But chiefly this waltz is an interior drama, within the wooden walls. Open, in front. Taken down, and put up again, on all the fairgrounds. And it ends as abruptly as it began.

But the musician has not changed his mood. With no longer pause than for another tune to come, he gives us one of the gods of comedy, descended to the muddy street, among the litter of the crowd. Standing on the boards, outside the frame, in the light of afternoon. For a moment only, and then he leaps onto the stage. But we see him by the wooden arch which imitates the colonnade. He has altered much from Bologna or Bergamo. For he is neither Pierrot, quite, nor Harlequin. He has the flaxen, peasant hair, the linen shirt of the moujik, the linen trousers and the Russian boots. Perhaps you would know he was a personage of comedy only from his collar, which is like a ruff, and from his wig, and painted cheeks. But none of the characters drink wine from a straw *fiasco*. They drink raw spirit. Their simulated drunkenness is more heavy and animal. Such is their metamorphosis amid the white lights of the North. We know that in the music. We can hear it.

And, preluding softly, he plays a tune that is entirely Russian in accent: a popular song. This he might play, in bed and ill, with his instrument on his knees, as Fétis heard him in his room in Brussels. For it requires no execution, but the expression lies in its poignant phrases. Nonetheless, we are in Mohilev in the open street.

Ah! This is different and nearer to the bone. Those others had wooden bones. But this is flesh and bone; or, at least, it bleeds. How can it be that this bare simplicity has such effect? For it is the bare bones of music. You can listen, and wonder how the heart beats in it. If he plays it once, or twice, or three times, it may resolve itself into mere notes at first or second hearing. That is the mystery of music. It may be the guile of the virtuoso to allow it to be bloodless once, and let it drop, lifeless and uninhabited, into your hands. Or it can be your own fault. But it returns. And this time it may miss another of the listeners and be dead and lifeless to his ears. Such are the cold hours of music. The chill dawn. This is when he strikes to light a fire. But it catches. The sparks begin to kindle. The next time the blood begins to flow. We get the sacred tingling of the skin. The god comes down to earth and there is magic in the air. In the streets of Mohilev. No one moves. It is impossible to stir or speak. It is too strong and overpowering, even in its weakness and simplicity. And what is it? Ah! No one can tell. There must be something animal in us that is entranced by music. A dumb nature, of which this is the word.

But he puts down the pair of hammers. These are but preludes to test the instrument.

For a few moments he tunes the notes, while two of his band of musicians kneel beside him, and without a word from him repair the slats of wood and tighten them in order that they should take the greater strain that he will put on them. It is even necessary that he should begin softly, but his months and years of practice while he made the instrument and perfected it have taught him how to strengthen his tone. At first it is no louder than a virginal or glass harmonica, partaking of both natures, if that be possible, and intended, therefore, for effects of infinite subtlety and concentration, like the music of a world in little, all things in proportion, so that a street song is the whole of ragged poverty in the motes of dust that glitter, and the entire theater and its actors are in a wooden booth that is no bigger than the hurdygurdy. You hold the stick in one hand, and turn the handle with the other. And thus you move with slow steps along the slums.

But we are to hear his instrument, like the cymbalom, lead the other instruments. It is tuned now, and on its mettle. Even the notes that he touches with his finger have the heroic twang. It is the dulcimer of Asia, no more in little, the music of the Balagani. No more the hurdygurdy. We are to hear tunes that have come at a horse's pace across the plains. From both the sunrise and the sunset. Part of the thrill of excitement is the pause and the anticipation, and he knows, cunningly, how to play on this. By making another adjustment at the last moment, when all was ready for him to pick up the pair of hammers and begin. Almost as though he wants a little time in which to mesmerize his audience. There are virtuosi of the concert platform who achieve this by looking round among their auditors. It was said of Liszt, by one who heard him: "He knows well the influence he has on people for he always fixed his eye on some one of us when he plays, and I believe he tries to wring our hearts. . . . He subdues the people to him by the very way he walks on to the stage." But the musician whom we see before us now hypnotizes by being impassive and expressionless. He has long hair and a long black robe, and looks straight down in front of him. In fact, the pause is for his personality to impress itself. This strange being, nurtured in poverty and misery, and belonging in dress and appearance to the ghettos of the Middle Ages, who played at dances and village weddings, is the genius of untaught and instinctive music. He attacks the heart and blood more than the brain. He entrances, and then intoxicates.

The moment has come.

He lifts the pair of hammers so that we see his wide sleeves tied at the wrists, pauses, to get the time, and strikes the bass notes, which roll like kettledrums. It is another instrument altogether. The loud and resonant dulcimer, rattling, rolling, in announcement. For this is how the cymbalom begins, imposing silence.

But his hammers run right up the instrument and, dividing, perform another shake, in bass and treble, both together, and still louder; and then, in short runs or rhapsodic openings, drumming fortissimo, with full force of both hammers, up and down the whole gamut of the notes, display the two and a half octaves, from end to end. Then, joining together, with both hammers on the middle notes of the keyboard, he gives a last great shake or rattle to the cymbalom, and the prelude ends with single, struck notes, in both directions, that give forth the masculine physique, the male architecture of the dance.

Now it comes. In a short stabbing phrase, slow and solemn, rattling from end to end, with another shake, and another phrase that bows low, as in the genuflection of the dance, quickening, ever so little, then slowing down to the formal conclusion. The other instruments come in. It is the Ukrainian tune "The Stork";* and now, softly and swiftly, the dance begins, as though with every kind of step worked into it, in endless variation, with fresh entrances, ever quicker, quicker, gathering as it goes. This he does with but half the force of the dulcimer, for the point is speed and nimbleness. But the major opening returns. We listen, unwilling to move or stir, to this most intoxicating of dances there has ever been. And the tune comes back, turning upon itself, faster, faster, and dies away, in magic, into the body of the dulcimer.

With only the interval of a moment, as though the dazzling effects of his preluding were necessary no more, he begins to play an air of different character. He contrives that his instrument should imitate the plucked string of the gusla. He gives us the music of the *Kalieki* and *Kasiteli,* street singers, beggars mostly, and those who sing in chorus on the pilgrimages. It is an archaic music, grand and primitive, like the sweeping of many harps. Dating from an age when music was near to plain chant. Religious in tone, but with the nip of strong drink in it. This is music of the great rivers and the plain: Dniester, Dnieper, Don and Volga; but the next tune comes from the birch forests, because it is less assured and more credulous. The horizon is hidden by the trees; but the tune is fanatical in meaning. Probably a hymn of the Raskolniki, or Old Believers; even of those

* This Ukrainian dance, "The Stork," was used by Tchaikovsky for the finale of his Second Symphony. It is among the most thrilling movements in all music, but of course altered or adapted by the composer from its original form.

who have been driven from their homes to the Arctic shores and call themselves Pomortsi, or dwellers by the sea. For there are Old Believers in this part of Russia, too, not far from Mohilev, and their religious choruses are characteristic of them.

Next, we have a curious Chassidic tune, one of the ecstasies of the Chassidim. This is a sensual poem, of many thrusting ornaments and regurgitations, but in the Babylonian mode it might be, so obscure and ancient is its form. Passionate, though, and ecstatic; more physical or, indeed, sexual than any other music, for it translates so easily into symbolism, and the flowers are ugly. Thus, Rabbi Israel Ba'al Schem, in his white robe, walked with his humble disciples in the Tatra hills, and it was the first time that the Jewish nation had invoked the trees and fields. After this, a wailing lamentation; then the blowing of the shophar, or ram's-horn trumpet; and he plays a Hebrew melody which could be of any place or time.

The secret of these extraordinary performances of natural music must be, in part, because the dulcimer is an unaccustomed instrument to our ears. This music would be prosaic on the piano or violin. But it has been necessary to create for it a vehicle which is capable of the highest degree of virtuosity. This is no simple dulcimer; the secret of it died with Gusikov. It is, of course, remarkable that a dying man should be possessed physically of such powers of execution. The reason is that nervous energy need not fail until the end. Perhaps, also, where it is an instance of tuberculosis, the very nature of that disease makes it that the powers or faculties of display are retained by the dying man, till long after they are any good to him. Certainly his feverish or febrile health affects his genius. We should never hear another performance that is like this. A healthy man, it may be, would not be capable of these superb strengths and subhuman subtleties. The gradations of tone are exaggerated to the point of being drugged. It is when a musician of genius throws the whole of his nervous and physical life into his music that such effects are possible. We shall see how quickly he can intoxicate; and, in another moment, make us weep.

But he is, again, the musician of the rustic dance and village

wedding. What can be the history of these melodies? Are they
composed by any one person; or do they take shape, imperceptibly, as they travel, and are they the work of many hands?
For the same tune alters as it goes. It can be found in different
villages in another version. It can be like the same story with
a different ending. This changes its meaning. But the lesson
of that has not been lost upon the virtuoso.

Looking up, for a moment, from his instrument, he begins a
simple, poignant tune. It is compact and square, and whatever
that may be, it has but that one meaning, which is as personal
as though it were a portrait. Nothing else could be intended.
But it is a peasant portrait; like an image upon a wooden panel.
It is full face, and looks straight out before it, with flat shoulders,
and arms straight down at its sides. Only in the first few bars.
Then we hear in it the red fire of a primitive sunset on black
earth. We see cabins or shelters of fresh boughs, where the
crowds eat or drink at the huge horse fair in the plain, while the
music turns into the discordant music that they listen to. Black
lambskin caps and shaggy sheepskin coats are worn. We are
looking for a race of strangers in the crowd. We shall know
them by their springing, limbered step. Here is one! He has the
insolent and peacock tread. Wearing a travesty of a beggar's
rags, with bared chest and brass-studded belt, long hair to his
shoulders, and mesmeric gaze. He has companions in the crowd,
but they keep away from him on purpose. For their trade is
cheating. The music has turned into a Ciganje tune. And it
ends with a run or glissando on the dulcimer, played, without
the hammer, by the fingers of one hand.

But he plays the same tune again, and it is entirely different.
Now, wholly in Ciganje rhythm. With wild runs and ornaments
hidden, before, in the body or fabric of that sheep-clad tune.
Without the addition of a note, but changing the time and altering the meaning. Fire, or sparks, are in its footsteps. Impossible
to let it bear images, for there is such entrancement in its time
and measure that the tune hypnotizes in itself, and has no suggestion but its own peculiar tread. The runs or shakes are like
flourishes. That plain tune is in another language, a secret

tongue of chicanery or subterfuge. With one finger of the right hand he runs from end to end of the keyboard, as though, for this sacred trance, he would tear the cymbalom to pieces. Loud and shrill, like the run of the Panpipes which are equivalent to bird whistlings or interjections played by the Danubian shepherds where the river becomes a swamp of huge willow trees, down by the delta, and storks and cranes and pelicans are seen. It must be in imitation of the Pandean pipes, which he may have heard once or twice and no more.* But now the glissandos sound soft and smooth for the expiring of the tune, and it dies into the great plain as the mists come up.

But we are to hear music of another order. Tunes, or their prototypes, that will be sung in another generation in the night cafés and restaurants of Moscow. Under the gaslit chandeliers of the Novo-Troitski Traktir or the Moskovski Traktir, where the Gypsy women singers of Moscow danced and sang. Not in hovels, but in all the luxury of gilded mirrors and plush sofas, among the barbaric wonders of Russian cooking, sparkling Crimean wines, and champagnes from the Don. Tunes to which we would listen all night through, and never tire. Not so monotonous as the Hungarian Gypsy music, which is too formal in its beginnings. Many accounts have been left of these famous Gypsy women singers. They sang both in Russian and in their own language, and there were among them artists who have never been equaled. No one could pass any length of time in Moscow without being seduced by these melodies, and carrying away the memory of them. The audience, consisting chiefly of rich merchants, was quite different from that of the capital, St. Peterburg. They called for the same tunes, over and over again, which they remembered all their lives. Melodies that evoke no imagery and, in fact, mean nothing else but the drug which is in their sentiment and rhythm. But this is, indeed, a craving which must be satisfied.

The long opening notes of the tune are repeated, two or three times over, like the casting of a net, which is thrown again and again so that nothing can escape it. Also, the musicians must

* Compare Fanica Luca, the Roumanian player on the Panpipes.

mesmerize themselves. They have to feel it working in them.
It quickens. The violins begin their wild leapings, and the abrupt
changes of key which are the means by which they work on the
nerves and gain their hold upon them. By now we can understand that old legend of the Orient according to which the rules
of music were formed in order to tame the wild animals, and to
bring harmony into the world. For it snares the senses. It is the
formula of the drug that it must be repeated again and again
monotonously. The *primás* or first violin ornaments the melody,
and then plays it, in variation, against the cymbalom, while the
spell works in himself, in the other musicians, and in the audience. Then it seizes him, and he leads the orchestra, playing
at furious speed in counterpoint against them.

So it is among the Magyars, but here in Moscow the fabric
of their orchestra is the balalaika, led by the cymbalom. We have
the slow melody again, again; then the chorus comes, and the
Gypsy choir begins to sing. After which a famous singer, one or
other, takes up the song. The night music spreads contagion.
Were you to walk into the crowded hall of the Moskovski Traktir, shaking the snow off your coat, or go up into one of the private rooms above, you would find half-drunken men and women
laughing, and others sitting weeping. On summer evenings it
is the same, in the cabarets outside the city.

Here and now, we hear these tunes on the dulcimer, and can
predict the future for them. But they are played in primitive or
embryonic form, not vulgarized. It is impossible they should die.
By some magical alchemy, they are crowd emanations or im-
personations. By the rule of numbers they must always have
existed as melodies, and can never have been written down. In
the sense that they were complete already, and only needed to
be gathered like the mushrooms in the field. We have said that
they are exhalations or interpretations of a mood; but, in fact,
they can create the mood. That must be why some tune comes
into the head for no reason when we are thinking of nothing in
particular. But, as regards the composition of these melodies,
they do not always visit the brains of those who are prolific of
such things. Did we know the true history we would find that

they come, impartially, to rustic musicians who have been visited before, and to those whom the god inhabits, this once, and never again. It is quite arbitrary. There are empty shells that murmur continually, and that bear his echo in them; and those may be persons who cannot read or write and are, in all else, of a low intelligence. Others may have a knowledge and an instinct surpassing that of most musicians. For fire and inspiration, when they play, there is nothing to be compared to them. This must be because it is still a wonder and a sacred mystery, beyond logic and beyond explanation.

The process is sensual and physical, and nothing else. We have to submit to it as the hooded serpent to his charmer. We have seen that one of the secrets is repetition or reiteration, and that it must begin slowly and gently, as though to rock or lull the senses. The ornament or arabesque is a part of it. Probably the purpose of that is to distract what is more critical or resistant, in order to cast the spell behind it. This is equivalent to the voice of the anesthetist; or to what the hypnotist may say while he bids us stare on some glittering object in order to fix the focus of the eyes. There must be submission of the will and senses. The slow prelude, or *lassú* as the Magyars call it, can be drawn out, delayed indefinitely, until the trance begins to show. It may even be that the secret lies in mastering the hours so that they merge into one another, and none of the audience have the will to get up and leave. They are willing to spend the whole night in listening. In effect, this music could be a drug put into their glasses that destroys their resolution. A narcotic that works collectively, as in the hegemonies of insects, where all obey instinctively and no individuals are outside the spell.

We are listening to "The Scythe" and "The Goosekeeper," two romances which, in later years, were favorites in the night restaurants of Moscow. And we hear their real character on this rustic instrument, where, by rusticity, we intend wooden houses and a far horizon. The tunes are potions or medicines that must be mixed with wine. But, in their simple state, we assist at the gathering of the herbs. In a dewy morning, while the rye is green. How can that be, while this simple tune turns in on itself? But it is as if the mere notes had a taste in them.

In that, they are minor enchantments, like a vision in the crystal or on the wall. It hangs on the notes, so that the picture does not exist without the music. So soon as he plays, it stands out clear before the eyes, and this could happen ten or twenty times, always the same. Precise in detail, fixed, and yet it fades with inattention, for before the end of the tune we can listen to nothing but the melody. And, as it dies, the picture comes up for a moment, but dies also, like a taste on the tongue.

How is it that the Russian accent can inhabit but a bar or two, and be unmistakable in that? In the opening phrase, merely, of a song. That is enough. So that if it broke off there, and went no further, there would be no mistaking it. Is it because music is a sort of shadow or parallel to speech? But let the song continue to its end! When the chorus comes, after the verse, the mystery appears again, immediately, in the shape and content of the strophe. It is not enough to say that the music follows certain racial and acknowledged lines. It is in the timbre and meaning of those rules, themselves; which accepts the explanation but carries it no further. The definition, that is to say, is a matter of fact; it states the formula, but does not tell us why, and how, it works. We know the ingredients, it may be, but are not told the secret of their quantities. That is withheld, as are the savors of the earth and of the rain. It is those which give the flavor, and no mathematical formula can imitate them. Can it be because the sensibilities have been bred and nourished in these lands? Would another human race, inhabiting the same country, work in that same idiom? Certain curious traits of resemblance there would be, ghostly parallels or identities, but no more than that. Music, then, must be the ghost of speech, when it comes spontaneously to simple souls, in inspiration: when it is born in minds that cannot read or write. But also it can be in the form of a riddle—that is, meaningless yet full of meaning. There can be themes that are like an epigram, a play of words, a catch, an apothegm. Freaks, like a double fruit, or the rose that has two hearts. We shall find instances of this magic. But later among the immortals. Not here, in this blossoming of the plains.

The player is a Jew bred to poverty and a life of misery. We must shudder when we think of the room in which he spent his childhood. Of the slum street: excepting, always, that it was a slum of the Middle Ages, and an Eastern slum at that, but with full rigor of the cold added to it, so that for winter raiment, the rat, the cat, the fox were skinned. But in all things the nationality of Gusikov must be considered, for it makes him different from the Gypsy players of the cymbalom. The genius of the race which excels in tragedy, and which interprets but does not create, found in him its opportunity. Fétis, describing Gusikov, speaks of the habitual melancholy expressed in his features, and mentions his pallor, which added to the interest aroused by his prodigious talent. To this we could add, for our part, his distinctive Jewish dress, in which he appeared condemned to the slums, the serf of the filthy streets. And, also, to be in some sort a student of alchemy, in the long gown of the priest or wizard.*

A musician of his race, even if he could not read the notes or write down music, even though he were an instinctive and not a learned player, would be possessed of more intellect than a Hungarian *tzigane*. But it is with those that he is comparable in temperament. Of the famous Bihary we are told by Liszt that: "When an orchestra alternating with his played at a ball he used, almost as soon as they had finished, to take up the same themes but with a new vigor. . . . They no sooner came to his hand than they became Bohemian." The performances of Gusikov, when we remember that he was a dying man, called for an altogether incredible expenditure of nervous and physical energy. But we should compare, for this, the accounts of how Chopin, another consumptive, had to be carried upstairs and into the room in order that he should be seated at his instrument, during the concerts that he gave in London and elsewhere in this country in 1848, a few months before his death. Even so, he had not to limit himself to the more simple items of his repertoire, but was able to give a full exhibition of his powers.

* A portrait of Gusikov appears as frontispiece to a little book by the Viennese music publisher, Schlesinger. It was printed in 1839. But I have failed to find a copy of this.

Chopin's songs, which were Polish and Lithuanian airs that he adapted, were of the type of melody played by Gusikov, who, once again we say, performed nothing but Russian, Jewish and Polish popular tunes and dances. But these took on immediately a character of his own, and became the vehicles of his mind and personality.

O, what a miracle! This is the damp mists, distilled, from a clearing in the forest. No! No! It is pure music. You must not move or stir. It is leagues from anywhere, too little to be found on a map. But its beauty is in its perfect form. This you would never be given by a *tzigane* player. Those have the fire—but not milk, not crystal, not perfection. Not milk of the udder, but the milk of plants and flowers. Weep! Weep! Not because it has a meaning, but because it comforts and assuages. It is as though the fingers of it touched or stroked our hearts. You will be awake when you remember this, and yet its message is of sleep. It tells you that you can sleep and dream of what you will. That is the way to die: when your hand is on the flower. For the music forgives and understands. How can that be? Ah! Do not ask. It is in the phrase, and is as clear as speech. It comes again, with no other meaning. There can be no mistaking it. That is its message. In a language that has no need of words.

And another, and another. These are not folk songs, but they are taken from little plays and dramas composed in popular style, and performed at fairs up and down the country. And they come back to us as popular songs and dances played in the *tzigane* style, like the tunes heard by Sarasate and transcribed by him for his violin. We can never tell, precisely, whether those are Russian or Hungarian, the truth being that they are theater music, of no defined frontier, but with the restaurants and cafés of Moscow as their capital. Here and now, we hear them before they reached the glitter of the gaslights. This is the music that transposes men and animals and makes them weep. For no reason. It is a spell or an enchantment. You may lose the focus, for a moment, in listening to the notes separately, and not surrendering to the tune, a sensation like that of moving swiftly past a fence or row of palings and counting them one after another, in isolation, until the eyes get weary and the stakes or hop-poles flow by once more in their patterns. In fact, you may break the magic, but can get back to it. Or, even, it allows you to drop out, on purpose, and pulls you in again. For the magic lies in the playing, not in the tunes themselves.

This is a song of the mushrooms in the woods. With no words; and, were there words, we should not understand them. It tells of how the mushrooms held a diet, a parliament, and went to war with the mushroom known as the borowik, the pine lover, for their leader. With but a pair of wooden mallets, tipped with felt, the damp, lonely wood becomes alive. Ah! But it is not the picking of mushrooms. What we have in the music is October and the hunter's moon. It is a ballad in rustic accents. And the melody, after it, is so haunting and beautiful that we must dwell on every phrase so as to remember it.

Next, a little drinking song which sparkles when shaken, as though from the flakes of gold leaf in the Danzig brandy. And a song of the linden flowers, a summer song, for the Poles take their name for the month of July, *lipiec,* from the linden trees, and drink a miot or honey mead in that month which is flavored with the linden flowers, so that it is in our own tongue a flowering mead and we would celebrate this hydromel that swims with flowers. If there be wine, it is the Hungarian Tokay, but mead is the national drink. Those are meadows of the red agaric and the chanterelle, or fox-mushroom, from northern parts of Poland or Lithuania, at the edge of the great forest, where the fields are damp and shaded from the trees. Here is nothing Russian. It is a different paganism, of another ancestry. We have village mazurkas and kolomyjkas coming from Ruthenia, down near Galicia, which is close to the Dniester. In order to bring back those tunes it is but necessary to cross the river.

There can be a mere phrase, of which it is not possible to bear the poignancy, that brings tears. The master of such emotions is Schubert. It has been written of the great Anton Rubinstein that he could play some simple piece by Mozart or Schubert and reduce his audience to tears. But the divine genius of those composers almost suffers from the fact of their having been human beings, having lodged, and fed, and done hack work for the publishers; it would be an advantage, positively, if those melodies were anonymous, for then we have the assurance, almost, that they existed in nature. The ancient instrument, and its particular and unique development into a perfection that will never be heard again—this, too, helps the music. For the more beautiful of these melodies have a natural or rustic spontaneity that could never be imitated by the masters. On occasion, too, a depth of meaning, as though dug into the soil and into the whole human past; or, again, sacred and wonderful because meaningless, or beyond meaning, in that manner of a riddle or conundrum, of an epigram or rebus, even, the theme being equivalent to a nugget or a meteorite of mathematical and magical properties giving forth sparks and radiations, capable, musically, of being read backward or in contrary motion, split into variations, and then continued, telescoped, as it were, in double counterpoint, or submitted generally to all the devices of the contrapuntist. This, in the hands of the greatest musical genius there has ever been, is a subject already dealt with in our episode called *Fugue*, hoping that the remarks and reactions even of an amateur may bear a little contribution to the sacred mystery. For this instant it is the lesser magic, but that is no less wonderful in its spontaneous flowering. Nearer, too, to the human emotions because it has no encumbrance. Laughter and tears lie as near together as flesh to the bone. They are contingent; or spring up in one another's footsteps as though their seed were carried on the winds.

Why should such gifts come, unsought, to ignorant minds; or be borne, as at this moment, from the hands of a dying man? Ah! This is something that we shall never hear again. The subtle genius of his race is inhabiting these others. The outcast, who has no home, possesses them and speaks their secrets. It is the hour of exception when all things are tranced. Persons who are under the spell will empty out the money from their pockets onto the table in order that he should continue playing. Meanwhile, they sit weeping as they listen. They are persons who keep quite alone, and do not move or stir. Such is the effect of music. It is an intoxication, certainly, or a hallucination. They are possessed by music, and are, mentally and physically, under its dominion. They are in his power completely. If he belonged to the race of vagabonds it would be all fire: the slow flame, and the raging, all-consuming fire. For that is the Gypsy style. In their own language, and none other. All that they play becomes Bohemian and uncontrollable. But this musician is priest or wizard, and not dervish. He is not the naked fakir who walks into the fire: who, in frenzy, tears and eats the living goat, stabs himself, gashes his own flesh and lets the serpent bite him.

This Jew with the dulcimer has more subtle magic. It may be that, because he has lived in houses, he is more understanding. Those others, who are nomads by blood, cannot know the pathos of these little things that are personal belongings. Their fire is inarticulate: it is of the blood, but not of the heart or brain. Therefore it is animal and not spiritual. It is communicable, by mass, as are sensations of fury or of panic. It requires incessant heating of the blood, for it appeals to passions that must never cool. Therefore their ornament and the headlong, vertiginous speed, with, immediately, the preluding of another melody on the violin or the cymbalom, already foreshadowing another climax in its long-drawn phrases.

The children of the tawny race are precocious, and at an early age they are in love. From birth they are young animals. It can be seen in their springing walk, and in the manner in which they raid the villages as if to rob them. Music, to them, is a sensual pleasure like the purring of the cat that stretches up, in ecstasy, and treads with velvet paw, and jumps into your lap. It is instinctive, like the displaying of the golden pheasant when he arches his back, or tautens it to one side, and runs up and down with leaping step, with flashing eye and golden hair, then stiffens and distends his cape or mantle, hissing, meantime, as it might be a serpent, in order to mesmerize the hen. His display is a dance of courtship, nothing else. But the hen pays little heed to his magnificence. The cock displays, or shows off, for his own pleasure.

This is the attitude of the Gypsy, in music, toward other races,

and the secret also of his own sensations. He makes use of it
as a means to hypnotize. It is his frenzy or delirium; but to himself, as well, an ecstasy of enjoyment. He does not even have to
learn as other men. When a violin is first put into his hand,
he imitates by watching the fingers of the other players, and has
to get the tunes by heart. To the Gypsy, and to the Jew as well,
music was a means of sorcery. A method of obtaining mastery,
and to be enjoyed as such. The child prodigy who is a Jew is
no uncommon phenomenon, but occurring nearly always in
Eastern Europe. At twelve years of age they have learned everything there is to learn. They may never play as well again,
probably because they lose their souls by constant repetition of
what is already flawless and cannot be improved on. We have
to consider what music can mean to a child prodigy. And our
argument points, perhaps, to the limitations of the violin. If it
were another instrument he might never tire of it. The clavichord, the harpsichord, perhaps the lute, are instruments capable
of lifelong improvement and exploration. Those are personal
instruments of fresh discovery and endless beauty, as, in this
instance, was the *straufiedel* or cymbalom of Gusikov. His ancestors, before they begged their way from slum to slum, could
have been minstrels in the Tartar camp.

Most of our music is Italian. Its line of beauty is from the
Mediterranean. Even if it comes from the green fields, or from
the stone walls and Border towers; even if it be a madrigal, a
fantasy for a chest of viols, a pavan, a galliard, or divisions on
a ground. Its greatness, when it flies with wings, is in an air
which is Italian, though permuted behind the mullions on winter nights of wind and snow. Toccata, pastorale or *passacaglia*
—all are Italian in origin and by name. But this is music from
another world. Blown by the long winds out of the kibitkas or
the tents of felt, moved with the nomads to where the grass was
sweet and the wilderness was pied with flowers. There you
could have heard this instrument, or its counterfeit. The germ
of this music was no Italian serenade, but an epic on the harp
and sheepskin drum, played at a moment when the conqueror
lifted up his victim's skull, and drank from it. Such was the

frenzy, or the seizure in this music. Its time for love was when
the khanum stood in her golden gown, stiff with gold, and with
her train held up by her maidens. Behind her mask of white
lead or antimony, which was white with the cosmetic, and like
a mask of paper. In the distance there were four towers of skulls,
built up as high as you could throw a stone—a row of skulls,
and then a row of clay. The countrymen told how, at night,
bright lights seemed to be burning on the tops of all the towers
of skulls. Behind that, the sky was pale and greenish and entirely empty.

The cymbalom, in spite of the extraordinary resources of his
particular instrument, is inadequate for so consummate a performer. It is the same sensation that is given by the greatest
pianists. The single keyboard is not enough. In much of his
music we hear the Berecynthian rattle. This was the giant cymbalom or dulcimer carried by the Scythian horde in the van-
guard of their battles. It was the ancestor, too, of the music of
the Turkish Janizaries. Their bells and drums and cymbals were
in imitation of its sound. Called Berecynthian after the clashing cymbals, drums, tabrets, bucklers of the Corybantes, who
were priestesses of Cybele. In fact, the giant cymbalom was the
consensus of that noise. But, in the Scythian horde, it preluded
among the horsemen.

The musician stood erect in a wagon that was a ten-wheeled
chariot, and played while it moved along the steppe. He played
them into battle, and at the feasting afterward, when they ate
horses roasted whole, entire, served up with their heads, and
drank fermented mare's milk. At such nomad feasts the musician was sometimes an "Indian," which is to say he may have
been a Gypsy, and at other times he was a wandering Jew. He
went everywhere with the Tartar warriors and formed part of
their military establishment. When great towns were captured,
musicians rode at head of the procession for the triumphal entry. They played the Tartar horde into the burning ruins. Historical survivals of this practice were the Gypsy violinists who
accompanied the Wallachian voivodes on their wars. It comes
down from Attila and his Huns, and is true of all the great nomad

conquerors down to Tamerlane. The Mongol, Batu Khan, who brought Gypsy coppersmiths from Central Asia with his army when he invaded the Danubian provinces in the twelfth century, which was the earliest irruption of the Gypsies into Europe, had "Indian"—that is to say Gypsy—or Jewish minstrels with him. No certain description of this instrument has come down to us. It is but a legend, and a name for intoxication and delirium.

But we hear wild cries and the beating of the cymbals. Then sharp blows, as it were the striking of an anvil. In imagination, these give sparks of flame. It is the nomad coppersmiths, or armorers, who come forth from their dark tents and take up the din. They have the long hair of the fire-eater or snake charmer, and wear rags that are singed and blackened by the flame. At that early date they are still Indian. The shadow of the great Indian sun is on their skins. For their burned bodies are the color of their copper caldrons. Now we hear a loud twanging, as of strings or wires that are tried, and then tightened. The same note is struck again, again, but with the fingers, which are more sensitive than the plectrum. Those chords suggest a race of archers. They must have bow-rings made of bone or ivory. From every direction there come the neighing of mares and stallions and the bleating of the herds of long-horned sheep. But, above that, comes the testing and the tuning of the strings. It must be a huge instrument, and there is more than one of them.

The ten-wheeled chariots have the mares attached to them, for part of the music is the stamping of the hoofs. Now, loud and tremendous, it begins. The players, like charioteers, are in long white gowns. But there are not fillets on their foreheads to bind their hair. Their hair flows, loose and long, on their shoulders. They are the furies, urging into war. They move their whole arms, as though they strike with blacksmiths' hammers. It is a giant dulcimer: the tremendous shakes and arpeggios sweep the air. There can have been no other such preluding. Two or more of the huge dulcimers sound forth together and strike out the theme, with that terrific rattle which commands and exults. Long as a death rattle, and leading into that. The wagons move forward. The horses paw the earth, and rear up on the rein. At the same moment all the tents are down. The Berecynthian sistrum is not one instrument alone, but the giant cymbaloms or dulcimers, and trumpets, drums and copper caldrons. But the players of the dulcimer are possessed by fury, as though they ran amuck, or slew in frenzy. It is darker, darker; and to more of the long tremendous shaken rattlings the whole horde moves on.

Now, with the fingers of one hand, he sweeps the notes. It is part of the *Midsummer Night's Dream* of Mendelssohn, as though played upon the virginals or clavichord. Preluding, in magic, with glissandos, up and down the scale, in the manner of the cymbalom or dulcimer. A magical underworld opens; as if to that wave of the fingers, as if they held the key. It is curious how, in this, he speaks with a foreign accent. A nocturne: Ah! But this is the greenwood of Arden on Midsummer Night, while the nightingale is singing and there are little mysterious noises that no one can explain. It is so exquisite that everyone is in tears. The little dance dies down. The glissandos come again. We hear the last notes played, which mean the ending. And the echoes of this magic die away.

It is impossible to move or stir.

Then, like someone who is dying, who puts out his hand, he takes up the hammers of the dulcimer, but as though the room was in darkness, or in a dying light, and preludes upon the notes. We are in that street of Mohilev; or near by, in the little town where he was born. For the music has the intonation of the spoken word: and these are the last words of a dying man. There will be no more. Only a phrase or two, and it is ended.

The whole town is in darkness as we drive away.

A PICTURE OF ROUMANIA *

The first impression of Bucharest comes from the wide extent of space that it covers. This is because there are so many houses standing in their separate gardens. Owing to this, Calea Victoriei, the main street of the capital, is as long as Oxford Street and Regent Street put together. You can dine at a restaurant just across the road; or you may have to traverse the entire extent of the town in order to get your dinner. It may take, in a taxi, nearly as long a time as it does to go down the Grand Canal in a gondola. Bucharest, then, is a town which is protracted and drawn out. So are the hours kept by its inhabitants; only you would not think so, for they pass so quickly.

It is a question of temperament and climate. In the summer it is as hot as India. No business can be done between midday and five o'clock. It is at that hour, or later, that the shops open for the afternoon, and they do not close their shutters till nine or ten. You dine, therefore, at ten or eleven, and no one would think of going to bed till three or four. This, again, explains the multiplicity of restaurants and cafés, and in its turn accounts for the popular music which is incomparable and haunts the mind. Not that the climate remains at that temperature forever. The autumn, which is the most beautiful season of all, lasting sometimes till early in December, is followed by a winter of deep snow and sledges. It is, in fact, the climate of Seville and St. Petersburg—for thinking of Bucharest and its languorous delights it must be St. Petersburg and not Leningrad—it is the climate of Seville and St. Petersburg in one. And this is the reason for the tempo of Bucharest, which is different from that of any other town.

I had been advised by many persons, when going to Roumania, to see the country first and the capital last. Bucharest, accord-

* From *Roumanian Journey*, 1938.

255

ing to this opinion, was no more than a bad copy of Paris. Actually, in Bucharest there is nothing whatever of Paris, except the one or two inevitable dress shops. The Chaussée Kisseleff may a little resemble the Avenue du Bois; but plane trees lining both sides of a road do not make a copy. It is the Chaussée Kisseleff, called after the general who governed Roumania during the Russian occupation of 1832, that leads straight into the Calea Victoriei. You can walk for nearly an hour down these two streets and the character of Bucharest will begin to form in your mind.

It is not only the larger houses that stand apart in gardens. Nearly every house has more space allowed to it than in any other town. This permits of much waste of room in courtyards, outhouses, stables and so forth, and, of course, increases the picturesque leisure of the place. Of dire poverty there are, unfortunately, some signs. No town can rapidly increase till it has a population of seven hundred thousand and not bring misery with it. But new buildings are springing up on every side. If you look down at Bucharest from one of the roof gardens of its modern flats, there are sights and sounds of rebuilding in all directions. And some of the buildings are more than creditable specimens of the modern style. Luckily, owing to the generous scale on which the city stands, this rebuilding has not entailed much destruction of the old. The character of Bucharest is, in fact, enhanced by new improvements, though there must come a point, before long, when improvement becomes spoliation.

Now the Calea Victoriei is not the magnificent tree-lined boulevard that the foregoing remarks might justify in the imagination. It is as narrow as Bond Street, and with more than one curve in its length. The first beginning of it, from the direction of the Chaussée Kisseleff, is disappointing. It is nondescript and meaningless. There are only small houses and no shops. It is like a quiet street in some country town, except for the line of passing motors. Then, gradually, the finer houses begin, one ministry after another lines the road and you pass the Royal Palace and the National Theater, until you come, in the end, to the quays of the river, the Dâmboviţa, or the Dumbovitsa, if it is written as pronounced. Such is the geography of Bucharest. It is simple enough; and anything else there is of interest lies to right or left of the Calea Victoriei in a narrow area to each side.

The character of Bucharest is in its personality, not its monuments. Even so, there are three or four churches that should be seen. The church, for instance, of the Colţei Hospital, belonging to a monastery that has been destroyed, is an interesting example of the bastard Byzantine of the eighteenth century. It has good frescoes and much gilt and carving. Other churches are the Biserica Doamnei, built by one of the Cantacuzeni; the Stavropolios; and, more especially, the church of the Patriarch Antime, dating from 1715 and containing some admirable carving. Outside the town, and requiring a special permit because its buildings have been made into a prison, is the monastery of Vacaresti, the most interesting sight of Bucharest, with a good stone porch, fine twisted columns in the interior and a frescoed decoration which is most interesting. A painted view of Jerusalem, occurring in midst of this, is no less than a landscape in the modern naïf manner, by the ancestor, it might be thought, of *douanier* Rousseau. And that is all that need be said about the ancient sights of Bucharest, for they amount to little, and that little is altogether overshadowed by the contemporary scene.

Or this statement may be qualified, at least, to include its inhabitants past and present. This is a land where till recently works of art consisted, in the main, of costumes and carpets. Anything more permanent was destroyed in the ceaseless petty wars and was, in any case, no safe possession with the Turks in sight. More than this the Turkish Empire, which in material riches was the greatest power in Europe during the sixteenth and seventeenth centuries, has left its Oriental influence on the land and its inhabitants. The Turks had inherited the legacy of splendor in dress from the Byzantines. There was even one body of the Sultan's bodyguard, the *peiks,* a branch of the tressed halberdiers, whose uniform had come down in direct descent from that worn in the household of the Palæologi. They wore a truncated conical hat, surmounted by a triple plume. The Sul-

tan in his progresses through Constantinople was attended by a
court, the splendid variety of whose costume defies description.
When, in the eighteenth century, the Phanariot Princes, Greek
families of the Phanar or Greek quarter of Constantinople, were
sent to rule the two principalities of Moldavia and Wallachia
they brought with them the customs and dress of their native
city, informed, it may be, by certain traces of French culture
and manners. Especially, they imported with them the dresses
of the Sultan's court. Our digression is in order to account for
the extraordinary costumes to be noticed in all old family portraits in Roumania.

But this brings us to a general consideration of the old noble
families, or Boyars, of Moldavia and Wallachia. The Cantacuzeni may be all but proved in descent from the Byzantine Em-
porers of that name; Brancovan, Kretzulesco, Philippesco,
Stirbey, Vacaresco, Baleano are families of Moldavian origin;
Catargi, Callimacki are from Wallachia; the Balsch family may
originate from Les Baux, in Provence; the Ghyka derive from
the Albanian Ghegs; there are other families of Ragusan, and
Trapezuntine origin, from Trebizond; Mavrocordato, Soutzo are
Phanariots from Constantinople; while the Rosetti, Moruzi and
the curiously named Regoli di Roma are Phanariots of Italian
origin from those Greek islands that were formerly Venetian,
such as the island of Naxos. It is this tradition of inherited
wealth and luxury that make of Roumania a different land from
the neighboring Bulgaria, from old Serbia, or from modern
Greece. At the same time, the complexity of the different races
from whom the modern Roumania is formed could not be more
evident than in this complicated tangle of descent.

During the eighteenth century Jassy was the capital of the
Phanariot princes sent to reign over Moldavia. Jassy, in all the
two principalities, was the most important town. Bucharest was
small by comparison. The Boyars, whether of Moldavia or
Wallachia, must be thought of as living, with a horde of servants,
in what we can only call a temporary accommodation. With
very few exceptions, nothing like the great town or country
houses of Western Europe was to be found. A house was built
to last a few years and was renewed with every generation. Its

riches, as we have said, were in carpets, in fine costumes and in jewels. At the end of the eighteenth and beginning of the nineteenth centuries there were built, in Moldavia, a few country houses, like Bozieni, or Stânca, in Russian Paul I "Adam" style, resembling "colonial" houses in America. Of old castles, or villas, there are none. A Phanariot prince reigned only at the whim of the Sultan, his liege lord, and was in perpetual danger of losing his life, if sent for to come back and account for himself to his master. Their temptation, therefore, was to make as much money as quickly as possible. Many of them reigned more than once, and for as many as three or four times. Such were the curious conditions of Bucharest, and still more of Jassy, during the course of the eighteenth century. The Boyars of more native descent kept as much as possible upon their estates. In the two capitals it was a completely Oriental existence. As late as 1818 there is an account by an English traveler of an audience with the reigning prince at Bucharest, in which he is described as being carried into the room in the old traditional manner, supported by the arm of a servant under each of his shoulders, as though he were too important a personage to walk. These were the manners and customs of the old Turkish court, or even of the Court of Pekin. It was remarked, too, that the Phanariot princes had no standing army. This was not allowed them. Their state consisted in a multiplicity of servants, and in a few Heyducks or Albanians gorgeously arrayed. I am even told, by Prince Matila Ghyka, that a Phanariot prince of the Mavrojeni family made his official entry into Bucharest riding in a sledge drawn by a pair of stags with gilded antlers.

If the Oriental, or even Byzantine, ancestral background to the capital is stressed it is because only in comprehension of this can its present unique features be understood. It is because the past of Bucharest, or that part of the past of Bucharest which devolved on it from Jassy, is of as much moment to its present psychology as the past of Rome or of Madrid, of London or of St. Petersburg is to their present tendencies and their appearance. But also, and we cannot deny this, its picturesque details have been irresistible and have cried out aloud for inclusion.

Perhaps the most interesting memorial, in Roumania, of this

time is the portrait by Liotard, which is the property of Prince Jean Callimacki and hangs in his house in the Chaussée Kisseleff. This is a rarity, too, among Liotards for it is a painting in oils and not a pastel. It will be remembered that Liotard, who was a native of Geneva, had established himself for five years in Constantinople where, it is said, he grew a beard and adopted the Turkish dress. He was invited thence by Constantine Mavrocordato, the Hospodar of Moldavia, of Phanariot family, and proceeded to his capital Jassy, where he remained for ten months. This was in 1742-1743. In Jassy he painted the portraits of the reigning prince, his wife, his son, that of the Patriarch of Jerusalem, who was on a visit there, the portrait of Prince Scarlati and many others, all of which would seem to have been destroyed in the great fire that burned down the palace of Jassy—all, that is to say, except the portrait that we are now considering. The painting of Prince Constantine Scarlati is, though, preserved in a contemporary engraving done from the drawing in sanguine that was a preparation for his portrait. It seems unlikely, however, that the painting we reproduce is that of the reigning prince. The young man that it represents is beardless, which must mean that he was painted in extreme youth. The probability therefore is that the tradition of the Callimacki family is correct and that the person portrayed is the son of the prince, Alexander Mavrocordato, known as Delimbey, "the mad," who was to reign at Jassy many years later, 1782-1785.

This portrait is a really charming thing. Especially, perhaps, because of the rose-colored pantaloons that the young man is wearing. But here another point arises—that it was not Turkish costume that Liotard adopted for himself. We are expressly told that he grew his beard and started to wear his peculiar costume, by which he was to become known all over Europe, while he worked at Jassy. It is, therefore, the dress and beard of a typical Moldavian Boyar that he affected; and in the portrait of himself, in this guise, we have the perfect representation of the dress of such a person. This is borne out in other portraits inherited by Princess Callimacki from her Vacaresco ancestors; one of which is full of character. It represents an old Boyar, blinded in one eye and wearing an immensely tall fur headdress, decorated with a red plume that was the insignia of his office. This again was an inheritance from Turkish or Byzantine tradition. Those persons who have seen the mosaics in the Kariye Djami at Istanbul will remember the kneeling figure of the Grand Logothete Theodore Metochitis presenting an image of the church to Christ, and wearing an immense striped turban that was the badge of his rank. This personage died in 1322; and the court costumes worn in Moldavia and Wallachia until 1848, even after the change of rule from Palæologus to Osmanli, are in the same living tradition.

It is most curious, therefore, to be shown the picture of a young lady, painted somewhere about 1810, and be told that it is the daughter of one of the Boyars. This portrait, moreover, which has some of the handling of a Goya, is remarkable for the beautiful diamond sprays worn by its subject. Nor, in spite of the fact that it is so manifestly of the decade 1800-1810, is this portrait at all conventional in its dress. Not only that, but the young lady has the joined eyebrows, the sprincene inbinate, which were so much admired in this country and that must seem to us as peculiar as the traits of Hindu or Rajput. This again is of the pure Orient and has not its equivalent in any Western land. We are told that this trait is still to be observed in a few old families, particularly the Stirbey.

But these old portraits, which will soon become a new interest to anyone who sees them, must be experienced in a house that is literally full of them, in what we might term the family museum of Monsieur Mano. This gentleman has collected every conceivable portrait of members of his family during this time, and where they were inaccessible he has caused copies to be made, or has copied them himself. The results of his energy make one of the most interesting collections in Roumania. They are not less absorbing to the student of costume, or of the history of taste. Several more female portraits are to be seen, by the hand that painted the Oriental Goya just mentioned. These are of rare beauty, and take, indeed, a high rank among late eighteenth-century portraits. But in this house, the paintings of men are even more remarkable. It is almost inconceivable that these Boyars in their fur-lined robes and immense fur hats should date from the early years of the nineteenth century. There are fur hats that must have been four to five feet in height, and, in the case of a tall man, adding this to his six feet of stature, there is a total of ten feet or more, a bearded Colossus, in fact, of altogether fantastic appearance. The young men, in a date equivalent to the bucks of the Regency, invented a bulbous form of headgear which came into fashion, a fur hat shaped a little like a Greek priest's hat, only more completely rounded, so that it had more of the appearance of a Russian bishop's miter. But this was the last decadence, the last flowering of tradition. In the next generation, as we have said, this characteristic costume went out altogether, after a slow development during what may have amounted to as many as fifteen centuries.

Underneath the fur robes, magnificent brocades were worn. Once more, this is of Turkish or Byzantine tradition. These silks and brocades are often very well rendered in the portraits, and their flowered materials deserve the attention of any competent professional designer. But the painters of these portraits remain a mystery. One painting in Monsieur Mano's collection is signed by a name that is something like Hayer, written in German characters. It is probable, therefore, that the artist was a Viennese who must certainly, to judge from the quantity of work that he executed, have lived for a considerable time in Roumania. But this subject, altogether, is one that deserves investigation by someone who has time, and who is living upon the spot. Whether it is the same hand that painted the Goya-like women is unknown. All those, at least, are by the same artist. As the Boyars are painted, as if by an identical person, at all dates between 1760 and 1820, it is evident that there must have been more than one artist at work, and more than one generation, even, of painters. The Boyars insisted on a close and exact representation of their features and the significant details of their costumes. Even in spite of these dead rules there were painters, probably from Vienna as we have said, who had enough personality to achieve these most interesting portraits. They are an important part of the history of Roumania and the names of their authors should be restored to knowledge. There is, by now, hardly another part of the world in which painters of their accomplishment, and with such obvious claims to attraction and interest, would be allowed to remain in oblivion.

While this subject is under discussion mention must be made of, perhaps, the only other artist who has left any traces in Roumania. We refer to Louis Dupré, a pupil of David and author of a delightful book, *Voyage à Athènes et à Constantinople,* published in 1819. This folio has colored lithographs that are masterpieces of the art, and is unique, besides, as being the only representation in art of Ali Pacha of Janina and his more than peculiar court. He is to be seen there, floating, narghile in hand, in a reverie, it may be, of future tortures to inflict on his friends and enemies. He glides along in his painted caïque, on the waters of the lake of Janina, attended by two Greek or Albanian youths with curled locks and of suspicious beauty. At the end of his volume Dupré gives a drawing of the Moldavian Hospodar's encampment, and mentions drawings that he made of various families, including the Soutzo. It is more than probable that portraits by his hand may still exist in Roumania. His stay in the principalities was of short duration, and he returned to Paris, dying at an early age, in 1837. Louis Dupré is, admittedly, a minor artist, but he was a clear and beautiful draftsman, especially of costume.

And, after Dupré, the list of foreign artists who have visited Roumania is completed with another Frenchman, Raffet, the military painter, who traveled in Moldavia with his patron, Prince Demidoff, in the '50s and has left many lithographs, in black and white, of Moldavian scenes. It is more than probable, too, that diligent search would yield drawings by a much greater man, Constantin Guys, who came out as war correspondent to the Crimean War, for the *London Illustrated News,* and is almost certain, in the course of his duties, to have visited Jassy, for the headquarters of the French army were at Varna, on the Black Sea. It is sad, if this surmise proves to be correct, that Constantin Guys arrived in Moldavia less than ten years too late to draw

the costumes that were worn until 1848. It is certain that they
would have had an appeal to his imagination. Also, he would
have drawn, inevitably, the Heyduck and the Albanian body-
guards, together with the French fashions that were worn by the
emancipated youth of the time. The principalities, in those days
of transition, must have formed a wonderful spectacle to those
who had the power of appreciation. Also, the horses and
carriages of Bucharest were subjects that might have been specially invented for the pencil of Guys.

There is more than one description of the capital during the
middle years of last century in which the extraordinary contrasts
are noticed that were to be observed in its streets. Horses and
carriages that would have been the pride of Hyde Park or the
Prater would pass within a few feet of hovels that were not fit for
animals to live in. A lady and gentleman dressed in the height
of Parisian fashion would walk side by side with a half-naked
tzigane. There were Armenian merchants, Turks and Greeks,
Jews and Russians, each to be known by his distinctive dress.
Later on in the century, after 1881, the year in which Bucharest
was declared capital of the kingdom, the increase of its importance and wealth did not diminish but rather accentuated
these living contrasts. A luxurious social life came into existence,
careless or oblivious of the intervening poverty. The reflection
of this is to be seen in a curious book, rare even in its own country.
It consists of a collection of the social paragraphs written in
French, for the fashionable newspaper of the early '80s. Every
week there was a gala night at the opera and a performance of
Norma, of *Ballo in Maschera*, or of *Don Pasquale* was made the
occasion for magnificent balls and supper parties. The sophistication of the language in which this odd book is written, with its
account of the jewels and the dresses worn, of the flowers and the
table decorations, is given an impetus, or is lifted to another
plane, when these hidden discrepancies are realized. This little
book is a complete exotic or Oriental commentary on fashion; it
is not literature but near literature, or, more exactly, notes for
literature. In the same way that there are books which could not
have been written without the help of a manual of dates, or of

a guidebook, this scarce little volume has a distant, or menial, relationship to Marcel Proust. This is the material on which he fed his intelligence, and perhaps the embryonic touch of Monsieur de Charlus revealed in its author may account for its quality. The heavy perfume of its pages, which are so meaningless and so strewn with cyphers, clings to every picture that the mind can evoke of Bucharest in the 1880s.

Bucharest, as revealed there, is a compound of many things—Russian, French, Viennese, Turkish, Phanariot. The fashion and luxuries were French; music for the ballroom came from Vienna; the extravagance and prodigality were Russian, for that country is neighbor to Roumania; while everything that was of the Orient had its origin in the background that we have sought to establish in the preceding paragraphs. We must think of the Chaussée Kisseleff on a summer evening when the carriages were driven at a furious gallop from end to end of the avenue. Everyone knew to whom each equipage belonged; while the demimondaines of the capital drove alone in their segregated glamour, the cause of varied feelings to those persons whom they passed. Their pace was swift but not headlong, for it was the gilded youth who urged their thoroughbreds to full gallop, being the same persons who, in the next generation, own racing motors and thunder along in the full noisiness of the exhaust pipe. Such was the fashionable glitter of a summer evening during the '80s and '90s, and for the first decade of this present century, during, in fact, all the best years of a lifetime. It was an atmosphere, we may conclude, that had not its like in any other capital of the West, owing to its hints of the Phanar, or even of Cairo, its South American languor, the Mexican luxury of its caparisons and harness. Meaningless it may have been; but we are thinking only of its appeal to the eyes.

But the present in Bucharest, the continuous present which consumes the living, has still a quality that must be put into words. This is the total of those different things that give it atmosphere. The popular music plays a great part in this; but music we have not yet come to. There are the primary or superficial traces of the Orient, the glass of water, perhaps, and the sherbet of roses that you find at three or four o'clock of the morning in your bedroom. This is the legacy from a not distant age when pure water was a luxury. In Turkey, and in the country in Greece, a glass of good water is still the greatest luxury that can be offered. As for the sherbet of roses, this is a spoonful of sticky paste, of the color of pink roses, lying on a glass saucer. Its taste is delicious, like the scented airs of Kazanlik, the valley of roses under distant Rhodope, where the attar is distilled; or sometimes the sherbet is changed for a conserve of cherries or blackberries. These sherbets are made, of course, in houses and cannot be bought in shops. I have been told, too, that in a particular nunnery in Moldavia a paste used to be made from lotus petals, but this water-lily sherbet seems to have vanished into the past. If these last attentions of the long, hot evenings are in living proof of this remoteness, so are the pair of Albanians attached to the house in which we stayed. Their lives, which seemed to pass in easy sinecure, were patterns, we are told, of fidelity to their masters. In no other country of Europe are these Heyducks still to be found, save in Roumania, where five or six families still maintain them. The two Albanians of whom we are speaking might be described as octavo editions of King Fuad of Egypt, himself of Albanian descent and of exactly the same physical type. There had always been Albanians in this household. When they wish to retire from service and go home, they send back another of their family or clan in their stead, so that the supply of Albanians is inexhaustible. It must, all the same, be a long and roundabout journey from Bucharest down the Black Sea, through the Bosphorus, to Athens and Corfu, and thence to Tirana or to Elbasan.

Many enjoyable hours can be spent in Bucharest looking for carpets. Down by the river, the Dâmbovița, there are carpet stalls where the wares are exposed for sale in the open air, as at a fair. Here it is sometimes possible to find a pretty rug for the equivalent of as little as six or seven shillings. These would be native rugs of the simplest patterns; but, also, some extraordinary relics of the last century are to be discovered, floral patterns of inconceivable hardness and complexity, or elaborate woven frames surrounding a poodle or a St. Bernard dog. The better rugs and carpets are, naturally, in the dealers' shops; but, although

their prices are far from high—an exceedingly fine Oltenian rug
costing no more than ten pounds in English money—the supply is
very limited. After a long search in the shops of Bucharest only
four Oltenian rugs could be found for sale. This is because the
area of manufacture was always small, and most of the good
specimens have, long ago, been bought by collectors.

Roumanian carpets fall into two main divisions, Oltenian and
Bessarabian. The Olt is a river coming from Transylvania and
running through the neighborhood of Hurez and Cozia (two
monasteries), due south into the Danube. It drains the chief
watershed of the Transylvanian Alps and is a region of pastoral
valleys, in that district from which the carpets came. The great
period of their manufacture would seem to have been from 1790
till about 1860. Their colors, often enough, are in wonderful
harmonies of red and blue, rivaling in softness the colors of the
finest Ghiordes, only it is a bold softness of pure reds and blues.
The patterns are, in simile, like strewed flowers; they are a pattern of flowers as thrown upon the ground, not held in bunches
or formally arranged. They are flowers, singly, or tied together in
twos or threes, with a border on another ground of smaller
bunches symmetrically arranged. The intervals between these
groups of flowers, in the main design of the rug, are kept to the
bare ground of the color base and are not worked over with the
minute interlacings and arabesques of the Persian rugs. The
Oltenian carpets, then, are bolder and less finished in design than
the rugs of Turkey or the Caucasus. On the other hand they are
both softer and more bold in color, so that by many tastes they are
preferred to any but the most valuable of Persian weaving.

The Bessarabian carpets are entirely different, and are, perhaps, better known in England. Bessarabia, it will be remembered, was a Russian province from 1812 to 1918. Its population
—it was, before 1812, part of Moldavia, and touching on Poland,
the Ukraine and the Tartar provinces—is, ethnographically, a
different mixture from that of Wallachia, of which Oltenia is
part. Bessarabian rugs are slightly later in date than those of
Oltenia, for their period extends from 1815 until about 1860.
They are to be known often by the black ground on which their

design is worked, and this, in its detail, is sometimes not unlike an English needlework carpet of the Georgian period, only greater use is made of the black background and the floral patterns are more successfully bold and unconventional in design. In fact a good Bessarabian rug looks as though it came from a land of carpets; an English needlework carpet, in spite of its beauty, always suggests that it was the recreation of the ladies in the house for which it was made. Another influence in Bessarabian design came from the neighboring Odessa, where the *émigré* Duc de Richelieu, founder of that city, imported, it is said, one of the directors of the Savonnerie factory from his native France and established him in a local carpet industry. There is a breath, then, of the sophistication of the French Empire in some of the more elaborate of the Bessarabian rugs; and yet the finer examples are unique in their way and to be recognized at a glance. Of these it may be said, at once, that there are more to be bought in London than can be seen in all Roumania. They were collected by Russian amateurs before the war and had found their way to London and Paris long before Bessarabia had become, again, a part of Roumania. It is almost hopeless to look for Bessarabian rugs in Bucharest; but the Oltenian are still to be found, though rarely and with increasing difficulty.

Besides the possibility of fine rugs, the antique shops of Bucharest contain the expected icons, silver work of no particular merit and, of course, peasant costumes, though not nearly to the extent that these are sold in, for instance, Budapest, where the multiplicity of peasant shops, beautiful as are the dresses and headdresses of Mezökövesd and Böldög, have become so numerous as to constitute a definite nuisance. Indeed, in Bucharest, by contrast, this industry has not been carried far enough, and some enterprise is badly needed by which the lovely costumes of Rucar, the Saxon dresses of the Siebenbürgen, the Ruthenian costumes of Bucovina, the distinctive Szekler dresses, the Suabian costumes of the Banat, all the wealth of Roumanian peasant art, which is the most rich and copious in Europe, should become available for purchase and for study. Equally, there can be said to be only the beginning of a museum of folk art. Its few rooms, in the

Chaussée Kisseleff, contain no more than the first scratchings of the surface. There is surely, here, an opportunity to do for the peasant art of Roumania what has been accomplished for Northern art in the wonderful Nordiska Museum at Stockholm, or in the open-air folk museum outside Oslo. The rugs of Oltenia or Bessarabia are only a fragment of this enormous peasant creation, though they constitute a part which can fit admirably into the most civilized surroundings. This art of weaving is only a portion of an enormous belt of such creation, extending from the Black Sea to the Baltic, giving on its way the Houtsoule crafts of the Polish mountaineers in their remote corner near the Bucovina, and ending with the elaborately embroidered aprons of Lithuania, or the *rjivy* rugs of Finland. The Nordiska Museum, which has extended its activities to demonstrate all the peasant arts of the Baltic, might be balanced and completed by a museum in Bucharest covering the whole area from the Bucovina to the Danube, for this is the richest part of the world in peasant costumes, peasant architecture, folklore and, it may be added, in folk music and folk dancing. The time is not yet too late. It is a still-living art; and without much difficulty or expense a museum could be assembled that would be, in its kind, one of the wonders of old Europe.

This would seem to be the moment, too, in which to speak of the wonderful collection of paintings by El Greco that are in the possession of the Royal family. Numerous persons are now familiar with these hitherto unknown pictures owing to the El Greco exhibition in Paris, in the summer of 1937, where they were the center of attraction. These paintings, which are nine in number, are distributed among the various royal palaces, at Cotroceni in Bucharest, and in Foïshor, Peleş and the smaller Peleşor at Sinaia. Their history is that they formed part of the collection of King Louis Philippe, sold after his death, and then resold in 1879. They were purchased by King Carol I, without the realization of their real value, for El Greco was then a forgotten painter, together with a number of indifferent late Italian paintings, in order to furnish the Roumanian palaces with a garniture of old masters. They had been gathered together for

Louis-Philippe by that mysterious character, Baron Taylor, who may have been his illegitimate son, a figure of mystery who makes an appearance in Borrow's *Bible in Spain,* and who for some strange reason has a street called after him in Inverness! Borrow, too, we must remember, was one of the first persons to appreciate the greatness of El Greco and he prophesied, in the 1830s, the high estimation in which the "Burial of Count Orgaz" would, one day, be held.

The most striking of these nine paintings by El Greco are a lovely "Marriage of the Virgin," a late work dating probably from the last decade of the painter's life, after 1600, and a large "Adoration of the Shepherds," also a late work, most wonderful in color and with huge soaring figures of frightening effect, a picture which is very similar in style and handling to "The Annunciation," in San Vicente at Toledo. A portrait of an ecclesiastic, a "Martyrdom of St. Sebastian," and one of the not uncommon paintings of St. Martin, on horseback, dividing his cloak with the beggar, are also in the royal collection. Very curious, indeed, is the small sketch of the "Legend of St. Maurice and the Theban Legion." That painting, which is the wonder of the Escorial, is quite different in this version. The color of that incredible masterpiece has, here, lost its fire. More peculiar still, the warriors of the Theban Legion are no longer in Roman kilts but are shown in Elizabethan trunk hose. The little boy in the foreground, holding a helmet, has become the image of the small orange seller in the bull ring at Seville, in the drop scene painted by Picasso for the Russian ballet, *Le Tricorne.* This version, in fact, cannot be described otherwise than as disappointing, in spite of its intensely odd and curious effect. Some authorities have suggested that it is a copy by Jorge Manuel Theotocopuli, the painter's son; but it seems more probable, owing to the different features and altered dresses of this version, that it is a very late painting by El Greco conceived, perhaps, as a kind of sketch from memory, for the original painting, it must be considered, had never been engraved. If Greco wished to see again that supreme work of his genius there was no other course than to go over from Toledo to the Escorial. This may have been, then, one of the replicas, in little, of his large paintings, for a contemporary writer tells us that Greco had, in his house, a finished sketch of each one of his big compositions. No fewer than three small versions of this subject are mentioned in the inventory of Greco's studio, taken after his death. "St. Maurice and the Theban Legion," in its Roumanian version, is an odd and weird work which adds little to our understanding or admiration of El Greco. "The Marriage of the Virgin" and "The Adoration of the Shepherds" are, contrary to this, two paintings, knowledge of which is necessary to all admirers of El Greco. They are late pictures of his most interesting period, and take an important place among those most extreme productions of the human spirit. They are, needless to say, the greatest works of art in Roumania.

The paintings by El Greco may be described as one of the invisible attractions of Bucharest. Even if they are not seen, it is interesting to feel that they are in the air. There is nothing incongruous in their presence in this town. Its aspect, which is unlike that of any other European city, most exactly suits their provenance and origin. If Bucharest be as essentially Roumanian as Toledo was particularly Spanish, there are other human elements as well which give a spiritual similarity to both towns. What was Moorish in Toledo is Turkish or Phanariot in Bucharest. It is not a question of architecture, or the comparison between Toledo and Bucharest would, at once, become ridiculous. But Bucharest is nearer to Turkey than Toledo to the Moorish town of Granada. So many persons now living in Bucharest have their connection with the Phanar. This would have been, had the Cretan painter aspired to ancient descent, the boast of his proud claim on the Byzantine tradition. The Phanar was the civilizing, if corrosive, influence on Roumania during the whole of the eighteenth century. Even the churches of Bucharest, in their bastard Byzantine style, have their frescoes based on the strict formulas of the schools of Mount Athos, conventions which were familiar to the painter since his Cretan childhood.

And there is even living, in Bucharest, a rich colony of Sephardim, or Spanish Jews, the descendants of those driven out from Toledo and from Granada, still speaking Castilian, and

forming part of that Sephardim population to be found in great
number at Salonica, at Brusa in Asia Minor, and throughout the
ancient Turkish empire generally. The Sephardim, who are the
aristocrats of the Jewish world, have families as ancient in origin
as any of the noble families of Europe. Their history, which has
never yet been written in detail, is a wonderful subject for the
historian. That they should still be speaking Spanish after an
exile of some four hundred and fifty years is astonishing in itself.
Their family lore, with its extraordinary ramifications, can have
no parallel in the traditions of any other race. It would be interesting to know what legends still persist among them of their
ancestry in Spain. The strict education of the Sephardim Jews,
their perpetual intermarriages which have fixed their physical
type to so remarkable a degree, their rules of family, the history of their synagogues—these are some of the mysteries of the
Sephardim. In Salonica, which is in some sense their capital—
for they have even newspapers printed in Spanish—the Jewish
women wore a particularly beautiful costume until the middle of
the last century. This will have been their costume as worn in
the fifteenth century in Spain; and it is probable that the colony
of Sephardim in Bucharest had also their distinctive dress.
Spanish folk tunes, or tunes with an unmistakably Spanish flavor,
have been collected within the last few years among the Spanish
Jews in Rhodes. This proves the inalienable tenacity of the
Spanish influence on them. It is remarkable, too, that the
Sephardim of Bucharest, in contradiction to the general political
tendencies of their race elsewhere in the world, are reported to
be warm in their support of General Franco.

But now we will confine ourselves to the physical appearance
of Bucharest. Its huge area and the leisurely spacing of its houses
are still of the Orient, while skyscrapers, more in model than in
fact, and blocks of modern apartment buildings rise in every direction. Bucharest is described in old books of travel as being
a town of woods and orchards. There are churches, or rather
chapels, now standing in its busiest areas of commerce that, until
the middle of the last century, were hidden from view in midst
of a patch of forest. In fact, the churches and monasteries now

engulfed among its modern streets must have seemed nearly as remote as the little convents still existing on the outskirts of the town. Most of these, which are the attraction of the country round the capital, stand on the edges of small lakes or lagoons. Such is the convent of Tigǎneşti, some twenty miles from Bucharest. A few miles farther in the same direction the forest of Snagov has, in its midst, a lake, on an island in which stands the monastery of the same name. There are others of this character, at Pasǎrea, or Comana, an equal distance from the town; none are of any great architectural interest, but all are picturesque, while the first two at least are romantic because of their situation by the blue waters of those still lagoons. Any convent or monastery the approach to which is by boat gains that much by its isolation and seems, more than ever, to exist in a sphere of life of its own. Equally a lake, which has little to recommend it except its waters to bathe in, has its surfaces broken, in these instances, by the reflection of cupolas and domes, while the music of bells, of the Eastern ritual, to the wooden mallet's stroke, comes over the long waters through the mists of evening.

In other respects the environs of Bucharest are not worthy of the town. A dusty, dry plain, with many marshes, stretches for an immense distance down to the Danube. Only in one direction does the scene improve, where a road with an appallingly bad surface leads to Mogoşoaia, the country house of Princess Marthe Bibesco. The beauty of Mogoşoaia is a tribue to the skill and good taste of its owner. An outside staircase and a pillared loggia in the style of those of Hurez make of this house the unique essay in its style. The material is a close, whitish brick, not unlike the brick architecture of Lombardy. At the other side of the house there is another loggia, and a series of flowered terraces go down to the lake, which is full of lotuses. The interior of the house, which we were allowed to see by the kind permission of its owner, is simple and beautiful, and must be the ideal retreat for a torrid summer. Of the Venetian architect who is said to have worked here and at Hurez I could see no traces. But the house contains a bedroom with splendid Empire furniture that belonged to Madame Tallien, from whom the Prince is descended, and in every detail in the interior the touch of an assured taste is revealed. The house, too, has a chapel near by, with an exceptionally good interior in that substyle of late Byzantine which is known as the Brancovan, from Constantine Brancovan (1688-1714), who was the great builder of his generation. It was this personage who built Hurez; and if that convent is the most charming and attractive in the whole country, Mogoşoaia must be its equivalent where the Roumanian country house is concerned. It must be said, though, that as it stands, Mogoşoaia is entirely the creation of its present owner. Before that time it had been empty and derelict for many years.

The excursion to this house occupied the afternoon of one of our last days in Bucharest. But before we close this subject, or, at least, end any individual day with a description of the music that is the creation of every evening there, another and most curious subject must be mentioned. In this city which has had so many polyglot influences, and in which the peculiarities of its character derive in so large a part from the Orient, there are the few remnants of one of the strangest and most extreme religious sects that has ever existed. One of the first features noticed by the stranger in Bucharest is the cabs, or droshkies, driven by Russian coachmen wearing long black velvet caftans and peaked caps, black in winter and of white linen in the summer. These Russians are often huge specimens of humanity, and their horses, in a land where it is better not to look at the horses, are glossy and well cared for. Generally they are a pair of a particular and valuable breed known as the black Orloff, though these fine horses are not to be seen now as often as formerly. These cabdrivers belonged almost entirely, in old days, to the Russian sect of Skapetz, or the Skoptzi, a sect who made it their practice to mutilate themselves.

The origin of these fanatics is obscure and undetermined. They were one of the numerous sects of dissenters from the Russian Church, of whom the Starosti, the Old Believers, are the most famous. A short digression into Russian history is necessary in order to explain these matters. They are concerned with the

Patriarch Nikhon, the reformer of the Russian Church during the reign of the Czar Alexis (1645-1676). The Patriarch Nikhon, it should be said, was a gaunt and terrifying figure, seven feet in height, whom we may imagine in his monastery of the New Jerusalem, or Voskresenski, daily repeating the curses in the 109th Psalm, with a nude hermit by his side. This was the perpetual and typical action of his extraordinary career. It was the Patriarch Nikhon, in the middle of the seventeenth century, who drove the Starosti into exile in the Northern or Arctic forests, where they built their characteristic wooden churches. They were known as Pomortsi, or Dwellers by the (White) Sea. Others of the Starosti fled to the southern confines of Russia and crossed into Bessarabia, where their descendants are still found, as we shall discover. If the general body of Old Believers was so numerous at one time as not to merit the name of a sect, there were others, and smaller, numbers of religious fantasy. Such were the Khlistovstchina, Jumpers or Flagellants, and the Bezpopovtzi or priestless. These rejected marriage, and believed that suicide by voluntary starvation or burning alive, which they called purifying by the immaculate baptism of fire, was the most meritorious action that a believer could perform. Two thousand seven hundred died thus, in 1687, in the Paleostrovski Monastery. Some readers may be reminded, in this, of a scene from Moussorgsky's opera, *Khovantchina*.

Another division comprised the Beglovestnie, those dissenters who simulated dumbness, and though tried with the most fearful tortures by Pestel, the governor of Siberia in the time of Catherine the Great, could not be induced to speak. Other votaries of silence were the sect of the Beatified Redeemer, who lived constantly absorbed in the contemplation of the holy portrait, which was supposed to produce heavenly bliss and ecstasy. Most extreme of all were the Stranniki, or Wanderers, who considered they must flee from the wrath to come by being homeless and houseless, and, especially, by dying in the open air.* Moscow, which the Orthodox Church considered to be the Third Rome,

* Rasputin is said to have been a member of this sect.

coming after Constantinople, was center and headquarters of these various sects. Archbishop Dimitri of Rostov, in his book on the different sects written early in the eighteenth century, mentions no fewer than two hundred of them. The Russian Church, in fact, persecuted all the sectaries and, not least, the Skoptzi.

Many of those mentioned are now extinct; but the Skoptzi, the most uncompromising of all, are still surviving. It is supposed that they had long existed in Russia, but did not form a religious body until 1765, when their doctrines were preached in the provinces of Orel and Tula by a fanatic called Kondrati Selivanov. Their dogma consists in the literal translation of such texts as "If thine eye offend thee, pluck it out," with others of the same import. The necessary operation was performed with steel and fire by the hands of this fanatic himself. Eventually he appointed a deputy, Silova Ivanovitch, who operated on the converts in Siberia and Eastern Russia. Selivanov was exiled to Siberia where he gave himself out to be Peter III, the murdered husband of Catherine the Great. Her son, the Czar Paul I, caused Selivanov to be brought to St. Petersburg, but deciding that he was an impostor caused him to be imprisoned in an asylum, an interesting decision when the mental balance of the Czar himself is taken into account. Selivanov was eventually released and placed in the monastery of Suzdal, in the Upper Volga, or of Spasso Euphemius—it is uncertain which—where he died in 1833, at well over one hundred years of age. The doctrines of the Skoptzi found a number of adherents. Many rich merchants were members of the sect. The jewelers and money-changers in Moscow and St. Petersburg, in Odessa and in Riga, were members of this community, and would offer large sums of money to induce converts to join them. For a time, under Alexander I, the Skoptzi even flourished. In that curious age and under that most mysterious of Czars, who later, it would seem, became a hermit himself, and went to live for fifty years in the Siberian forests, there were even instances in which officers of the Guard became converted by their soldiers and took the irrevocable decision by which they joined the Skoptzi. It is even claimed that Field-Marshal Count Souvarov became a Skapetz. In 1856 it was estimated that there were thirty thousand of them in Russia; while, in the Urals and on the confines of Armenia, whole villages had nothing but a Skapetz population.

These various details should give the background of fanaticism in which the Skoptzi had their origin. They were exiled to the farthest corners of the Russian empire, or crossed the frontiers into neighboring lands. Of their present condition in Russia I can find no mention in any account published during the last twenty-five years, but it is to be assumed that they must still exist, though the cult is likely to be extinct as far as its proselytyzing energies are concerned. And having said so much about the origin of the Skoptzi in Russia, we now return to Bucharest, where this discussion was prompted by mention of the Russian or Bessarabian droshky drivers. We have described their fine black Orloff horses and the long black velvet caftans that give a look of Russia to the streets. Until twenty or thirty years ago the droshky drivers were almost always eunuchs of the Skoptzi sect. Their practice is to marry and have two children, or at least a son, after which they submit themselves to this cruel operation which alters all the rest of their lives. The story that this operation is the culmination to a licentious orgy I take to be very far from the truth. On the contrary, after having done their military service and had the requisite children by whom the future of their tenets is assured, they carefully undergo an operation at the hands of a surgeon, but, it is natural, in circumstances of deep secrecy. It is said that, according to the strictest tenets of their creed, their wives also go through an operation which is directed to the same purpose, of stopping procreation, and that, at this time of sanctification, even their domestic animals are emasculated. This would be the case only in rare instances of fanaticism.

The interest of this peculiar creed lies in the metamorphosis of its victims. Practically none of the present droshky drivers in Bucharest are Skoptzi, but it is still possible, on careful inquiry, to discover some old adherents to their faith. I was taken to a suburb of the town where several whole streets of prosperous-looking houses were pointed out as having been the homes, until a few years ago, of the Skapetz cabmen. Side by side with the houses were the stables for their horses. This was a relic of the days when Bucharest had as fine equipages as any town in Europe. Every person approaching middle age remembers these Skapetz cabdrivers who had the status of confidential servants and, being in possession of many persons' secrets, could be relied on never to divulge them. This inquisitiveness, this passionate passive interest, were the signs of their physical condition. In no instance is anything but good to be heard of them. They are given the character of pathetic and deeply religious persons condemned to this fanaticism by their beliefs.

But there is still a small quarter, even in this area, which has altogether changed its inhabitants, where you can see the Skoptzi. We stopped at a stable yard where some personal inquiries were made, and in a moment the old cabman Vassili emerged. He was tall and heavily built with a completely smooth and hairless face, ageless features and the high-pitched voice that was to be expected. Like the few remaining Skoptzi of Bucharest he was prosperous, and had let out most of his stables for a garage, only keeping one carriage and a pair of horses. He was born in Moscow and had come to Roumania with his parents when a child. The next day we saw him driving in the streets, where he is still a well-known character. When asked his age, with a touch of that pride and mystery that are noticed in all accounts of the Italian *castrati* singers of the eighteenth century, he refused to answer until a correct guess was made. He was, actually, sixty-eight years old, but was not sure of this within a year.

Round the corner we were in midst of a whole street of them. All are prosperous, living on the rents of their stables, and in a few moments we were drinking Russian tea with them and eating honey underneath a pergola of vines in someone's garden. There were eight or nine of these metamorphosed beings, all with the intense inquisitiveness of their kind. They will not drink or smoke, and an inquiry after one well-known Skapetz was answered sadly with the phrase, "He is lost to us." The meaning of this was that he drank and smoked and had, therefore, forfeited their friendship and his own chances of salvation. All these Skoptzi, being old men of between sixty and seventy, had been born in Russia. Only one of their number had the appearance of middle age, but he avoided conversation, and so deceptive are the effects of their condition that he may have been as old as any. Their intensely religious atmosphere is most impressive.

The cruel mutilation they have undergone alters their physique in a variety of peculiar ways. It is this which should interest the student of psychology and also, it may be added, the medical profession. They become large and feminine round the hips and can, with a little acquaintance, be known at once by their disproportionate limbs, which seem curiously articulated, by a shambling walk, and even by the shape of their backs. More curious still, after several generations who have mutilated themselves, it is said that these physical characteristics appear even in the normal individuals who have not submitted themselves to emasculation.

No history of fanaticism—and one has never yet been written —can ignore the Skoptzi. But it is palpable that their character has been grossly misrepresented. The sacrifice of their virility is, for them, the supreme renunciation and must have been attended in the past with the death of by far the larger proportion of its votaries. There was no greater sacrifice that they could make. The pathos of all religious belief could not be played to more bitter effect than by such ruthless protagonists. The Skoptzi are not vile and sensual but are pathetic to a degree that is hardly to be believed. Human beings have, it is probable, never had a more terrible illusion to trick them into felicity and ultimate salvation. But their appearance in Bucharest, in the middle of the last century, coincides with the extinction of all that was Byzantine in the neighboring Turkey and is, therefore, a fictitious reinforcement of the Orient into a country that will never cease to be of the Orient, as to a large part of its idiosyncrasy. The old and tortuous Orient is not real without the eunuch. The very presence of the Skoptzi is like the wind that never ceases to blow out of the steppes. But this vilified sect has the virtues, also, of the Quaker or the Moravian. It is difficult, indeed, not to feel some sympathy for them. It must be sufficient to say that they deplored, in Bucharest, that no new converts ever came now to increase their number. In Bucharest they are nearly extinct and in another ten years there will be none of them left. But the Skoptzi still flourish in another Roumanian town, in Galați, and it is in Galați that we must describe a visit to their homes, and the impression of true religion, and almost of sanctity, that is shed about them in their pathetic lives. At the present time the Skoptzi claim to have three hundred and forty adepts at Jassy, of whom one hundred and eighty are women, as many more at Galați, many fewer at Bucharest, and some five hundred scattered along the Delta. In all, they are numbered at fifteen hundred. In my opinion this is an underestimation.

It was in the knowledge of having seen some of the most curious individuals left in Europe that we came away from that suburb of low houses. Row after row of those one-storied dwellings stretched in every direction; but the Skoptzi had gone, and no stranger could ever find his way back to them through this maze of little streets. And here, walking in twos and threes, were the typical Russian peasant women, looking, even, like the peasant dolls of childhood. Their heads were hooded in white shawls that entirely hid their faces, they had blue cotton dresses printed with white or red flowers, and, of course, heavy wooden clogs. Because of their hidden features they were like painted wooden ghosts. These were the wives of the droshky drivers, with, it is probable, the wife of a Skapetz among them. And, in another moment, this suburb of old Russia was entirely left behind.

Life in the poorer quarters of Bucharest must be far from unpleasant. Food is plentiful and extremely cheap; in fact Roumania has a cheaper rate of living than any country in Europe. Bulgaria or Yugoslavia may approach to it in these matters, but the greater fertility of Roumania produces crops to which those colder countries cannot aspire. Chickens are the equivalent of tenpence each; turkeys are little more expensive. They have excellent fish, fresh water from the Danube and salt water from the Black Sea. There are a variety of fruits, from the apples of the colder north to watermelons, ending with those huge gourds that have flesh the color of blood oranges and are a favorite food with the

populace, that are typical, therefore, of the extreme south of
Europe. Yet this town which had such tropical heat during our
visit in September lies pale and noiseless in winter, under a thick
covering of snow. Sledges make their appearance, and the cold
of St. Petersburg has succeeded to the fire and languor of Seville.

It must be because of this variety of foods, and for the torrid
heat, that Bucharest possesses an altogether inordinate number of
summer restaurants. The same thing is to be seen in the places
where many of the population of Bucharest spend their summer.
The road, for instance, between Predeal and Sinaia, a distance of
twelve miles, appears to be lined on both sides with open-air
restaurants, over the greater part of its extent. In Bucharest they
are to be found in all quarters of the town. The name of these
garden restaurants is *grădină*. Dinner—though it is difficult to
call it dinner if it begins near midnight—will begin with a
glass or two of țuica. And now we come to the Roumanian cuisine.
This, to gourmets, was the surprise of the Paris Exhibition. The
Roumanian pavilion was thronged, night after night, for this
reason. It is probable that, after pre-Revolutionary Russian, the
Roumanian is the best native cuisine in Europe. Dinner, in even
these inexpensive *grădinăs* of Bucharest, will consist of *ciorbă*, a
fish or chicken soup made with sour cream; and will be followed
by carp, perch or sturgeon. Other dishes are *mititei*, a compound
of grilled sausages; *tocană*, veal with a tomato sauce; *sărmala*, rice,
balls with chopped meat, wrapped in winter in a cabbage leaf
and in summer in a vine leaf, similar, in fact, to the Greek *dolma;*
a tender saddle of lamb; or *mușchiu de vaca, filet de bœuf*, always
excellent. There are, as well, *fleiça*, beef roasted on a spit; or
ardei umpluți, paprika pods filled with rice and minced meat.
Poussins roasted on a spit are a specialty of Roumania. Other
things which can only be described as delicious are a *pilaff* of
quails, and the crayfish, or *queus d'écrevisses*, which are cooked
in a variety of ways, with saffron or paprika, and have better
flavor even than the crayfish, or *kraftor*, in Sweden. Roumania
also has its own caviar, which they prefer fresh, though this does
not make instant appeal to those who are used to the salt beluga
or molossol. The fresh caviar is infinitely more expensive, having

been brought the same day from the Black Sea; but it must be said that the Roumanian salt caviar is only just less good than that of the Caspian. There are a great many dishes that are eaten with a sauce or dressing of sour cream. For dessert there will be fresh peaches and *fraises des bois,* or wild raspberries; bunches also of the small white grapes; and, of course, Turkish coffee.

The wine in Roumania is generally, or universally, good but never exciting. A wine is but seldom to be met with that can be thought of as a discovery. Individual proprietors make enough only for their own needs, and it is only the rich vineyard owners who will take trouble over their products. On the other hand, the wine seems never to have the heavy sulfurous taste of most of the wines of southern lands. No similarity can be noticed between Roumanian and Sicilian or Southern Italian wine. There are wines made with imported Tokayer grapes, but possessing quite a different flavor from those of Tokay. As a rule, though, the red wines are more interesting than the white. The Crown wines are usually to be relied on; as are those of Cotnar, Odobeşti or Drăgăşani. These are, perhaps, the best; there is not much to choose between the others. Many of these wines could probably be much improved on with care, by the selection of the best vintage years, by careful maturing, and so forth. But these processes require many years before they can be brought to perfection and, in the meantime, the Roumanians seem content to drink the wine as they find it. A tolerable brandy is made, resembling the Greek cognac. Many homemade liqueurs are distilled on country properties—good cherry brandy particularly, and also peach or apricot brandy. Finally, it must be said that Roumania seems sadly deficient in mineral waters, Borsec being the invariable reply to every inquiry. There must be many excellent waters in the mountains; but either these have not yet been exploited, or else it is that the Roumanians prefer to drink the local water with their wine. Perhaps, until this custom has stopped, their wine will never receive the attention that it deserves.

Persons who have spent a two-month holiday in Bucharest have assured me that, on leaving, they have realized there remained twenty or thirty of these small restaurants or *grădinăs,* to which there was not time to go. And if there is this bewildering choice of food, the same thing is true of character and locality. There are, of course, the expensive restaurants to be found in every capital; places like the famous Capşa, which well deserves its reputation, and has a *confiserie* and sweetshop attached to it that has, perhaps, no equal in Europe; and Capşa's pupils, Angelescu and Grigorescu. But the true character of Bucharest is to be found much more in smaller places of less international repute. A summer day, which is divided into two by the siesta, a device, incidentally, that gives the illusion of prolonging human life, could find no more pleasant ending than dinner to the accompaniment of music. This, indeed, is the culminating pleasure of Bucharest. It may be said, in a phrase, that there is as much music here as there used to be in Naples when the *festa* of Piedigrotta still brought out, every year, the new songs that were to sweep like fire all over the Italian peninsula within a few weeks.

This music is of many different sorts. The expensive restaurants have American bands, as good as any to be heard in Paris or London, and playing the new tunes that have only been surreptitiously released and are still played, as it were, by the favor of the conductor. The players in these bands are all of Roumanian nationality. No one would know that they were not American. If this music has to exist it must, at least, be as good as possible, and this is our excuse for mentioning these places. There are, as well, the bands that play Viennese waltzes; and the fact that so much of the present Roumania was part of the Hapsburg empire will sufficiently account for the ease and grace of their performance. Gypsy bands also abound, but are not as good as in Hungary. The Roumanian *ciganje* have not yet developed a sophistication that can be adapted to the restaurant life of a big capital. Their performances are rough and uncouth. To be properly heard they should be listened to in the remote country where their genius keeps to the soil and invents those tunes that are collected by Béla Bartók and by Kódaly. In them the true Romanian speaks; but it is in a dialect that is not understood in great cities.

There is at least one *grădină* where a Russian orchestra can be heard. This particular band is of superlative merit, in its kind. They sing the tunes that were sung in Moscow before the Revolution, many of which are familiar tags, as hackneyed as the cheaper Spanish tunes that are the commonplace of circus or bull ring. One Russian singer, living in Bucharest, was mentioned, who had an extreme renown before the Revolution; but this person was, unfortunately, ill and could not be found. This band, probably because in Bucharest they cannot actually be said to be in exile, possessed a quality that I have never heard before in a band of their description. The banality of those Russian Gypsy songs, and the songs which go with drinking toasts, had never appealed to me before, heard now for the first time, away from the Russian restaurant or tea room of conventional exile. There are some Russian tangos, such as the well-known *"Dwe Gitare,"* that have a peculiar nostalgia in these circumstances. The origin, too, of that traditional song is mysterious, for if it is a tango it can hardly have been composed before the war. Many of them come, of course, from Russian musical comedies; but nearly all are now anonymous. One of the best known of all, which passes always for a Russian Gypsy song, is in reality by the Spanish violinist Sarasate, who died some thirty years ago, and it is to be recognized in his *"Zigeuner-weisen."* Perhaps he may have heard this air in Russia. If that is so, then this tune and many others of its kind may be nearer sixty than thirty years old. Later on, at Vâlcov, on the Black Sea, we were to hear many more of these Russian tunes, and some of them, we were told, had come lately from Russia.

But the real beauty of these evening entertainments are the Roumanian songs. By now, after three weeks in the country, the dawn of them had broken on one's mind. They come at first only with the recognition that they have been heard before. A day or two later they are in your mind and you cannot remember where you have heard them. Next time, it is that the tune is in your ears and you cannot quite get it. Like something unattainable it hangs beyond the reach. That very evening a band may play it, but when you get home, you have forgotten the way it went. It comes back to you in the middle of the night, and next morning has gone from you again. In the end, when I knew these tunes, I could be kept awake thinking of them, such is their impalpable nostalgia and the mystery of their quality.

I have compared them with the songs of Piedigrotta, but this is a comparison in popularity. It does not attempt a description of their merits. They are the popular songs of a great town and have nothing in them of Moldavia or Wallachia. This is not peasant music; it is the music of the inn and the *grădină*. Neither does it show any American influence. But many of these tunes, again, are a mystery as to their origins. Some of them, people remember in their childhood; others that are just as good come from the latest revue, at the Carabus, for instance, or from some other summer theater. There is nothing whatever of Vienna, nothing Hungarian, still less Russian, in their style. Neither are these the French chansons of the music halls, although their purpose approximates more to that than to anything else. They are partly that, and in part the popular song, as of Piedigrotta, where the new tunes were tried over for the first time every year, and still the old favorites never died. They are less sentimental than Neapolitan songs, not set out expressly for the tenor, nor giving him the high notes that all Italians would want. On the contrary, they are better when sung by a woman's voice. It does not even appear that their composers are at all well known or popular. There must be new songs every year for the revues, and the best of them blend irrevocably with the old. It is, thus, a convention that has been in existence for a long time. Its mannerisms are perfectly well known and, in fact, in order to be a good song the new must fit exactly within these limitations of the old.

To the many persons who will have heard the band in the Roumanian pavilion at the Paris Exhibition it must be said that Fanica Luca, the virtuoso who played on the syrinx or Panpipes, would appear to be unique of his kind. There is no one else in Bucharest who plays on that instrument. But that particular band, which is famous, consists principally of *ciganje,* and they played Gypsy music. Neither can I say that I altogether admired his performance. The Panpipes, besides their Papageno qualities, possess, as it were, a propensity to impertinence, and the shrill whistle which terminates every tune comes to spoil all that has gone before. Also, the noise of it quite overpowers the band. Even so, this first introduction to Roumanian popular music will have been a revelation to many people. Nothing of its kind has ever reached Western Europe before, though its true quality may have been forced or obscured by that too exuberant performer. I find that my view of this instrument was shared also by Liszt. In his book, *The Gypsy in Music,* talking of the Gypsy musicians of the Danubian provinces, he says: "There is, also, great use made of an instrument consisting of several pipes placed in a row, similar to that which we call Pandean pipes, the honeyed tones of which would quite sufficiently cancel the verve of their orchestra, without the further effeminating effect produced by the equally free use of a kind of mandoline." And yet the effect of these Panpipes is, surely, to be heard transcribed and reproduced toward the end of Liszt's Tenth Rhapsody.

This is the only good popular music that I have ever heard in the knowledge that it was living. New York, or Harlem, are of a different order. This is living music in the sense that it was alive in Vienna in the day of Ziehrer and of Johann Strauss. It transmutes every memory of Bucharest. The point of these songs is that they are like images or clichés of the town, giving you its feeling and atmosphere within a breath or two of its air. At the same time, I wish it had not been necessary, in order to illustrate my meaning, to write the names of Ziehrer or of Johann Strauss, for they infer an entity that is entirely alien to that of which we are speaking. This is much more the *café chantant* of Degas; but as if its cafés were at no inordinate distance from the Black Sea, or even from the Bosphorus. It is essentially the music of a southern land. If the *fados* of Lisbon were all that they are said to be, this music would be their equivalent.

Toward the end of a few days in Bucharest this music will take up an extraordinary share of one's unconscious attention. For most of the day, or night, it is at the back of one's mind. This, indeed, is the true nostalgia, in music, for the import of these tunes is undeniably sad and disillusioned, in spite of their words, which may have an entirely opposite meaning. The hot September nights always hold the echo of them from some café. They seem to utter, cynically, their message of the little chance there is in life and the small meaning there is in happiness. All the same it is a land of summer heats and fruits. The climate, as in songs of Naples or Seville, has circumscribed their shape. By now their burden becomes unbearably sad. Yet, since this is its expression, and it has none other, it would be useless to seek for an explanation. The message of it is in the music.

For night after night this can continue. "Ionel, Ionelule," that masterpiece of disillusionment, though a moment later it may be fraught with another meaning altogether, can easily become an obsession. It opens like the popular songs of Seville or Valencia; and then in a moment is itself again. This is its nostalgia. At every reiteration it comes back again. On the last night of all, just before I fell asleep, I remembered it once more. And then, immediately, the strains of it came from the open-air café next door, in the Chaussée Kisseleff, from under the trees.

It was four in the morning. There was no other sound but the footsteps of one of the pair of faithful Albanians, enjoying his sinecure of night duty and listening, no doubt, like myself, to the music. Outside, the long avenue lay quiet. How curious it seemed, lying there, to think of the Chaussée once full of carriages, of the Skapetz coachmen, of those Laetzi Gypsies at the fair, only two days before. This was Bucharest, a town that is like none other. And once more the refrain came back incarnating the nostalgia of my thoughts. All, all was implicit in that tune.

The valley of the Danube is a corridor along which horde after horde of barbarians has come into Europe. But, if we think of it in the direction in which it flows, the Danube passes out of civilization into nothingness, toward the Tartar steppe. It is more than seventeen hundred and fifty miles from its source at Donaueschingen, in Bavaria, to its ends in the Black Sea, passing Linz and the huge convent of Melk, past Vienna and Budapest, through the Iron Gates, past the bridge of Trajan built by the Greek Apollodorus, past the little Turkish island of Ada-

Kaleh, through the great Wallachian plain, down to Dobroudja and to Galați. But before Galați, even before Braila, it is entering on its delta: it has huge lagoons that appear to be lost in their immensity, and it is from this point down to the Black Sea that the Danube is no longer like a part of Europe, and that it has begun to assume the quality of those mysterious lands toward which it flows. It is this portion of Roumania that bears no resemblance to any part of the Western world. Travelers have compared these last reaches of the Danube with the Yellow River, flowing into the China Sea.

In prosaic contradiction, the train from Bucharest to Galați, is nothing less than an express of English Pullman coaches. It is the journey down to Dover or to Brighton, but without the teacups or assorted biscuits, and passing on the way—for it is evening—some oil towns that light the air with their flares, while poisoning it with their unpleasant fumes. Galați, a huge river port with a hundred thousand inhabitants, seemed dark and endless; but it was here, at the very station, that by good luck we met Pedracchi, the giant Skapetz cabdriver, an immensely tall and thin figure, some six feet eight inches in height, and wearing a long black caftan that seemed further to increase his stature. He stood by his black Orloff horses, a head and shoulders taller than their manes, and before he had driven us for more than a few minutes it was discovered he had been coachman, in Galați, to the grandfather of a friend, in the days when Galați was headquarters of the Danube Commission and a center of life and gaiety. This made him an old acquaintance. He came with us on board the Danube boat, in a flow of anecdote and reminiscence. It was after midnight when he left and not before a promise had been given to visit him on our return. That, indeed, as we shall see, was to take up all our time at Galați. Not that there is anything else, there, at which it is necessary to delay, unless it be the tomb of Mazeppa in the Church of St. George; but this had been violated by the Russians a hundred years ago. The mention of Mazeppa, though, is in proof of the Russian or Cossack steppe that is so near.

An afternoon had to be spent in Galați before the train left

for Bucharest, hours that held no promise, for the town has
nothing interesting except its Gypsy quarter, which we had no
time to visit. It is said that from Galați, and the neighboring
Braila, come many of the Gypsy musicians who lead the restaurant orchestras in all parts of the world. Most of these Gypsies,
in their early youth, will have had exceptional quality as musicians. But, once more, as if predestined to this meeting,
Pedracchi, the giant cabdriver, appeared. He looked even taller
than before in his long black caftan, and by daylight it was
possible to admire properly his pair of black Orloffs. He repeated the invitation to his house. Within a few moments we
had reached the road in which he lived and could begin a most
interesting investigation. Like all his coreligionists, Pedracchi
leads a prosperous and happy life in close contact with others
of his race and creed. A whole street seemed to be inhabited by
them. But our friend must be wealthier than most. His house
was spotlessly clean, and its walls were stenciled with the bright
flower patterns that are so popular in Roumania. Perhaps he is
a trifle more sophisticated than his fellows, for the sitting room
had an icon but none of the other special features that we shall
soon notice. Delicious Russian tea was handed round by his
sister, for he has never married; but she remained standing and
would not take a chair, and it was explained to us that their
women never sit down when there are guests in the house. Instead of sugar he put spoonfuls of honey into our tea, while
talking of his youth in Russia and extolling the country in which
he had settled, for it left him and his friends in peace to earn
their living and did not interfere with their beliefs. The modern
Russians he regarded as lunatics, saying that liberty no longer
existed there. Roumania was a land of freedom where persons
were allowed to worship their god and follow the precepts of
life that appeared right to them. Nothing more friendly and hos-
pitable could be imagined than our reception in this house; in
fact any of our party who came to Galați again were invited to
stay there instead of at the hotel, an invitation which would be
warmly accepted. As was natural, we asked no intimate questions of him; but it transpired that his community go to the

Russian church and have no priests of their own, that they are, indeed, the Bezpopovtsi, but in the milder sense, not of denying the very idea of priesthood, but in accepting the existing priests and having no special pastors of their own denomination.

And then, taking off his caftan and putting on a linen coat and an odd, old-fashioned Panama hat, Pedracchi took us along to visit his friends. His height looked positively gigantic in this costume, but he assured us there were two Russian coachmen in Galați even taller than himself. First of all we went to see his beehives, for they are all great apiarists or beekeepers. This is their other industry, after what would have been called, in another century, their livery stables. He had thirty or forty beehives, which were inhabited by as many millions of bees, to judge from the dense clouds of them that we disturbed. The other coachmen, who were in poorer circumstances, lived in a double row of one-storied wooden houses running at right angles to the street outside.

It was the interior of these little houses that was a revelation of taste and style. They are cleaner than the Dutch houses of Marken or Volendam, and have a profusion of the finest white linen, elaborately worked by hand. These houses have, in fact, a linen decoration, where the walls of other Roumanian houses are hung with striped stuffs or embroidered cloths. This is their difference in style; the reception rooms of some of the convents I have described elsewhere as being typical of the Roumanian style. These, on the contrary, are Russian houses; but it can only be the Staroviri or Dissenters, generally, who are distinguished for cleanliness. The next thing that is noticeable in their houses is, always, a portrait of the Czar, not the unfortunate Nicholas II who was murdered, but his father Alexander III, the giant Czar, and then it is to be seen that there are engravings also of Alexander I and of Nicholas I.

But always, in a place of honor, is to be seen a more ancient portrait, that of the Czar Peter III. This portrait is to be found everywhere among them; Peter is invariably painted bareheaded, with a short black beard, wearing a blue caftan trimmed with black fur from top to bottom; on his right knee lies a red cloth

on which rests his right hand. There is some curious significance
about this gesture, for the secret sign that one Skapetz will make
to another consists in placing a red cloth on his right knee and
striking it with his right hand. Peter III, the grandson of Peter
the Great, was the husband of Catherine the Great. It was by
her orders that he was murdered in 1762, the year in which he
came to the throne. He had never been crowned or consecrated;
and only one person, an Archbishop, knew the secret spot where
his bones rested, unmarked by either monument or inscription.
His son, or putative son, the mad Paul I, caused the tomb of his
father to be opened as soon as possible after Catherine had died,
but only a few bones were found within, and the Czar's boots.
These were exposed for three days and, having had the services
of consecration and coronation read over them, were removed
and buried with the remains of Peter the Great and others of
his family.

It is the belief of the Skoptzi that Christ never died, but
wanders constantly, without sex and in different forms, over the
earth. They believe that He assumes the form of Peter III, who
they say was never murdered, but fled to Irkutsk. Soon he will
come again and sound the great bell of the Uspenski Sobor (the
Cathedral in the Kremlin), in order that the Skoptzi may assemble round him and inaugurate their everlasting empire over
the world. It is for this reason that they make a point of possessing his portrait. The fanatic Selivanov, who first preached their
faith in about 1765, claimed, it will be remembered, to be the
Czar Peter III.

It is apparent that the mystery of Peter III's death made imposture nearly a certainty. He was the last male descendant of
Peter the Great, which made his life the more valuable from a
traditionalist view. It was, though, Peter the Great who particularly persecuted the Russian Dissenters and exiled them abroad,
which makes their attachment to his grandson less easy to understand. The Skoptzi were, of course, of more recent origin,
occurring within a few years of the death of Peter III. But Peter
III must have had the reputation of wishing to restore the old
Russian customs. It is to be observed that in these strange icon-

like portraits of Peter, which are venerated by the Skoptzi, he is represented with a black beard. This is, in itself, of significant importance, for his grandfather, Peter the Great, taking a beard as the symbol of Russia's backwardness, imposed heavy penalties on the wearers of beards. He would even, it is said, wait behind a corner armed with a heavy pair of shears and would spring out and clip away with his own hands the beard of any passer-by. Beards, in short, were practically abolished from Russia by Peter the Great. He was as stringent in their suppression as his historical parallel, Kemal Ataturk, toward the wearers of the fez.

Their appearance, once more, in the person of Peter III, might be taken as the symbol of a wish to go back to old customs, to restore the old worship and to return to Russia as it was before the reforms of the Patriarch Nikhon, or of Peter the Great. Even so, it is, within modern times, one of the most extreme aberrations of the human spirit that should seek to invest as unworthy and obscure a figure as Peter III with the attributes of divinity, while imposing, at the same time, such a terrible penalty of pain, such a lifetime of sacrifice, on its sectaries. How, indeed, this religion —for it can only by circumlocution be called a branch of Christianity—can ever have possessed sufficient appeal for its votaries still to be numerous, more than a hundred and fifty years later, is quite impossible to comprehend. It entailed, as well, lifelong persecution and, at the least, exile far from home.

The appalling stringencies that they have imposed on themselves would seem to have their reward in increased prosperity. Even the minor hardships of neither drinking nor smoking must increase the income of all abstainers, in this class of life, by a minimum of something like ten per cent of their weekly income. It appears, too, as if their energies are forced into supplementary directions. One source of livelihood is not enough. They keep beehives, as well as their livery stables, and, in the country near Galaţi, are possessed of big orchards. For in the neighborhood of Galaţi there are villages, or settlements, in which they form the majority of the population. At Galaţi, or in its neighborhood, and perhaps nowhere else in the world, there are young Skoptzi to be seen, men of twenty-five years of age or under, who have submitted to emasculation. If they have performed their military service, paid their taxes, more still, if they have married and had children, there seems no valid reason for interfering with the liberty of their lives. It is, at least, the strongest possible argument that Roumania is the land in which minorities are treated with the most consideration and allowed the fullest freedom. As to the ethics of it—is this worse than allowing a celibate priesthood, or permitting the voluntary incarceration of men and women in monasteries and nunneries? The Skoptzi, at least, fulfil their duties to the state in greater measure than is the case with the religious orders.

This is all that need be said for or against the strangest of all religious communities in Europe. We will hope that enough has transpired, in the course of it, to set on record the very touching and pathetic character of the persons concerned. In those places in which they have been mentioned elsewhere in literature, their virtues have been denied them and they have been termed licentious and depraved. On the contrary, they are a deeply religious body, in whom the good qualities of the Quaker or the Moravian are to be found, but in humbler circumstances.

It was with very real feelings of regret that we parted from this friend whom none of us is likely to see again, and in the conviction that this body of Russian or Oriental zealots live in the ideals of a thousand years ago and are, thus, of a rarity and humility that are never to be met with elsewhere in this modern world. There are instances, we are told, in which, paradoxically, the Skoptzi have progressed with the times and own taxicabs instead of droshkies. But it is with their carriages and their black Orloff horses that they will always remain a memory, and in the thought of that strange figure with his *imberbe* features and ageless countenance, living, owing to his gigantic height, in the canon of El Greco or of the Byzantine mosaics, and remembered in the hospitality of his house, or stooping over the beehives in his apple orchard.

DRAMAS AND DANCE CYCLES OF THE ISLANDS:
THE AREÖI SOCIETY*

We arrive in a vessel after a long voyage. "Our ship is rocked by the sunset wind."**

All morning we lay against the reef, grinding on the walls of coral, casting the lead, calling out the fathoms. For the coral atoll is but just below water. Looking down, we see patches of clear white sand for floor, and fishes with spots and stripes of gold, like birds on the trees, among the branches of the corals. Of these, later. For they live and breathe in their own element. That is Poseidon's kingdom, though he is known by other names.

Over and upon this, with a long swell, the ocean lifts and hurls itself in an unbroken wave. But we are within the reef and have before us high hills and a dazzling white strand. Instantly, the canoes come out. The first is filled with gifts of fruit and flowers. In another are the high priests and their idols. The King comes last with his attendants. They are dressed in brilliant cloaks and helmets of red feathers. But the King's cloak is entirely yellow, and shines in the bright sun like gold. Climbing on board, they throw their cloaks on our shoulders, place their feather helmets on our heads, put their fans into our hands. "An hour later the hood of night comes on the land."**

And so we have reached an island, big or small. No need to be precise. It is all Oceania; the coral sea of many isles and archipelagos. Oceania of the light-skinned races. Not the Negritos, nor the Melanesians. But the voyage was a necessity. This cannot be written of as though we were native to the islands. Nor, entirely, as if we came from their Antipodes. We are a

* From *Primitive Scenes and Festivals*, 1942.
** Quotations from one of my first poems, "Tahiti," written in 1917.

disembodiment, and write of what we see with the eyes of the poet or the artist, having all antiquity for our journey here, until the recent past. It is a subject for a composition, to be judged by intrinsic, not by literal truth. We will allow ourselves, after being carried here, to enjoy the recreation of this enchanted spot. For that, we will wait for the voyages of the Areöis. That is our subject.

Meantime, for accuracy, we return to the large red feather caps, for that detail may give identity to what will become general to this coral sea. Their cloaks and helms of feathers are made, more often, of the red, yellow and green feathers of a small bird. Another bird, *Melithreptes pacifica* of the ornithologists, inhabits the mountains and has under each wing a single yellow feather only, an inch in length. They are caught with birdlime smeared on poles, and the pair of feathers taken from them. The yellow war cloak of the King, which we saw shining on the strand and that became more like a cloak of gold as he was rowed nearer to the vessel, is four feet long and eleven and a half feet round the hem, made entirely of these feathers. It was formed during nine successive reigns. Dating from the antiquity, therefore, of this paradisal shore. "For the most prominent feature in the character of the islanders appears to be their love of indolence, in which the too great bounty of nature has permitted them to indulge." This much may we read, even of a hundred years ago: "And that they appear hitherto to have been an exception to that common law of nature, which has seemed everywhere else to have imposed toil in greater or less degree upon all men." Shall we continue?

But these shores of fragrance must display their population. The women dress in long, loose calico gowns of gaudy colors, preferring red or yellow; some of them wearing a small girdle or gay handkerchief tied round their waists. Over their calico gowns they wear silken shawls, with a wreath of red or yellow flowers, or an ornament of red or yellow wool on their heads. They walk barefoot. The girls in their dances form headdresses of living fireflies, which they impale on slips of bamboo and fix in such a manner that for hours they wear the glittering diadems in their

hair. Their chiefs are clothed in pieces of snow-white tapa, made
from the paper mulberry, and allow the trains to drag after them
along the ground.

Husbandmen have aprons of red dracæna leaves, ornaments
made from the pearly nautilus, and chaplets of flowers of the
scarlet hibiscus. Their tattooing is plainly visible. One pattern,
varying in its details, is like the crown of a palm tree. It springs
from the central line of the back, and gracefully curls round
both sides of the body. They also wear a picturesque kind of
hat made of palm leaves, which, in the words of an eyewitness,
gives an interesting finish to their manly figures. And the fishermen, in their canoes, use long bamboo rods and lines, from
which a pearl imitation of a flying fish is attached, for the cap-
ture of the bonito, dolphin or albacore; or plunge into the water
with a hand net, when they come in danger from the sharks, or
their long black hair may get entangled and held fast in the
branches of the corals.

That is Oceania, from end to end. Not a particular island, but
the consensus of its Pacific sands. Paler than our shores, as
though there were more pearl shell here. For the waves roll from
half across the world, and in a million years have ground the
shells into a fine white dust. They are shores of coral, too. It
is, in fact, the coral sea.

And among one group of islands we find the Areöis. The
Jesuit fathers describe something similar in the Caroline and
Ladrone Islands. The Areöis—for we must quote again—"were
a sort of priviliged libertines, or strolling players, who formed
themselves into a society for the worship of the god Oro, and
the practice of immoral dances and pantomimes. They spent
their time in travelling from island to island, and from one district
to another, exhibiting their performances, and spreading a moral
contagion throughout society. The numbers connected with this
fraternity, and the magnitude of their expeditions, will appear
from the fact of Captain Cook witnessing, on one occasion, in
Huahine, the departure of seventy canoes filled with Areöis. On
board the canoes in which they travelled they erected temporary
altars, for the worship of the tutelary deities of their society. On
public occasions they painted their bodies with charcoal, and

stained their faces with a scarlet dye. At times they wore a girdle of ripe plantain leaves, and ornamented their heads with the bright yellow and scarlet leaves of the barringtonia. Their entertainments consisted in delivering speeches ludicrously referring to public events, in pantomime exhibitions, in wrestling, and in dancing during the night to the music of the flute and drum. In the constant display of these often obscene exhibitions, they passed their lives, strolling from one place or island to another."

In our eyes they are South Sea Islanders. To themselves, they are inhabitants of the living world. But, for our purposes, they are neither the one, nor the other. Not more than the personalities of universal legend. Their fruits and flowers, as much as the fragrant winds and coral shore, are the classic architecture of this myth. If we impute to them more of beauty and intelligence than they possessed, it is in the interest of the ideal, and no more, it may be, than to the eyes of their beholders.

This may be the moment, too, in which to discredit the stories of the Protestant missionaries. It was not long before, under their influence, the women and girls at Sunday service wore hideous bonnets, like huge coal scuttles, based on the middle-class fashion of the '40s, when the missionaries first arrived. The islanders fell out of an earthly paradise into a Sunday slum. The conch shell was made silent by the harmonium. We attach little more importance to their stories than to their promises of heaven. The one, indeed, contradicts the beauty of the other. That the Areöis were immoral is not to be denied. And it may be inquired what is meant by morals, where are neither palaces nor slums, nor sound of marriage nor funeral bell? But the wheezing harmonium must be forever banished. It has come and gone. It came with measles, whooping cough and colds, and other and more wasting ills. So the tin chapel is not yet put up. We could have wished it was but an interlude, a day and night in prison; but what it touched has been destroyed forever. It has been the hand of death: and, in life, it is better not to think of that.

In effect, we land on this shore with all the technique learned of other lotus-eating lands. It is a food that, like fancy, has no substance. True lotus-eaters are, generally, more famished than

well fed. But the Lotophagi are no parallel: for the Areöis led
active, and not passive, lives of pleasure. In virtue of this they
become a concept that we clothe, or unclothe, with our preju-
dices. They are the instruments of pleasure, not the audience.
Here, the Areöis spread a moral contagion throughout society,
journeying from isle to isle. In a paradise where there is no poverty nor cold. Nor excessive heat; but the seasons are tempered
day by day, instead of month by month: a little rain in the early
morning so that earth wakes freshened. No floods nor gales.
But, for excitement, the lightning and the thunder.

We will take the climate and the scene in order to have those
skies and that brilliant light for background. For it is, precisely,
"that indolence in which the too great bounty of nature has permitted them to indulge," together with the information that the
Areöis "were a sort of privileged libertines, or strolling players,
who passed their lives in travelling from island to island"—it is
these statements that intoxicate the imagination and make the
Areöis, to our eyes, brothers and sisters to the comedians in Watteau's paintings. "Their magnificent valleys abound not alone
in luxuriant forests that attract and charm the eye, but also in
trees bearing sufficient fruit to supply all their proper wants. The
trees which produce the bread fruit, the banana, orange, coconut, and the cheremoya, seem to contend with one another for
the palm of superior strength and beauty, and for the quantity
of their spontaneous abundance. Their hogs require no care,
and feed upon fruits which would otherwise rot and waste upon
the ground; and their coasts abound in fish of every kind, which
can be obtained at the price of no more labor than such as might
be termed an agreeable pastime." It reads like an account of
paradise.

But where to begin? Along the white strand; upon the scented
hills; or in Poseidon's kingdom? So many thousands of leagues
of blue weather, in every direction, into the four winds, have
given to these islands a character of light that is their own. As
much as to oases among the yellow sands; but Oceania is a continent of islands. A coral sea of many isles and archipelagos, with
an entity as of Asia or Africa, and attributes that could be per-

sonified into a statue or a painting. Unsullied of history. So that its physiognomy has no likeness to another. A continent of islands, inasmuch as Africa is black man's land. That is its meaning, that it is isle upon isle. That it has been built up in a million years out of the blue main. The marine Indies—for where the past of poetry or painting is concerned, the Oceanians are Indian, to be known by what ocean has yielded to them the pearl, the scepter of narwhal ivory. There are a million wonders in half the world of ocean; and those living in their midst could rightly be called the Poseidonians.

But here it is not Neptune, but another god, who has given colors, also, to the trees and flowers. Not a snowy landscape lighted by the prisms in the crystal; nor that which lies yellow in a grain of sand; the chalk hills; the plain of shards and broken marble under the acanthus and the asphodel; where the blue campanula grows from cracks in the granite; the blue delphinium from the moraine; where the oleanders in the dry river bed compose into a myth; or an almond in blossom is the antique world on a youthful morning; where the hills and high places are trodden by the Muses; here is nothing familiar, or that has a token meaning. All things are soft and clear as in a drop of water, but of blue water, as it might be a drop of water on the back or shoulders of the god himself, youth or maiden, as he climbs out of the sea.

Day and night, here, are spent half in, half out of water. Amphibian noons, cooled by the surf for snow. The kingdom of the trident. Their legends are of the vast spaces of the ocean. How they beached their canoes after many days at sea, and were the first to set foot on this isle of flowers. How they plucked, at once, the jasmine for their hair. Not a bird flew away. All stayed, or came up near, as though their bidding was to wait for man. During the first years they could be struck down like flowers. Their wings were but to float them in the pleasant winds. Flight has but one meaning. It is pure pleasure. Far away, where the sun sank, there were other isles where no one died. In other ways it was the same there. They had night and day, for none feared the dark. The nights were too beautiful to lose, crowned with nocturnal blossoms that lived for this hour and only opened now. The winds, too, breathed differently, and you felt the sea plumes waving in them. The clang, even, of their feathers, now and then, and the breaking of a gigantic wave. Their paradise, in fact, was but another island, for the imagination could conceive of no more fruits or flowers.

Listen! It is a huge roller breaking. And we hear laughing and singing. The fishermen are far out on the reefs, crossing what has been uncovered by the tide; and women and girls go with them, lighted torches in their hands. They will come back with pearls. The ocean gleams and drips with phosphorus. It is easy to be a maiden and return a woman in the morning. The rosy shell of Venus is a sign of that, held in the hand, for the rosy awakening of day. All will carry back shells for ornament. Their pleasure gardens are out on the coral, which we will see, later, pool by pool, in all their wonder. What we would have, for the moment, is laughter and singing on the coral reef. For, near at hand, the blue moonlight shows us chieftains in togas made of snow-white tapa; tattooed like the drawing of the body on the human body, only it is an abstraction, a mere pattern of dots and lines, or an arabesque of leaves and shells, but it moves with the body, it lies on the body, it is a sculpture to be felt by the fingers on the living flesh, it is the lunar outline on the solar body, a form seen in double silhouette, a flickering and pursuing shadow, a shade on a shade. These are moonlight warriors in white cloaks, beaten out of the tree bark, and all day you would hear the hammer, hammer, of the wooden mallets. Such is the loom or distaff of the islands, for it is common to them all. There are the different qualities but this is the snowy white, without pattern. The textile of the Polynesians has another sound and one to which our ears must get accustomed, for we will never hear it but on the coral islands and it is much different from that of silks or cottons, to the point that it is the Oceanian fabric. Their ghosts would walk in snow-white tapa, the cloth of blue ocean. It is grown in the sea gardens, so near to the marine that at the sound of a bare foot the tree crabs will drop like apples from the boughs and scuttle into the sands. Here, in the moonlight, we are under other branches—flowering branches—the tamanu,* with white flowers and a perfumed bark, held sacred, so that it is death to break a bough—or the coral tree itself, with scarlet blossoms that cannot be described in moonlight, for they are blind or muted, yet burning like flames of coral in a moonlit water, until torchlight falls on the gleaming trident, and laughing and singing, some with pearls, or some with cockle shells, the young men and maidens come in, wandering, from the reef. Then the clusters keep their scarlet color. It is retained, or muted, in them until the torches light the lower air.

What other flowers are there? A hundred that we could not name. But the white clematis has a sugary or spiced starlight of its own, as it trails on the darker trees. A starlight of a few inches in density, blowing sweeter up to its petals; while the fragrance of hyacinth and jasmine mingled comes from a low shrub, the horopito, with bright green leaves as of a nutmeg tree, and waxen bells or trumpets that hang in clusters, of white, and pink, and crimson, and all shades of red. Come down to the shore, where the red fuchsia creeps out of the sands! Or but a few steps into the forest! That is another, or an underworld. Huge fungi, sprouting from the tree foot, are so broad and strong that you may sit on them; while, on the ground, luminous toadstools of enormous size gleam with phosphorus and shine like evil stars or constellations out of the damp.

But we seek, once more, the moonlight and the cloaks of snow-white tapa. Near to them sits a queen or a princess, scepter in hand, of sea ivory, made of the tusk of a narwhal or sea unicorn, one of the wonders of the Southern Seas. This monster, could we but see it, is as white as snow, marked with a few dark spots or blemishes; its belly, white and glistening, and as soft as velvet to the touch. With their tusks they break the thin ice, to breathe, down in the dreadful South where the Pacific becomes Antarctic. The explorer Scoresby remarks of the narwhal: "A great many were often sporting about us, sometimes in bands of fifteen or twenty together. . . . They were extremely playful, frequently elevating their horns out of the water, and crossing them with each other as in fencing." That was in the old days of the sailing ships. In our time such a sight could not be seen.

* Tamanu: *Calophyllum inophyllum*. Coral tree: *Erythrina corallodendron*.

The herds of narwhals are all slaughtered. This twisted scepter came from one that drove in to shore, after a storm; or, more probably, pursued a shoal of fishes and was stranded in the shallows. Its horn was bartered from isle to isle along the coral reefs, passing from queen to queen out of their dusky hands: carried in canoes close to the triton shell, which is their war horn or trumpet blown out on the deep. You would hear—for it is still night —the voice of the triton and the splash of many oars. And the canoe comes past, at high speed, navigated by the Southern stars which lie in countless archipelagos into infinity, until the eyes can stare no longer, and a meteor glides out of the zenith, without a sound, like some portent, but dies above the sea. Another, and another, fall. They shoot, like golden bolts, out of the firmament, living only for that moment, to portend a mystery. Such was the coming of the narwhal scepter. Listen! Listen! It is the sweeping of a snow-white toga. That is the noise they make. We see a shell bracelet and a dusky hand.

How wonderful are the clear colors of the morning, in Oceania, on the Southern Seas. The pandanus trees droop their fronds almost into the waves. Here is shade, instantly, of a fernlike kind. The coconut palm is in ecstasy, dancing in every wind, while the substance of shade is as much from blossoming branches as from green leaf or hoary stem. There could be, here, such an experience as to lie down to sleep in the shadow of the orange, or the shaddock, not of their leaves, but of the fruit itself, red globe on globe, or of the swollen and distended yellow moons. At foot, the pine pricks almost out of the sand. The sunlight comes down, with no dilution, for the hills are not high enough for clouds to gather. No more than terraces, or pleasant eminences from which to take the cool. And covered, from head to foot, with trees in flower. Here, by falling waters, grows the South Sea chestnut, *Inocarpus edulis*, with dark green leaves, white flowers in season, and aerial roots, like buttresses, that join the branches to the checkered earth; a bower wherein the shepherd—but there are no flocks to watch—could look, instead, down to the coral reef.

The morning and the evening breezes, playing from the shore, waft these many scents on their wings, so that, at dawn and sunset and long after, "while our ship is rocked by the sunset wind," every breath is perfumed. "Shrill voices from the town cleave the air like darts." Far into the night. Thus, the evening and the early morning. Noon is the hour of distillation, when they wax and strengthen in the stillness, in the shade of their own leaves; a spiced breath, but it hangs on them and is not blown away. Scent of the flower mouth is part or parcel of the noonday heat. Look how it lies blue upon the dryad body! For a maiden, naked to the waist, lies in the shade. We will have music. The earth is all dappled with its cloaks of shadow and the open sunlight. Call it golden! But it is the golden yellow of a dancer's body that is painted with turmeric and coconut oil. Not yet. We are to embark, later, with the Areöis.

And crossing from shade to shade, a girl passes in a snow-white shaggy dress. Of cotton-tree fiber, loosely woven, and on purpose for coolness much too big in size, hiding all her body. Like a pearl in the oyster shell, or the chrysalis in the cocoon. Within that white shagginess, her nude figure is to be guessed, or dreamed of. That is the purpose in her loose white dress. For it hides her from neck to foot.

We called for music. A dryad sings from under every tree, hidden in the bracts or flowering boughs. You have but to look between, or lift them aside, and she will be lying with her companion at the tree foot, one with an empty turtle shell strung for a harp, or the sea conch to his lips blowing a mournful and a shaggy music. Always a vibrant or a wavering music, such being the nature of their South Sea throats, or in order to be heard above the sound of sea, which is never still for long on the islands, but like the voice within the sea shell is ever hidden there. A voice, and a sea harp or sea trumpet, that is all. It is more in the melody than in the instrument. And more in the singer than in the song.

But of an isle in utter ocean, until the dancers come in pearly coronets and necklaces of flowers. Not yet. This is the long and lazy noon. There is music, and a pause of heat. For the leaves are as hot as flames; and in those colors, burning in a steady fire. The flower bracts burn like candles. There are feathery fires upon the hills, where the tufted palms grow; and a shrill fire in the groves of bamboos, given from the green rods. That, and the deep heat of the timber trees; the teak with scarlet fruit or scarlet flowers; trees which are poisonous—the itchwood, or the leper tree; trees which give a black dye; the pine tree; or, for the haunt of music, the glorious barringtonia with red flowers; the banyan with its flying buttresses; or the sandalwood tree, smelling warm and fragrant, which, when the traders come, will bring death and destruction to the island.

It is a scented indolence. Not the siesta of green shutters, nor of the fountain. Here you cannot lie on cool marble in a pillared shade. Walls that sport the snapdragon do not throw down their shadow. The hours do not chime with bells, nor does a voice call from the minaret to where merchant and beggar lie sleeping. To the court of waters, and the trellised alleys. To the mules tied up in the shade. To the honeycombed vault, and arch of stalactite opening to the orange grove. Here are no colonnades, nor dancing waters.

But it is an isle of indolence. The lustral shadows reach between the trees; flower shadows, not the shade of leaves; the form of the scarlet cone, or fiery cluster. There can be lawns of white or red sloping to the waters; or fields, more cerulean than ocean, breaking on the scarlet bough, or at the hanging fruit. A rosy soil, on which you tread the blossoms, but only in token, as though it were moonlight, for the color comes from the loaded branch. A near shadow can be as blue as the lotus pool, and as translucent, with that same lightness as of the lotus cells, glistening in texture, as of a blue light upon the petal, blind or matt, because there is no white on it, and it is blue through and through in all its particles, an interior blueness as though you lay within the lotus. And, near by, a tree of white flowers, smelling like hyacinth and jasmine mingled, until its difference is recognized and it becomes a person, a hand that sheds incense, a guttering candle, for it is weighed down with flowers. Here are flowers—there is no word for it—that are muted and have no smell, by that much more creamy or more velvety, like blind persons who love music or who live by touch. Each of the shades has its philosophy—those that lull; or are intoxicant; that bring

discontents; or sensual longings; that are sufficient in themselves
so that the imagination calls for no more than that; or by something missing are more lovely in their imperfection; that remind
one of a forgotten name; or, in extension of that, are as though
one is so much in love that the eyes, from too much looking, have
forgotten what is out of sight; others to inspire music; or build
a policy or a culture that is peculiar to themselves, as it could be,
cities of the gondola; melon domes; or palaces of coral, all rusti-
cation, rising from the shadowed waters. All day you could lie
in a tree shade and go no further in your thoughts. It is in the
Southern Seas. Here are, in fact, no more than flowers or persons. There are no great causes.

No horror but the feasts of human flesh. We may find a victim trussed and bound, sitting ready, his feet drawn up below
his thighs and his arms folded, tied tight so that he cannot move,
then lifted onto the hot stones of the oven with leaves and earth
thrown upon him, or put to the huge caldron. When cooked,
his face is painted black; and the flesh is eaten with great forks
of many prongs, made of the hard wood of the casuarina, a
drooping tree which grows about the burial places. Such are the
cannibal hearths. You could see joints of human flesh hanging
on the trees.

This is the landscape in islands that have hills, that are not
the simple atoll. In New Caledonia, Tahiti or the Marquesas;
mainlands where you could make a journey of a hundred miles,
or be lost three days' march into the interior. In Fiji, Samoa or
Hawaii; in New Britain; or New Ireland, off the coast of New
Guinea, where the stone men were undisturbed until a year or
two ago, and tilled their terraces and stuck their wigs of hair
with flowers, living in plenty, having heard no rumor of the turning world. But, in order to comprehend the immense Pacific
and its archipelagos, its lonely islands that may be destined to a
bloody fame, and the reefs of coral, that ocean must be seen in
entirety from the Arctic Aleutians down to the roaring South.
Then we can return and set forth with the Areöis on a voyage
of pleasure.

A map of the Pacific Ocean gives the following as the most

curious in shape of the coral atolls. Aitutaki and the Hervey
Islands, among the archipelago of the Cook Islands, midway, it
could be said, between Tahiti and Fiji. Niafuoo, between Samoa
and Fiji, is almost a complete coral circle with a round lagoon
three miles across in its middle. And three islands are more
curious still: Tongareva, Rakahanga, Manihiki, isles of euphony,
lying northwest of Samoa. The first is nearly a hexagon of coral,
in no place wider than a hundred yards or so, with a lagoon
twenty miles long and ten miles across inside it. Rakahanga is a
distorted square of the same pattern; and Manihiki a square with
bending sides, so that it is broken nearly into a pentagon of coral.
The other is Wake Island, halfway between American Hawaii
and the Philippines, an isle like a coral arrowhead, with a safe
lagoon within, and lying open for the seaplanes. Guam, not less
notorious for its potential future, lies much nearer to Manila, an
ordinary isle of hills and valleys. These islands are important
enough to be inset on the map; how many more must lie all but
virgin! There are still the islands, Los Jardines, marked "existence doubtful," five hundred miles or more west from Wake
Island toward the concealed mysteries of the Japanese Mandate.
A seaplane from Wake Island, maybe, could solve this problem.
There is no other quite like it in the world today. The Japanese
Mandate extends over the Bonin Islands, the Mariana or La-
drones, and the Caroline Islands, coral atolls about which it is
next to impossible to discover anything in the present for it is
the policy of the Japanese to keep them, on purpose, in obscurity.
Of old they were Spanish settlements and the resort of South Sea
whalers. Guam is an American outpost in midst of these. Tinian,
in the Marianas, has the remains of old buildings, left by an unknown race; and when Admiral Lord Anson called there, in
1742, the isle was deserted but it was remarked of the wild cattle
that "it is not uncommon to see herds of some thousands feeding
together in a meadow. They are all of them milk-white, except
their ears, which are generally black." The Carolines lie south
of these, toward New Guinea, including Yap, which is the Japanese answer to Wake Island and to Guam. These islands, too,
have ruins; while, of the inhabitants, we are assured that "their

dances are by no means indecorous, and are performed by the un-
married men and girls, who stand in a row on a plank, and with
graceful movements of the arms and body keep time with their
feet to the song. . . . They bathe three times a day, and anoint
their bodies with scented coconut oil and turmeric."

Other wonders of the Pacific are Easter Island, Christmas
Island, and the now notorious Pitcairn. The Solomon Islands
are, probably, the only cannibal islands of the modern world.
Their population must be related to the stone men of New
Guinea, but they are thieves and prodigals, the degenerates of
that antique world. Their patriarchs are different in expression
from the elders of that lost nation. Where shall we sail next?
To the frightful landscape of the Galapagos, four thousand miles
away, and half of that across an open ocean? A scene like Pluto's
underworld; isles of the damned, for their arid hopelessness
breeds suicide; igneous rocks whereon the maned lizard creeps;
where the droppings of the sea birds make a night soil many
fathoms deep. Or south, a thousand miles, to Easter Island,
where the giant images stand on the coast in mystery. No living
person knows the whole Pacific. Melanesia, Micronesia, Polyne-
sia could be called three continents of islands. In respect of arts
and customs, New Ireland may be the most interesting of the
whole Pacific Islands. Its natives were masters of what could be
termed outrigger sculptures, wood carvings into which the image
or fantasy of the war canoe had passed, so that they are made for
speed and lightness, incased, often, in an open framework which
suggests the bounding of a craft on the patterned waters; some
great amphibian gliding in the reef pool; or even, in extension of imagery, a bird flying, or static, but in symbol of its
powers of flight. New Ireland carvings are to be known at once.
They are not dramatic and obscure, like Negro sculptures, suddenly sensual, and exquisite by moments and by feeling, but
always of the animal in man. Negro carvings can be nearly great
art, through intensity and meaning. But New Ireland carvings
have, as it were, the flying fish for canon. It is an imagery of
much fin and wing, with scale and ridgeback, and the dolphin
tail, which delights in springing over the billows and enjoys the

resistance of the waves. All this, in terms of the tutelary deities. So that they are more excitant and poetical than wrought in terror. What must have inspired them are the forms and colors of the coral reef.

It is among the Melanesians and Papuans, and principally in New Britain, New Ireland, the Solomon Islands, the New Hebrides and New Caledonia, that the dance and the savage arts have come to their fullest development. These groups of islands follow in a curve the western coast of Australia and are, as it were, in parallel to the tribal ritual of the aborigines in Queensland, or throughout that continent, dances and initiations, arts of the masker and of metamorphosis pursued with the intensity of total war, all else subordinated so that the drama or dance cycle can play through the seasons. The shadow life of these savages is more complex than slum life, or life in a council house in any modern town. Nearer, too, to the realities than in a city of wet pavements and back windows. In comparison, Hawaiians, Tahitians, who are Polynesian and live in an earthly paradise, have the languor of the South and are less serious in their pleasures. They are Sicilians of the Southern Seas. And, in fact, of another race. Down south, where it is colder, there were the Maori warriors; while Hawaii, Tahiti, the Marquesas are the temperate isles, far removed from steaming Papua and equatorial heats of the Melanesian or Negrito. But, in those tropics, the primitive savage still flowers in his prime.

It is here then an anthropologist can spend a lifetime in an island; where a river pours the rains of Papua into the coral sea; or in an unknown archipelago, moving from isle to isle, watching the kitchen middens rise, as it might be a hundred thousand years ago. Not in a whole lifetime could be exhausted the treasures of the land or sea; for a language must be learned, and another tongue is spoken but a few miles away; the shadowy taboo must be explored, which is the subconscious given phantom form; and their involved imagery of belief and superstition be correlated and its shadow illusions understood and explained. Works such as *Drama of Orokolo* or *Stone Men of Malekula* are in evidence of

this.* The time traveler could have no experience to compare
with these. They are the complete antithesis, while an airplane
passes over the coral reef and is gone before the next wave breaks.

Concerning life in the coral pool it would be impossible to be
both sober and exact. For the fishes surpass in color all that the
imagination could conceive of. Blue and silver, ultramarine, or
scarlet, striped, pheasant marked, or golden spotted with drops
that are of liquid gold and fade while the eye looks at them as
the fish is caught; fishes that are the macaws of the coral grove,
but in greater variety; that bask or glide, or flaunt their parrot
skins; or are singular in shape as well as color; monstrous and
creeping, or shooting like Xiphias through the olivine, for the
waters are of every color beside the blue of Amphitrite. Their
form is of a million experiments to devise beauty and swiftness;
but, as well, for pure ornament, for there could be no other purpose than their mutual pleasure. The entire conspectus of these
South Sea fishes must be impossible of attainment, for many
species are in variety beyond number; nor, in a thousand years,
could it be feasible to search all the coral reefs and be certain
which are peculiar to what set of islands, for they may be as re-
stricted in their habitat as the birds of paradise. Some may haunt
one reef only, or be found in their millions all through the coral
seas. Their color mutation is no mere development of new
shades and markings. But it is as though from the full palette the
most opposite colors had been chosen, and growth, from the beginning, had been for clash and contrast, a sort of shadowy
scheme, if the light and luminous took the place of shade.
Not in dun colors, but in blues and scarlets for the *poissons-
perroquets,* cockatoos of the coral reef; so individual it could be
a suit of colors dyed for one fish alone, until another gleams above
the floor of snow-white sand. Others have their fins prolonged
into a pair of scaly wings; into fringed oars or rudders, according
to their motion; they sail, or fly, or float, or skim on the waters.

* *Drama of Orokolo,* by F. E. Williams, and *Stone Men of Malekula,* Vol. I,
The Coral Islet of Vao (4 vols. in all), by J. Layard—two of the most interesting
anthropological works published in our time.

The commonplace, the vernacular of fishes is, here, all gold or silver. They are netted, splashed or striped with it; or, like the macolor, one of the kakatoes, are all black and gray and white, but so disposed that it is in the colors of the whale or dolphin, but as pretty as a golden carp. A hundred painters, content with these wonders, could not portray them in a thousand years; and, as well, there are the different sorts of shells from the Red Sea, across the Indian Ocean, from Amboyna in the Moluccas to the Galapagos.

The true and veritable Poseidonia, the kingdom of the islands lying half across the world from Africa to the Americas. Seas of the pearl scepter, the chambered or pearly nautilus; the Latirus, which, when dry, is dull and colorless, but, on being wetted, as though in its own element, gleams like a rainbow; terrestrial mollusks which, like little painted shells, climb into the trees; two hundred species of achatinella in the Sandwich Islands, which are their habitat; the spotted or banded land shells of Papua and the Solomon Islands, belonging, in the language of science, to the trochiform group of helices, known as geotrochus, their lips brilliantly tinted with scarlet, rose or yellow; the Bulimi of the forests, one of which, from the isle of Guadalcanal only, is of a delicate greenish straw color, with the edge of the lip bright vermilion; glittering fishhooks made from the pearl shell of the haliotis iris; the shells of New Caledonia, which are more wonderful than any; canoes that are patterned or inlaid with shells; the clamshells that are big enough to use for fonts in churches; and the *Triton variegatus,* war horn or trumpet of the islands. They are found on the beaches and in the pools, and, as a rule, their beauty lasts. This is not so with the fishes. They lose their color when they are lifted from the waters. They are as far from their own element as meteors that fall on the earth. In a moment they have lost their fire, and die dully, as the light dies.

There is the truism, also, that shells do not journey for long distances, unlike the migrant shoals. They may have their summer or their winter pastures, and change a tropic for a temperate isle. Their lanes are by instinct along and under the blue main. It is impossible, in fact, to know them all or to calculate their numbers. On a day, at any coral shore, they may appear in their nations. How, therefore, to make them tally with another shoal a thousand miles away! A race of fish may be so rare as to appear extinct; and then be found, in multitude, where they have wandered in the waters. The hidden droves of the deep seas must be included, which are unknown save for what the net brings up. This is of no more moment than the arrow that falls on the plain. The huge depths are untroubled and hold to their secrets. It will be impossible ever to explore them thoroughly. They are dark pits or caverns illumined by strange gleams. But what necessity is there to look down into those valleys! The coral ramparts come up from the bed of ocean. Not exactly. It would be more true to say they are forts or breakwaters built by the madrepores upon the summits of marine mountains. Bastions of coral a hundred or two hundred feet in height. Not more than that. Coral-capped mountains, for the sheer cliff or precipice may fall for a thousand fathoms, and near the shore be as deep as the Himalayas. It is upon this outer rampart that the ocean lifts and hurls itself in an unbroken wave. It is deep blue, and curling over, breaks into a roar of foam, white as foam, or as the blue hair of the sea god. Thousands of rainbows shine along the spray, as though ten thousand fountains were splashing. Within the atoll the coral artisans are found, for the outer fortifications are formed by their slaves or peons. Here, in the lagoon, are brain coral (for it has the shape of that) or moeandrina; astroea; and the branching madrepores and explanaria; corals that are all shades of colors, not alone the red and white, but browns and yellows, pink and vermilion and deep blue. Bright red, yellow or peach-colored nulliporae; the pearl-shell eschara and retipora. Such are the coral groves and coral branches.

Where to choose to study this! The first coral reefs are in the Red Sea; and from the east coast of Africa to the west coast of America there are coral isles. The Cocos or Keeling Islands in the Indian Ocean, eight hundred miles to the south of Java, are as typical as any; or Christmas, halfway from there to Java, where Captain Cook lay to, in 1777, for turtles, "perhaps as good as any in the world." Near by, the Indian Ocean is six miles deep. There are the Maldive atolls, below Ceylon; the Nicobars which

were famed for shells; Celebes; Amboyna; and so into the Pacific.
The Great Barrier Reef, a thousand miles long, runs parallel to
the coast of Queensland and nearly touches on New Guinea.
Sometimes but ten miles from the shore, or, in places, a hundred
miles or more. It is here that the waves break on the longest
terraces of coral. But the madrepores never build out of the
water. Their labors are done when the reef, at low tide, is an inch
or two below the surface. So that you can climb out from a boat
and walk along it. And, in places, the broken pieces detached by
the waves have been piled up, like blocks of cement where a pier
or breakwater is unfinished; while, upon these, the softer corals
have been powdered into sands, and the seaweed and the guano
forms a soil, until it is a little coral island. Months, or years,
could be lived on the Barrier Reef. Or but a few moments, in
imagination. There is no time for more. It is the primitive
world, not in its scenes and festivals, but in the untainted mornings. We are far enough from the savage men to keep them, in
contemplation, across the Coral Sea. Opposite are the Louisiades,
where the communal houses are built down to the shore, and the
men are all fishermen.

The catamaran is poled along the shallows. A raft, made of
planks lashed together; or they push it in front of them, wading
on the reef. They are savages of bestial feature, with frizzed-out
mops of hair, their ears and noses slit for ornament and pierced
by a piece of shell. A man of thirty is like an old man; black as a
Negro, but of the Papuan race, which means more hirsute, and
with a sloping or receding head that expresses cruelty or cunning,
filed and blackened teeth and the mouth of a carnivore, or cannibal. All his ancestors have fed on human flesh. He is an eater
of raw fish, an ichthyophagite, the man of the kitchen midden,
collateral of the beachcomber along every shore, groping for shellfish with his hands, but, the next moment, throwing a line which
is baited with the pearly nautilus. A primitive of the coral seas,
where the green iceberg never comes. An amphibian, for half his
days and nights are spent in the shoal water. His catamaran
could be lying off Golconda's coasts, it is so heaped with shells.
Many of those, in the antique world, would be bargained for by

kings. One of their number, *Cypraea aurantia,* "the morning dawn" or orange cowrie, when found on the reefs is so rare that its wearer is given the dignity of a chief. The philosopher may wonder why the most beautiful is the rarest. But the savage is old enough in wisdom not to be astonished. He finds other shells, little less wonderful, which are so common they are no concern of his. They are thrown, one by one, where the waves wet them, or they even crawl along the boards. In the meantime, we will have it night. He baits his hook again with a bit of pearl shell. It is low water and he wades on the rocks. A meteor falls across the sky. There are myriad lights burning and no heat from them. It is the Southern starlight. This warmth of the waters is no part of that. But the planets throw down their fires which lift into long lines on the swell. And so it is for long hours in the catamaran until the morning.

The thought of those curious nights and days takes us to one more locality before we set out with the Areöis. It is to the Sulu Islands in the Philippines, between their southern mainland, or Mindanao, and North Borneo. In the Celebes Sea. And the sound of that gives us the high eaves of the houses, built side by side, their huge gables hanging above them like tents or crooked steeples, like the poop of a junk or the fo'c'sle of a galleon. Not all shaped alike, except in principle, so that they could be as many boats drawn up on a beach, out of the monsoon wind. These houses of Celebes or of the Sulus are a fantasy of ship-builders, and the ribs of their eaves are carried through. They are boats, keel upward, and the ribs have sprouted into horns or antlers. It is a wooden architecture influenced by pirate seas and by the deer or antelopes of the forest. By affinity, if not directly through suggestion. Seas of the lateen sail, for the junk has sailed here from the China Seas. The war canoes, with foam at their prow, are oared on another ocean. Here, in a storm, a huge junk has been shivered on the reefs. And, on a lacquered noon, the lateen sails have often come and gone. The water towns are on the far shore; floating cities of the sampan with their own joss houses and their dens of infamy. Thousands of souls are born, and die, on the river. Beyond these islands are the China Seas; so that their southern winds are from the Pacific, but the weather can change and blow down to them from Bantam China or Cochin. The Malay seas, the haunt of Malay pirates. Beside Borneo, but the archipelagos lie from here to Honolulu. This is the last mainland, for Borneo is big enough to be the terra firma, so that the Sulu Islands are between several worlds, and it is here in obscure corners that fishing villages are built on stilts into the sea and every conceit of seafaring finds expression along the shores. For the seas could be said to be more fertile than the land. They are more punctual than the cornfields, and have not to be tilled or sown.

Here, then, are the Sea Gypsies, round and about Sibutu, the nearest of the Sulu Islands to North Borneo. The southernmost of all the Philippines. The Sea Gypsies are born in the sailing canoe and pass their lives in it. Having no villages, nor houses on land. Their sails are made of matting, and they know the ins and outs of all the winds, how and when they freshen and exhilarate from isle to isle. Or creep, turtle-footed, as though they trailed in weeds. There are the steady winds that, month after month, would speed you out to ocean and offer no return. Rare winds, once in a lifetime, that break the laws and blow back whence they came. A north wind breathing out of the south, in prelude to an earthquake and a tidal wave, when an island, like Krakatoa, could be blown out of the bed of ocean. They do not even pitch the tents. They are wanderers on the seas. Their stolen food is there for all to steal. And their sea voyages are mostly made by night. Dawn comes to meet them on another shore, rising like naked Venus out of her pearly shell, and wafting to land upon the cat's-paw calm in the opaline or milky waters. Where else could you find Gypsies walking on the coral reef? Or their naked children paddling on the rocks? What signal or indication will they leave behind them to guide their friends? Broken coral stems piled up into a pagan altar? A mound of oyster shells? And with what intent?

That the dappled herds—only they are dipped with gold and vermilion and deep blue—have moved away? That the golden fin no longer waves above the sand? Sometimes, like the Gypsies, they have destroyed just for destruction's sake. A coral pool has been entirely pillaged. The fronds and coral stems have been chipped down with the hammer. Or so it would seem. The broken shells, from which their inmates have been gouged away, float on the calm, as sordid as the ship's refuse on which the sea-gulls feed. They are like the cracked eggshells that the cuckoo has thrown down from the nest. It is, of course, in hyperbole that we call them Sea Gypsies. They are a tribe who have taken to the waters. But like breeds like; and there are points of similarity in the nomads of the coral reefs. They move by stealth. The fraternity do not meet by chance. They are liars and dissimulators. And they will spread false news. They will come ashore at some village, bringing triton or cowrie shells hidden in a piece of matting. By fire of personality they barter these for other things; and, always, the purchaser loses in the bargain. And they are off to sea before he knows this. That contrast between the Gypsies on the road and the motorcar that passes them, or the airplane overhead, is present here in the difference betwen this naked poverty and the primal colors of the coral sea. There is no taint on the fishes or the sea shells. Was there, once, a golden age when *Cypraea aurantia* was as common as the cockle-shell? Has the race perished? Or were they, purposely, made few in number? If they show themselves, they will be stolen. In this they are blond children whom the Gypsies kidnap.

And there are lights and music. It is the embarkation. Men and women and young girls climb, laughing, into the canoes. There are many farewells; but no tears, for they will come back again. It is but a journey from island to island, and the wind will carry them all night. No need to use the oars; or more than dip a hand into the milky waters. It cools the pulse. For the night is warm; and there is music without end.

The Areöi Society, in sixty or seventy canoes, take the sunset wind and are gone. But we go with them. It does not matter where. As long as there is music, and at dawn and all night through we have the scents of the paradisal islands. And more than music. Or that much more which music brings. For there is much else besides; and we would talk of it in our own symbols.

What is there in the color of a skin? These are the Tahitians, and
the women are no darker than Sicilians. The Sicilienne could be
danced here. Forty or fifty Siciliennes promised long ago, and
unfulfilled.* By the net of waters. Against the netted foam.
But not the Sicilienne alone. That measure must mingle with the
other music. As dew falls, even out on the waters.

We will not exaggerate the beauty of the songs; but, as with
all music, it is what it seems to be. And we will have it in our
idiom. This is a troupe of players and comedians, with flowers
at the wrist and neck, and in coronals of flowers that will keep
fresh until the morning. This is the primal world in decadence.
And there are parallels in all the full-blown flowers of decay.
Music, itself, is first and last of the arts. If ever there comes a
lull, listen, and you will hear the conch shell blown in the prow
and at the helm! That is primitive music. It is thus the wagons
or the moving tents are kept together. It is the long horn of the
shepherds in the mountains—the *bucium*** that echoes along
the valleys.

Dew falls on the sea trumpet. Dusky goddesses, in plenty, dip
their wrists into the water. You could see a dark hand below a
moonlit wave. And the goddesses, or Columbines, are in gowns
of calico. Many of them wear the scarf or handkerchief of the
rumba dancer. Or the snow-white shaggy dresses that we saw.
Others wear dryad blue, and are naked to the waist. A lute is
held in a hand of amber—for we would have it a lute—and amber fingers touch the strings. What shade of petal are the lips
that sing? A shell ornament glitters at a shadowed ear. The
figure is a smoky column rubbed with rose and jasmine oil. It is
rare to meet with this on the waters, as the armada moves above
the madrepores and knocks at mullions into which the moonlight
falls. For all night long it is the coral reef.

Who would not disembark on this dazzling white strand? And
watch these shadows become living girls and women? Here!
Ah! Here, the Sicilienne can begin. But we do not call it that.

* Title of a projected book of poems announced in 1933.

** This is the Roumanian name for the bronze trumpets, eight or ten feet long,
blown by the Wallachian shepherds.

This is the youth of the world and there are no complications. So it may be many other things besides. How can it be a Sicilienne with waist and breasts of amber? With a body rubbed yellow with turmeric? And another smells of sandalwood. Like the opening of a little box or casket. But a pillar, nonetheless, of naked sandalwood. Another has stained her face with a scarlet dye, but it is no more than rouge on her skin of cloves. And her limbs and body are not altered by it.

Such are the dryads whom we watched beneath the boughs. But the men are actors or musicians. Some wear their feather helmets in the moonlight. In a moment we will have dance and pantomime. Where are the moonlit currant bushes? Like those bunches that are dipped in sugar. No! No! It is not that. And here are neither asphodel nor myrtle. Not ilex, nor the tamarisk. These are the South Seas. What is fanciful is not architecture but the structure of the shells. Can we have the mime of the nautilus, or of the shell of Venus? For we see this as a huge composition of goddesses or women bathing. But on the coral shore. That is the difference. There is this much in the color of a skin. It is thus, and thus, that the moral contagion spreads throughout society. But no one dies of it. We are alive but once; and in this mood would pass our lives, strolling from one place or island to another.

MEXICO *

Our Conquistadors are on the point of starting. The masts are
flapping under every conceivable piece of bunting and the whole
ship is held back on its cable only with difficulty. Don Antonio
Gonzalez is in command once more, with his old charge Luca
Giordano on board, and the latter's pupil, Solimena. They are
bound for Mexico.**

The provisions are already below, part of the ship's ballast
consisting in bales of canvas, so determined are these artists to
find material ready to their hands on landing, for with the help
of their gang of assistants they can paint at the rate a spider
spins its yarn.

The port, of course, is Cádiz—beyond the Pillars of Hercules
—and it wanted only a few minutes' sailing to get out of sight of
these lintels to the Mediterranean. So narrow is this water gate
that it is unbelievable that ships sailing back from the Indies can
arrive in front of this open arch at the first attempt; it is more
likely they will be driven in and battered on the rocks of Africa,
which should be red as the coals in a fire from the torrid heat, so
that the water hisses up in steam as it reaches them.

Very different is the objective for their expedition. They must
crowd on all the sail they can, to get them across the deathly calm
of the Sargasso Sea, so that they may arrive in its midst with as
loud a flourish of trumpets as possible. If dramatic and piercing
enough, one of the sleepy winds, waiting like a sentry or a porter,
will be stirred out of his slumber to come to their rescue, and pull
the ship out to the far side of the calm, where the gales are at
their usual work again. If this does not happen, they must trust
to the lazy currents to drift them out; but this is the slowest of

* From *Southern Baroque Art*, 1924.

** Earlier pages of my first prose work *Southern Baroque Art* being concerned
largely with Naples, I placed the Neapolitan painters Luca Giordano and Solimena
on board this fanciful expedition bound for Mexico.

progresses, as though drawn by the huge turtles that are crawling over the sea floor. Once out of the Sargasso, they can sail again under the same Trades they started with from Spain, so that the cause of this sudden calm lay only in the distance between the center of the ocean and the nearest mountains; for out in the midst here the winds are far away from their nests and breeding grounds in the crags. The expanse of sea is too great for them to manage, and the center lies too far to be reached from either side. It is true that the Sargasso Sea is only half the distance from Mexico that it lies from the cliffs of Europe; but, while too far away for the gales from the east to interfere, equally it is undisturbed because the Mexican breezes are enervated and weak from the tropical conditions of their life; they are powerless to interfere. There is no narrow and defined point, like the Pillars of Hercules, for their ship to aim at. They may strike anywhere on the huge length of coast, and then, having found their position, move south or north toward Veracruz, the port of Mexico.

The coast lay far down, with no cliffs and a great extent of sea apparently sloping toward it; an effect which made the journey half round the world more realistic, as though part of the unavoidable terrestrial curve of this straight voyage was visible, inclining down gently from the heights of mid-ocean. They came near to shore and lowered a boat to make inquiries, then rowed off; the boat crew quickly found a village of half-breed turtle fishers living in arbors made from leaves. It was low down in the Gulf of Mexico, near the island of Cozumel, along the huge coast of Yucatán, that they had arrived, with a long coast voyage before them until they reached the port of landing. They stayed for an hour or two at this small settlement, to take supplies of water and fresh fruit and vegetables on board. Meantime, some of the important passengers who had been landed to get an early impression of the new continent took a walk along the beach, to while away the time of waiting.

Along the shore, at no great distance, was a funeral pile of the carcasses of turtles, half burned and covered with countless millions of flies, actually heaving and moving as if alive; and near this hideous mound, as if to draw a contrast in beauty and de-

formity, was a tree covered to its topmost branches with the white
ibis, its green foliage appearing like an ornamental framework to
their snowy plumage. Some fishermen near by dragged across
the beach two large turtles, leaving the carcasses to swell the
funeral pile; they brought down to their arbor strings of eggs, and
the parts that served for food or oil, and hung them quivering in
the sun along a fence. Walking farther along, toward the end of
a sandy beach was a projecting point, on a line with which they
noticed on the water what seemed to be a red cloud of singular
brilliancy and, at the same time, delicacy of color, that, on drawing nearer, they found to be a flat covered with flamingos.

High overhead, on a solitary cliff-like piece of hill which broke
down into the water with a precipice edge, was a ruined tower
or temple; one of those ruins which the Spanish sailors who first
came to this shore describe every few miles along the immense
Yucatán coast. In their day the ruins were still inhabited, with
the altars smoking and with the weapons of the warriors leaning
against walls that are now the hiding place of snakes and every
kind of venomous reptile. The hill was not so high as to be inaccessible, and it afforded the widest view to be got over this
wild and unknown region of the Indies. Near the mouth of a
creek, on their way to the foot of this hill, a flock of roseate
spoonbills flew overhead.

They climbed up, hacking their way through a dense jungle
of creepers, looking carefully where they trod for fear of snakes.

At last they came to the first of the fallen stones, lying moss-
covered in the damp undergrowth, and after following along the
line of wall, looked out on the boundless ocean. There below
them, deep in the clear water at the foot of the cliff, they could
see, gliding quietly by, a great fish eight or ten feet long. Inside
the walls, in a dark, cell-like room, were many carvings in hard
stone of human figures, all of them crowned with immense
plumed headdresses. But before there was time to investigate
these birdmen, they were signaled to by the boat crew below, and
had to climb down as hurriedly as possible, for it was time to be
off. As they came back along the shore, the snowy plumage of the
white ibis still appeared among the green of the trees, and a

heron stood like a statue in a river pool, just where the creek
reached the sea, turning his long neck almost imperceptibly to
look at them.

In the coast voyage, sailing slowly along, the same experiences
were repeated over and over again. Every few miles they passed
below one of these white gleaming ruins, which shone out so
mysteriously at sunrise or sunset when the beams of light came
toward them at their own level. They were so many signal towers
to warn the Indian cities, far inside, of the presence of enemies,
for it was impossible to believe that they had been deserted by
their sentries for many years, and that the thriving and teeming
cities they were guarding were no longer anything but a metropolis for snakes. This island of Cozumel had been the last center
of Indian civilization to be taken by the Spaniards, and the center
of Yucatán has remained unexplored down to our own generation,
so that in the days of Luca Giordano there was more than a possibility of the existence of great Indian towns hidden away in the
interior.* It was this that gave a peculiar danger and excitement
to the coast voyage, for at any moment the sands might be covered
with a horde of feathered warriors, plumed and winged for battle.
They were quilted with their cotton armor to the extent that you
could hit as hard as you liked without hurting them; and from
their hiding places among the trees, where their bright colors
were indistinguishable from the leaves and flowers, they made
the best use of poisoned darts from bows and blowpipes. They
were an enemy dangerous not so much from strength as from
skillful defense, for fighting the Indians was like an attempt to
gather the fruit from a prickly tropical plant, which infects you
with poison every time you are scratched by its thorns. It was
only the sight of a horse which reduced the Indians to obedience,
and the landing of a specimen was a difficult undertaking on so
surfy a shore.

As soon as Yucatán was left behind, the coast grew flatter and
more sandy, and the chance of meeting a buccaneer become the

* The island of Pelen, with the town of Itzen, was subdued by the Spaniards
only under Don Martin de Ursua in an expedition that sailed from Campeche
in the year 1697 (cf. A History of the Conquest of Itzen, by Don Juan
Villagutierres, a native of Yucatán, Madrid, 1701).

only offset to the monotony of the view. The beach was more and more monotonous to look at, while the sea, as if to enhance the dullness of land, put on every variety of color. The ship sailed in to shore like a horse galloping over the fields. Veracruz appeared depressing in the extreme. The town had been founded by the Viceroy, Conde de Monterey, at the end of the seventeenth century, in front of the small and heavily fortified island of San Juan de Ulua, on the same shore on which Hernán Cortés landed; and the parched and arid desert, so different from the green West Indian Islands, was no encouragement to march inland. All round the town were low reddish sand hills which had been heaped up and were gradually blown from place to place by the north wind, which still blew cold after its handling of the icebergs far away in the Arctic Seas. The houses of the town were as if blackened by fire, and the long straight streets were always full of wind and blinding dust. Hordes of sopilotes, the huge black "police" birds, were flapping heavily along, or hovering over some carcass on the road outside the town. They had black feathers, with gray heads, beaks and feet, and always flew about in troops searching for their prey, while at night they perched, still in their regiments, on the trees.

Only a few miles through this Arabian desert the country blossoms into a magnificent and almost eternal paradise. The fruit and the flowers seem in themselves sufficient to sustain human life without the carrion diet which a less favored climate imposes, but there are other aspects to be considered before we can make a map of the paradise and describe its towns and gardens.

In Mexico, and there alone, is to be found the most perfected flowering of the architecture we have traced through the kingdom of Naples, and growing from a separate and independent center in Spain and Portugal. Here, in Mexico, where more money was at its command, the style reached to its fullest expression. The City of Mexico itself I am not proposing to examine in close detail, because its fine buildings are, for the most part, the work of architects imported from Spain, and they have a certain dignity and sobriety suitable to the capital, but dividing them apart from the class of buildings that we have come here to examine. Nowhere else in the world, except in Austria, at this period were convents being built on the same tremendous scale that made the medieval monasteries as powerful as a small principality. On the higher reaches of the Danube, at Melk, at Göttweig and at Klosterneuberg, near Vienna, the last Roman Emperors employed the best Italian or Italian-trained German architects on buildings that were hardly finished before the reforming spirit of Joseph II, their descendant, caused them to be emptied and to lie desolate. Out in Mexico the size and magnificence of these last of Imperial works were far outdone, and the classical, if flowery, lines of the Italian façades were changed and transmitted into something more suitable to the extraordinary concourse dwelling inside their walls.

Added to all the influences traced in former chapters of *Southern Baroque Art,* there were at work on the buildings of Mexico two strains which are found only in that country. In the first place, obvious traces remain of the ancient Aztec work, because the architectural details were carried out by Indians who had been hurriedly converted to Christianity and could not forget their ancient temples or the figures from their own mythology. They could not avoid—for no other method of expression was familiar to them—the treatment in Aztec fashion of the Christian legends on which they were at work.

It must be remembered that the great time for emigration from Spain to the New World took place in the generations immediately succeeding its conquest by the Spaniards. In the seventeenth and eighteenth centuries Spain was poverty-stricken and falling into disrepute as a military power because of the drain of emigration from the peasant and soldier-producing classes. The Moriscos (Moors converted to Christianity after the conquest of the Caliphate in 1492) were not driven out from Spain till the year 1609 by a decree of King Philip III. A large proportion, therefore, of the emigrants to Mexico and other Spanish states of America were of Moorish, and perhaps also of Jewish, blood, for the most useful trades and occupations in Spain were in the hands of the Moors and the Jews, and these classes were the most likely to be called on for emigration. In Mexico there are very patent signs of Moorish influence, and, indeed, there are as striking examples of the Mudéjar* style in Mexico as there are in Spain. These two facts, the Aztec and the Moorish influence, taken together explain why the Mexican buildings are unlike any others in the world.

The native craftsmen, living contentedly in an easy slavery to the Church, were content to spend a whole lifetime carving the *retablo* of an altar or inlaying the presses of a sacristy. Their labors were directed by an Indian or Creole architect, who, in most cases, could not write and was not draftsman enough to draw a plan. It is related of one Indian architect, whose extremely interesting work will be described later on, that he used to scratch his plans with a pointed stick on the sand, while the workmen gathered round him or could look down on his plan from the scaffolding above. The sand below acted like a mirror to their labors, for the actual and the intended states could be examined together; and when they were in need of a detailed instruction, the information they wanted was sketched out in the same scale on the sand.

The dress of the Indians is to this day well calculated to enhance the effect of their architecture. The women can be seen at work, or on their way to and fro, carrying the youngest child slung on their backs; while the pointed Mexican hats with their immense brims make a fine finish to the white pantaloon clothes of the men. Market day is like a parliament of the birds, so far removed do the scene and its characters seem from ordinary human activities. But this scene we must describe in its proper setting under the shadow of the great church at Taxco.

---

* The Mudéjar influence is especially noticeable in the polychrome tilework decorations on the buildings of Puebla. Travelers have always remarked on the resemblance between the district of Puebla and Andalusia, both as regards the architecture and the character and appearance of the population. All the Spanish settlers in this province were of Andalusian origin, with, of course, a strong element of Moorish blood in them, and the situation of Puebla between the coast and the city of Mexico made communication easy with Seville and the ports of Southern Spain.

Another example of the Mudéjar style is the Casa de los Azulejos, or the House of Tiles, in Mexico City. The Capilla del Pocito, or the Chapel of the Sacred Well, at Guadalupe, is also a first-rate example of this manner.

Each province shows differences in its architecture. For example, the buildings round and in Puebla have domes covered with glazed tiles, which are arranged in formal patterns after the fashion of the domes to the mosques in Persia, and the roofs can be seen gleaming far away, their visibility from a distance being very much increased by the bold and lavish color on them. Then, again, there are the buildings in quite a separate manner at the rich mining towns of Taxco and Cuernavaca; while Celaya and Querétaro have the finest work of the great Creole architect, Tresguerras.

The place names of Mexico, whether Spanish or Indian in origin, never betray the souls committed to their charge, for the remotest and most fever-haunted village has a name magnificent enough for a dynasty to call itself by. They have very often an effect of onomatopoeia, as though, in an obvious instance, imitating the perpetual prospect of a volcanic eruption. In less known and more remote examples the name is still better, and distance and inaccessibility are balanced by the sonority of the word. The names are a skillful imitation of the sounds that nature makes: the heavy rain tumbling clumsily from leaf to leaf till it booms down on the sodden soil; the sawing noises that the jagged-edged cactuses make upon the wind; and high up, but always in sight, the snow biting into hard rock.*

We will begin our survey with the greatest name among Mexican architects, Francisco Eduardo Tresguerras. The bearer of this curiously militant surname was born in Celaya on May 13, 1745, and, let me add at once, he died at the mature age of eighty-eight, on August 3, 1833, of fever, so that it was not old age that removed him. He was a Creole—that is to say, a Mexican of Spanish blood—and at various moments was sculptor, painter, etcher, engraver on wood, musician and poet, as well as architect.

---

* Wherever the Aztec tongue is in use, the letter R is unknown, while in the Otomi dialect it occurs in nearly every word. Thus, Popocatapetl, Iztaccihuatl, Tenochtitlán are Aztec names, while Ocambaro, Puruundiro, Litacuaro and Cinapecuaro, in the province of Valladolid, are Otomi in origin. Humboldt quotes, as a record in impossibility of utterance, the word meaning "venerable priest whom I cherish as a father," which runs as follows: "Notlazomahuizteopixcatatzin." But is this more frightening to a neutral observer than: "VenerablepriestwhomIcherishasafather"?

He worked entirely in the district immediately surrounding his birthplace—in the Bajio, that extensive, low-lying plain in the midst of the central tableland of Mexico, at Celaya, Querétaro, Irapuato, Guanajuato and San Luis Potosí; and now we may examine his work without the statement of any more leading facts.

We will take, first of all—because it was his earliest work—the buildings for which he was responsible at Querétaro, beginning with the church and convent of S. Rosa de Viterbo. Here and at the convent of S. Clara in the same town Tresguerras produced the most perfect and complete examples of the Churrigueresque to be found anywhere in the world. An enormous sum of money, realized from the merchandise seized from *contrabandistas*, had been placed at the disposal of the convent of S. Rosa de Viterbo. In both churches the choir screens and the screened balconies for the Mother Superior show the most extraordinary development of this, one of the strangest devices of monasticism. They are of wrought ironwork and are designed not for themselves alone but so as to form a decorative composition with the rest of the architecture. In that of S. Rosa the balcony for the Mother Superior has its elaborate golden base supported by the carved *retablo* of an altar, and in S. Clara it stands like a bridge over a richly carved doorway below. The confessionals of S. Rosa are designed in keeping with some of the rest of the color scheme, so that their gilding is sharpened with shrill touches of metallic luster, an effect which is obtained, in the medieval fashion, by mixing the colors with a transparent varnish medium applied over a ground of gold leaf. In this way ruby and emerald-green effects of great violence and brilliancy are procured. His use of color is seen all over the building, and, for example, the reredos of the altar of S. José has its picture by Miguel Cabrera (the greatest Mexican artist and master of Tresguerras) framed with garlanded lines that are treated in emerald in the process I have described, making a beautiful contrast with the rich gold masses about them. The pulpit of S. Rosa is a superb piece of inlay in ivory, tortoise shell and mother-of-pearl, the tortoise shell being underlaid with thick gold leaf.

S. Clara has a fine example of the tiled domes which Tresguerras brought to perfection. It has a pattern of blue on a yellow ground, like the smaller dome of the lantern; while the base is of white and blue. The lowest belt of the tower has a pattern of blue and white on yellow and light green; the two middle belts are blue, yellow and white below, and blue and white above, the dome of the tower being blue and white over a belt of yellow and white.

Of the convent of S. Clara it is, unfortunately, only the church that now remains, but the convent covered with its buildings alone several acres of ground, and was the home of as many as eight thousand nuns. The whole of this huge building has been designed by Tresguerras, who was responsible for all the details, and supplied rough sketches, even, from which the best of his band of sculptors, Mariano Arce and Mariano Peruzquia, carved their figures.

In S. Rosa there is a great deal of decorative painting by Miguel Cabrera, and in the sacristy there is the famous performance of Tresguerras, the *"Hortus conclusus,"* a huge painting as a background to wooden polychrome figures, which shows the nuns of the convent and their pupils at work in the garden. This picture has, unfortunately, some of the woolly softness that characterizes Murillo's work, but in every other respect it is a most extraordinary proof of the varied powers of this Mexican genius, who had the ability to make successful every scheme to which his exuberant imagination directed him.

This convent, as I have stated, was the home of some eight thousand nuns before the dissolution of the monasteries, out of whose number only a small proportion can have been of pure Spanish blood. A large detachment was permanently engaged on the embroidery of all the vestments that the splendor of the church required, but large numbers of them found work in the convent sugar plantations and on the fields. The bombardment of wild flowers in the early spring was something from which a stranger might recoil in fear, and the saw blade of the cactus was as dangerous as an armed sentry; but under all these alarms the nuns kept up their daily routine. In the course of a year enough cloth of gold and silver was woven to clothe every one of them with a rippling gown that would make a better mirror than any water film, but all this splendor was denied by them and kept only for the pompous ceremonial of the church.

They were hidden from view during the service behind the huge flying metal lattices that I have described. It was like looking through the meshes of a fan down into the body of the church below, and all round, lining the whole wall of the church, were more of these boxes full of nuns. Higher up still, where she could see into every box and observe every corner of the building, was the Mother Superior, waited on and guarded like a queen bee; behind her was a group of servants, waiting like aides-de-camp to take her orders. The highest lattice of all sprang right up, starting almost from the ground, and, spreading out its wings to protect the balcony full of nuns, mounted still higher and burst in a kind of golden spray on the roof. There was a full military band, mainly of Indians, joining in the service down in the aisle below, and the heroic players were prevented from any view of the Creole beauties above by the contrapuntal intermixture and flow of metal screens. Some of the nuns were in boxes facing straight down at right angles to the nave of the church, and the lattice that guarded them was like a palisade of sun rays, for their strength of defense lay in blinding light. So brilliant was the gold leaf laid over this metal work that, after looking at it for a few seconds, the different rails and bars did actually seem to move and drift into and among each other, like intermingling sunbeams. Above the heads of the nuns in this balcony was the organ, and the angels that leaned out blowing their trumpets were actually sounding out of the lattice, in special places where room had been designed for them, so that they were crying out shrilly from the very heart of this splendor, and were no nearer to heaven than this, when sounding their fanfare out of the actual sun rays, as they dart into space over a cloud edge. The balconies along the side walls were more difficult to examine because of the steep and neck-craning angle up to their height. They were so many boats riding a sharp sea and hidden in the spray they cut out of the waves, for the lattice in front of them had the flung-up and curving line of foam.

After mass was over the nuns left their boxes and made for the door in the organ loft that led from the church into their sequestered life behind. Their bare feet sounded from below as they walked along the narrow gangways leading from balcony to balcony, like a flock of birds, a tribe of pigeons, half walking and half flapping along to their dovecots. The refectory where they were eating their evening meal was throbbing with music again from another band which had taken up its station in the musicians' balcony. The Indian servants came in carrying huge platters piled up with fruit, while others went round pouring out water or wine from a hollowed-out gourd. The band now playing consisted entirely of the nuns, and there were none of the heroic brass or percussion instruments that give character to a military band. There were, instead, the long and sliding measures of a string band, to which the abbess of the convent came in with her retinue, and they dined off the produce of lands that belonged to, and had been mostly worked by, the nuns, while the pastoral music suggested a landscape in which there was no human violence.

The entire and splendid isolation which these two convents afforded their regiments of nuns, the demands even that these two small universes made on the invention of Tresguerras represent only one half of his output of work; since Celaya, his birthplace, four leagues from Querétaro, is the scene of his other great labors. The huge five-spanned bridge, as you come near the outskirts of Celaya, over the River Laja, is to the design of Tresguerras, and has splendidly rolling send-offs in the form of four great stone finials at each end of the bridge on either baluster. The whole four of them roll in the direction of the center of the bridge, so that whichever way you are crossing there is a demonstrative farewell. On the center of the bridge, before you have got to the entrance into the town, you can see the dome of the Church of Carmen, the greatest triumph of the architect.

The main plaza of the town is an example of his garden planning: in the center there is a fine column from his design as a celebration of Mexican independence, and he felt this change in the national life to the extent of writing a long patriotic hymn in its praise and winning the reputation of having been mentally affected by the news; while all round the square there are secular buildings planned by Tresguerras, including two splendid private palaces. The churches, like the plaza, are the late work of Tresguerras. He had built, in the church of S. Rosa, the finest example of the Churrigueresque, while S. Clara showed him working in a more directly Rococo manner; and now, in the Church of Carmen, at Celaya, Tresguerras changed into the classical mode that was then spreading all over Europe, but, instead of the pseudo-Greek, he adopted a classical Renaissance manner. The date of this church (1803-1807) seems anomalous beside the huge classical line of this building, for which Wren might have been responsible. The famous dome, covered with glazed tiles that alternate from yellow to green, he might have copied from a mosque in Persia, so perfectly does the brilliant color suit the rounded lines of its architecture. Inside the church the sculpture and the mural paintings are his work, and there are three large frescoes (the only works in pure fresco that he ever executed) in the Chapel of the Juicio. Here also are two medallion-shaped portrait frescoes of himself at the ages of thirty-five and sixty-three.

There are many other buildings at Celaya of which he was the architect. The tower and Church of S. Agustín are his work, and in the parochial church of S. Francesco his tomb lies in a little mortuary chapel that he built against the side of the church. Inside it he painted a frieze of the twelve Apostles, and there is his own portrait again to the left of the entrance. Various poems by him in manuscript and signed with his name hang in frames on the walls, and a door leads into a small room in which there is a shrine, over which hangs a crucifix carved by his hand.

This little chapel sounds a depressing end to the gorgeous and exuberant life of Tresguerras. He died just at the worst period of art, and had he lived a few years longer we might have had to describe a Mexican rival to Pugin. It was, as I have hinted, only a putrid fever that prevented this. He had lived, if we really search for the truth about him, some forty or forty-five years too long, and though he had the ability to change with the times, his real work lay in the eighteenth and not in the nineteenth century. In spite of this he considered Mexican independence, which was proclaimed when he was over seventy-five years of age, as a culmination in the history of his country, which he was lucky to have lived to see; and yet, within ten years, it was to lay waste and leave empty the convents that were his lifework. It is a very remarkable feature about his buildings that there is no trace of provinciality about them; they are not second-rate, and there is no feeling that they would have been better if nearer a capital. How a completely uneducated Creole can have attained to the degree of mechanical knowledge necessary for this work is in itself difficult to understand until it is realized that, from the very first, the Spaniards had embellished their colonies with the most magnificent churches that money could produce, and there was, therefore, in Mexico a tradition of magnificence that even in the early life of Tresguerras was two centuries old.

It is not the work of Tresguerras alone that makes these two cities of Celaya and Querétaro so interesting to study, for there are in both places other and earlier traces of this tradition of building which explain the apparently miraculous endowment of talent on him. At Querétaro there is a famous aqueduct spanning the valley, like the work of the Romans, in one flight of seventy-four arches, and two thirds of the cost of this huge work was contributed by the local nobleman, the Marqués de la Villa del Villar de la Aguila, whose share alone came to one hundred thousand Mexican dollars. The palace of this grandee in the chief plaza of Querétaro is as fine a building as any in Naples or Seville, with its frieze of glazed tiles and the splendid wrought iron balconies; and the descendants of this public benefactor are still in possession of the property, ruling the town like one of the lesser principalities of Italy.

The monastery of S. Agustín, built in the middle of the eighteenth century by the two Augustinian monks, Luis Martinez Lucio and Carlos Benito de Butrón Moxica, is so remarkable in style that it is impossible to suggest a date for its construction without definite knowledge of its history, for the building has the appearance of being earlier than its real date by at least two centuries. There is, to begin with, the unfinished and extraordinary-looking tower. This rises up above the body of the church, carved elaborately in a kind of flat bas-relief, in which the figures have the still but complicated pose of the Aztec and Maya carvings, and then suddenly, just as the tower is collecting itself for the final leap up above the roofs of the church, it stops short, where even the Mexican gold and silver mines were unequal to the strain put on them. So the tower ends just above the knees of the huge statues at each corner, and it is as though these archangels had their feet on the earth, but were yet, as far as the rest of their bodies were concerned, in a kind of lambent invisibility. They can be seen to the knees, and up to this point they show the strained and leaping muscle of a dancer who relaxes as soon as he stands still for a moment; and these four dancers have the strong light thrown on them so far as this, but all the rest of them is cut off and hidden in the darkness of the theater, while everything round them is burning in a white heat of sunlight. At any minute they will shift their position and walk round carefully like dancers, to take up a new position for the music to begin. Then they will, all at once, emerge into the dazzling light, which will show up the rainbow feathers on their heads, and their breastplates shooting out gold and silver rays. Farther off, at the side of the dome, there is a seated archangel waiting for his turn and clothed in the full heroic costume, in a breastplate and with a profusely feathered hat. At each corner of the dome there stand the more than life-sized figures of angels, who wear enormous plumes on their heads, and are like the statues of Indian caciques executing a pagan dance.

At the side of the church the convent encloses a cloister of large dimensions, and it is on this that the two monk-architects have engaged their strongest powers of ingenuity. Between each pair of arches the pillar that acts as the separating bar between them has been changed from its ordinary business as a pillar into a caryatid. The cloister has two stories and, in consequence, two tiers of caryatids, those in the upper tier being allowed the greater freedom of expression. Each caryatid represents a differ-

ent individual in this strange race: some are bearded like a patriarch, some have the aquiline warrior features of the Indians,
while others are fauns laughing over the frightening effect their
appearance always exerts on mankind. They are holding their
giant hands, with the fingers outstretched, to the full height
above their heads, in order to support the arch for which each
hand is responsible. All this time they are talking to each other
in the deaf-and-dumb alphabet, for each one of them is spelling
out different words with his fingers, and at the appointed moment
they will throw down the loads they are carrying and let fall
the whole mass of building, to crush those walking in the cloister
beneath. Their faces are actually carved with the derisive and
cynical smile that is ready for this signal, and till that comes
they call across to each other in their disconcerting, quiet
fashion.

The two convents at Querétaro, the churches at Celaya and
the other buildings in both towns that I have described, may
serve to give some idea of the huge mass of material that is still
waiting in Mexico to be investigated by someone in sympathy
with this class of building, and who is, at the same time, well
enough informed of contemporary work in the Spanish
peninsula and in Southern Italy to be able to present the one
in relation to the other. In the villages round these two towns
there are numerous large churches possessed of the same characteristics as those of which a description has been given, and
even in the two towns themselves there are many similar remains just as interesting in their detail. Nor has the complete
work of Tresguerras been described. There is, not far away from
this district, in the mining town of San Luis Potosí, a great
theater, the Teatro Alárcon, which was designed by him, and
for the performances at which he doubtless on many occasions
designed the scenery. In Querétaro itself there is the Palacio
del Estado, or State Palace of the Province, where the government offices and the governor's residence are situated, and this
palace is a superb example of the more restrained Churrigueresque. Its gleaming white façade can be seen, as if bathed in a
diurnal moonlight, through the shafts and broad-bladed leaves

of the palms that grow in the public square, and it affords at once a most interesting comparison with the Town Hall in the chief plaza of Salamanca, which is one of the most successful of those buildings for which Churriguera gave the designs. It is extremely difficult, owing to the bad repute in which this architecture is still held, to discover writers who have been conscientious enough to describe and investigate what they know will not interest readers of the class who buy such works, and, in consequence, there are many contradictory points to be solved before the work of Churriguera can be disentangled from that of the plethora of architects working at the same time and involved in the general confusion and disgrace. But Salamanca was the birthplace of Churriguera; and should this argument not carry weight there is, in the building that he designed, his actual model for it—a fact which must be allowed to dispose of the problem once and for all. The palace, then, at Querétaro may be compared with a building of exactly the same character and built for the same purpose in Spain itself, and this analysis will reveal to what a wonderful degree this architecture is elastic in scheme; for, while preserving all those characteristics that contribute its point and give it the bad name, it has, at the same time, transmuted itself from being the one point of elaboration in a stern and rock-laden Spanish landscape into the only quiet but consistent relief in this country, where the sun is a scorching fire and the vegetation a cannonade.

There is now time to examine for a short space the scenes by which these buildings are surrounded, so as to arrive at some estimate of their suitability to the country they are situated in. The convent of S. Clara, at Querétaro, with its army of eight thousand nuns, is a sufficient proof of the enormous and plutocratic scale of things. There was such a concatenation of influences that something transcendental in its effect was inevitable, if only the various factors could be fused together so that their result was not wasted on one another, and this cancellation into one movement was achieved by the power of the Church, which, in Mexico, was preternaturally endowed with wealth. So skillful were their dispositions that, within fifty years of the Conquest, all the great monastic orders were established in Mexico on the most permanent of scales, and the Jesuits, as we shall see later on, in discussing their work down in the wildernesses of South America, were training and employing the Indians in those particular directions to which their racial ability was most suited. In a climate so enervating, and where the labor of agricultural work is reduced to an absolute minimum of trouble, it may at first seem a surprise that the native workmen and carvers should have attacked their material with so much energy. The carvings and ornaments are all executed in the very hardest of wood or stone and with the most simple of instruments, so that the thoroughness and elaboration of the work is a topic of endless surprise. But the answer to this question is that, far from these ornaments being a test of disconcerting energy from the Indians, they are, on the contrary, a tribute to their slow and contented laziness; for, like patient beasts of toil, once secure in the prospect of the little food and the shade rather than the shelter that they require, they were content to while away the whole of their lives over the carving of a panel or the inlay of a cupboard. No one admires the beasts of the field because of the amount of grass they eat in a year, by patient and long-continued labor; nor should the Indian, who sits year after year working gently, be a subject for astonishment. He works to while away the time, and probably even the cow would complain were everything else except sleep forbidden to it.

The three zones of Mexico, disposed like as many terraces, add enormously to the peculiar character of the country. The big landlords, by skillful preparation, could procure tropical summer foods during winter from the low-lying *tierra caliente,* and, in the most torrid of weathers, could cool themselves on early summer fruits from the highest tableland of all, the *tierra fria.* There was a year's climate in all its different stages within a day or two's traveling, and when you reached the point where one zone melted into another, within the space of a few yards, there was an intermingling of tropical and European vegetation, for on the slopes of the low hills there would be woods of fir and oak and in the plain below plantations of sugar cane, divided by woods of bananas and orange trees. A river came tumbling down, falling in small cascades among the rocks on its way to fertilize the plain with snow water from the mountain heights above.

"The parasitic plants of the tropics are exchanged at a very early period for the evergreen oak, and the deadly atmosphere of Veracruz for the sweet mild air of Jalapa. A little farther the oak gives place to the fir, the air becomes more piercing, the sun, though it scorches, has no longer the same deleterious effect upon the human frame, and nature assumes a new and peculiar aspect. With a cloudless sky and a brilliantly pure atmosphere there is a great want of moisture and little luxuriance of vegetation; vast plains follow each other in endless succession, each separated from the rest by a little ridge of hills, which intersect the country at regular intervals and appear to have formed, at some distant period, the basins of an immense chain of lakes. Such, with some slight variations, is the character of the table-land from Mexico to Chihuahua.

"The transition is sometimes extremely sudden, for a ravine or cañada is sufficient to occasion it. Thus, in the cañada of Querétaro and in the famous barranca of Regla, at Real del Monte (both of which places are situated in the middle of the central tableland of Mexico), a few hundred yards change the face of Nature entirely. The luxuriance of tropical vegetation replaces the stunted growth peculiar to the central plateau; the birds assume a more variegated plumage; the inhabitants a more relaxed and indolent expression; and the whole scene the characteristics of another world."*

The music in the villages was of a character in keeping with the country. Each tune had the long termination which the Arabs brought with them to Spain, and the drawn-out close of the melody was accentuated by the clashing of little bells and any metallic shaking sound which could be contrived, as if the precious metals of Mexico were playing their share in the music.

* Such is the description given by H. G. Ward in his book *Mexico in 1827*; and, in further proof of the diversity of climate, Humboldt mentions the valley of Rio Verde, where sugar is raised with success at nearly four thousand feet above the degree of elevation which previous experiments had induced him to fix as productive of the minimum of heat requisite for its cultivation.

The stringed instruments, far from being taut and flat in their sound, as they are in Spain, produced an effect as if the actual strings were of a different material and were made out of the longest quills that could be plucked from the tropical birds. The liquid sounds were more gurgling, and the loud passages far more fiery in their speed.

The big towns celebrated their religious *festas* with an even more fervent enthusiasm than the Spaniards. A love of flowers is the most permanent quality of the Indians, and they took part in these processions wearing long garlands that they had hunted for through the woods the previous evening, as they attached a peculiar significance to their choice of flowers. When the evening service was over they spent the rest of the night dancing and playing their instruments. Farther south, in Yucatán, a great feast day of this character would be celebrated for as long as three days and nights, with a fair, and huge arrangements for gambling to add to the entertainment.

These were the conditions of life in the mild and rather sleepy market towns of the countryside, where the peasants got their livelihood from working on the *haciendas,* or large estates of the landed proprietors. To the Spaniards it was nearer to the pastoral life than anything to be found in Spain, except in those southern provinces to which the Moors clung with a desperate tenacity, knowing them to be more alluring and fertile than the burnt wastes or the overstocked oases of their native Africa. The *haciendas,* seldom visited by the owners, who lived in the capital or passed a month at most on their country property, were under the direction of an overseer, whom we may imagine cracking his whip like any driver of a galley team. But his charges were large-eyed and gentle, unlike the savages who were shipped from the coasts of Africa to North America and the West Indian Islands. Every traveler records the submissive way in which they accepted punishment, and they always showed an astonishing resistance to pain, so that an Indian seriously injured in a fight or by some accident, bore his sufferings with a stoicism which seemed to argue his belief in one recipe or other of philosophy. This insensibility to pain holds true of the Indians in every part of the continent, for in the north there are the tribes of Indians, whom the cinema has made the heroes of Homeric campaigns of skirmish and outrage, while in the south the death of Guatemozin proves the truth of this generalization as regards Peru.

The Spaniards, once they had built their cities, treated the Indians as though they were a race of mild antelopes or gazelles. They must be broken in, but after that they might be allowed a certain amount of freedom and a few of the rights of Christians. They had been given away with the land to the Spaniards by a Deity still grateful to them for their expulsion of the Moors, and it was the triumph of a Spaniard or two, here and there, over the flowerlike multitudes of Indians that inspired many a Captain Fracasse to give the Italian comedians those models of the Spanish captains, who strutted up and down the trestles that they set up on feast days all over Europe.

The religion to which the Indians found themselves converted became, under the hands of the Jesuits and the monastic orders, the purveyor of more general and better regulated pleasures than had fallen to the share of the natives as a reward for attentions to their own pagan deities. The numerous Church *festas* were organized by the priests in such a way that the Indians found their own simple and childish delight in music, in bright color and in flowers, changed from an amiable weakness into a religious duty. These very safe indulgences were not likely to find a recusant, for returning to the old pagan times meant worship combined with danger, and the fires of the auto-da-fé confined themselves in Mexico to those Indians of the far backwoods who were too stupid to seize at the bargain that the Jesuits dangled before their eyes.

Let us examine, as an example of their powers, one of those districts in which the Indians form almost the entire population; for in such circumstances they are taught the method, but themselves provide the style, and the buildings they put up are, in consequence, a real expression of how the new civilization mixes itself with the ancient traditions. Tlaxcala is a case in point. It is to this day almost wholly Indian, and we may be certain that at the date the churches were built, European influence

came simply from two or three priests who could train their
workmen in the process of carving or carpentry, but had to leave
them to themselves over the details. We may let the churches
of the town go undescribed, as the example we want to discuss
is a pilgrimage church, the Santuario de Ocotlán, which stands
on a high hill some three miles outside the town. It is in this
church in particular that there occurs the theaterlike arrangement of the whole space between the end of the aisles and the
altar, that I have mentioned a little way back. There are huge
retablos and carved wooden panels reaching right up to the ceiling, and the golden glitter and droop of their ornament makes
this open space like a grotto, at the back of which, through a huge
open proscenium, the high altar appears like the stage beyond
these effective footlights. When hundreds of lamps were strung
from every corner and point and the great crystal chandeliers
hung down scintillating, with their candles burning again like
sparks in the waterlike fronds and leaves of crystal, the ordinary daylight glamour of this grotto was transmuted into a darkness more played on and pierced through with artificial light
than any stage. The priests were moving slowly from altar to
altar, lighting fresh candles, and they were followed and waited
on during the service by barefoot Indian servants, who moved
about through the fields of light like birds treading golden lawns.

The whole of this grotto, with its carved walls, the drooping
stalactites among the figures of saints, and the roof inlaid with
precious woods, was the work of a pure-blooded Indian, Francisco Miguel, who spent twenty-five years of his life on this work.
Leading out of this part of the church is the *camarín*, a word for
which it is difficult to find the counterpart in English. These
rooms are to be found only in Mexico, and are really a kind of
boudoir in which the vestments for the image of the Virgin are
kept, and where the image is dressed with an elaborate ceremony.
On this *camarín* Francisco Miguel spent the remainder of his
years, and, to judge from the work it contains, his life must have
been healthy and protracted. The decoration is gold and green
on white, with other brilliant colors used as accent. The dome
has a blue ground, with a circle of gold on scarlet. A circle of

polychrome Apostles stands round a blue ground in the act of receiving tongues of flame from the Holy Spirit, here symbolized by a white dove in the center. The feet of the Apostles stand on a white and gold cloud. The altar beneath the dome is silver and the figure of the Virgin is of pure gold, while round the walls, the doors, the cupboards and the presses are carved and inlaid by this Indian. The floor, of inlaid marbles, is covered with a piece of ancient Mexican figured tapestry.

Immediately after this, so that comment may be made on these two churches together, I will describe a rather similar group of buildings at Tepozotlán. In this case, again, they are situated outside the town, about an hour's drive away from the station, and on this occasion it is not a pilgrimage church but a Jesuit seminary that I am describing. The Seminario de San Martín was built as early as 1584, but it was very largely rebuilt again in mid-eighteenth century, and the work of this latter date is, in some respects, the finest example of the Churrigueresque to be found in Mexico. The convent was, naturally, dissolved a hundred years ago, at the time of the confiscation of all the monasteries; but being Jesuit and not strictly monastic it is now once more in the hands of that order, and in consequence the church is still splendidly kept up, unlike nearly every other institution in the country. There is an elaborate façade, so fabulously intricate in design that one may imagine the most staring of Suns might blink his eyes for a moment before he looked down to investigate the detail. The floors of all the chapels are in glazed tiles of yellow, blue and white, and above this checkered field rise the huge carved altars, like knights and castles ready to move at the right moment, however heavy their clanking armor. The *camarín* built onto this church is the most splendid example of its class, far surpassing even that described at Tlaxcala. It has, to begin with, a domed ceiling lighted by a triple lantern. These following colors flash out, one after another—gold, scarlet, blue, light and dark green, and silver, all of them obtained out of this metallic luster. As each new color meets the eye it is as if the one before had been extinguished, and the whole room thrown suddenly into darkness, for the force of every one of them blinds the eye for a moment, and the whole lot of them together flare out, one after the other, like the beam in a lighthouse, which owes part of its strength to the darkness between each flash. For the rest, the *camarín* has the usual inlay on doors and presses; there are huge panels of wood carving, big groups of polychrome sculpture, and great oil paintings framed in panels.

Tlaxcala and Tepozotlán, taken together, show that the line, which even a photograph of these buildings will show, has color to support it; so that, when standing actually in front of one of them, it is difficult to say whether it is the color or the drawing that gives the better effect. They are both there in equal proportion. No feather tapestry could be more gorgeous and flashing, and not one of those sea shells that are washed up like a magical castle on the sands is more delicate and touching in its design. The imagination of Gracián or Góngora would be satisfied with these transcendental qualities built into and over the mortal fabric of stone, for they realize in the most permanent form those superstructures that these authors had attempted out of ordinary words, above the printed line and the cut page of a book.

We will amplify and fulfill this remark. The lantern to the dome of the *camarín* of Tepozotlán is in three stories. From each of the two lower stories, heads of cherubs, angels and saints lean out sculptured in relief, looking down almost as though they were all the stars of the universe concentrating their gaze on this one miserable globe. The light from the windows in these two stories is modified by screens, but from the third and highest floor the full illumination is admitted, so that the emblem of the *Espiritu Santo,* the white dove on a ground of azure, sculptured up there, seems to be floating on a veritable sea of light. It is such a Gloria as no words and no music can convey, for speech is dwarfed by the symbols in which it has to be written, and music is dead as soon as ever the instruments and the voices have stopped.

I will now give, in rapid succession, nearly the whole remainder of the buildings that must be described, so that when their account is safely finished there may be no data wanting in the discussion of the whole. By this method we may, first of all, state the facts and then prove the case, while for final evidence South America can be searched and I can keep, for my peroration, the finest example in the whole of the repertory of Mexico.

There is Oaxaca,* the most southerly town of any interest in Mexico; and it may please American statisticians to know they live on the same continent as the Church of Santo Domingo in this town, on the building of which twelve million dollars was spent. The ceiling of this church, now largely in ruins, has so elaborate a system of inlaid coffering that such a sum of money might well have been spent on this piece of work alone. To the side of the church is an immense convent, and consideration of the whole affair induces the opinion that labor here must have been as cheap as in China, so that work of the same proportion in Europe would have been perhaps a hundred times more expensive.

Almost at the other end of the country is the town of Zacatecas, in which the church was continuously building for a space of one hundred and thirty years—from 1612 till 1742. Here, again, the traces of purely Indian workmanship are to be seen at the first glance. Before the confiscation of Church property the interior decoration was rich beyond belief. I will mention the font, which was of solid silver, so that every child baptized in Zacatecas may be said to have been born with his head in a silver spoon; but I refuse to divulge at what figure this piece of metal has been valued.

Then there is Morelia, the capital of the state of Michoacán, with an early sixteenth-century church of Plateresque design. And there is Tzintzuntzán (how the Mexicans like the letter Z!), on the lake of Pátzcuaro, with a picture sent over from Spain by Charles V and reputed to be by Titian. The church was built at the expense of the famous lawyer, Quiroga, for a town which contained at that date not less than forty thousand inhabi-

* The palace in Mexico City of the Marqués of the Valley of Oaxaca is the finest example of Churrigueresque domestic architecture in the country. This gentleman, of an obviously geographical import, died in the year 1771, leaving the palace unfinished, in spite of the huge sums he had lavished on it. The architect was Francisco Guerrero y Torres, and the palace is called by the people the Casa de los Mascarones, because of the huge grinning masks with which its four façades are adorned.

tants, while it has now shrunk into an insignificant hamlet, with only one priest left in charge of the church.

There is quite a distinct difference in style between any of the buildings already indicated and the churches in a group of mining towns I shall now describe. One of the finest of this class is the Church of San Cayetano, in the town of Guanajuato. This was built for the miners of the Valenciana silver mine by the proprietor, the Conde de Rul. During the years of its productivity the output of this mine was eight hundred million dollars; now it is worked out, and the town, like Tzintzuntzán, has shrunk back into a miserable hamlet, with but a handful of population. Here, again, the church is in the charge of one lonely priest; while, in the days of its plenty, the scale of extravagance on which it was built can be indicated by the elaborate temporary ornament that was provided for the ceremony of dedication when the church was opened on August 7, 1788, for the tissue that entered into its composition cost three hundred Mexican dollars a yard.

At Cuernavaca, in the state of Morelos, besides the church and what ruins there are left of the castle that the Conquistador Cortés built here for himself, there are the remains of what is more unusual in Mexico—a great formal garden. This was made by the millionaire mineowner, José de la Borda, whose work at Taxco we shall describe at the end of this chapter. There are terraces now overgrown, statues lying in the undergrowth, and pavilions on islands that are inaccessible for want of a boat. The man who built it came as a young boy, penniless, from Bordeaux, his native town, at the very beginning of the eighteenth century, and made a colossal fortune out of the mines of Taxco, with the proceeds from which he built the church there, and the palace and gardens in which he spent his old age at Cuernavaca. The palace is in ruins and the garden desolate and snake-haunted. All round the garden stretches an immense sugar plantation, which was established by Cortés and now belongs to his descendant, the Sicilian Duke of Monteleone; but he is not allowed to enjoy the revenues, which go, by the will of Cortés, to support the Hospital de Jesus in Mexico City. The Marqués de la Borda

344 Selected Works of Sacheverell Sitwell

lived, as I say, with his garden entirely surrounded by the property that was conferred on Cortés, but this oasis was laid out by him in a way that utilized every slope of the ground for a terrace and every hollow for a tank of water, just as though he had to defend his ground against the sugar canes. Their hollow, reedy music, when the wind blew through them, was like a perpetual sighing that came from behind every tree and through each spray of water.

After this group of mining towns, in which the dust and the darkness of work in the mines is compensated for by an intensity of color not obtained anywhere else in the country, there remains to be discussed the work of an extremely interesting architect of pure Indian blood who was working in the '70s and '80s of the last century, and who is very probably still alive at this date. He worked entirely in his remote native province of Guanajuato, and chiefly at San Miguel de Allende, a town which already possessed some interesting buildings for a local architect to found his studies on. There is, for instance, the Oratorio de San Filippo Neri, a building in the richest of Jesuit styles; and near to it is the chapel of the Santa Casa de Loreto, built in 1735 by Don Manuel Tomás de la Canal and his wife Doña Maria Heras de Flores; its superposed dome is very like that described of the *camarín* at Tepozotlán.* This is quite sufficient to show that there was already a tradition for Ceferino Gutiérrez to work in. He did, in fact, rebuild the dome, in a drum of two stories, of the convent church of La Concepción in the town of Guanajuato, not far from San Miguel de Allende, in a pure Renaissance style that he may be said to have refined out of the later and more elaborate work of his native town. The two markets, with their deep-shadowed colonnades, are his work, but his distinctive originality appears in the new façade and tower that he added to the Church of San Miguel, the parochial temple of the city. Gutiérrez had never in his life seen any building in the Gothic style, but he had arrived at some idea of what it must look like from studying the early Victorian steel engravings of the cathe-

* There is also an extremely fine private house at the corner of the Plaza Mayor, the Casa de la Canal, with balconies and the most elaborate of carved doors.

drals of Northern Europe. It was he who, as we have said, could not even draw a plan, but used to scratch out on the sand, with a pointed stick, a huge sketch of what he intended his building to look like, and from their perches high up on the scaffolding his workmen would look down and follow his suggestions. In this way the building was finished piecemeal, until, on the day when the church was finished and ready for service, the whole town was dominated by this barbaric and tropical interpretation of the icy pinnacles and dripping grottoes of the North.

With the work of Tresguerras and Gutiérrez we arrive at so recent a period that, in the case of the former architect, tradition is still in existence about him, and with the latter, many of the workmen, and very probably the architect himself, are still alive. The Indians, far from being reduced by the Spaniards to that abject submission and impassivity in which they are usually depicted, have produced, as we have seen, as many great works of architecture after as before the Spanish Conquest. The churches are bigger than the ancient temples, better planned, and show a more successful expression of exactly those emotions that they tried to give shape to in their pagan temples. It was because life was more secure under the Spaniards that the Indians, in the three centuries of Spanish rule, were able to finish more great works than their ancestors had achieved during a much longer lapse of time. The ruined Indian cities, with their traces of a huge population before the Conquest, can be paralleled by the mining towns like Oaxaca, Zacatecas and Guanajuato, that once held a population of forty or fifty thousand in their times of prosperity, when the mines were working, and have now shrunk back again into hamlets and a collection of tumbling hovels. The mixture of strange blood among the inhabitants is exactly what is wanted to produce those conditions in which a vigorous tradition of art may flourish. Now that the emigration of Japanese to Mexico has reached such a scale, there is an even stronger probability of the rebirth of a great barbaric art, for none has existed in the modern world since the collapse of every Mohammedan power, and the Westernization of Japan. The Japanese artists, so unlike the Chinese who love repose, find their subjects in the violent exploding curves of vegetation, and in flowers that open wide, as though detonated by the first touch of sun. The dizzy perspective, the volcanoes, the tropical flowers and birds, the huge cactuses with their sawlike leaves and the tiny flower, so seldom in blossom, at the top of an inaccessible ivory tower rising out of the heart of the guarding saw blades—all these ingredients of the noisy and melodramatic Japanese art are present in Mexico. If only Japan should ever conquer and occupy Mexico, the third religious state to which the Indians would be converted should produce more rhapsodies in all the arts than ever music has given birth to in itself.

Now that the country is in a state of transition, in order to realize how it looked in a period of productivity, we need carry ourselves back only eighty years, to that decade after the separation from Spain, before the Republic and the revolutions had ruined the work of three centuries. It is of this period that the diary in Mexico of Madame Calderón de la Barca treats,* when the waltz had just reached to those far shores and the romantic operas of Donizetti and Bellini were played by a military band in the gardens of the chief plaza. All the balconies were hung with tapestry, the church doors were open; and glittering brightly in the darkness down at the end of the church, the jeweled cups, the relics and the vestments of the priests could be made out like some fiery creature moving slowly in the mud at the bottom of a pool.

With an appalling rumble a great gilded coach would lurch along, while the postilions cracked their whips as though to disperse the evening mists and restore the air. The horses had broken into a wild gallop in their attempts to get free from the coach they were dragging, which had the appearance of being about to topple over at any moment on to the horses' backs. Behind the windows the residents in this glass palace were glittering with such a steady fire from their jewels, that to see them through the window as they passed was like leaning over the side

* Cf. *Life in Mexico during a Residence of Two Years in that Country*, by Madame Calderón de la Barca. First published (with a Preface by W. H. Prescott, the historian), London, 1843.

of a boat to watch the stars reflected in the sea below; for however much the water shook and trembled, the stars were still
there a moment later, blazing away through the glassy depths.
At other times, when the roads were too difficult for a coach, a
person of great importance would come riding along in a cluster
of mounted attendants, and their huge Mexican saddles were one
mass of jewels, with gold and silver fastenings to the harness.
It may be imagined, if such was the appearance of an ordinary
country landowner, to what a far greater degree of splendor the
progress of the Viceroy was carried. He would appear in the
plaza of a town in the middle of a tragic blare of trumpets announcing his arrival. The Corregidor and his Alguacils, the
attendants of office, were waiting there to receive him, standing
perfectly still at attention, as though in terror at his coming.
The crowd, also, was still, with the words hardly dead yet from
their mouths, like a wind that dies down suddenly before the
leaves have time to hush their low voices.

Traveling over the countryside you were continually meeting
with these traces of the peculiar terror with which Spaniards
have always contrived to invest their public ceremonies. In every
big town, and all along the chief roads, you met companies of
traveling matadors, like a small army in perpetual readiness for
a campaign; for the chief matador had his officers with him and
the rank and file, all of them in condition for battle. They rode
along on the miserable cheap horses they bought in each town
to carry them through to the next, where these steeds would die
as an offering to the bulls. Their fine clothes they kept for the
fight, and, except in the case of the one or two chief matadors,
the bullfighters rode past in ragged bloodstained clothes, that
were a witness to the hard lives led by their wearers. A day or
two later you might meet with very different traveling companions, like the experience of an English traveler of the period,
who complains that, by he knows not what accident, the whole
country was covered with a deluge of monks, who took up all
the easy carriages, so that it was impossible for him to travel any
farther in one of the Mexican mule carts, but had to ride the rest
of the way on a slow and famished-looking horse. This deluge,

spread over the countryside like the rain you may read of in
Australia, which comes down and covers the country with
millions of frogs or small fishes, was a section of the inmates of
some such monastery as those I have described a few pages back,
who were on their way to one of the monastic *haciendas* where,
by rotation, and a certain proportion at a time, they went to pass
the heat of summer, moving in this way from the *tierra caliente*
to the thicker shades of the *tierra fria*. Nearer the central tableland, where most of the big towns are situated, you met the
companies of traveling Italian opera singers on their way to con-
vert, for a few nights, the stage in one of these bare Spanish
theaters into the shadow beneath a Neapolitan balcony, or into
one of those shuttered but still fiercely lighted rooms in which
the Italian women are secluded, while, as though borne in on
the yellow bars of sunlight that are creeping between the black
lines of the shutters, you can hear the rattling nasal voices singing outside in the street, and now and again the church bells, that
give the only indication of flying Time, who, in this easy climate,
seems to have no divisions to mark his progress.

The Cardinal of Mexico was a greater, because a rarer, figure
than the Viceroy. He moved about as though protected and
hedged round by the fires of the auto-da-fé; and to the supersti-
tious Indians the ease with which the Inquisition could commit
its victims to the flames bespoke the Cardinal's authority, and
made him not less dangerous than their pagan high priests, who,
before the Conquest, arranged for the sacrifice of human victims to placate their bloodthirsty gods; while the form of sacrifice was no more awful in the latter than in the former state.
The Church found an audience of Indians as enthusiastic and
impressionable as a congregation of Italians or Spaniards; so that
the love of splendor, which was part of the doctrine and most
of the instrument of the counter-Reformation, found itself with
full occasion for use, and with no Calvinist criticism as a set-
back against its employment. The extraordinary mineral wealth
of the country made this lavish expenditure easier than anywhere
else in the world, and the gold and silver of Mexico found its
first application, on being recovered from the mines, in the

service of the Church. As an example of the methods of this direct utilization of wealth from the mines, I will give the Church of San Cayetano, which I have already mentioned, as having been built in the town of Guanajuato by the Conde de Rul, for the use of the miners of La Valenciana silver mine. For the use of this church, every one of the thousand of miners employed was compelled to give, each week, a piece of ore called a *piedra de mano,* a stone the size of the hand, or of a size that could just be held in the palm of the hand. This produced a sum of fifty thousand dollars a year, and in addition to this there were the customary church tithes and the revenues derived from the huge estates which the mineowner, the Conde de Rul, had handed over for the endowment of the church. From endowments and revenues of this nature a huge army of priests was supported, and the works of carving and building were maintained on the generous and apparently permanent scale that I have indicated. Vast sums were expended on vestments and jewelry, and the church *festas* were organized with their fireworks and triumphal decorations, so that every inhabitant could play his part in them and feel that the entertainment had been devised for his own special benefit.

The lake, in the center of which the Indian city of Mexico stood till the Conquest, had dried up until nothing was left to show where it had been except a few areas of plain, which shone out like beds of snow under the incrustation of salt which the waters had left behind them when they sank back again into the depths of the earth. Over these plains, and some ten or twenty feet above their present level, the Indians had glided along in canoes over the mirror face of the water, just at the height of the best leaves of a tree above where you can stand now, crunching the soft salt with your feet. The little waves overlapped and broke on each other just like the feathers, which melt from one color into another, on a bird's breast and wings; while the canoe itself glided along like a bird sweeping down from the heights of air with just a stroke of the wings now and again to change its direction on the stream of speed which is rushing by, for it is always the air that is moving and not the bird or the airplane, and the canoe itself is filled with a crew of Indians, plumed and feathered as though born into the world with these sails and rudders. As though their appearance was not ornithological enough, the Indians kept the feathers of one or two particularly rare species of birds for the insignia of royal blood, while, in drawing or carving the human figure, they imparted a fluttering air to each being, so that he looked as if just caught for the moment on the ground beneath the flowers, trees and clouds, among which his occupation lay. These transmutations of the human physique they carried still further in their feather tapestries, the most supreme of all Indian arts. These were made of the most delicate and brilliantly colored feathers obtainable, and more especially of the soft downy breast of the picaflores, the humming-birds, called by the Indians *huitzitzlin*. Each of these tapestries, according to the description of Madame Calderón de la Barca, was the work of many different hands. Each person finished his part and then all the different pieces were sewed together to form the whole. After the sketch had been made the feathers were first taken up with some soft substance with the greatest care, and fastened with a glutinous matter on a piece of stuff; then the different parts, being reunited, were placed on a plate of copper and gently polished, till the surface became quite equal. The nuns were still making these tapestries at Pátzcuaro, the chief center of manufacture, in the days of Madame Calderón de la Barca's visit to them, but they imitated, in a poor fashion, the original art, which had become extinct only some twenty years before, with the death of the last real artist of this nature. Unfortunately, for some two or three generations before its extinction a century ago, these tapestries, though perserving the original method of manufacture, had fallen on evil days, for, as subject, they reproduced sacred pictures by Murillo or Sassoferrato, and these timid performances gave no indication of what the Indians had produced by this method before and for a generation or two after the Spanish Conquest. With the exception of one or two pieces in Spain, and a cope and miter of this material in the treasury of Milan Cathedral, there would appear to be no specimens existing now of the Indian work, for the

color was not permanent for more than the space of a century,
and, if exposed to strong sunlight, all the feathers crumbled into
dust, and the whole design disappeared as rapidly as the Indian
civilization before the Spaniards.

Besides the Spaniards and the Indians there was a large population of half-castes of different degrees; for some were the compound of the two races named, while others were half Spanish
and half Negro, or else Negro and Indian mixed. It was from
these mongrel races that the soldiers and the men of violent lives
—matadors and bullfighters of every rank—were drawn. These
half-breeds were, in fact, more energetic than the Indians, and
not so disdainful of trade, or any work except fighting, as were
the Spaniards. It is also established beyond contradiction that
it is the Creoles who have a love of music, for the Indian music
is monotonous and depressing almost beyond endurance. In
Mexico it is the Creoles who both compose and perform the
native tunes, and the beautiful Brazilian dance music is produced by the same race. It is sometimes a Spaniard, more often
a Creole, but seldom an Indian, who discovers the secrets of
this new music that will one day improve on and drive out the
Negroid tunes of North America in its appeal to the popular
sentiments in every country.

In the same way that it is difficult to arrive at any just perspective of the ancient Mexican civilization, that has no parallel
in any other continent of the world, without some knowledge of
its sister culture in Peru, so is it impossible to see the results of
Spanish settlement in Mexico without some small acquaintance
with the fruits of Spanish rule in other parts of the American
continent. Such a reconnaissance is a continual journey toward
the south, for the mission settlements started by the Jesuits and
Spanish monks in Texas or California are not large enough to
repay a close investigation.

Leaving Oaxaca, the most southern town of Mexico that has
any architectural pretensions, you come to the Republic of Guate-
mala. It is in the jungle to the east coast of this state, and bor-
dering on its frontier with Yucatán, that the ancient Maya
civilization flourished, producing more works of art in sculpture

than any of which traces can be found in Mexico or Peru. Yucatán, to this present day, is still the property of some three or four great landowners whose estates are worked, almost exclusively, by slave labor; and their *haciendas* are on a scale of size and strength that is to be compared only with the colonial villas of the rich Roman patricians in Africa or Syria, and with the castles that the Normans built wherever there was a subject race to hold in check. Each one of these gigantic properties has been developed with the completeness of an Italian principality, for religion, education, health, the printing of books, and the teaching of every skilled trade are entirely dependent on the munificence and liberality of the landowner. There are the remains of big Indian cities still lost in the jungle and waiting for the explorer's spade some two or three days' journey inside the impenetrable wilderness; while nearer at hand are found ruined monasteries still more imposing in their remains, and lying desolate for only a century past, but overgrown by the jungle as luxuriantly as the ruins of three centuries ago. It is the island of Pelen, with the Indian town of Itzen, lying off this coast, that the Spaniards subdued as late as the year 1697, when it was still inhabited by myriads of Indians, as the Mexican towns had been nearly two centuries before this date, at the time that Cortés first marched inland from Veracruz.

The remaining states of Central America have, all of them, many traces of the first conversion of their natives to Christianity, but we can pass through Panama, and Colombia, where the purest Castilian is still spoken, before we come to the first signs of civilization on a settled scale once more, at the frontier of Ecuador. It was in the big indenture on the Ecuador coast—the Gulf of Guayaquil—that Pizarro and his sailors first caught sight of the Indian boats moving slowly across the bay toward their journey's end; for this gulf was the farthest north to which their voyages reached, and its Indian harbor was the port for Quito, one of the two capital cities of ancient Peru, which lay a long distance inland from this harbor, to the north. The ancient empire of the Incas included the whole of the modern Ecuador and Peru; the northern capital, Quito, was in what is now Ecuador; while the southern, Cuzco, lay in what is, at this day, called Peru. These two cities, Cuzco and Quito, contain many ancient Spanish buildings; they have convents and monasteries in a number quite out of proportion with their population, and at Cuzco there is a monastery built on the site, and actually made out of the cyclopean stones with which the Incas had built their convent for the Sacred Virgins of the Sun. To the south of Cuzco, toward the Pacific coast, the town of Arequipa stands, which has great Spanish buildings in a style of architecture quite unlike that in use at Quito and Cuzco, for the stone is much softer and requires an altogether different architectural treatment. In all of these places mentioned, the carving inside the churches was carried out by the Indian population, and reaches to a degree of delicacy and invention that had died out in Europe many generations before this, when the Gothic art drank itself to death on such occasions as Brou in Burgundy, and Louviers in Normandy. The Jesuits built their churches in situations that have become accessible again only in the last half century with the aid of railways and river steamers; for even a settlement so remote as Putumayo, the place of torture for the Indian rubber-gathering population, on a river which is one of the most distant tributaries of the Amazon, hundreds of miles inland over the snow mountains from the Pacific, and literally some thousands of miles from the Atlantic, where the Amazon flows into it, has a Jesuit church of beautifully worked stone, the most elaborate internal carving, and a pharmacy and refectory to the finishing of which many Indians must have devoted their lifework.

Lima was the residence of the Viceroy, and his palace still stands there with the portraits of the Incas, whose aquiline features are so different from those of their placid and complacent descendants. There are also many faded family palaces and a great deal of that splendor, as regards the churches, which one would expect to find in the port at which the Spaniards first landed after leaving their harbor of Cádiz and rounding the dangerous Horn. But in the whole of this region under discussion, although the Spaniards produced many great buildings, there is nothing comparable to the Mexican remains; for there is nothing Andalusian about the high stony deserts and the violent precipice edges of Peru. The snowy mountains can be seen, as you come near the coast in your ship, until they loom like forbidding cliffs straight out at the water's edge; and there is none of that gradual accommodation to the climate, so that you may try one terrace after another till your taste is suited, which helped the Spaniards to adapt themselves to the Mexican atmosphere. Peru is a sterner and more forbidding land; and there is a monstrous distortion, like the human disease of acromegaly, about the very bones of the country, for the stony ridges, alike with the high snow-capped mountain ranges, are swollen out of all perspective and proportion. The animals of the country—the llama and the vicuña—are uncouth and clumsily contrived, while the Indians bear out, in their distinctive appearance, the modern theory of a separate human creation for the ancestors of the Indian races of America. It is from their understanding of this, perhaps, that the Spaniards, in this region of South America, so seldom intermarried with the Indians; and the two races remain apart as rulers and conquered, in quite different circumstances from those prevailing in Mexico. All the provincial towns are purely Indian in population, and the Spaniards form the bulk of the big towns and the harbors, and in the country are only landowners or officials. It is only in the Republic of Colombia, for some peculiar reason, that you find a village population of pure Spanish blood.

We now move across the Andes to the Atlantic seaboard of South America, and before we come to the Portuguese settlements of Brazil there remain to be described the Jesuit settlements in Paraguay, that were the most southerly of all Spanish works, and, indeed, farther to the south of the world than any other works of Catholic activity. The Jesuits landed in this part of South America toward the end of the sixteenth century, and they marched far inland on their missionary enterprise till they came to the huge rolling pampas of the interior. These districts were inhabited by the Guarani Indians, a race of absolute savages, who, now that the Jesuits have left them, are back again once more in their primitive condition. The Jesuits set about the immediate conversion of these natives, and within twenty-five years of their first arrival in the country the Guaranis had altered their mode of life and were living peaceably in the *Misiones,* or settlements designed for them by the Jesuits. These villages were uniformly alike in arrangement; the church, with its monastery, was in the plaza, and the long tenement houses of the natives lay along the roads radiating from this center. The houses were built on a fixed plan, and the Indians wore a costume which the Jesuits had designed for them. There were altogether thirty settlements of this description, eight of them being in the modern Paraguay, and the rest of them in Brazil, and in the Argentine provinces of Entre Rios, Corrientes and Misiones.

This territory, which was ruled like a republic by the Jesuits, lay far concealed, some one thousand or fifteen hundred miles up country from the Gulf of La Plata. The Guarani language was studied and written down, and the Indians themselves taught to print books or, where this was impossible, to copy with a pen the printed letters of a book in so close a fashion that the forgery could not be told from the original. The great missionary, Ruiz de la Montoya, who traveled for some thirty years through the wilderness among the savage Indians, was the author of the first book on the Guarani language, while the Bible was soon after this translated and printed in Guarani, and there is a book of sermons in this language by the Indian Jesuit, Nicholas Yaparaguey. These books, which are some of the most valuable of bibliographical rarities, were printed and finished entirely by the Indian workmen and they bear the imprint of the various settlements, principally that of the Misione de S. Loreto.*

The Indians were taught, also, every art connected with the science of building; they carved the statues and painted the altar pictures. Many of these churches were of very great size, sometimes with as many as five aisles, for the Jesuits were very rich from their cattle ranches and from the various objects that they exported, on a fleet of their manufacture, down the La Plata

* Manuale ad usum Patrum Societatis Jesu qui in Reductionibus Paraquariœ Versantur, ex Rituale Romano et Toletano descriptum (Misione de S. Loreto). And for a description, with maps, of this region, La descripción geografica del Gran Chaco, Padre Pedro Lozano (Córdoba, 1733).

River to Montevideo and the great ports at its mouth. Maté, the South American tea, coffee, and sugar were part of the sources of their wealth; while some of the medicines—as, for example, quinine—that they extracted from the herbs and flowers of this region were held in such value that the Jesuits were directed to send every year a quantity of their balsam of the Misiones for the use of the pharmacy in the palace of Madrid. They supported an army of Indian troops, and on more than one occasion drove back the marauders, who had come eight hundred miles through the wilderness to attack them—from the robber state of San Pablo de Piritinanga, the so-called Paulist Republic, a colony of all the desperadoes who could reach it from every country.

It was their wealth and military strength which brought about the downfall and expulsion of the Jesuits, against whom charges of cruelty and extortion to the Indians were raised by their jealous neighbors. It is well established that these charges were unjustified; but so great was their wealth at the time of their expulsion, in 1767, that in cattle alone their possessions reached the following figures: cattle, 719,761; horses, 27,204; sheep, 138,827; and oxen, 44,183. As soon as the Jesuits were removed (there were apparently only some four hundred of them among a population of as many hundred thousand Indians), the whole region fell back again into barbarism; the churches and settlements were lost in the jungle, the Indians forgot everything they had been taught and became savages again, while so complete was the ruin that it is only within the last twenty years that settlements have sprung up again in the neighborhood of these towns, where the Jesuits once lived in peace among their Indian dependents for the space of a century and a half.

The scene of their labors was of extreme beauty, hundreds of miles removed from snow mountains or dangerous volcanoes; and apparently so far away from human interference that war or pestilence did not enter into the calculations of those who built these colonies. There are huge rolling plains, with blue or red hills far away, perhaps one hundred or one hundred and fifty miles into the distance; and to describe the flowers and trees with which they were familiar, I can only quote a paragraph from Mr.

Cunninghame Graham, one of the few travelers who have visited this remote region:* "The Croton Succirubrus (from which a resin known as the sangre-de-drago is extracted), the Sumaha (bombax—the fruit of which yields a fine vegetable silk), the Erythroxylon or coca of Paraguay, the Incienso, or incense-tree of the Jesuits, are some of the most remarkable of the myriad shrubs. But if the shrubs are myriad, the flowers are past the power of man to count. Lianas, with their yellow and red and purple clusters of blossoms, like enormous bunches of grapes, hang from the forest trees. In the open glades upon the Trandu-bays, the Algarrotos, and the Espinillos, hang various orchidaceæ, called by the natives *"flores de aire,"* covering the trees with their aerial roots, their hanging blossoms, and their foliage of tender green. The Labiatæ, Compositæ, Daturæ, Umbelliferæ, Convol-vulaceæ, and many other species cover the ground in spring, or run up trees and bushes after the fashion of our honeysuckle and traveller's joy."**

Like all the aborigines of the American continent, the Indians had a very highly developed cult for these flowers, in connection with which they believed in many pagan traditions as to the origin or the different uses of each blossom. On particular feast days they would decorate the whole interior of the church with flowers, and used to build up triumphal arches of them along the roads leading to the church door, while even the very trees by the roadside would be hung with flowers in such profusion that the branches seemed to be festooned with different-colored snows. The uniforms worn by the Indian notabilities on such occasions as this were of a gorgeousness in keeping with the colors of nature. "All the militia of the town"—I quote again from Mr. Cunninghame Graham—"were in attendance, mounted on their best horses, and armed with lances, bolas, lazos, and a few with guns. The officers of the Indians rode at their head, dressed out in gorgeous clothes, and troops of Indians, at stated intervals, per-formed a sort of pyrrhic dance between the squadrons of cavalry.

* A *Vanished Arcadia*, Cunninghame Graham.

** For a study of the flora, see Vasconcellos, *On the Flora of Brazil*; and the works of Montenegro, Sigismund Ansperger, and Lozano.

In front of all, on a white horse, rode the Alferez Real, dressed in a doublet of blue velvet richly laced with gold, a waistcoat of brocade, and with short velvet breeches gartered with silver lace; upon his feet shoes decked with silver buckles, and the whole scheme completed by a gold-laced cocked hat. In his right hand he held the Royal Standard, fastened to a long cane which ended in a silver knob. Behind him came the Corregidor, arrayed in yellow satin, with a silk waistcoat and gold buttons, breeches of yellow velvet, and a magnificent hat. Other officials—the Commissario, the Maestro de Campo, and the Sergente Major—were in scarlet coats, with crimson damask waistcoats trimmed with silver lace, red breeches, and black hats adorned with heavy lace."

All of these settlements are now a melancholy ruin, and the very stones of the building are covered under such a growth of tropical jungle that it is almost impossible to discover their whereabouts. There are a few carved stones, and one or two mutilated and broken statues, but, except for these, every sign of ornamental work has disappeared many years ago, for after the expulsion of the Order, every object of value was removed, and those that were too heavy were broken up and thrown out to rot away in the wet woods; while the very natives, as I have said, relapsed again into barbarism, until, at this day, the Guarani Indians are among the most savage of the aborigines of South America.

In Brazil, as we leave the Misiones and make for the Atlantic, the race of conquerors changes from Spanish to Portuguese. I have described, in an earlier part of this book, the sources from which so much wealth was drawn by the Braganza family early in the eighteenth century, and without enumerating these again it is enough to say that the riches of Brazil drew away from Portugal huge numbers of the peasant classes, and many of those younger sons of the nobles who would be likely to depend on war and adventure for their livelihood. The emigration from Portugal grew, in fact, to so serious a pitch in the Algarve (the part of Portugal lying south of Lisbon and the River Tagus), that Negro labor had to be imported from Africa, by which expedient the Portuguese living in this part of the country are now very Negroid by race and appearance. Meanwhile the most energetic of their

countrymen had sailed across the Atlantic to Brazil, where they
founded great cities and started valuable industries. Earthquakes,
fires, many revolutions and a century of desolation have nearly
destroyed the buildings with which the Portuguese colonists
adorned their towns, and it is only safe to surmise their activities
by drawing a parallel with the remains of the days of Portuguese
colonial supremacy elsewhere. Macao, an ancient Portuguese
city on the Canton River, some forty miles from Hong Kong,
has huge churches and decaying palaces that testify to her former
importance; but it is at Goa, on the west coast of India, south of
Bombay, that these energies can be seen working to their fullest
extent. Old Goa, which is some five miles from New Goa, to
which the Viceroy removed in 1790, had at one time a population
of some two hundred thousand; while in the year 1890 there
were only eighty-six fever-haunted inhabitants remaining.

There are, in this ruined town, four or five churches of great
splendor. The Church of Bom Jesus, built in 1594, contains the
body of St. Francis Xavier, and is the principal building of the
place. Its high and complicated façade runs straight on into that
of another huge building with lofty halls and immense corridors,
the Convent of Jesuits, which was finished in 1590, some forty
years after the death of St. Francis. This was the college from
which so many missionaries were sent forth to India, China and
Japan; but the Jesuits were expelled by Pombal in 1759, and their
property confiscated by the government. The other monastic
orders were driven out in 1835; but the endowments of the
churches have never been forfeited, and so the archbishop and
secular clergy of Goa still receive large allowances from the
government. The Church of Bom Jesus is entered by a side door
from the Jesuits' College, through the sacristy, a huge room with
wardrobes filled with embroidered vestments. The tomb and
shrine of St. Francis occupy a side chapel; and this monument
consists of three tiers of sarcophagi made of jasper and marble,
and given, in the year 1696, by the Grand Duke Cosmo III of
Tuscany. The upper tier is decorated with inlaid panels in
Florentine mosaic, representing scenes in the life of the saint,
and on the top of this is his body in an enormous silver coffin;

while on the altar is a life-sized statue in solid silver of the saint, which was given by Queen Maria of Portugal late in the eighteenth century.

A little distance away is the Sé Primaçial, the Cathedral of St. Catherine, built between 1562 and 1623, which still has a staff of twenty-eight canons, who live in the archbishop's palace, a magnificent building next door; the archbishop yet, on occasions, lives here, while the Viceroy, on his periodical visits, stops in the neighboring monastery. In front of the cathedral the Palace of the Inquisition used to stand; and it was in this square that the terrible autos-da-fé were held at which, so typical of a religious controversy, the Nestorians, the primitive Christians of India, suffered so much more than the Hindus. At the other corner of this huge square were the buildings of the Misericordia which enclosed the Church of Nossa Senhora de Serra, a building made in fulfillment of a vow taken on one of his sea voyages by Albuquerque, and in which he was originally buried.* The palace of the viceroys is nearly a complete ruin, but it still shows traces of its once famous windows, in which the panes were made not of glass, but of sheets of mother-of-pearl. Beyond this there lie the Great Bazaar, the vast domed and doubled-towered Church of San Cajetano, the convents of the Dominicans and Carmelites, and the renowned missionary College of St. Paul, or Santa Fé.**

These details of Goa may give some idea of the extent to which colonization was in those days associated and connected with building, for Goa was intended as the metropolis of a Christianized India. In the absence of any good photographs it is almost impossible, without a personal visit, to describe the nature and appearance of the churches and palaces that the Portuguese erected; but their activities in India were not on a greater scale than their South American adventure. The settlements of Brazil were, of necessity, strongly fortified, for the Dutch had a power-

---

* The body of Albuquerque, who died near Ormuz in 1515, now lies in the Church of Nossa Senhora de Graça at Lisbon.

** Goa, about the year 1700, is said to have contained as many as thirty thousand priests, monks and nuns in its population.

ful colony on the same coast, and there were, in addition, huge bands of mamelukes, as they were called, and marauders from the robber republic of San Pablo de Piritinanga* to be reckoned with.

A little later than this, by the time that the Paulist Republic had been subdued, and the Spanish and Portuguese had expelled and absorbed the wealth of the Jesuit Misiones, Brazil received an additional dignity by the presence of the Braganza family at Rio de Janeiro, who had fled there on a British man-of-war, before the victorious French under Junot, in the year 1808. Ten years later, when the Braganzas were compelled by public opinion to return from Brazil, that they preferred, to Lisbon, the elder son of the King of Portugal was proclaimed Emperor of Brazil under the title of Dom Pedro the First. His son, Dom Pedro II, who was only expelled by the revolution of 1889, was a suitor for the hand of Queen Victoria; and the writer of a recent book of memoirs, who was a diplomatist at Rio de Janeiro in the days of the last Emperor, tells a curious and fascinating story of the peculiar etiquette with which his court was conducted. It appears that the natives of Rio de Janeiro were under the necessity of leaving early each day, by train, for the suburb in which all the business houses are situated. It was Dom Pedro's custom to attend every day the departure and arrival of the businessmen's train. At sixty-thirty each morning it started, and Dom Pedro appeared at this ceremony in top hat and evening clothes; there was a brass band always in attendance, playing to the Emperor, who stood in the waiting room. It was a moment of tense excitement for all concerned when the train drew out of the station, with the band at full blast and the Emperor on the platform surrounded by his staff and the foreign diplomatists. The evening train, that brought the businessmen back to their homes and suppers, was equally an excuse for ceremonial on the part of this really democratic monarch. On days of particular splendor—a national fete or a religious *festa*—he would appear less soberly

---

* *Histoire de Nicolas Neenguirui (Nicholas I), Roy de Paraguai et Empereur des Mamelucs, San Paolo (de Piritinanga)*, 1756. This book, according to Cunninghame Graham, was, if really printed in Piritinanga, the only specimen known from any printing press in that region.

dressed, in his Imperial mantle of the pink and scarlet feathers
of the toucan, providing in his person a parallel with the plumed
and feathered American kings of the Indies, at a time when those
could direct their cotton-quilted warriors under no menace from
Spanish aggression.

The Emperor has been gone more than thirty years, and most
of the businessmen ride to their work now in motorcars, so that
the suburban railway also is out of use; but Rio de Janeiro still
lies there, sheltered between the two rocky hills at each corner of
its wide-spreading bay, and there is still the avenue of trees, one
hundred and twenty feet high, that flower like gigantic roses,
leading up to the palace where the Emperor used to live, for it is
a town better suited than any other to be the culmination of a
huge empire. Brazil is nearly double the size of India, and contains more possibilities of new and strong developments in human
history than any other country in the world; for, like all the other
Latin republics of America, it was colonized from Europe in the
days of the greatest fertility of European culture, and once this
immense land has become peopled to the extent of the United
States, she may surpass the Northern Republic in her influence on the decaying European civilization.

The other great cities of Brazil, towns that are simply names
to all who have not visited them—Bahia and Pernambuco on
the Atlantic coast, and Pará, the gigantic settlement at the mouth
of the River Amazon, where that river at last flows out into the
Atlantic, attacking its tumbling waves on a perpetual battle front
of some three hundred miles—these three towns will one day
become provincial centers for a culture that, while it shows a
strong unity, will allow as much diversity in its different parts
as you may find between Hindu and Mohammedan in India.
Bahia is, for example, already a center for music, and the
Brazilian dance music is more continual and complicated than
anywhere else in the continent: it is there that they invent the
most languorous and the most fiery of measures, which, indeed, is
only natural, as they have bands playing dances in their streets
all day long, from one early morning to the next. Between these
dawns that they contrive, by this method, to telescope into each

other, hoping, perhaps, that the collision will flare up into a brighter conflagration, they discover the beat and the rhythm that are caught and handed on from one band of music to the next, like a sacred fire that is never allowed to die out. At Pará, where the millionaires outnumber the beggars, and the rubber that has been collected all over the interior of the continent enriches all the hands it passes through, the perpetual drift of life is so quickened by the flow of fortunes and the endless motion of the river that is like a huge sea moving uniformly in one and the same direction that you seem to grow old almost before you have had time to draw the Brazilian air into your lungs; it is alternately fiery white and then tropically dark, like the alternating squares of a chessboard; the air scorches, and then freezes as though the sky has as many icy shafts and pinnacles glittering there as it has soaring flames; time, flying with strong wings, or rolling its wheels lazily along—these two conditions are simply a brake or a higher speed at work on the continual flow of the waters: they laugh out loud or whisper softly like young leaves in the wind: it is a steady flame or a whorl of sparks . . . golden lawn or black chasm . . . fire or ice . . . eagle or tortoise . . . the lion or the crooning turtle . . . staring sun or drooping, heavy eyes . . . sleep, out of which we were born, and into which we die . . . till once in each life it is a dream, and we can wake again and find ourselves in the great plaza of Taxco; from its high tower I now deliver my peroration.

The house where we slept was in the street of the Flamingo, built of stone and in one story, with a big *sala* covering most of the space, and a courtyard behind the kitchens, where a great flame was used to temper the strange steely fruits of the land, for their core underneath this armor is cool and refreshing; while the fire has also to draw out the golden ore from the sugar canes, where it is hidden behind glass walls, and the brittle music that the wind makes when it sighs through these golden groves. The sugar cane was imported from the Canary Islands to Santo Domingo, whence quickly it passed to Cuba, and was introduced by Cortés into Mexico. The descendant of the Conquistador, the Sicilian Duke of Monteleone, as heir of Cortés, and Marqués of

the Valley of Oaxaca, still holds these sugar plantations, especially in the neighborhood of Cuernavaca, where they still produced a rental of thirty thousand arrobas of silver,* and these
sugar orchards fill all the valleys toward Taxco, which is high on
the mountain slopes, five thousand feet above the sea. The
gardener, Don Juan by name, with an immense black beard, a
Mexican hat, and a silken sash of military crimson, will offer you
orangeade; he sends to the house for sugar and tumblers, pulls
the oranges from the trees, and draws the water from a clear tank
overshadowed by blossoming branches, and cold as though it
had been iced. This is the evening of the first day's journey, for
Taxco is still three days' ride on muleback over the stony mountains of the state of Guerrero.** Behind the *hacienda* there is
a courtyard round which stand the house for boiling the sugar,
wherein furnaces blaze night and day, another house with machinery for extracting the juice from the cane, the refining rooms,
and the place where the cane is dried. As this is a coffee plantation, here also there are the great mill for separating the beans
from the chaff, and buildings in which they make brandy; while
there is lodging for the four hundred men employed, exclusive
of boys, one hundred horses and a number of mules. Outside are
the fields of sugar cane, the plains for cattle and the plantations
of coffee, this one containing upward of fifty thousand young
plants, all fresh and vigorous, besides a great deal of uncultivated
ground abandoned to the deer, hares and quails, of which there
is a great abundance. The second day's ride brings you higher,
onto the cold outer slope of the hills; and on the evening of the
third day you arrive at Taxco, tired out and hardly able to stagger
on foot up its narrow streets, that are paved in a flowing pattern
of pebble mosaic, like the Italian grottoes, and are too narrow and
steep for even a mule's sure feet to tread them.

Our lodging was a house, as I have said, in the street of the
Flamingo, and coming out of its shade the next morning at ten
o'clock, the Festa of San Christoval was in full swing: Grand Mass
was over, and the bullfight, the *corrida de toros,* ready to begin.
It was to take place in the square in front of the cathedral, this

* The Mexican arroba contains twenty-five pounds.
** This state of Guerrero alone is three times greater than Wales in area.

spot being the only piece of level ground for miles around. The enclosure took up nearly the whole extent of the square, and was in the form of a gigantic circular scaffold, some fifteen hundred feet in circumference, with room for about four or five thousand spectators. The whole of this huge wooden structure was built up and held together without the help of a single nail, being made of ordinary poles, standing just as they had been cut in the woods, and tied together with withes. The interior was enclosed by long poles crossing and interlacing each other, leaving only an opening for the door, and was divided by poles, in the same manner, into boxes. This made a gigantic frame of rustic latticework, admirably adapted for the hot Mexican sun, as it admitted a free circulation of air. The top was covered with an arbor made of the leaves of the American palm, a suitable finish to a building of this simple nature, which every Indian could help to build, and when the *festa* was over it could be torn down and the materials used for firewood.

High above the poles and the roof of palm leaves stand the two high towers of the Church of S. Sebastián y Santa Prisca: this is indeed the finest and culminating work in Mexico.* The *corrida* was on the point of beginning, and the place was already thronged, all the cheaper seats being in that part which was

* The man who paid for it was the Marquis José de la Borda, before mentioned, and the whole building was finished by the year 1757, by which date de la Borda is supposed to have spent some 8,000,000 Mexican dollars on its construction. The material is a hard and fine-grained brownstone, and there is a most fantastic façade with two towers and four windows in each, while the balconies with which the four faces of each tower are decorated have a sardonic and leering mask to support their weight. Inside the church there are twelve altars with retablos of carved wood, and gilded and polychrome sculpture. All the altar paintings are by Miguel Cabrera, and there are eight huge panels by him in the sacristy, which is filled with the most elaborate and fanciful chairs and tables that can be imagined, of such character and force that something transcendental has been arrived at in their making. Next to this is the Sala Capitular, in which there are portraits of de la Borda and other great dignitaries, and the floor was originally entirely covered with a superb India carpet imported to Taxco by way of Manila and Acapulco, of which a small fragment is still in use as a rug in the sacristy. Such is the church, described in the baldest and most uncompromising reality, but it would be impossible to describe in words the majesty and phantasm of its appearance. Underneath, as you look down from one of the towers, are the huddled roofs of the town, the tumbling, hilly country, and the plaza, which from above looks so small, although this is compensated for by its whiteness in the sun and by the feeling that it is the only level ground, apart from the floor of the church, for a huge distance round.

exposed to the full blaze of the sun. Outside the door of each box stood the proprietor with a rickety little stepladder of three or four steps, inviting customers to buy the seats inside. Everyone was scrambling for his seat, and in this general stampede and confusion the whole of the huge scaffold was trembling and swaying to and fro under the load of spectators. Above all this din, and coming out louder and louder as everyone settled in his seat and the hub of all the voices calling out at once began to die down, came the noise of the bells ringing out of the two towers, with a vehemence that seemed to express the relief of this building at being left empty again for the day's heat, after the appalling crush at mass earlier in the morning. All the masks carved on the façade and by each window in the towers wore an intensified leer, as if in preparation for the animal auto-da-fé; while those of them who were turned away from the direction of the bullfight were preparing to watch it reflected in one of the little mirrorlike clouds, or projected photographically onto one of the facets of the fathomless sea of space.

On ordinary days the plaza was allowed to sleep contentedly in the sun; but three or four times every year there was a bullfight, or a market and fair, which was about the only opportunity the inhabitants of this faraway town were afforded to buy cloth, jewelry, and all the other products of the capital. A market day, then, was the occasion for as much excitement as a bullfight. The pebble mosaic with which the square was paved had a fluttering air about it from the canvas shades of all the stalls that had been set up, as though it was a bed of flowers on which a whole tribe of butterflies had swarmed. The people who were buying and selling from these canvas windows were of, at any rate, four entirely distinct and separate colors. These were the Spaniards, the Indians, the mestizos or half-castes (and some of these were a mixture of Spanish and Indian, while others were mixed Indian and Negro), and, to finish with, there were quite a number of pure Negroes, imported from the Gold Coast to perform the most arduous and unhealthy tasks on the plantations and in the mines. The Spaniards, and those half-castes who were rich enough to afford it, had the utmost magnificence of costume, with gold and silver embroidery and fringes, and jeweled rings and earrings; the peons—that is to say, the Indian laborers—the Negroes and despised half-castes wore the wide, flapping, white pantaloons of the Neapolitan peasantry; and the stunted aquiline features of the Indians were of a perfect fitness for the Punchinello costume, while an occasional Negro in this dress looked like one of the dark spirits of the air masquerading under the sailcloth of these birdmen. No surmise could be too fantastic for the objects they were bartering at the stalls. The immense high-crowned and broad-brimmed hats of the peons were whiter than the snow on the high mountains that ended every view, and they looked as quenching and cool as those white capes round the shoulders of the fiery Mexican volcanoes. Some of the peons who had ridden in from the country villages had a blunderbuss, an enormous pistol, or a curved, cutting sword at their side, and they recalled what must have been a familiar sight in parts of Southern Italy till sixty years ago; for until the expulsion of the Bourbon Kings, in 1861, the brigands in Apulia, and more especially in the district between Brindisi and Taranto, and Lecce and Gallipoli, roamed about in their bands, armed to the teeth, and completely masked in the guise of Pulcinella. It was that birdlike nose you saw peering in through the window at an hour when you should have been asleep; and it was the phantom, with wings growing weak from disuse and only capable of a little flying jump like the ostrich, or a quickened walk like the penguin, that terrified travelers on a lonely road, and took away their money and valuables. Out here in Mexico the black mask was unnecessary for a disguise, for the Indians were swarthy and difficult to tell one from another, while at times, as I have said, the mask was made really necessary by the fact of its wearer being a Negro.

This particular week the market and fair were to be held for three successive days after the bullfight, and the dry wood with which the ring was built could be pulled to pieces with an hour or two's work after the *corrida* was over, so as to give torches and bonfires to light them at their second task of putting up the stalls for the traders, and the platforms for charlatans and mountebanks. But before this could come about there was another whole day to be lived through, and the *corrida* was just about to begin, punctual to its appointed starting time of ten o'clock.

High up, on the top of the scaffold, and above the gate through which the bulls would charge into the ring, was a big band of music, the conductor of which wore a shining black mask to caricature a Negro. This orchestra was continually playing, but its notes sounded soft and far away against the background of shouting and laughing voices. They seemed far removed from the purpose of this gathering, aloof and independent, like the orchestra you can hear playing, during a silent moment, in the theater next door, through the flimsy walls. But all of a sudden there came the sound of a squawking trumpet, dying away almost before it had begun, and the whole audience became silent and attentive in a single breath. The gates were flung open and the band came nearer, and rang out loud all at once in the strains of a heroic march to which the toreadors came in, headed by the president of the fight on horseback. The burlesque Negro who conducted the music gave it a specially exaggerated air, as though he, at any rate, knew the weak side of this mercenary warfare. They marched in procession right across the arena to the president's box opposite the entrance; the matadors first, and then the toreadors, the mounted picadors and their attendants, and, last of all, the most menial of the gladiators, those whose duty it was to kill with their stilettos the horses that were too badly gored by the bull to be of any further use, and had to be finished with a knife thrust into their spinal marrow; these men wore plain red pantaloons and shirts, in contrast to the other gorgeous uniforms, and their other duty was to drag out, with a team of mules, the dead body of the bull, after the matador had drawn his smoking sword out of its body.

There was now silence for a little, while the bullfighters took up their different positions; and they were hardly in their places before a general murmur ran round, and everyone looked attentively toward the gate. The manner of introduction for the first bull was brutal in the extreme. It was by a rope two or three hundred feet long, passed through the fleshy part of the bull's nose and secured at both ends to the saddle of the *vaquero*, one

of the band of cattle tenders, hard riders, and brought up to deal
with cattle that run wild in the woods, who came in for these
fights from the neighboring *haciendas*. In this way the bull was
hauled through the streets and into the ring. Another *vaquero*
followed close behind, with a lasso over the animal's horns, to
hold him back and prevent his rushing upon his leader. When
this pair appeared, hauling and beating the bull between them,
there was a hurricane of laughter, and everyone all round the
ring waved their handkerchiefs, making an indescribable effect:
it was as though every law of nature had been contradicted and
there were two huge waterfalls dashing at each other with equal
force, one from above and the other from below, so that when
they met, and as they passed each other, you could see the little
detached heads of foam falling in either direction so quickly that
you could only distinguish their mass, and were not able to follow
each one separately up or down. These were the waving handkerchiefs. At the same time, through their flutter, a fanfare of
trumpets could be heard announcing the animal's torture. In the
center of the ring the leader loosed one end of the rope and, riding
on, dragged it trailing on the ground its whole length, perhaps a
hundred yards, through the bull's nose, leaving a crust of dirt on
one side as the rope came out bloody on the other. The bull, held
back by the rope over his horns, stood with his neck outstretched
and when the end of the rope passed through, he licked his gory
nose, pawed the ground and bellowed.

The *vaqueros*, who were dressed in pink shirts and trousers
and wore small hats of thick-plaited straw with low round crowns
and narrow brims turned up at the sides, settled into their huge
saddles, the flaps of which covered half the body of each horse,
and dug their iron spurs, which were six inches long and must
have weighed some two or three pounds, into their horses' flanks.
One of them rode up and started the bull, and, chasing him round
the ring, with a few throws of the lasso caught him by the horns
and dragged him to a post at one side of the ring, where, riding
off with the rope, he hauled his head down to the ground close
against the post. Keeping it down in that position, some of the
others passed a rope twice round his body just behind the fore-

legs, secured it on the back, passed it under his tail and, after returning it, crossed it with the coils around his body. Two or three men on each side then hauled on the rope, which cut into and compressed the bull's chest, and by its tightness under the tail almost lifted his hind legs off the ground. The animal bellowed, threw himself on the sand, and kicked and struggled.

After this he was charged on and goaded by the undaunted picadors with their lances until the blood streamed from his shoulders, and he stood quite still, desperately pawing the ground and not knowing in which direction to turn and face his enemies. At this moment the toreadors ran toward him and threw their sharp barbed *banderillas* into the sore wounds on his shoulders, and then, when his neck and shoulders were quivering under a whole sheaf of these darts, they would twist their ropes or throw their red cloaks round one of the darts so as to pull and tear the wound still further. This particular bull was to be killed by the picadors: they formed in front of him, each with a black and yellow poncho in his left hand, and with a spear poised in the right. They stood with legs extended and knees bent, so as to keep a firm foothold, changing position by a spring forward or backward, on one side or the other, to meet the movement of the bull's head. The deathblow had to be between the horns into the back of the neck. Two or three struck him fairly with a cutting, heavy sound and drew out their spears reeking with blood. One man misdirected his blow: the bull threw up his neck with the long handle of the spear standing upright in it, and rushing on the picador, hurled him to the ground and passed over his body, seeming to strike him with all four hoofs. The man never moved, but lay on his back with arms outstretched, as if dead. The bull moved on, with the handle of the spear still standing up in his neck. The *vaqueros* went in pursuit of him with their lassos, and chasing him round, the spear fell out and they caught him. The bull was again assaulted, worried out and dragged away, while the wounded man was carried off, doubled up and apparently gravely wounded. Other bulls followed, making eight in all. At twelve o'clock the church bells rang out and the fight ended; but it was only a truce, for another was timed to begin at four o'clock in the afternoon.

This later fight was the last *corrida* of the season, and some of the best bulls had been kept in reserve for it. The first that was dragged on was received with acclamations by the crowd, for he had distinguished himself by his bravery in a former fight; but he bore an ugly mark of favor, having been dragged by the nose till the cartilage was completely torn out.

The victim was then let in, lassoed, dragged up to the post, girt with the rope round his body like the other, and then again let loose, amid bursts of music, rockets and loud shouts. The *chulos*, fighters on foot, went at him, flaring before him with the left hand red and yellow ponchos, and holding in the right darts containing fireworks and ornamented with streamers of yellow paper. These were thrust into his neck and flanks. The current of air quickened the ignition of the fire, and when the fireworks exploded the paper still rattled about his ears. The picadors then mounted their horses; but after a few thrusts of the spear the bull flinched, and the spectators, indignant that he did not show more fight, cried out for him to be taken away.

The next bull was led in by the same method, with a long rope passed through his nose, and after this preliminary torture was goaded with darts and speared fiercely by the picadors, while each time he received a blow, or one of the *banderillas* stuck in his shoulder, the whole crowd shouted out like one man, and laughed in great bursts like a cannonade. Each new torture was announced by a fanfare, which sounded forth like a shrill voice, and its metallic syllables held out no hope of mercy. He was then lassoed and dragged up and tortured at the post. But as even this did not goad him to enough fury, the crowd called out loudly for fire to be applied to him. Watching narrowly that the ropes around his horns did not get loose, they fixed on his back the figure of a soldier in a cocked hat, seated in a saddle. Both the saddle and the figure of the soldier were made of wood, paper and gunpowder, making a formidable and dreadful firework. When this was fairly secured to his back they all fell back, and the picadors, mounted and with their spears poised, took their places in the ring. A *vaquero* with a pointed and sardonic chin set off large and furiously whizzing rockets within a few feet of the bull; another fired in the heel the figure of the soldier on his

back; the spectators shouted, the rope was slipped, and the bull
let loose. His first dash was furious. Maddened by the shouts
and laughter of the crowd, and by the fire, the smoke, the explo-
sion and the awful whizzing of the engine of torture on his back,
he went for the first picador, and ran his horns into the horse's
belly, lifting it up and nearly tossing it over the barrier onto the
crowd behind. The laughter was louder than ever, and the bull
dragged out his bloodstained horns with a horrible slipping sound.
The horse's entrails came out, splaying themselves into a horrible
resemblance to some sea animal, with their red pipes and smoking,
seething mass. After its wound was stuffed with straw, the animal was quickly stitched up, beaten onto its feet again and led
out, blindfolded, once again toward the bull. Meanwhile he had
charged another horse, and received a second awful thrust of the
picador's spear in his flank. The first horse gave a moaning, pitiful cry as the horns opened its wound once more, and the bull,
rejoicing in its revenge, stood over the prostrate body, digging its
horns again and again into the stomach, trying to enlarge and
make fatal his first stab. He was at last tempted away with a red
cloak and a furious rocket, and fixed his attention onto the second
horse, which was being beaten toward him with a timid but
brutal-looking picador on its back. The animal could hardly
stand, and was dropping great gouts of blood onto the sand from
the terrible grapelike bunch of entrails that was hanging out from
below its belly. The picador's lance went right into the bull's
shoulder with a clenching, grating violence, while the horns dug
themselves savagely into a fresh place on the horse's neck. The
bull all this time was bleeding from scores of wounds, his neck
and back were a fluttering mass of darts, the firework was burning furiously into his flesh, and he was fighting with fictitious
strength.

He made a ferocious advance toward a third horse, lifted it
high up on his horns, while both of them bled together and made
the sands dark with blood. He was thrust at by four picadors, had
fresh darts thrown at him, and his burned fat was sizzling and
scenting the air. In the corner, a few yards away, knelt some half
dozen *chulos,* two or three of them holding the head and tail of
each of the two dying horses, while the most experienced pair of

them drew a little stiletto from their belts, and seemed to be
gently stroking the necks of the horses as they felt for the right
spot to plunge their daggers in.

The powder was now burned out, and the bull, with gaping
wounds and charred, smoldering flesh, turned and ran, bellowing
for escape at the gate of entrance, and then crawled round the
wall of the ring, looking up at the spectators, and pleading to the
mild faces of the women with imploring eyes. A matador stepped
up, motioned with his left hand, and thrust a straight long sword
into his back up to the hilt. The bull sank on to his knees and then
stumbled up again, peaceful and calm, while the matador went
over to him, drew out the sword, and then pressed it back again
in a new place: the knees gave way, he gave one moan, rolled
his eyes and lolled his stained tongue. A moment later, when
they had all stood at his deathbed, he was dragged out by a
jangling mule team, which drew out the three horses that were
his victims with him.

It was almost dark, and the last bull was dragged in. He was
stabbed, fringed with darts, tortured with the rope and burned
with fire. But the vesper bell rang out suddenly, and with this
the ring was opened to the boys, who, amid roars of laughter,
pulled, hauled and hustled him till he could hardly stand. No
one moved from his place yet. The bells rang out louder and
louder as their metal seemed to grow molten with the heat of the
blows rained on them, and the conductor of the band, in his
shining black mask, directed and sounded forth a fine burlesque
march, to which the toreadors filed away, grumbling at their pay,
but resolved to gamble it away that evening. They were shabby,
with wet and ruffled plumes, torn shirts and brown stains on each
arm and leg—blackened hands from the smoke, singed, even,
with the fire, and still slippery and wet with the promiscuous
blood. The most heroic of the company carried a bull's head
with glassy eyes and lolling tongue, the blood still hanging con-
gealed, like a rich and fantastic lace, round the jagged skin edge
of the neck. They limped, stumbled, and some of them were so
tired that they seemed to walk on air, with their legs cut off at
the knee; but the music got the lot of them safely over its
tightrope to the benches and the brandy behind.

FESTIVAL AT NOLA *

1. Night at Santa Lucia

"Rends-moi le Pausilippe et la mer d'Italie."—GÉRARD DE
NERVAL

On such a night as this it is impossible to sleep. All Naples
sings, or strums the mandolin.** It is because the god of music
has persisted here, but lingers only in the trembling of the lute
string. The mask of Pulcinella is scribbled on the walls. A man
runs past in rags; and the mules and horses are thin as ghosts
from the knacker's yard.

Here are booths of amulets and sacred emblems. There is a
smell of wax. These are the candle shops. Little plaster statu-
ettes show saints or sinners writhing in the fire. We are among
the statues. You will see wings being fitted to a wooden doll.
Gods and goddesses are for sale in the workshops. And, at the
corners, there are barrows for old clothes.

Here are watermelons—"Redder than the fire of Vesuvius,"
as the peddlers cry them; apricots—"There's cinnamon inside";
pears are "Ladies' thighs. We adore them!" Grapes are "Gold,
not grapes"; nuts—"As fine as quails' legs." Here are booths of
lemonade with festoons of lemons. Here are the stalls of *pizza*—
flat pancakes cooked with cheese and tomatoes; and bladders of

---

* From *Primitive Scenes and Festivals*, 1942.

** The Festival of St. Paulinus, at Nola, is described in *Siciliana: Sketches of
Naples and Sicily in the Nineteenth Century*, by Ferdinand Gregorovius, translated from the German by Mrs. Gustavus W. Hamilton (London, G. Bell & Sons,
1914), pages 111-123. It is taken from *Wanderjahre in Italien*, published in
German in 1853. My account of the festival is based on this. The translation by
Mrs. Gustavus W. Hamilton is, in itself, a work of art. A few of her sentences
and phrases I have quoted in entirety, because it is impossible to improve upon
them. My account of the festival, indeed, is a picture based, as it were, on a
sketch by Gregorovius. This is the place, perhaps, in which to remind readers not
only of the *History of the City of Rome* by Gregorovius, but also of his *Roman
Journals, 1852-1874*, translated by Mrs. Gustavus W. Hamilton (G. Bell & Sons).

374

goat's cheese, or *mozzarella*. Men, old and young, and a few
women drink *sanguinaccio,* made from chocolate and pig's blood,
which improves the constitution. Here are stalls of syrups; and
flower stalls of roses and carnations. You cannot see the sky for
strings of washing.

It is a phantasmagoria, an hallucination. What we see are living phantoms. For this is ninety or a hundred years ago. Here are
the Pulcinella theaters, with Pulcinella's house at the entrance,
whence the snapping tones of the mannikin are heard above the
siren waves. For stone steps descend to the water's edge, and it
is an open paved foreshore, as it could be the stage of a huge
theater set for a crowd scene. A sea piazza for a marine festival.
The lazzaroni sleep everywhere, on the pavement and the sea
wall, in their rags and stocking caps, the cap of a tarantella
dancer. The mask of Pulcinella on the wall becomes the symbol
of the town.

It is Santa Lucia, the fisherman's quarter down by the waters
of the Bay. Here are the oyster stalls. But, as well all kinds of
shellfish are offered in this horn of plenty. It is like a fair or
market. Here, too, the nymphs of night cast their nets for
strangers. This is the city of Parthenope, a siren or sea nymph
whose naked body was found upon the shore. These are her
daughters.

This is Santa Lucia of old Naples, long pulled down.

Tomorrow we rise early. But who could sleep tonight? We
can see the volcano and the rock of Capri. It all lies before us.
In their season there are cliffs of violet and narcissus where
Procida and Ischia float upon the milky seas. With vales of lemon
and pomegranate trees. The goatherd stays upon the mountain,
looking down:

> To isles of fragrance, lily-silver'd vales
> Diffusing languor to the panting gales:
> To lands of singing and of dancing slaves,
> Love-whisp'ring woods and lute-resounding waves.

It is late: but there is no end to the music and the singing in this town of the volcano and the tarantella. The town of Southern superstition. The urn into which Campania pours her grapes; while the Bay loads the cornucopia with shells and fishes.

We hear, all night, the twang of the guitar. Through the open shutters, from the balcony. While the bells of many convents, some cracked, some strident, strike the restless hours. Here is the tunnel, hewn by convicts. And the tomb of Virgil. The oleander, even in the darkness, blooms before the palace of pink walls. In wooden tubs at foot of the great stair. But we would have no palaces. We would, sooner, the oyster stalls and fishing nets. And the mask and cap of Pulcinella.

The early morning is virginal, but sordid. On the way to the railway station, through the mean streets, we meet the galley slaves, guarded by soldiers, and marching two by two, clanking their heavy chains. Some are wearing blood-red, the color of fraud and infamy. Turning a corner, we see Vesuvius and the Bay. It is June 26: the morning of the festival at Nola.

2. *Festival of St. Paulinus*

For an hour, or a little more, the train goes through the Campanian plain. On every side are vines as high as houses. Nola is twenty miles from Naples,* and not far from Aversa, the birthplace of Pulcinella; whose image, or prototype, works in the vineyards in soiled white linen coat and cap and trousers. In the dog days of August he may be nearly naked in this classic land. For it was at Nola that Augustus Caesar died; and the peasant still drinks red wine from a two-handled amphora of terra cotta.

---

* Nola was an important town in classical antiquity. Hannibal was defeated here by Marcellus; while Augustus Caesar died at Nola in A.D. 14. At the present time it is a town of some ten thousand inhabitants. St. Paulinus was born in Gascony in A.D. 351, his father being a Roman Prefect of Gaul. He was converted to Christianity at Bordeaux, and having been made Consul was appointed to Campania. He became Bishop of Nola, and was famous as a poet and religious author. He died A.D. 431, and is buried in the Church of S. Bartolommeo in Rome. While he was Bishop of Nola, the only son of a widow in that town was taken by the Vandals into slavery in Libya. St. Paulinus set out to rescue him, and became a slave himself. It was on his return to Nola from servitude that he was met by the inhabitants of Nola, dancing and carrying obelisks in front of them. The festival was celebrated, ever after, on June 26. St. Paulinus was made the subject of a Latin epic by Saverino de Rinaldis, in imitation of Virgil, called the "Paolineide." This poem may contain further clues to the festival.

But Nola has its own Campagna, where the vines are trained on stunted elms and apple trees, and there are terraces of lemon and pomegranate trees. They are apples, indeed, of a special and late sort, that taste of lime and honey. Never hidden for long, we see the cone and plume of smoke from Vesuvius.

But the excitement grows. It is not enough that the flat-topped houses of one story are the home of Pulcinella. For we are approaching the most extraordinary of all festivals in a Mediterranean land. And the roads have become long clouds of golden dust. Through these dash the *calessos* and *carricolos,* two-wheeled open carriages going at full gallop, crowded with anybody who can cling to them. Cross-gartered peasants in the peaked hat of Fra Diavolo; monks and priests; children beyond counting; and peasant women wearing the striped dresses with puffed sleeves of the district, and the *mucador* or headdress of the country, a veil folded in classical manner upon the back of the head. As to the galloping horses, they have loud and jingling harness, their manes are twisted with flowers, and pheasants' tail feathers nod above their necks. Crowds are pouring in from Naples and from all Campania to the festival.

We have arrived at Nola. But no one can walk at his ordinary pace toward the town. All are hurrying, or running. The railway station is a little distance from the walls. And here the fair and the great festival begin. More than ever it is a phantasmagoria, an hallucination. One must go carefully and forget nothing of what is to be seen.

The walls of the town have been covered with gigantic pictures, painted in a frenzy, where the masters of old Italy have come down to the gutter, working all night and for a day before. Decorations for a slum inferno; painted wings of houses; Cupids of the mean lodgings; a garlic-eating Harlequin; the family of Pulcinella; the volcano and the golden Bay; and the *gran Foca marina,* the monster, or sea calf, shown to the public in an ancient tower. Musicians and town criers make incessant fanfares and trumpet blasts, as though for a circus entrance, and the effect of this perpetual repetition of an opening phrase or flourish is both exciting and pitiful. These fanfares, which will linger for long afterward in the memory, sounding suddenly, for no reason, in the silence of the night, are so many frantic appeals to be heard above the others, and not to be allowed to starve. They are military ghosts: trumpeters dying on the field of battle, who with their last breath lift the trumpet to their lips. Yet pariahs, street Arabs of the Neapolitan slums. Tritons too, who play their conch horns before the shell of Amphitrite, the sea goddess, who, in metamorphosis of the fair is none other than the *gran Foca marina,* the sea calf who is an exhibition in the tower. With a hired band of music to proclaim her, she journeys from town to town, and came to Nola last night, drawn in a tank of water on a wagon. Mute goddess, who lifts her seal-like neck and looks pitifully around her in her prison tower. The trumpet blasts that surround and accompany her can mean nothing to her animal mind but cries for food and cries for love. Her mammal soul, and the souls of ten or twenty men, are in a drove, a finny herd, together.

Every kind of stall has been set up at the entrance to the town. Their purpose is to catch the crowds before they get into the streets. The hucksters are calling out with all the force of Southern lungs. It is not exactly a market, for the crowd pours through it in one direction toward the town. Most of them are carrying little colored flags, and have bought emblems or amulets of St. Paulinus, as well as food and flasks of wine. But, as well, every conceivable object is for sale. Green umbrellas, pigs and sheep, strings of sausages, *mortadella,* cheap crockery.

But a strange and wonderful sight makes one breathless and gives the sacred tingling to the skin. It is announced by the trumpet and the drum. Something moves: it is a curtain drawn aside. The actors come out onto a trestle, and the curtain falls back behind them. We behold another race, of Areöis, of strolling players, who spend their lives in traveling from town to town, exhibiting their performances, and spreading the contagion of the stage. Some instinct tells one they are of different race. They are standing on two planks set up on trestles before their booth or theater. There is no time to stay. The crowd press us on. But it is something that will forever haunt the memory. Four or five actors and two women, or soubrettes. Of a race apart, as it could be priests or temple prostitutes. Where are they now? Still traveling with some fair? For the circus music does not change so much. But it is wonderful to see them in the sunlight of an early morning amid the fanfares and the frenzied voices. A mandolin hangs by a ribbon from a nail. Columbine, the dove, the gentle singer, lifts it down and holds it in her hands. It is impossible to hear her; but she begins to sing. The other dances, and holds a tambourine. There is a clown, a comic Bacchus, camp follower of his Indian triumph; a young man who is poet or pierrot of the company; and a person cast for tragedy. Their voices are quite lost in all the din, so that it could be one of those common nightmares in which you call for help and cannot make a sound. No one listens, or looks at them for longer than a moment. Everyone is hurrying, or running past.

We are carried on, as though to an assault on the town. Looking back, we see them work their blandishments; but all in vain. No one has the strength, or patience. All press forward into the town; entering through a breach in the walls or fortifications, a place where those have just crumbled and the fallen stones lie, one upon another. Not a gate or solemn entrance into Nola. But there are many lanes and alleys leading from it, into which the crowds disperse to find the quickest way to the piazza. For the Piazza del Duomo is the center of the festival. But these alleys are dark. The sun has not yet come down to them. And in their silence, where there is no other sound than that of hurrying footsteps, we hear behind, in front of us, and to every side, the noise and music of the fair.

But, of a sudden, noisy and discordant music bursts upon the ear. Of a curious, halting, swaying rhythm. As though it is moving slowly forward. Tottering from side to side. Can this be imagination? In the distance there are shouts and fanfares. Furious blasts of the trumpet; and the fevered sensation that every window in the tall houses may open like a showman's box, a Punch and Judy theater. With gaunt and bright movements of which we will not know the hidden drama. But it grows louder and steadier. It is coming in our way. We are to see the pagan mystery.

Here it is. Down this side street, and moving toward us.

A tower, or monster, tottering in its steps, in midst of an immense crowd. Taller than the houses to either side; and rushing one in ecstasy or delirium from Campania to India. For it is entirely Indian in this moment. Yet, not. It is a tower, or obelisk, of five stories. We recognize Corinthian columns in every story, and a frieze and niches. But the whole obelisk glitters, or coruscates, red and gold and silver. The columns are bright ruby red with tinsel; and, in their shadows, red like Bengal fires. The tower is gold paper and gilt paint, figured with saints and angels on a golden background. Paladins, also, in gold or silver armor, troops of cherubs, painted genii, false draperies and curtains, golden arabesques and flowers; while this painted population hold in their hands gilded palm leaves, wreaths of flowers, and the spilling cornucopia. Many of the saints are dressed like Roman warriors, or wear the golden buskins of an actor. In the lowest story of the obelisk there sits a choir of young girls, virgins, dressed in white and garlanded with flowers. Above them, on a level with the first-floor windows of the houses, there is a band of trumpets and kettledrums, with triangles and cornets. The obelisk is borne upon the shoulders of about thirty porters, and has just begun to move. It had been waiting, and is now ready. It advances. Tottering, and swaying like a palanquin.

It has passed us, and moves slowly on, standing higher than the roofs of the houses, with an extraordinary sound of creaking and fluttering, a straining of ropes, and a shaking and jostling of its many statues. Down one street, and then another, this huge obelisk proceeds, directed, it would seem, by instinct or the group soul of the bearers. At its apex, a saint with a golden nimbus glitters in the sun, above the tiled and lichened roofs. We follow, walking in the crowd. And now there is a burst of music from a different side, and the summits of another and then another obelisk appear above the housetops. All these moving towers are proceeding in the same direction toward the cathedral.

What are these gigantic obelisks?

They are the *guglie di San Paolino*. The *guglia* is a form of

religious monument that is peculiar to Naples, and found nowhere else. A marble obelisk in several stories—or we could
call them members—topped by a statue of the Madonna or a
saint. Their shape is that of the flame of a candle, the jet of a
fountain, and up all their height they have masks and bas-reliefs,
and balustrades and statues. There are three of them at Naples.
The *guglia del Gesú,* outside the church of Il Gesú Nuovo, with
its façade of stones cut into diamond points, is the most elaborate of all, and springs sixty or seventy feet into the air, surmounted by a statue of the Virgin, an exuberant and bubbling
monument of marble, diamond-shaped, itself, in plan, and set
at an angle to the Gesú.* Nothing in architecture is more ex-
pressive of the vitality of the Neapolitans than these Baroque
obelisks. Here, at Nola, the marble of the *guglia* (which means
lily) has been metamorphosed into an obelisk that moves, and
is inhabited by living persons. It is a tower with motion. A
triumphal car, a juggernaut made from a pyramid, a living
fountain.

As to the origin of the *guglie di San Paolino,* it is probable
that some form of triumphal car had been used in the festival
since early times. They were, as we shall know presently, made
anew every year by the different Guilds of Nola, and we may
assume that they followed in their decoration the fashion of the
day. They will have been late Gothic, according to the Neapolitan Gothic of their time; and have gone through the various
phases of the Renaissance to Baroque. But, when the *guglie*
were set up in the squares of Naples, the inspiration communi-
cated itself immediately to the inhabitants of this provincial
town, and the pattern became fixed. They designed a *guglia*
that could be carried through the streets; that could tower up
above the houses; that carried living persons, singers and musicians; and that gave such opportunities to the carver and the

---

* The other two *guglie* in Naples are that of San Domenico, in front of the
church of that name; and of San Gennaro, which is in a piazza at back of the
Cathedral. Their date is approximately 1690-1730. There is a connection between
these Neapolitan *guglie* and such monuments of the Austrian Baroque as the
Trinity column in the Graben at Vienna, designed by the Italian theater painter,
Burnacini.

gilder. At the time when we see the moving towers of Nola, in the last days of the Kingdom of the Two Sicilies, the type had been followed in its deviations for a hundred years and more. Being so essentially Neapolitan, the spirit of it faded with the passing of their independence. A few years later it had lost its force. We see it, therefore, in its prime, when Campania down to the city and the Bay was a land of singing and of dancing slaves.

The *guglie* of Nola are constructed in this manner. A high wooden scaffolding with canvas sides is set up in the street close to the house of the head of each Guild. This screen of canvas keeps the work secret, and protects each obelisk and its artificers against the weather. And so the *guglia* begins to grow; hidden on three sides, and with boughs of myrtle and green branches on the fourth, where the obelisks nearly touch upon the houses. The work continues for six months. By early June the *guglia* has begun to rise above the roofs. It is growing like the Indian mango tree.

Each Guild, or *Arte,* makes its *guglia.* And every one of them is to be known by the principal statue on its front. Judith, glittering with gold, holds a dripping head of Holofernes upon the obelisk of the Husbandmen or Reapers. But this group of sculpture only fills the niche on the middle story. On the highest floor of every *guglia* there stands an angel swinging a censer; above this a golden cupola or a gilded flower; and, on top of all, the statue of a saint. On the *guglia* of the Husbandmen or Reapers it is St. George with the cross of Malta and a white flag in his hand. But besides this, as a distinguishing sign, each obelisk has an emblem hanging from the frieze of its main story. The Husbandmen and Reapers have a sickle, the Bakers two huge loaves, the Butchers a joint of meat, the Gardeners a pumpkin, the Tailors a white waistcoat, the Cobblers a shoe, the Grocers a cheese, the Wine Merchants a fiasco. And, as well, each obelisk has a man to walk in front of it, carrying a particular emblem. A silver pillar is borne in this manner before the obelisk of the Wine Merchants; and on this pillar lies a wine barrel, held by two little statues of St. Peter and St. Paul. The Guild of Gardeners is more fanciful. It is preceded by a handsome youth who holds a cornucopia, and smiles upon the crowd.

Standing in the Piazza del Duomo we see, and hear, the coming of the *guglie*. From every quarter of the town the obelisks are on the march. Each has a choir in its lowest story; and above that, the cornets and kettledrums, the triangles and trumpets. There are nine obelisks in all. They advance, tottering in their steps, and halt every now and then to give a rest to their bearers. No sight could be more thrilling than the convergence of so many marching towers. Several streets lead into the piazza; and one or more obelisks, to their own music, advance down every street. The giant of giants belongs to the Guild of Farmers. It is one hundred and two palms in heights, or between sixty and seventy feet from the shoulders of the bearers up to the golden nimbus of the saint. As it comes forth into the square we see the living actors in the lower stories, and young girls or boys above them in short tunics and helmets of gilded paper, holding in their hands gilded wands or golden bulrushes. Above and around them are the hundreds of golden statues, big or small.

This greatest of the obelisks is preceded by two little pasteboard towers, in which sit children crowned with golden wreaths. Behind them, a pasteboard caïque, or pleasure boat, on which a boy sits, crosslegged, in a Turkish costume, holding a pomegranate flower. After this comes a galleon, floating in a little painted ocean. At the prow there is a young man in Moorish dress; and on the poop a statue of St. Paulinus kneeling at an altar. At the back the towering *guglia* of the Guild of Farmers comes forth with bursts of music, and as it appears in all its height there is the detonation of ten thousand crackers, thrown down not only on the piazza, but in all the streets that lead to it. The church bells ring their loudest, and flocks of pigeons fly round, volleying their wings, and casting swift shadows out of the cloudless sky. Every balcony is full of people, and hung with flowers. Below, nearly all the crowd are carrying little banners of gold and silver paper; while we begin to hear, at once, the music of as many obelisks, marching, one behind another, into the square.

The giants of pantomime are now visible in all their strangeness. Like so many marching, golden fountains. The gilded saints at their summits, balanced by the golden jet, are theatrical and extraordinary in their attitudes, praying, preaching, or bestowing blessings. Some gaze from their pedestals, in ecstasy, into the sky; or look down from their giddy height upon the crowd. One is a kneeling saint, borne on his totem pole down every street toward the altar of the Duomo. Another stands like an Indian fakir on his mango tree. One rolls in triumph upon his gilded car. Another strides the golden lotus petal. For, in symbol, they are Indian; and the procession of these towers is like some Hindu festival. Not in its decadence, but it could be a thousand or two thousand years ago. They could belong to that sect of Brahmins in whose name it is denoted that "their covering is the air"; or to those others who are "clad in white," or "saffron yellow." And we would think of these towers, accordingly, as wagon-temples built to receive the god for his yearly visit of one day only in the golden month of June. In reason of this the *guglie di San Paolino* are so many pagodas by their multitude of idols. Of that legendary India where Krishna, a lovely youth of Ganges in a yellow robe, played his flute and all living beings were entranced.

The procession of these Stylites on their pillars is purely pagan as a spectacle. It is thrilling and intoxicating like a draught of pagan wine. We are carried back to the arcana of the ancient gods. We are to see other mysteries. But the discordant music of so many bands grows loud and louder. Nine towers are advancing; and there is time to see the different nimbus to each statue of the saint. For no two are alike. A wild fantasy has set the constellations on their heads. There is the simple nimbus, a circle like the bands of Saturn, or Orion's golden belt. A half-moon nimbus in emblem of the months above the pagoda of the Gardeners, for the weather alters with the new moon. A fuller moon, that is like a sickle, above the Reapers' golden tower. A golden barley moon above the Bakers' wain. A circle of golden stars upon the great obelisk of the Guild of Farmers, which, in their golden multitude suggest the sheaves of corn. But, also, there are other fantasies of the golden nimbus. One

pagoda—could it be the obelisk of the Tailors?—has the statue
of St. Paulinus in a shepherd's or a pilgrim's dress, with staff in
his hand and wine flask at his side, wearing a rakish tricorne or
a corded hat, and the nimbus behind his head is the stylized
counterpart of that. The obelisk of the Wine Merchants has its
statue backed with a sunburst of golden rays, as it could be the
smiling face of Bacchus looking down on the vines. And it is
not only golden. It has strips of mirror set in it, which glitter
like diamonds. At each halt of the obelisk, as the bearers set
it down, the nimbus sparkles or trembles in its fire. It burns
with a steady light; and, again, flashes as the march proceeds.
It has advanced into the square. This golden rocket hangs, in
perpetuity, upon the air. And, round it, the lesser fountains
leap continually to their appointed height.

All nine towers, tottering and swaying, are to be seen at once.
And so many mysteries are contained in them. Each obelisk is
in the pattern of the *guglia,* that Neapolitan invention which
was derived from the great machinery of the old Italian theater,
with its "clouds" and the "heaven" or "Parnassus" of its trans-
formations. The *guglia* belongs, in fact, to the school of Bibiena,
and is related to the huge funeral catafalques, or to the staged
mysteries of the Passion erected in their churches by the Jesuits.
But here, at Nola, the *guglia* is not static. It has been given
movement. It is a living monument that moves and . . .

For we will know in another moment! It is Indian in its
exuberance. This pagoda has its idols of the living and the dead.
We are in the nodding plain of India, among its temples. Indus,
Ganges, Brahmaputra roll their waters. It is a sacred spell, or
an intoxication. But, as well, the nine towers, the nine obelisks
of Nola, are nine holy mountains. A sacred Thebaid of a night
and day. These are its crags and pinnacles. The cliffs of
Meteora, the Cappadocian mountains hollowed out with grottoes.
There are hermits upon the summits of the hills. Not the
nymphs of old, who cried out aloud upon the rocks; but holy
anchorites, the athletes of religion, advancing on their pillars.
For the nine towers are tottering forward. They are coming out,
all nine of them, into the square.

And the tallest tower of all sets out dancing to the music of its band. A man with a conductor's baton stands in front of it, and gives the time. In the beginning it is as though it is about to fall. It totters, while its population of the living and the dead rattle in their bones. Then it steadies.. The obelisk lifts its feet and dances. It treads the measure. The thirty bearers move in rhythm, stepping this way and that. The colossus dances: or it could be a huge elephant and its howdah. Dancing in this manner, each obelisk takes up its place before the Duomo.

Now comes the counter dance. With two men to beat the time, one obelisk dances against another, in a solo dance and counter dance of swaying towers. One moment they are leaning towers or campaniles, at a slant, in different angles, in outward perspective, sloping from old age, or in a subsidence of the soil beneath the ancient city; but then they come together into time, and bow in rhythm. They shake and tremble, as though seized with the ecstasy, while they dance side by side. Then move apart again and dance, one against another, in cross rhythm to the music of their choirs and bands. And now they dance in pairs, the whole nine of them changing partners, a dance of giants who are clumsy in their movements. We can hear the music of four obelisks at once, while the other five towers hide behind them, and we know only the stamping feet, and that the piazza is full of dancing pyramids. The dance and counter dance of each pair of obelisks lasts for a few moments, for as long as the bearers can support the weight, after which each tower comes to a standstill and the trumpets play a wild flourish to announce the end, and the start of a new mystery.

About twenty men and youths begin to dance round each obelisk in turn. Each puts his hands upon the shoulders of his neighbor, making a ring or circle in midst of which two solo dancers move in counter rhythm, with a third youth whom they lift up in their arms. While they dance with him, he is in a lying or recumbent posture, but goes through the motions of dancing with his limbs. He grows more languid and more lifeless. He droops; he shuts his eyelids; he is dead, or sleeping. The music quickens: and the circle dances round him, faster and faster, to a quickening measure. And now comes the mystery of the festival. For the dead or sleeping youth returns to life. He smiles and lifts his head. He raises himself upon his shoulders. He has awakened. He stretches his arms. And, with a sudden movement, he strikes his castanets in the air.

This dance is performed in front of every obelisk. No one can explain it. The meaning has been lost far back in antiquity. It has been suggested that the rites of Adonis are portrayed in it. In the Adonia, the festival in honor of Adonis, celebrations were held for two days, the first of which was spent in howling and lamentations, the second in joyful clamor, as if Adonis was returned to life. This youth, we would recall, was the favorite of Venus. He was killed by a wild boar, while hunting, and Venus after many tears changed him into a flower called anemone. He was restored to life by Proserpine, on the condition that he should divide the year between herself and Venus, living six months with each. This is symbolical of the alternate return of summer and winter.

But the rites of Adonis are identical with those of the Egyptian Osiris, which also began in lamentation and ended in rejoicing, when Osiris returned among the living. Osiris was a legendary King of Egypt, who brought the fruits of civilization to the earth. He was murdered; and Isis, his wife, wandered through the world seeking for her husband. He was magically restored to life by his son Horus, and continued to rule the land as King of the dead. It has been written that nothing could give a clearer idea of the power and greatness of Osiris than this inscription, in hieroglyphs, which has been found upon some ancient monuments: "Saturn, the youngest of all the gods, was my father. I am Osiris, who conducted a large and numerous army as far as the deserts of India, and traveled over the greatest part of the world, and visited the streams of the Isther, and the remote shores of the ocean, diffusing benevolence to all the inhabitants of the earth."

Osiris, we may add, is more generally given as the son of Jupiter and Niobe. It is stated that after his golden reign in Egypt, Osiris resolved to go and spread civilization in the other parts of the earth. He left his kingdom in the care of his wife

Isis, and of her minister Hermes or Mercury. The command of his troops at home was left to the trust of Hercules, a warlike officer. Osiris was accompanied on his expedition by his brother Apollo, and by Anubis, Macedo and Pan. He marched through Ethiopia, where his army was increased by the addition of the Satyrs, who made dancing and playing on musical instruments their chief study. Afterward he passed through Arabia, and so to India, or its borders. As to Saturn, his also was the golden age. During the festival of the Saturnalia, held in Rome, which is not far distant from Nola, the chains were taken from the statues, to intimate the freedom and independence enjoyed by mankind during the golden age. It was permitted, too, for slaves to ridicule their masters. The festival itself had been instituted by Janus, the most ancient king who ruled in Italy, in gratitude to Saturn from whom he had learned agriculture.

Whether the march of Osiris into India clashed with that of Bacchus, we are not told, and can but conjecture. It is more probable, indeed, that Bacchus was identical with the Osiris of the Egyptians. The festival of Nola would seem to be in classical descent from the Bacchanalia or Dionysia of the Ancients. Or, equally from the Saturnalia or Adonia. It had become involved, somehow, in the return of St. Paulinus from his slavery in Africa. Or was made the occasion or the excuse for that. When he came back to Nola, so the legend runs, he was met by the citizens, dancing and carrying these obelisks or towers before them. It would appear, then, that an old feast of fertility, of a golden age, held in a Roman provincial town, took on a Christian meaning and survived till modern times. The youth who returns to life is none other than Adonis, in the guise of that only son of the widow of Nola, who was carried by the Vandals into slavery in Libya. St. Paulinus set forth to become a slave in his stead and rescue him. Hence the dancing obelisks: in time, influenced in their shape by the *guglie* of near-by Naples. The Indian or Hindu aspects of the festival are brought about by the circumstance that the feat itself, in origin, was something of an Indian triumph, considering the legends of Bacchus or Osiris; and by the fact that the prolixity of both ornament and imagination in Southern Italy, during the Baroque age of the seventeenth and eighteenth centuries, produced effects in sculpture and in architecture that are almost Indian, as many authorities have noticed when discussing the Neapolitan churches, or the churches and palaces of such towns as Lecce, in Apulia. Here, in Nola, it is not a church, nor a palace. It is the whole procession that is Indian.

The nine towers glitter in the blue Campanian sky. Preceded by many monks of all the orders, and by bishops and deacons in the miter of Osiris, amid the shouts of thousands, they start upon a round of the whole city. The church bells ring their loudest; while myriad crackers, thrown down and bursting, make the sound of innumerable instruments of percussion. Perhaps the crackle of the castanets when Adonis, the sleeping youth, raised his hand was the signal for this.

The gilded galleon dances before them. And so the procession sets out. The huge obelisk of the Guild of Farmers is the first to move. Its bearers take away the props of wood and lift it to their shoulders. It sways and totters, and begins to march. Behind it comes the pyramid of the Husbandmen and Reapers; and the heroic figure of Judith, holding the head of Holofernes high before her, appears to shake and tremble. Obelisk follows obelisk: Cobblers, Tailors, Gardeners, Butchers, Bakers, Grocers and Wine Vendors. All advancing. A procession of pyramids, of obelisks, of marching towers. The whole town seethes, and roars, and surges with excitement.

The rites of the golden age are restored, for a day and night. Osiris, the son of Saturn, comes to life. He has returned from India. The chains are taken from the statues; and images of the gods are carried in triumph. It is his golden reign. He is met with dancing towers. There is magic in the air. It is a festival of fertility. Why does the youth in the caïque, which is borne along, hold in his hand a pomegranate flower? Why could the statue of Judith be holding a sheaf of corn, and not a severed head? Or the obelisk of the Gardeners be preceded by a youth who holds a cornucopia? Why had dead Adonis a castanet in his hand? We meet a troop of children who have gauze wings on their shoulders; and a full brass band plays the march from *Moïsé in Egitto*. The shepherds' bagpipes, the *pifferari* or the *zampognari*, that come up at Christmas from Calabria; is it imagination? Do we not recognize their sound? And we hear, on all sides, the rhythm of the tarantella. They are dancing in the wine shops, in the streets, in the vineyards. The wreathing, twining tarantella danced among the vines, in sight of distant Vesuvius. The tambourine is struck in frenzy. It is midday: the golden noon has come. There is the firing of cannon from the barracks. And a fanfare of bugles. Wherever we look, an obelisk, a pyramid, walks or dances. The Stylite gods are carried on their towers, with choirs and bands of music in their lower stories.

The tower of the Reapers or Husbandmen emerges. A golden sickle is its emblem. Will it not march with its flail into the harvest? It must be a statue of Priapus upon the obelisk of the Gardeners. He is the god of orchards and of gardens, born to the goddess Venus after she had gone to meet Bacchus coming back in triumph from the Indies. Or some say Adonis was the father. What, then, of the tower of the Wine Vendors? And of the seven others?

It is a delirious and haunting dream. Are the actors still shouting on the board outside their theater? Noises of the fair mix with the festival. Booths or shops were open on the day Adonis died. Someone haggled for a pomegranate, for a clutch of eggs, for a lark in a wicker cage. And so it must continue. What is that droning? Will the nine towers go toppling down? Ah no! It is the golden age. Or the noon of that, declining to a golden sunset. With singing and dancing, and crashing of cymbals. The pagan gods have been restored to life. There go their palanquins, in the streets and squares of Nola.

BATTLE IN THE STEPPE*

Listen! Listen again! Did you hear nothing? Now again! Then, then! Could you not hear it? It was quite distinct. And again. Ah! That was but a shooting star. It must be the battle many hundreds of miles away, in the cornlands of black earth. During all August, which is the month of harvest. Along the plains of Tanais. It is where the world will be lost or won. In the name of what god? Ah! Do not ask. It is enough to watch the battle.

Did you see another star fall out of the heavens? Noiselessly, without a sound.

We will suppose there is wanton moonlight, for it is full moon. The moon of the barcarolle. But this is the lantern held up in the murderer's hand. The lighted candle stuck by its end upon the mantelpiece, until the deed is done, and found there in the fearful morning, fallen into the ashes of the grate. Among the burned matches and the stumps of cigarettes.

The whole battle is in monstrous parody on the harvest. It has continued all night long, but we will meet it at the morning. There are chained lights, or at least they hang in chains, that float in the heavens, and come slowly down. And red flares. And moths that court the flames. The night must be weary with the noise of wings. And there is the beating of the flail, as well. The cranking, cranking of the caterpillar that crawls upon the leaf, but never turns into a butterfly. That is the panzer column. Where are the spearheads? They have eaten deep into the harvest. They have cut lanes that lead for miles and miles.

Lie down and hide! Lie flat! First comes the shadow, but it has gone by. The moon is yellow as barley sugar, immense and doltish, like a rural comedy, and leaning on one side. The most perfect weather in memory for the cutting of the corn. Surely

* From *Splendours and Miseries*, 1943.

391

you heard that? But it was far away and did not come in our direction. The plain is so immense, between the Dnieper and the Don, that they are harvesting in certain places. And the battle, and the harvest, are in parody on each other. For the corn stooks are tied like prisoners, in bundles, hand and foot. They take the form, too, of a line of tents. It is curious to watch the sorting of the corn sheaves, for they are laid out, like wounded, on the ground while one harvester attends to a whole row of them. Where we find them kneeling, to tie up the sheaves, it would seem sometimes, from their attitudes, that they are lifting in their arms a god of reeds or straw, or some fantastic head-dress. Behind them stands the golden honeycomb, just as though a spoon had cut into the cells. A spoon, but not a knife, for it is not as sharp as that. The cells are still brimming over. They cloy with sweetness, and you could count the drooping heads of rye.

It is waist high, and thick as honey; and, elsewhere, dead, or stacked upon the ground. Some of the husbandmen are sitting on the bundles while they eat their breakfast. But stand them on end, tie their necks with a rope of straw, and they are the corn stooks of the harvest. Of three armfuls, each, with a space of light between, just like the door of a tent or, for that matter, of a house of cards. Yes. They are straw houses. Uninhabited. It is a kind of children's game. They have pitched these tents in make believe. One after another, unnecessarily. It is a need-less slaughter. As much so as when holiday makers, young men and women from the town, raid the spring woods, and come back with bunches of bluebells, roots and all, tied to their bicycles.

One or two persons come, walking slowly, hidden to their shoulders up the lanes of corn. They are carrying corn stooks upon their backs, and go, one behind another, like maskers in heavy costumes; or as though they are carrying dead men of straw. Back to back. The dead man's head and face are behind the living head. What is the meaning of this? Is it that, Janus-like, they know the past and future; and, as harvesters, open the day with the sun and close it at his setting? A covey of partridges, with whirring wings, rises out of the corn. And, at the side, a hare runs this way and that, and doubles on its traces. Poppies and cornflowers are in bloom, but in the golden underworld below the heads of oats or rye.

There are cliffs and sudden segments in the corn. It rises steeply, for no reason, as if at a tumulus, or tomb mound in the plain. Then we get curves and softness, like the clipping of a horse's mane, as it climbs and comes up, and is level on the summit, makes an edge against the landscape, and drops down again. Indeed, a whole section of the uncut corn, solid, like golden bread or golden honeycomb, has been left till last. In its shade, for it has a shade, the husbandmen are resting. But there are one or two who cannot stay their hands, and go on reaping.

Away in the distance are the collective farms. The motor tractors are at work. We hear them, up and down the cornland, binding as they go. But the country is so immense that they are lost to sight in it, and we have to look for them until they turn and come reaping in our way. Then it is slow, and takes the corners carefully and we hear the motor louder, at times, just as though it was a paddle steamer lifting on the waves. Long white buildings, far away, are where the workers live and sleep. They are not dressed as peasants, but men and women alike, as dancers in the rehearsal room.

From every point of the horizon there comes the noise of motor engines. Far and near, but more generally, invisible. Therefore this primitive harvest is but a vision or hallucination. But we shall see that the machines are at war with one another. In pursuit: and they will pass by the dolt who walks on foot. We are hidden here. Lie down and keep low! It has gone by as swiftly as the swallow. The husbandmen still eat their bread and honey. And in the ghostly dawn they drink their mead or hydromel.

What do we see? A plain which lies for miles and miles into infinity. Do you not get the smell of burning? Of burned tinder. Or of whole woods on fire. It is in the air all the time. It is stronger now than ever. But from far off. That is a column or pillar of smoke, over there. It may be thirty or forty miles away. It is difficult to tell the distance in this immensity. But it has not moved all the time we have been looking at it. Nor altered shape. But it must climb halfway into the sky. It must have the hornets flying round it. And there is something else, low down. We know that is where the river runs. They are trying to cross the river under an artificial smoke cloud which was laid down during the night. In a Stygian darkness of their own making. But that, too, is many miles away. Did you hear that? Or, rather, did you feel it, behind your ears, for it is a pressure or a feeling, more than it is an actual sound? There is a white flash in midst of the fog, and long after that, the detonation, so far off that it is difficult to be quite certain.

Look in another direction! And there are torn locks of smoke blowing on the air. And not a sound, nor any flame. These travel, or dance, upon the horizon. And one of them lifts, or curls away, as we are staring at it. Just as though it shrinks into its own stalk and vanishes. If you did not search for it, you would not know that anything was happening. Except for that smell of fire. Or it may be that there is unrest and dread in the very landscape and in the color of the corn. For, in the whole distance, it is silvery white. It is not honey-colored as ripe corn should be. It is white, like the flaxen hair of children. As if it has been bleached. Down in the south there is the coal basin. And the new industrial towns of the Five Year Plan, from which the workers have issued who are like dancers at rehearsal. Can this be a blight or pallor from the colleries? But it is in character with this land of birch trees. And there can be huge floods higher than the sighing reeds. Not now. This is the summer drought. Lanes of fire have been driven through the harvest. It is the singeing of the flaxen hair. That is this smell of burning.

One quarter of the heavens is entirely black. It is where the oil wells are on fire. Could you behold the oil fields you might wonder what they are. So many pyramidal tents of wood and steel, as regular as the crosses in a war cemetery. Termite town; or where the lemmings swarm. Put up with gnawing teeth and clawlike, rodent hand, as ingenious as where the beavers build their dams in the flaming maple woods, but, here, to an unknown purpose. For, tombs or tenements, they are untenanted. But for the incendiaries with their fiery torches. The wreckers have put down their mines and fuses. The black earth is being scorched. The bowels of earth are burning. The lakes of petroleum are on fire. Here is the burning river Phlegethon, near to Cimmerian Bosphorus, and flowing out of Tartarus. The smoke hangs like a black pall along the heavens. Here, according to Virgilius the sorcerer, are punished those who have undertaken unjust and cruel wars.

A sudden wind brings up the sound of cranking. From far below. Just as though we listened for it at the pit shaft; or leaned over and looked down into the well. Then, silence. But it starts up again; but wearily, as though wound up with the handle. The machines have come a long distance. From half across the world. It misfires and splutters. It refuses. Can it have a soul? But it has been brought to obedience. It roars out, clear and vibrant, over the white harvest. Where is it? And what can it be? They are still reaping with the tractor. We see them on the brow of the hill, going down from us into the hollow, and binding as they go. Their white barracks is unchanged. No dead bodies dangle from the apple trees.

Now that, certainly, was gunfire.

Like a sharp stroke upon the drum that imitates the shaking thunder. Struck with the hand, not with the drumstick. A stroke and a recoil, like a head that lifts up and barks, lowering itself again. All in a moment. Before there is time to look. And another, and another voice of anger. They snarl. But that was something deeper and much bigger. It is as when the heavy raindrops come. And again. Down there. Yes, down along the river. And there is the crunch, crunch of bombs, sometimes with a ring of metal. A dumb, senseless crunching, a disintegration, choking in its own earth, as the muddy fountain falls. Ah! But that grated, it had the clink of steel. A stick of bombs, six at a time; one after another, dropping in a pattern, so close there is no time to escape. All the eggs are falling from the basket. But no. They are dropping like the grains of sand. They are deliberate, and will not be hurried. They are in entire control. It has been planned where they shall fall. All in the distance. So far away, it is inhuman. But the sky above has little puffs of white smoke, which drift, and do not come down. They are not parachutes. It is but antiaircraft fire. And suddenly, with screaming engine, as though the metal cried in pain and fear, an airplane plunges wildly down, in flames, and there comes a crash, like an empty bottle thrown against a wall. And no more. So die the moths and flies. So die the sons of the morning.

Another and another swarm come out of the sun, drop their load, and are gone. It is the law of nature that they should lay their eggs and fall into the flame. Not all. But they come back again. It is the nuptial flight of the adolescent, and sooner or later it must end in death. Such are the nuptials of *homo sapiens* and his machines. It is the marriage in the cockpit. It must be some kind of atavism when they die above the oil derricks. For that is the trend of the battle. It is for this they devastate the cornlands. They are passing through with fire and sword. The rivers wash the blood down into the salty sea. For the rivers are terrible to cross. There are rivers three or four miles wide. But drowning is more merciful than burning. And it is quicker than to be left dying in the harvest, near to the red poppies. In a space of trampled corn. The heads of oats or rye, after a day and night of agony, take on those attitudes of the waiting, staring furniture in a room. In dumb attendance upon their owner or inhabitant. It is their inanimate personality, and fever and dying thirst can give them all a meaning.

There are bodies lying in perfect little nests of straw. You could find a crumpled cornstalk clenched tightly in a hand. That is the moment of his appearance at the gates of death. That is the scepter or talisman held in his hand. He is lying in the fouled nest with an arm above the corn. Little mysteries surround.him. How could one, so maimed, unlace his heavy boots and leave them in the virgin corn? It is the mystery of the tramp's fires where there is always an old boot, and sometimes a woman's shoe, among the tins. Ah! But they lighted the dry sticks and cooked themselves a meal. They had enough life to quarrel; or to sleep holding hands. But this is the wounded insect that drags itself upon the blades of grass. He has not moved, except to roll over and lie upon his face.

In places the corn has become a sickroom, or the bay of a hospital to which they bring the dying. But there are no screens put round the beds. It is part of the degradation that they lie in heaps as though tipped out of a cart. There is a fatality that forces them to crawl on one another, like puppies in a newborn litter. Their agony makes them blind and oblivious. Only the rare spirit tries to creep away and die. The others, like lower forms of life, climb upon the bodies. It is not that they seek company. But theirs is the clumsiness of those who have lost perception through all the faculties being expressed in pain. Nothing is left over. They choose the short road, and like Hydra, the many-headed monster, lie huddled close. For it is a multiple agony. It is not enough for one to die. Each head, separately, must be deprived of life.

They babble, too, in unknown tongues. In the thick speech of the Turcoman, and in the dialects of beyond the mountains. Some are lying near their enemy. There is this horrible truth of battle, that one is male and the other female. There is always this between the combatants. It is not the weaker, necessarily, who is the female. Neither brute force, nor guile, are the property of one sex only. Both can be combined in one body. Those, also, who have become weak as babes can be killed by a weak woman. When the night turns cold, in the dawn, at the hour when many babes are born. The dealing of the deathblow has a parallel in life, as all lovers know. But of this other, none alive can tell. Nor if they meet again in death. But the *actus tragicus* must be more compelling than the casual acts of love. Or its long habits. For love has many meanings. There is but one death. But many sorts. It is a casual death to be killed by someone whom you have not seen. Who fired at random, or but pulled a lever. Will they meet each other in another world? No. No. There are no more meetings. But death comes in many moods. In a dream; or when wide awake. Here it creeps, night and day, among the wounded bodies. Some have lived for a week, sucking the dew from the cornstalks, chewing the white heads of clover. Others were left behind, last night, when darkness fell. This is their first morning in the trampled corn.

Some have been quick to learn. For it is like living on a raft far out at sea. There is the chance of rescue. But the horizon shakes with fires, and the battle passes. Behind it, huge areas have been burned down to a blackened stubble. It is as bad as when the oil from a tanker catches fire. Then the water will be quite calm, but blazing. Here, the first sparks fall, and lodge in the beards of corn like pretty fireflies. Soon the heat begins. It is smoldering a few feet away, and brands of fire fall on their hands and faces. The crackling flames come licking up, and the whole cornland is ablaze. Some escape, by miracle, who were in a ring of fires. But many others have been consumed, or suffocated.

Gigantic efforts have been made to get in the harvest and gangs are at work who sleep for an hour or two in the fields and then take their turn upon the tractors. But the Cossack villages are on fire. If you listen you will hear them burning. They have been bombed from the air without discrimination and for the sake of terror. A day or two, usually, before the battle comes to them. It is this that makes the harvest like a vision or hallucination. For it continues in spite of everything. And the harvesters themselves are lying shattered in the corn. It is even difficult to tell the difference in the wrecked machines, whether tank or tractor, when they have been blown to fragments. When they have been disintegrated to their metal parts, and are lying in a pool of oil, with their crew beside them. Some, of course, have been caught in the machinery, or are underneath the engine. It is worth no one's while to lift them out. They are left with the machine on top of them. Later, friend or foe will look for scrap iron. The lorries will come round for rags and bones.

Which way is the battle going? I can see nothing. Do you see nothing? I can see nothing, nothing. I hear the humming of the winged insects, for they are insects in structure, they are not birds of the air. They have their sting. They do not fight with beak and claw. They are mischievous like insects and attack in swarms. Their blood diet makes them dangerous. The wings of man are fatal as the anopheles. There can be no mercy from the air.

How many millions hear the humming while they go to sleep! I have had dreams in which fantasy, born of the imprisonment of war, has brought long aerial convoys flying low, and in the locomotion of a dream, traveling no swifter than a railway train, but painted in the bright colors of the totem pole and passing with the noise of plowshares along the air. The shapes of Leonardo's fancy: dragon devouring tiger, or eagle fighting lion, not the slate-gray steel and canvas.

For no one can be rid of the humming while he sleeps. It is universal to all mankind. And those who do not hear it, dream of it. The youth of the world plunges down into the fires. They fall in flames: even when the earth does not burn below them. This is the horror behind the shuttered window. For all blinds are drawn. While they fly at night it is as though a perpetual funeral was passing down the street. They have imposed the symbols of death, and of a dead body lying in the house, on the living. These dragging years must be the climacteric. There are so many broken nights. For the sweet peace of night has gone. If there is no noise, the thoughts of evil are always present, and the wings of evil beat about the room. The body rushing through the night means some deviltry, it may be half a continent away. Women and children will be weeping, and at four and five in the morning there are the returning wings. In imagination those pinions must drip with blood. The lone flier comes limping home. The others arrive later, flying line-ahead, in Indian file, as braves in the dark forest. Their eagle plumes are gory with blood, and they circle and come down.

It is a little before dawn. Soon they will be awake in Dachau. The sirens sound an hour before dawn in the concentration camps. They are wakened by the loud-speaker. In the huge camps of the starving and in the dreadful ghettos. In every hell in Poland and in Russia. But the reign of hell may be extended. It may reach to other lands. Evil does not always perish. The camps spring up like fungi in the footsteps of the conqueror.

There are weeds that grow only where blood has flowed, and plants that carry poison. Not for themselves. They are the poison bearers. The deadly nightshade offers its black fruits near to the purple bilberries, and for further enticement still hangs its flowers of evil.

It is singular that you can listen and hear no human voice. But the pilots call to each other on their radio telephones. There may be some creature in the harvest that can communicate, that listens and answers while it gnaws the leaf. That was born only for destruction and has no other instinct; that has come over the immense distance only for this purpose, but, always, from one direction, out of the further immensity. While this blows the other way: it is the anticyclone. It has never succeeded before in human history. And, indeed, it blows all ways at once. What is left of the world watches in dumb horror. We can hear nothing. We are too far away. We are hidden, in imagination, among the shocks of corn. Among the primitive harvesters who reap until they fall down reaping and are left, unburied, in the corn. Who take bread out of a basket and sit down to eat their dinners in the white light of midday, and then work on through the August afternoon. We find a party of reapers standing in a circle on a rising ground, holding their sickles aloft. One in the middle holds up some ears of corn tied together with flowers, and they call out three times together, in words that are unintelligible. This is their harvest cry. It is the cutting of the last sheaf of corn, and the "crying of the neck." Toward nightfall we shall hear them cry again, from far off, through the quiet evening air. For we are lost here, or becalmed, in the old pagan customs.

The scythes come from an ancient smithy, near the pagan dew ponds. There they have forged for many centuries the swords that cut the harvest. Do you remark the curve of the sickle, in the gesture of gathering in? For cutlass or scimitar have another meaning. Their blade curves back, and the sharp edge is outward, for striking down. They do not cut at the foot of the cornstalks and pull them in. They strike down, but they do not reap. That is the difference. And now the husbandman takes up the whetstone. It is so familiar; the awkward balancing of the scythe pole upon the ground, and the slow sharpening of the blade. More in keeping with August than the cranking of the tractor engine, which splutters and refuses, or reaps mercilessly and does its bidding. He whets the scythe and bows his back to reap again. The cut sheaves are laid in rows upon the ground, and in this moment they are like dresses put upon the floor. Women's dresses. The dresses of mummers or of masqueraders.

There is an appalling fight, with flame throwers, in the village street. Devils out of the medieval hell have come up with liquid fire. They wear suits of noninflammable skin, and walk slowly, with the heavy tank or container strapped on to their backs, and the hose pipe and the nozzle held in both hands. No one who has ever seen it will forget these masked men in their heavy fireproof boots. They go in with as much caution as though they have set foot on another planet, three abreast, and then turn on the fire. It is a burning jet. It burns holes in walls. They direct it onto other human beings as you might stop to kill an insect, and pass on. They do not waste the liquid fire. They are gloved and masked as though the air and light contaminate. They have been trained specially, and are not often used. We could have seen these monsters laughing and joking in the lorries, with their helmets off. For their only use is to advance and burn things up. They are young men, heavily built, who might work with the road gang, or as navvies. But, in the street fighting, they are automatons, and their only analogy is to gladiators in the Roman games. When one of them has exhausted his supply of liquid fire he can only put the nozzle down and walk away. Then he is vulnerable. But the street is littered with dead bodies. It smells of burning oil. The black smoke smudges upon the bloodstained walls. Bombs and grenades are being thrown. There is desperate resistance in cellars and from upper floors. A tank drives straight into a house and knocks it down. Mortars are firing at point-blank range, and land mines are exploding. The dogs of the town run about with their tails between their legs.

The cleaning up may last until tomorrow morning. But there is a village every few miles. More odd, still, there are monasteries and churches which have been made over into schools or barns. The retreat and advance are terrible, alike. Over this endless distance which is, in fact, a beginning with no end. For even the huge rivers are no obstacle. It is only a question of so much time and so many lives, until the pontoons have been put across, until the rubber boats and rafts have been brought up. The tanks have been refueled and overhauled. They are ready to begin again. Already the enemy planes are dive-bombing the towns and villages that lie beyond. The further horizon is ringed with fires. Pillars of smoke rise, steadily, one after another. But the women and children and old men are left behind. They must hide in the houses until the enemy has gone on. The police come later and a census of the slaves is taken. After, all are driven back into that other distance.

The cornland is all stubble now, and on fire in many places. The land of Cockaigne is laid flat and bare. The dead bodies feast, in mimic, and are heaped together as though they have fallen at the banquet table. They are left, like weasels on the string, to wither. Like the rats, and owls, and other vermin. Like the hawks and jackdaws. You can tell them by their skulls. Sometimes by a tattered coat; or, by his clothing, if he has fallen from the air. Whether he fell out of a tank or lorry, or crawled into the corn to die. The plain is thick with broken, burned-out fuselages. And the plain darkens into the distance, and the contagion spreads. The wings of death fly on.

FINALE IN FORM OF A BACCHANALE *

The antique magic is in the air again. Forget the present and the future. Nor, in particular, is this the past. Like music, it must live in its own melody and make its shape. The ram's-horn trumpet blows. It is the Bacchanale. The breath winds long and steady in its twisted volutes, more pastoral than the conch shell which calls the tritons and divinities of ocean. Again and again it blows. They come from teeming India down the dusty plains, gods rubbed with sandalwood and powdered blue, youths of the cassia flower with towers of jasmine in their hair, the sacred milkmaids, the rout of the flowering precincts, male and female, and dark cupids. Their tamed animals are led along, peacocks which dance to music, the striped tiger and the purring lion. It is their ecstasy. They close their eyes and listen motionless; or start to weep. The living gods are carried past, mute and ineffable, their followers in frenzy.

Some walk slowly with iron barbs in their flesh, dragging great weights with them, quilled like the porcupine with hooks and wire, in a halo, a palisade, the points all trembling. Some hold the trident and come forward, dancing. Others are naked, but for ashes, with circles and ugly signs painted on them, the wild men, the sacred vagabonds who sleep beneath the trees. There are Brahmins in yellow robes, whom none may touch, who perform miracles; those who control their breath and are suspended between life and death; others who, by fasting, hover over their bodies and are rapt in contemplation. The long sleep of the lotus tank and the slow unfolding. The inscrutable smile, and darting and swaying of the serpent neck. Language of the wrist and hand to hypnotize the senses, for such are the flower-soft Indies, now advancing. Monks, in their colleges of red or yellow, where the pearl-red pillars look toward the mountains. The ponds bear on

* From *Sacred and Profane Love,* 1940.

403

their surface the blue lotus. It is the Abbey of Nalanda. Time was nodding, nodding, in those flower-hung days.

But there are contingents, too, from across the Indian main. Their ships of sandalwood churn the foaming ocean. And the flowers and winds are different. It is another world. Their men and women have the pose of dancers and move with hieratic step, but softly as animals. Their king rides on an elephant, and none may pronounce his name, it is so holy. Before him march a company of Amazons, and in the procession there are carriages drawn by goats. It is a circus triumph, but the visitors are of another creation from ourselves, with a different tread, passing us like flowers blown by.

And the scene alters to the lacquered Indies. It is the land of the palanquin. There are golden plains and the pale shadow of the gingko. But we take it in its islands, far from the rites of the Shaman and their Northern fogs. There are mimed plays and antique legends danced to music of the gamelan. To our untrained ear it is the only music of the Orient: announcing a god out of a waterfall, out of a moonbeam, a sea god glittering in his pearl-shell armor, always an entrance and a diminishment, a dying off, as though the bells and gongs died down in another world, of unknown crops and harvests, where the temples are built up in a day and destroyed at the golden dawn, being but scenery for the sacred trances. The gamelan, too, is music of the child actor: the sacred serpent coiling from the ground: a myriad heroes and divinities with supple limbs in the long-drawn epic: poetic images interpreted by the wrists and hands, after which the dancer is a child again. Suddenly the wind of inspiration seizes on young and old alike, and all descend into the nether world and come back, fainting, in poetic stupor. They lie prostrate on the earth, and for an hour or two are senseless, in the way of persons who have tasted death. This is their formal ecstasy, while the dying gamelan announces a new drama.

We have, as well, the third or mock scepter of the Indies, submissive races who bowed their necks and died. They amble along the wide causeways, bringing fruits and flowers that are unknown, to market. The shell trumpet sounds thrice from the high pyramid, and priests, who do not change their raiment, and whose long hair is matted with gore, plunge a jade knife into the victim and hurl his heartless body to the crowd below. In a distant land of this continent there are golden figures of the sun and moon: golden images of the fruits and flowers: and, for clue to the contrary, llamas, life-sized with golden fleeces. The stone walls of the temple are joined without mortar, and the work of giants. Within are virgin priestesses. In another place a huge pole like a ship's mast is set up. In their yearly festival, Indians, six at a time, climb to the top of this and, standing perilously for a moment, lash the long ropes to themselves and leap toward the earth, spinning, like lunar satellites, around their parent maypole. Head downward, in feathered headdress they revolve, until the rope unwinds its length and brings them down to the crowd who wait below and lift them from their sacred ecstasy and lay them on the ground, their Daedalean flight accomplished.

But there is the crash of cymbals and of tambourines. These are milky lands of the violet and the cyclamen. Music itself is a bacchanale in shape, starting, again and again, and returning in its form, crowned and wreathed in flowers, shaking the lilied thyrsus, garlanded with ivy, the fig leaf and the vine. It is the return from Bacchic India. The world was taught the use of wine, the cultivation of the earth, and the manner of making honey.

There are signs of India. The priests have put serpents in their hair, and in the wildness of their looks feign madness and the sacred frenzy; while virgins carry baskets filled with gold and fruit, and snakes writhe and crawl from these to daze the senses. The hiss and coil of serpents are in the music, which darts and trembles in its rhythms, and proclaims the theme. Their prisoners accompany them, though it was a conquest without bloodshed. There are tumbrils loaded with purple grapes, beside which walk the captives, behind the chariot, and the lion and tiger.

When men were taught to till the earth, and the use of wine and honey, this was all, and enough, for most of them to know. What they have learned since is mostly folly. The arts came from the vineyard and the olive grove. They learned letters from the patterns of the constellations, to foretell the truth, and translate the dead. These are mysteries still, and no one is the wiser. The lyric moment is still a mystery between the vine and olive. Sacred and Profane are two schools of thought, two hemispheres, two continents, a heaven and a hell, in accordance with the winds that blow.

But the music grows louder. The living have no time to think. They must take one side, or other. The siren and the time signal have been music in their day; but the bacchanale will drive away the present and the future. Here the crocus grows beneath the cedar tree in a vernal forest giving on the vines. All the airs are perfumed and sigh sweet with resin. The music thrills and empties in the hollow valley. Here Sacred and Profane meet together in the dance, which loudens with the shaking of the lilied scepter and beats with the tambourines and crashes with the cymbals. There is one god, or many gods, but all are worshiped here. Or no god at all, but what the music means. Is there not word enough in the vineyard and the cedar breath? The creaking tumbrils pass by in a dream, while the bacchanale comes back again in louder triumph.

Where, then, is wisdom? In the arts, and not in war. In the cold and in the heat. In this music and its lilies. In shocks of corn and in the golden locks of children. In the arts and in the senses. In the bright wing and in the golden leaf. In night and day, or sun and moon, but not among the dead. In this there lies no difference: Profane or Sacred. Sacred or Profane.